Gaussian Processes for Machine Learning

Adaptive Computation and Machine Learning
Thomas Dietterich, Editor
Christopher Bishop, David Heckerman, Michael Jordan, and Michael Kearns, Associate Editors

Gaussian Processes for Machine Learning

Carl Edward Rasmussen
Christopher K. I. Williams

The MIT Press
Cambridge, Massachusetts
London, England

MIT Press books may be purchased at special quantity discounts for business or sales promotional use. For information, please email special_sales@mitpress.mit.edu.

Typeset by the authors using LaTeX2_ε.
This book was printed and bound in the United States of America.

Library of Congress Cataloging-in-Publication Data

Rasmussen, Carl Edward.
  Gaussian processes for machine learning / Carl Edward Rasmussen, Christopher K. I. Williams.
    p. cm. —(Adaptive computation and machine learning)
  Includes bibliographical references and indexes.
  ISBN 978-262-18253-9 (hc. : alk. paper)
  1. Gaussian processes—Data processing. 2. Machine learning—Mathematical models.
  I. Williams, Christopher K. I. II. Title. III. Series.

QA274.4.R37 2006
519.2'3—dc22

                                                                              2005053433

20 19 18 17 16 15 14 13

The actual science of logic is conversant at present only with things either certain, impossible, or entirely doubtful, none of which (fortunately) we have to reason on. Therefore the true logic for this world is the calculus of Probabilities, which takes account of the magnitude of the probability which is, or ought to be, in a reasonable man's mind.

— James Clerk Maxwell [1850]

Contents

*Sections marked by an asterisk contain advanced material that may be omitted on a first reading.

Appendix A   Mathematical Background   199

Appendix B   Gaussian Markov Processes   207

Appendix C   Datasets and Code   221

Bibliography   223

Author Index   239

Subject Index   245

Series Foreword

The goal of building systems that can adapt to their environments and learn from their experience has attracted researchers from many fields, including computer science, engineering, mathematics, physics, neuroscience, and cognitive science. Out of this research has come a wide variety of learning techniques that have the potential to transform many scientific and industrial fields. Recently, several research communities have converged on a common set of issues surrounding supervised, unsupervised, and reinforcement learning problems. The MIT Press series on Adaptive Computation and Machine Learning seeks to unify the many diverse strands of machine learning research and to foster high quality research and innovative applications.

One of the most active directions in machine learning has been the development of practical Bayesian methods for challenging learning problems. *Gaussian Processes for Machine Learning* presents one of the most important Bayesian machine learning approaches based on a particularly effective method for placing a prior distribution over the space of functions. Carl Edward Rasmussen and Chris Williams are two of the pioneers in this area, and their book describes the mathematical foundations and practical application of Gaussian processes in regression and classification tasks. They also show how Gaussian processes can be interpreted as a Bayesian version of the well-known support vector machine methods. Students and researchers who study this book will be able to apply Gaussian process methods in creative ways to solve a wide range of problems in science and engineering.

Thomas Dietterich

Preface

Over the last decade there has been an explosion of work in the "kernel machines" area of machine learning. Probably the best known example of this is work on support vector machines, but during this period there has also been much activity concerning the application of Gaussian process models to machine learning tasks. The goal of this book is to provide a systematic and unified treatment of this area. Gaussian processes provide a principled, practical, probabilistic approach to learning in kernel machines. This gives advantages with respect to the interpretation of model predictions and provides a well-founded framework for learning and model selection. Theoretical and practical developments of over the last decade have made Gaussian processes a serious competitor for real supervised learning applications. {kernel machines}

Roughly speaking a stochastic *process* is a generalization of a probability distribution (which describes a finite-dimensional random variable) to *functions*. By focussing on processes which are *Gaussian*, it turns out that the computations required for inference and learning become relatively easy. Thus, the supervised learning problems in machine learning which can be thought of as learning a function from examples can be cast directly into the Gaussian process framework. {Gaussian process}

Our interest in Gaussian process (GP) models in the context of machine learning was aroused in 1994, while we were both graduate students in Geoff Hinton's Neural Networks lab at the University of Toronto. This was a time when the field of neural networks was becoming mature and the many connections to statistical physics, probabilistic models and statistics became well known, and the first kernel-based learning algorithms were becoming popular. In retrospect it is clear that the time was ripe for the application of Gaussian processes to machine learning problems. {Gaussian processes in machine learning}

Many researchers were realizing that neural networks were not so easy to apply in practice, due to the many decisions which needed to be made: what architecture, what activation functions, what learning rate, etc., and the lack of a principled framework to answer these questions. The probabilistic framework was pursued using approximations by MacKay [1992b] and using Markov chain Monte Carlo (MCMC) methods by Neal [1996]. Neal was also a graduate student in the same lab, and in his thesis he sought to demonstrate that using the Bayesian formalism, one does not necessarily have problems with "overfitting" when the models get large, and one should pursue the limit of large models. While his own work was focused on sophisticated Markov chain methods for inference in large finite networks, he did point out that some of his networks became Gaussian processes in the limit of infinite size, and "there may be simpler ways to do inference in this case." {neural networks} {large neural networks ≡ Gaussian processes}

It is perhaps interesting to mention a slightly wider historical perspective. The main reason why neural networks became popular was that they allowed the use of *adaptive* basis functions, as opposed to the well known linear models. The adaptive basis functions, or hidden units, could "learn" hidden features {adaptive basis functions} useful for the modelling problem at hand. However, this adaptivity came at the cost of a lot of practical problems. Later, with the advancement of the "kernel era", it was realized that the limitation of fixed basis functions is not a big restriction if only one has enough of them, i.e. typically infinitely many, and one is careful to control problems of overfitting by using priors or regularization. The resulting models are much easier to handle than the adaptive basis function models, but have similar expressive power.

many fixed basis functions

Thus, one could claim that (as far a machine learning is concerned) the adaptive basis functions were merely a decade-long digression, and we are now back to where we came from. This view is perhaps reasonable if we think of models for solving practical learning problems, although MacKay [2003, ch. 45], for example, raises concerns by asking "did we throw out the baby with the bath water?", as the kernel view does not give us any hidden representations, telling us what the useful features are for solving a particular problem. As we will argue in the book, one answer may be to learn more sophisticated covariance functions, and the "hidden" properties of the problem are to be found here. An important area of future developments for GP models is the use of more expressive covariance functions.

useful representations

Supervised learning problems have been studied for more than a century in statistics, and a large body of well-established theory has been developed. More recently, with the advance of affordable, fast computation, the machine learning community has addressed increasingly large and complex problems.

supervised learning in statistics

Much of the basic theory and many algorithms are shared between the statistics and machine learning community. The primary differences are perhaps the types of the problems attacked, and the goal of learning. At the risk of oversimplification, one could say that in statistics a prime focus is often in understanding the *data* and relationships in terms of *models* giving approximate summaries such as linear relations or independencies. In contrast, the goals in machine learning are primarily to make predictions as accurately as possible and to understand the behaviour of learning *algorithms*. These differing objectives have led to different developments in the two fields: for example, neural network algorithms have been used extensively as black-box function approximators in machine learning, but to many statisticians they are less than satisfactory, because of the difficulties in interpreting such models.

statistics and machine learning

data and models

algorithms and predictions

Gaussian process models in some sense bring together work in the two communities. As we will see, Gaussian processes are mathematically equivalent to many well known models, including Bayesian linear models, spline models, large neural networks (under suitable conditions), and are closely related to others, such as support vector machines. Under the Gaussian process viewpoint, the models may be easier to handle and interpret than their conventional counterparts, such as e.g. neural networks. In the statistics community Gaussian processes have also been discussed many times, although it would probably be excessive to claim that their use is widespread except for certain specific applications such as spatial models in meteorology and geology, and the analysis of computer experiments. A rich theory also exists for Gaussian process models

bridging the gap

in the time series analysis literature; some pointers to this literature are given
in Appendix B.

The book is primarily intended for graduate students and researchers in
machine learning at departments of Computer Science, Statistics and Applied
Mathematics. As prerequisites we require a good basic grounding in calculus,
linear algebra and probability theory as would be obtained by graduates in nu-
merate disciplines such as electrical engineering, physics and computer science.
For preparation in calculus and linear algebra any good university-level text-
book on mathematics for physics or engineering such as Arfken [1985] would
be fine. For probability theory some familiarity with multivariate distributions
(especially the Gaussian) and conditional probability is required. Some background mathematical material is also provided in Appendix A.

intended audience

The main focus of the book is to present clearly and concisely an overview
of the main ideas of Gaussian processes in a machine learning context. We have
also covered a wide range of connections to existing models in the literature,
and cover approximate inference for faster practical algorithms. We have presented detailed algorithms for many methods to aid the practitioner. Software
implementations are available from the website for the book, see Appendix C.
We have also included a small set of exercises in each chapter; we hope these
will help in gaining a deeper understanding of the material.

focus

In order limit the size of the volume, we have had to omit some topics, such
as, for example, Markov chain Monte Carlo methods for inference. One of the
most difficult things to decide when writing a book is what sections not to write.
Within sections, we have often chosen to describe one algorithm in particular
in depth, and mention related work only in passing. Although this causes the
omission of some material, we feel it is the best approach for a monograph, and
hope that the reader will gain a general understanding so as to be able to push
further into the growing literature of GP models.

scope

The book has a natural split into two parts, with the chapters up to and
including chapter 5 covering core material, and the remaining sections covering
the connections to other methods, fast approximations, and more specialized
properties. Some sections are marked by an asterisk. These sections may be
omitted on a first reading, and are not pre-requisites for later (un-starred)
material.

book organization

*

We wish to express our considerable gratitude to the many people with
whom we have interacted during the writing of this book. In particular Moray
Allan, David Barber, Peter Bartlett, Miguel Carreira-Perpiñán, Marcus Gal-
lagher, Manfred Opper, Anton Schwaighofer, Matthias Seeger, Hanna Wallach,
Joe Whittaker, and Andrew Zisserman all read parts of the book and provided
valuable feedback. Dilan Görür, Malte Kuss, Iain Murray, Joaquin Quiñonero-
Candela, Leif Rasmussen and Sam Roweis were especially heroic and provided
comments on the whole manuscript. We thank Chris Bishop, Miguel Carreira-
Perpiñán, Nando de Freitas, Zoubin Ghahramani, Peter Grünwald, Mike Jordan, John Kent, Radford Neal, Joaquin Quiñonero-Candela, Ryan Rifkin, Stefan Schaal, Anton Schwaighofer, Matthias Seeger, Peter Sollich, Ingo Steinwart,

acknowledgements

Amos Storkey, Volker Tresp, Sethu Vijayakumar, Grace Wahba, Joe Whittaker and Tong Zhang for valuable discussions on specific issues. We also thank Bob Prior and the staff at MIT Press for their support during the writing of the book. We thank the Gatsby Computational Neuroscience Unit (UCL) and Neil Lawrence at the Department of Computer Science, University of Sheffield for hosting our visits and kindly providing space for us to work, and the Department of Computer Science at the University of Toronto for computer support. Thanks to John and Fiona for their hospitality on numerous occasions. Some of the diagrams in this book have been inspired by similar diagrams appearing in published work, as follows: Figure 3.5, Schölkopf and Smola [2002]; Figure 5.2, MacKay [1992b]. CER gratefully acknowledges financial support from the German Research Foundation (DFG). CKIW thanks the School of Informatics, University of Edinburgh for granting him sabbatical leave for the period October 2003-March 2004.

Finally, we reserve our deepest appreciation for our wives Agnes and Barbara, and children Ezra, Kate, Miro and Ruth for their patience and understanding while the book was being written.

errata

Despite our best efforts it is inevitable that some errors will make it through to the printed version of the book. Errata will be made available via the book's website at

http://www.GaussianProcess.org/gpml

We have found the joint writing of this book an excellent experience. Although hard at times, we are confident that the end result is much better than either one of us could have written alone.

looking ahead

Now, ten years after their first introduction into the machine learning community, Gaussian processes are receiving growing attention. Although GPs have been known for a long time in the statistics and geostatistics fields, and their use can perhaps be traced back as far as the end of the 19th century, their application to real problems is still in its early phases. This contrasts somewhat the application of the non-probabilistic analogue of the GP, the support vector machine, which was taken up more quickly by practitioners. Perhaps this has to do with the probabilistic mind-set needed to understand GPs, which is not so generally appreciated. Perhaps it is due to the need for computational short-cuts to implement inference for large datasets. Or it could be due to the lack of a self-contained introduction to this exciting field—with this volume, we hope to contribute to the momentum gained by Gaussian processes in machine learning.

Carl Edward Rasmussen and Chris Williams
Tübingen and Edinburgh, summer 2005

Second printing: We thank Mikhail Parakhin, Leif Rasmussen, Benjamin Sobotta, Kevin S. Van Horn and Aki Vehtari for reporting errors in the first printing which have now been corrected.

Symbols and Notation

Matrices are capitalized and vectors are in bold type. We do not generally distinguish between probabilities and probability densities. A subscript asterisk, such as in X_*, indicates reference to a *test set* quantity. A superscript asterisk denotes complex conjugate.

Symbol	Meaning
$\backslash$	left matrix divide: $A\backslash\mathbf{b}$ is the vector $\mathbf{x}$ which solves $A\mathbf{x} = \mathbf{b}$
$\triangleq$	an equality which acts as a definition
$\stackrel{c}{=}$	equality up to an additive constant
$|K|$	determinant of K matrix
$|\mathbf{y}|$	Euclidean length of vector $\mathbf{y}$, i.e. $\left(\sum_i y_i^2\right)^{1/2}$
$\langle f, g\rangle_{\mathcal{H}}$	RKHS inner product
$\|f\|_{\mathcal{H}}$	RKHS norm
$\mathbf{y}^\top$	the transpose of vector $\mathbf{y}$
$\propto$	proportional to; e.g. $p(x|y) \propto f(x,y)$ means that $p(x|y)$ is equal to $f(x,y)$ times a factor which is independent of x
$\sim$	distributed according to; example: $x \sim \mathcal{N}(\mu, \sigma^2)$
∇ or $\nabla_{\mathbf{f}}$	partial derivatives (w.r.t. $\mathbf{f}$)
$\nabla\nabla$	the (Hessian) matrix of second derivatives
$\mathbf{0}$ or $\mathbf{0}_n$	vector of all 0's (of length n)
$\mathbf{1}$ or $\mathbf{1}_n$	vector of all 1's (of length n)
C	number of classes in a classification problem
cholesky(A)	Cholesky decomposition: L is a lower triangular matrix such that $LL^\top = A$
cov($\mathbf{f}_*$)	Gaussian process posterior covariance
D	dimension of input space $\mathcal{X}$
$\mathcal{D}$	data set: $\mathcal{D} = \{(\mathbf{x}_i, y_i)|i = 1,\ldots,n\}$
diag($\mathbf{w}$)	(vector argument) a diagonal matrix containing the elements of vector $\mathbf{w}$
diag(W)	(matrix argument) a vector containing the diagonal elements of matrix W
δ_{pq}	Kronecker delta, $\delta_{pq} = 1$ iff $p = q$ and 0 otherwise
$\mathbb{E}$ or $\mathbb{E}_{q(x)}[z(x)]$	expectation; expectation of $z(x)$ when $x \sim q(x)$
$f(\mathbf{x})$ or $\mathbf{f}$	Gaussian process (or vector of) latent function values, $\mathbf{f} = (f(\mathbf{x}_1),\ldots,f(\mathbf{x}_n))^\top$
$\mathbf{f}_*$	Gaussian process (posterior) prediction (random variable)
$\bar{\mathbf{f}}_*$	Gaussian process posterior mean
$\mathcal{GP}$	Gaussian process: $f \sim \mathcal{GP}\big(m(\mathbf{x}), k(\mathbf{x},\mathbf{x}')\big)$, the function f is distributed as a Gaussian process with mean function $m(\mathbf{x})$ and covariance function $k(\mathbf{x},\mathbf{x}')$
$h(\mathbf{x})$ or $\mathbf{h}(\mathbf{x})$	*either* fixed basis function (or set of basis functions) *or* weight function
H or $H(X)$	set of basis functions evaluated at all training points
I or I_n	the identity matrix (of size n)
$J_\nu(z)$	Bessel function of the first kind
$k(\mathbf{x},\mathbf{x}')$	covariance (or kernel) function evaluated at $\mathbf{x}$ and $\mathbf{x}'$
K or $K(X,X)$	$n \times n$ covariance (or Gram) matrix
K_*	$n \times n_*$ matrix $K(X, X_*)$, the covariance between training and test cases
$\mathbf{k}(\mathbf{x}_*)$ or $\mathbf{k}_*$	vector, short for $K(X, \mathbf{x}_*)$, when there is only a single test case
K_f or K	covariance matrix for the (noise free) $\mathbf{f}$ values

Symbol	Meaning
K_y	covariance matrix for the (noisy) $\mathbf{y}$ values; for independent homoscedastic noise, $K_y = K_f + \sigma_n^2 I$
$K_\nu(z)$	modified Bessel function
$\mathcal{L}(a, b)$	loss function, the loss of predicting b, when a is true; note argument order
$\log(z)$	natural logarithm (base e)
$\log_2(z)$	logarithm to the base 2
ℓ or ℓ_d	characteristic length-scale (for input dimension d)
$\lambda(z)$	logistic function, $\lambda(z) = 1/\big(1 + \exp(-z)\big)$
$m(\mathbf{x})$	the mean function of a Gaussian process
μ	a measure (see section A.7)
$\mathcal{N}(\boldsymbol{\mu}, \Sigma)$ or $\mathcal{N}(\mathbf{x}|\boldsymbol{\mu}, \Sigma)$	(the variable $\mathbf{x}$ has a) Gaussian (Normal) distribution with mean vector $\boldsymbol{\mu}$ and covariance matrix Σ
$\mathcal{N}(\mathbf{x})$	short for unit Gaussian $\mathbf{x} \sim \mathcal{N}(\mathbf{0}, I)$
n and n_*	number of training (and test) cases
N	dimension of feature space
N_H	number of hidden units in a neural network
$\mathbb{N}$	the natural numbers, the positive integers
$\mathcal{O}(\cdot)$	big Oh; for functions f and g on $\mathbb{N}$, we write $f(n) = \mathcal{O}(g(n))$ if the ratio $f(n)/g(n)$ remains bounded as $n \to \infty$
O	*either* matrix of all zeros *or* differential operator
$y\|x$ and $p(y\|x)$	conditional random variable y given x and its probability (density)
$\mathbb{P}_N$	the regular n-polygon
$\phi(\mathbf{x}_i)$ or $\Phi(X)$	feature map of input $\mathbf{x}_i$ (or input set X)
$\Phi(z)$	cumulative unit Gaussian: $\Phi(z) = (2\pi)^{-1/2} \int_{-\infty}^{z} \exp(-t^2/2)dt$
$\pi(\mathbf{x})$	the sigmoid of the latent value: $\pi(\mathbf{x}) = \sigma(f(\mathbf{x}))$ (stochastic if $f(\mathbf{x})$ is stochastic)
$\hat{\pi}(\mathbf{x}_*)$	MAP prediction: π evaluated at $\bar{f}(\mathbf{x}_*)$.
$\bar{\pi}(\mathbf{x}_*)$	mean prediction: expected value of $\pi(\mathbf{x}_*)$. Note, in general that $\hat{\pi}(\mathbf{x}_*) \neq \bar{\pi}(\mathbf{x}_*)$
$\mathbb{R}$	the real numbers
$R_{\mathcal{L}}(f)$ or $R_{\mathcal{L}}(c)$	the risk or expected loss for f, or classifier c (averaged w.r.t. inputs and outputs)
$\tilde{R}_{\mathcal{L}}(l\|\mathbf{x}_*)$	expected loss for predicting l, averaged w.r.t. the model's pred. distr. at $\mathbf{x}_*$
$\mathcal{R}_c$	decision region for class c
$S(\mathbf{s})$	power spectrum
$\sigma(z)$	any sigmoid function, e.g. logistic $\lambda(z)$, cumulative Gaussian $\Phi(z)$, etc.
σ_f^2	variance of the (noise free) signal
σ_n^2	noise variance
$\boldsymbol{\theta}$	vector of hyperparameters (parameters of the covariance function)
$\text{tr}(A)$	trace of (square) matrix A
$\mathbb{T}_l$	the circle with circumference l
$\mathbb{V}$ or $\mathbb{V}_{q(x)}[z(x)]$	variance; variance of $z(x)$ when $x \sim q(x)$
$\mathcal{X}$	input space and also the index set for the stochastic process
X	$D \times n$ matrix of the training inputs $\{\mathbf{x}_i\}_{i=1}^n$: the design matrix
X_*	matrix of test inputs
$\mathbf{x}_i$	the ith training input
x_{di}	the dth coordinate of the ith training input $\mathbf{x}_i$
$\mathbb{Z}$	the integers $\dots, -2, -1, 0, 1, 2, \dots$

Chapter 1

Introduction

In this book we will be concerned with supervised learning, which is the problem of learning input-output mappings from empirical data (the training dataset). Depending on the characteristics of the output, this problem is known as either regression, for continuous outputs, or classification, when outputs are discrete.

A well known example is the classification of images of handwritten digits. digit classification
The training set consists of small digitized images, together with a classification from $0, \ldots, 9$, normally provided by a human. The goal is to learn a mapping from image to classification label, which can then be used on new, unseen images. Supervised learning is an attractive way to attempt to tackle this problem, since it is not easy to specify accurately the characteristics of, say, the handwritten digit 4.

An example of a regression problem can be found in robotics, where we wish robotic control
to learn the inverse dynamics of a robot arm. Here the task is to map from the state of the arm (given by the positions, velocities and accelerations of the joints) to the corresponding torques on the joints. Such a model can then be used to compute the torques needed to move the arm along a given trajectory. Another example would be in a chemical plant, where we might wish to predict the yield as a function of process parameters such as temperature, pressure, amount of catalyst etc.

In general we denote the input as $\mathbf{x}$, and the output (or target) as y. The the dataset
input is usually represented as a vector $\mathbf{x}$ as there are in general many input variables—in the handwritten digit recognition example one may have a 256-dimensional input obtained from a raster scan of a 16×16 image, and in the robot arm example there are three input measurements for each joint in the arm. The target y may either be continuous (as in the regression case) or discrete (as in the classification case). We have a dataset $\mathcal{D}$ of n observations, $\mathcal{D} = \{(\mathbf{x}_i, y_i) | i = 1, \ldots, n\}$.

Given this training data we wish to make predictions for new inputs $\mathbf{x}_*$ training is inductive
that we have not seen in the training set. Thus it is clear that the problem at hand is *inductive*; we need to move from the finite training data $\mathcal{D}$ to a

function f that makes predictions for all possible input values. To do this we must make assumptions about the characteristics of the underlying function, as otherwise any function which is consistent with the training data would be equally valid. A wide variety of methods have been proposed to deal with the supervised learning problem; here we describe two common approaches. The first is to restrict the class of functions that we consider, for example by only considering linear functions of the input. The second approach is (speaking rather loosely) to give a prior probability to every possible function, where higher probabilities are given to functions that we consider to be more likely, for example because they are smoother than other functions.[1] The first approach has an obvious problem in that we have to decide upon the richness of the class of functions considered; if we are using a model based on a certain class of functions (e.g. linear functions) and the target function is not well modelled by this class, then the predictions will be poor. One may be tempted to increase the flexibility of the class of functions, but this runs into the danger of overfitting, where we can obtain a good fit to the training data, but perform badly when making test predictions.

The second approach appears to have a serious problem, in that surely there are an uncountably infinite set of possible functions, and how are we going to compute with this set in finite time? This is where the Gaussian process comes to our rescue. A Gaussian *process* is a generalization of the Gaussian probability *distribution*. Whereas a probability distribution describes random variables which are scalars or vectors (for multivariate distributions), a stochastic *process* governs the properties of functions. Leaving mathematical sophistication aside, one can loosely think of a function as a very long vector, each entry in the vector specifying the function value $f(x)$ at a particular input x. It turns out, that although this idea is a little naïve, it is surprisingly close what we need. Indeed, the question of how we deal computationally with these infinite dimensional objects has the most pleasant resolution imaginable: if you ask only for the properties of the function at a finite number of points, then inference in the Gaussian process will give you the same answer if you ignore the infinitely many other points, as if you would have taken them all into account! And these answers are consistent with answers to any other finite queries you may have. One of the main attractions of the Gaussian process framework is precisely that it unites a sophisticated and consistent view with computational tractability.

It should come as no surprise that these ideas have been around for some time, although they are perhaps not as well known as they might be. Indeed, many models that are commonly employed in both machine learning and statistics are in fact special cases of, or restricted kinds of Gaussian processes. In this volume, we aim to give a systematic and unified treatment of the area, showing connections to related models.

two approaches (margin)

Gaussian process (margin)

consistency (margin)

tractability (margin)

---

[1] These two approaches may be regarded as imposing a *restriction* bias and a *preference* bias respectively; see e.g. Mitchell [1997].

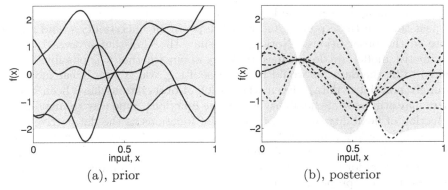

(a), prior   (b), posterior

Figure 1.1: Panel (a) shows four samples drawn from the prior distribution. Panel (b) shows the situation after two datapoints have been observed. The mean prediction is shown as the solid line and four samples from the posterior are shown as dashed lines. In both plots the shaded region denotes twice the standard deviation at each input value x.

1.1 A Pictorial Introduction to Bayesian Modelling

In this section we give graphical illustrations of how the second (Bayesian) method works on some simple regression and classification examples.

We first consider a simple 1-d *regression* problem, mapping from an input x to an output $f(x)$. In Figure 1.1(a) we show a number of sample functions drawn at random from the *prior* distribution over functions specified by a particular Gaussian process which favours smooth functions. This prior is taken to represent our prior beliefs over the kinds of functions we expect to observe, before seeing any data. In the absence of knowledge to the contrary we have assumed that the average value over the sample functions at each x is zero. Although the specific random functions drawn in Figure 1.1(a) do not have a mean of zero, the mean of $f(x)$ values for any fixed x would become zero, independent of x as we kept on drawing more functions. At any value of x we can also characterize the variability of the sample functions by computing the variance at that point. The shaded region denotes twice the pointwise standard deviation; in this case we used a Gaussian process which specifies that the prior variance does not depend on x.

Suppose that we are then given a dataset $\mathcal{D} = \{(\mathbf{x}_1, y_1), (\mathbf{x}_2, y_2)\}$ consisting of two observations, and we wish now to only consider functions that pass though these two data points exactly. (It is also possible to give higher preference to functions that merely pass "close" to the datapoints.) This situation is illustrated in Figure 1.1(b). The dashed lines show sample functions which are consistent with $\mathcal{D}$, and the solid line depicts the mean value of such functions. Notice how the uncertainty is reduced close to the observations. The combination of the prior and the data leads to the *posterior* distribution over functions.

regression

random functions

mean function

pointwise variance

functions that agree with observations

posterior over functions

If more datapoints were added one would see the mean function adjust itself to pass through these points, and that the posterior uncertainty would reduce close to the observations. Notice, that since the Gaussian process is not a parametric model, we do not have to worry about whether it is possible for the model to fit the data (as would be the case if e.g. you tried a linear model on strongly non-linear data). Even when a lot of observations have been added, there may still be some flexibility left in the functions. One way to imagine the reduction of flexibility in the distribution of functions as the data arrives is to draw many random functions from the prior, and reject the ones which do not agree with the observations. While this is a perfectly valid way to do inference, it is impractical for most purposes—the exact analytical computations required to quantify these properties will be detailed in the next chapter.

The specification of the prior is important, because it fixes the properties of the functions considered for inference. Above we briefly touched on the mean and pointwise variance of the functions. However, other characteristics can also be specified and manipulated. Note that the functions in Figure 1.1(a) are smooth and stationary (informally, stationarity means that the functions look similar at all x locations). These are properties which are induced by the *covariance function* of the Gaussian process; many other covariance functions are possible. Suppose, that for a particular application, we think that the functions in Figure 1.1(a) vary too rapidly (i.e. that their characteristic length-scale is too short). Slower variation is achieved by simply adjusting parameters of the covariance function. The problem of *learning* in Gaussian processes is exactly the problem of finding suitable properties for the covariance function. Note, that this gives us a model of the data, and characteristics (such a smoothness, characteristic length-scale, etc.) which we can *interpret*.

We now turn to the *classification* case, and consider the binary (or two-class) classification problem. An example of this is classifying objects detected in astronomical sky surveys into stars or galaxies. Our data has the label +1 for stars and −1 for galaxies, and our task will be to predict $\pi(\mathbf{x})$, the probability that an example with input vector $\mathbf{x}$ is a star, using as inputs some features that describe each object. Obviously $\pi(\mathbf{x})$ should lie in the interval $[0, 1]$. A Gaussian process prior over functions does not restrict the output to lie in this interval, as can be seen from Figure 1.1(a). The approach that we shall adopt is to squash the prior function f pointwise through a response function which restricts the output to lie in $[0, 1]$. A common choice for this function is the logistic function $\lambda(z) = (1 + \exp(-z))^{-1}$, illustrated in Figure 1.2(b). Thus the prior over f induces a prior over probabilistic classifications π.

This set up is illustrated in Figure 1.2 for a 2-d input space. In panel (a) we see a sample drawn from the prior over functions f which is squashed through the logistic function (panel (b)). A dataset is shown in panel (c), where the white and black circles denote classes +1 and −1 respectively. As in the regression case the effect of the data is to downweight in the posterior those functions that are incompatible with the data. A contour plot of the posterior mean for $\pi(\mathbf{x})$ is shown in panel (d). In this example we have chosen a short characteristic length-scale for the process so that it can vary fairly rapidly; in

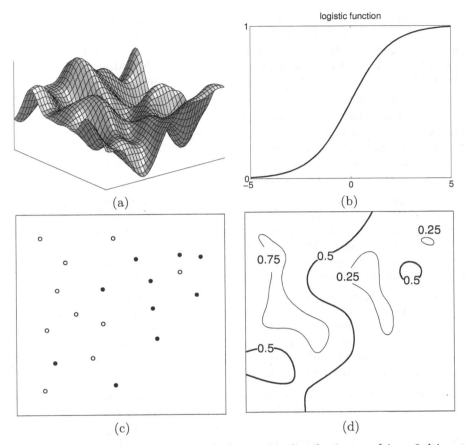

Figure 1.2: Panel (a) shows a sample from prior distribution on f in a 2-d input space. Panel (b) is a plot of the logistic function $\lambda(z)$. Panel (c) shows the location of the data points, where the open circles denote the class label $+1$, and closed circles denote the class label -1. Panel (d) shows a contour plot of the mean predictive probability as a function of $\mathbf{x}$; the decision boundaries between the two classes are shown by the thicker lines.

this case notice that all of the training points are correctly classified, including the two "outliers" in the NE and SW corners. By choosing a different length-scale we can change this behaviour, as illustrated in section 3.7.1.

1.2   Roadmap

The book has a natural split into two parts, with the chapters up to and including chapter 5 covering core material, and the remaining chapters covering the connections to other methods, fast approximations, and more specialized properties. Some sections are marked by an asterisk. These sections may be omitted on a first reading, and are not pre-requisites for later (un-starred) material.

regression   Chapter 2 contains the definition of Gaussian processes, in particular for the use in regression. It also discusses the computations needed to make predictions for regression. Under the assumption of Gaussian observation noise the computations needed to make predictions are tractable and are dominated by the inversion of a $n \times n$ matrix. In a short experimental section, the Gaussian process model is applied to a robotics task.

classification   Chapter 3 considers the classification problem for both binary and multi-class cases. The use of a non-linear response function means that exact computation of the predictions is no longer possible analytically. We discuss a number of approximation schemes, include detailed algorithms for their implementation and discuss some experimental comparisons.

covariance functions   As discussed above, the key factor that controls the properties of a Gaussian process is the covariance function. Much of the work on machine learning so far, has used a very limited set of covariance functions, possibly limiting the power of the resulting models. In chapter 4 we discuss a number of valid covariance functions and their properties and provide some guidelines on how to combine covariance functions into new ones, tailored to specific needs.

learning   Many covariance functions have adjustable parameters, such as the characteristic length-scale and variance illustrated in Figure 1.1. Chapter 5 describes how such parameters can be inferred or learned from the data, based on either Bayesian methods (using the marginal likelihood) or methods of cross-validation. Explicit algorithms are provided for some schemes, and some simple practical examples are demonstrated.

connections   Gaussian process predictors are an example of a class of methods known as kernel machines; they are distinguished by the probabilistic viewpoint taken. In chapter 6 we discuss other kernel machines such as support vector machines (SVMs), splines, least-squares classifiers and relevance vector machines (RVMs), and their relationships to Gaussian process prediction.

theory   In chapter 7 we discuss a number of more theoretical issues relating to Gaussian process methods including asymptotic analysis, average-case learning curves and the PAC-Bayesian framework.

fast approximations   One issue with Gaussian process prediction methods is that their basic complexity is $\mathcal{O}(n^3)$, due to the inversion of a $n \times n$ matrix. For large datasets this is prohibitive (in both time and space) and so a number of approximation methods have been developed, as described in chapter 8.

The main focus of the book is on the core supervised learning problems of regression and classification. In chapter 9 we discuss some rather less standard settings that GPs have been used in, and complete the main part of the book with some conclusions.

Appendix A gives some mathematical background, while Appendix B deals specifically with Gaussian Markov processes. Appendix C gives details of how to access the data and programs that were used to make the some of the figures and run the experiments described in the book.

Chapter 2

Regression

Supervised learning can be divided into regression and classification problems. Whereas the outputs for classification are discrete class labels, regression is concerned with the prediction of continuous quantities. For example, in a financial application, one may attempt to predict the price of a commodity as a function of interest rates, currency exchange rates, availability and demand. In this chapter we describe Gaussian process methods for regression problems; classification problems are discussed in chapter 3.

There are several ways to interpret Gaussian process (GP) regression models. One can think of a Gaussian process as defining a distribution over functions, and inference taking place directly in the space of functions, the *function-space view*. Although this view is appealing it may initially be difficult to grasp, so we start our exposition in section 2.1 with the equivalent *weight-space view* which may be more familiar and accessible to many, and continue in section 2.2 with the function-space view. Gaussian processes often have characteristics that can be changed by setting certain parameters and in section 2.3 we discuss how the properties change as these parameters are varied. The predictions from a GP model take the form of a full predictive distribution; in section 2.4 we discuss how to combine a loss function with the predictive distributions using decision theory to make point predictions in an optimal way. A practical comparative example involving the learning of the inverse dynamics of a robot arm is presented in section 2.5. We give some theoretical analysis of Gaussian process regression in section 2.6, and discuss how to incorporate explicit basis functions into the models in section 2.7. As much of the material in this chapter can be considered fairly standard, we postpone most references to the historical overview in section 2.8.

two equivalent views

2.1 Weight-space View

The simple linear regression model where the output is a linear combination of the inputs has been studied and used extensively. Its main virtues are simplicity of implementation and interpretability. Its main drawback is that it only allows a limited flexibility; if the relationship between input and output cannot reasonably be approximated by a linear function, the model will give poor predictions.

In this section we first discuss the Bayesian treatment of the linear model. We then make a simple enhancement to this class of models by projecting the inputs into a high-dimensional *feature space* and applying the linear model there. We show that in some feature spaces one can apply the "kernel trick" to carry out computations implicitly in the high dimensional space; this last step leads to computational savings when the dimensionality of the feature space is large compared to the number of data points.

training set

design matrix

We have a training set $\mathcal{D}$ of n observations, $\mathcal{D} = \{(\mathbf{x}_i, y_i) \mid i = 1, \ldots, n\}$, where $\mathbf{x}$ denotes an input vector (covariates) of dimension D and y denotes a scalar output or target (dependent variable); the column vector inputs for all n cases are aggregated in the $D \times n$ *design matrix*[1] X, and the targets are collected in the vector $\mathbf{y}$, so we can write $\mathcal{D} = (X, \mathbf{y})$. In the regression setting the targets are real values. We are interested in making inferences about the relationship between inputs and targets, i.e. the conditional distribution of the targets given the inputs (but we are not interested in modelling the input distribution itself).

2.1.1   The Standard Linear Model

We will review the Bayesian analysis of the standard linear regression model with Gaussian noise

$$f(\mathbf{x}) = \mathbf{x}^\top \mathbf{w}, \qquad y = f(\mathbf{x}) + \varepsilon, \tag{2.1}$$

bias, offset

where $\mathbf{x}$ is the input vector, $\mathbf{w}$ is a vector of weights (parameters) of the linear model, f is the function value and y is the observed target value. Often a bias weight or offset is included, but as this can be implemented by augmenting the input vector $\mathbf{x}$ with an additional element whose value is always one, we do not explicitly include it in our notation. We have assumed that the observed values y differ from the function values $f(\mathbf{x})$ by additive noise, and we will further assume that this noise follows an independent, identically distributed Gaussian distribution with zero mean and variance σ_n^2

$$\varepsilon \sim \mathcal{N}(0, \sigma_n^2). \tag{2.2}$$

likelihood

This noise assumption together with the model directly gives rise to the *likelihood*, the probability density of the observations given the parameters, which is

---

[1] In statistics texts the design matrix is usually taken to be the transpose of our definition, but our choice is deliberate and has the advantage that a data point is a standard (column) vector.

factored over cases in the training set (because of the independence assumption)
to give

$$p(\mathbf{y}|X,\mathbf{w}) = \prod_{i=1}^{n} p(y_i|\mathbf{x}_i,\mathbf{w}) = \prod_{i=1}^{n} \frac{1}{\sqrt{2\pi}\sigma_n} \exp\left(-\frac{(y_i - \mathbf{x}_i^\top \mathbf{w})^2}{2\sigma_n^2}\right)$$

$$= \frac{1}{(2\pi\sigma_n^2)^{n/2}} \exp\left(-\frac{1}{2\sigma_n^2}|\mathbf{y} - X^\top\mathbf{w}|^2\right) = \mathcal{N}(X^\top\mathbf{w}, \sigma_n^2 I), \qquad (2.3)$$

where $|\mathbf{z}|$ denotes the Euclidean length of vector $\mathbf{z}$. In the Bayesian formalism
we need to specify a *prior* over the parameters, expressing our beliefs about the   prior
parameters before we look at the observations. We put a zero mean Gaussian
prior with covariance matrix Σ_p on the weights

$$\mathbf{w} \sim \mathcal{N}(\mathbf{0}, \Sigma_p). \qquad (2.4)$$

The rôle and properties of this prior will be discussed in section 2.2; for now
we will continue the derivation with the prior as specified.

Inference in the Bayesian linear model is based on the posterior distribution   posterior
over the weights, computed by Bayes' rule, (see eq. (A.3))[2]

$$\text{posterior} = \frac{\text{likelihood} \times \text{prior}}{\text{marginal likelihood}}, \qquad p(\mathbf{w}|\mathbf{y},X) = \frac{p(\mathbf{y}|X,\mathbf{w})p(\mathbf{w})}{p(\mathbf{y}|X)}, \quad (2.5)$$

where the normalizing constant, also known as the marginal likelihood (see page   marginal likelihood
19), is independent of the weights and given by

$$p(\mathbf{y}|X) = \int p(\mathbf{y}|X,\mathbf{w})p(\mathbf{w})\,d\mathbf{w}. \qquad (2.6)$$

The posterior in eq. (2.5) combines the likelihood and the prior, and captures
everything we know about the parameters. Writing only the terms from the
likelihood and prior which depend on the weights, and "completing the square"
we obtain

$$p(\mathbf{w}|X,\mathbf{y}) \propto \exp\left(-\frac{1}{2\sigma_n^2}(\mathbf{y} - X^\top\mathbf{w})^\top(\mathbf{y} - X^\top\mathbf{w})\right)\exp\left(-\frac{1}{2}\mathbf{w}^\top\Sigma_p^{-1}\mathbf{w}\right)$$

$$\propto \exp\left(-\frac{1}{2}(\mathbf{w} - \bar{\mathbf{w}})^\top\left(\frac{1}{\sigma_n^2}XX^\top + \Sigma_p^{-1}\right)(\mathbf{w} - \bar{\mathbf{w}})\right), \qquad (2.7)$$

where $\bar{\mathbf{w}} = \sigma_n^{-2}(\sigma_n^{-2}XX^\top + \Sigma_p^{-1})^{-1}X\mathbf{y}$, and we recognize the form of the
posterior distribution as Gaussian with mean $\bar{\mathbf{w}}$ and covariance matrix A^{-1}

$$p(\mathbf{w}|X,\mathbf{y}) \sim \mathcal{N}\left(\bar{\mathbf{w}} = \frac{1}{\sigma_n^2}A^{-1}X\mathbf{y}, A^{-1}\right), \qquad (2.8)$$

where $A = \sigma_n^{-2}XX^\top + \Sigma_p^{-1}$. Notice that for this model (and indeed for any
Gaussian posterior) the *mean* of the posterior distribution $p(\mathbf{w}|\mathbf{y},X)$ is also
its mode, which is also called the *maximum a posteriori* (MAP) estimate of   MAP estimate

---

[2]Often Bayes' rule is stated as $p(a|b) = p(b|a)p(a)/p(b)$; here we use it in a form where we
additionally condition everywhere on the inputs X (but neglect this extra conditioning for
the prior which is independent of the inputs).

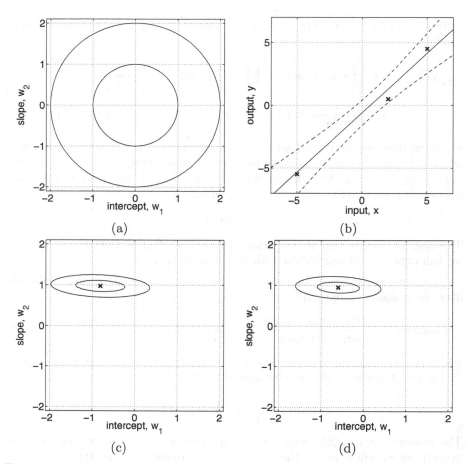

Figure 2.1: Example of Bayesian linear model $f(x) = w_1 + w_2 x$ with intercept w_1 and slope parameter w_2. Panel (a) shows the contours of the prior distribution $p(\mathbf{w}) \sim \mathcal{N}(\mathbf{0}, I)$, eq. (2.4). Panel (b) shows three training points marked by crosses. Panel (c) shows contours of the likelihood $p(\mathbf{y}|X, \mathbf{w})$ eq. (2.3), assuming a noise level of $\sigma_n = 1$; note that the slope is much more "well determined" than the intercept. Panel (d) shows the posterior, $p(\mathbf{w}|X, \mathbf{y})$ eq. (2.7); comparing the maximum of the posterior to the likelihood, we see that the intercept has been shrunk towards zero whereas the more 'well determined' slope is almost unchanged. All contour plots give the 1 and 2 standard deviation equi-probability contours. Superimposed on the data in panel (b) are the predictive mean plus/minus two standard deviations of the (noise-free) predictive distribution $p(f_*|\mathbf{x}_*, X, \mathbf{y})$, eq. (2.9).

w. In a non-Bayesian setting the negative log prior is sometimes thought of as a *penalty* term, and the MAP point is known as the penalized maximum likelihood estimate of the weights, and this may cause some confusion between the two approaches. Note, however, that in the Bayesian setting the MAP estimate plays no special rôle.[3] The penalized maximum likelihood procedure

---

[3]In this case, due to symmetries in the model and posterior, it happens that the mean of the predictive distribution is the same as the prediction at the mean of the posterior. However, this is not the case in general.

is known in this case as *ridge* regression [Hoerl and Kennard, 1970] because of the effect of the quadratic penalty term $\frac{1}{2}\mathbf{w}^\top \Sigma_p^{-1}\mathbf{w}$ from the log prior.

ridge regression

To make predictions for a test case we average over all possible parameter values, weighted by their posterior probability. This is in contrast to non-Bayesian schemes, where a single parameter is typically chosen by some criterion. Thus the predictive distribution for $f_* \triangleq f(\mathbf{x}_*)$ at $\mathbf{x}_*$ is given by averaging the output of all possible linear models w.r.t. the Gaussian posterior

predictive distribution

$$
\begin{aligned}
p(f_*|\mathbf{x}_*, X, \mathbf{y}) &= \int p(f_*|\mathbf{x}_*, \mathbf{w}) p(\mathbf{w}|X, \mathbf{y})\, d\mathbf{w} \\
&= \mathcal{N}\big(\frac{1}{\sigma_n^2}\mathbf{x}_*^\top A^{-1} X \mathbf{y},\ \mathbf{x}_*^\top A^{-1}\mathbf{x}_*\big).
\end{aligned}
\tag{2.9}
$$

The predictive distribution is again Gaussian, with a mean given by the posterior mean of the weights from eq. (2.8) multiplied by the test input, as one would expect from symmetry considerations. The predictive variance is a quadratic form of the test input with the posterior covariance matrix, showing that the predictive uncertainties grow with the magnitude of the test input, as one would expect for a linear model.

An example of Bayesian linear regression is given in Figure 2.1. Here we have chosen a 1-d input space so that the weight-space is two-dimensional and can be easily visualized. Contours of the Gaussian prior are shown in panel (a). The data are depicted as crosses in panel (b). This gives rise to the likelihood shown in panel (c) and the posterior distribution in panel (d). The predictive distribution and its error bars are also marked in panel (b).

2.1.2   Projections of Inputs into Feature Space

In the previous section we reviewed the Bayesian linear model which suffers from limited expressiveness. A very simple idea to overcome this problem is to first project the inputs into some high dimensional space using a set of basis functions and then apply the linear model in this space instead of directly on the inputs themselves. For example, a scalar input x could be projected into the space of powers of x: $\boldsymbol{\phi}(x) = (1, x, x^2, x^3, \ldots)^\top$ to implement polynomial regression. As long as the projections are fixed functions (i.e. independent of the parameters $\mathbf{w}$) the model is still linear in the parameters, and therefore analytically tractable.[4] This idea is also used in classification, where a dataset which is not linearly separable in the original data space may become linearly separable in a high dimensional feature space, see section 3.3. Application of this idea begs the question of how to choose the basis functions? As we shall demonstrate (in chapter 5), the Gaussian process formalism allows us to answer this question. For now, we assume that the basis functions are given.

feature space

polynomial regression

linear in the parameters

Specifically, we introduce the function $\boldsymbol{\phi}(\mathbf{x})$ which maps a D-dimensional input vector $\mathbf{x}$ into an N dimensional feature space. Further let the matrix

---

[4]Models with adaptive basis functions, such as e.g. multilayer perceptrons, may at first seem like a useful extension, but they are much harder to treat, except in the limit of an infinite number of hidden units, see section 4.2.3.

$\Phi(X)$ be the aggregation of columns $\phi(\mathbf{x})$ for all cases in the training set. Now the model is

$$f(\mathbf{x}) = \phi(\mathbf{x})^\top \mathbf{w}, \tag{2.10}$$

explicit feature space formulation

where the vector of parameters now has length N. The analysis for this model is analogous to the standard linear model, except that everywhere $\Phi(X)$ is substituted for X. Thus the predictive distribution becomes

$$f_* | \mathbf{x}_*, X, \mathbf{y} \sim \mathcal{N}\left(\frac{1}{\sigma_n^2} \phi(\mathbf{x}_*)^\top A^{-1} \Phi \mathbf{y}, \ \phi(\mathbf{x}_*)^\top A^{-1} \phi(\mathbf{x}_*)\right) \tag{2.11}$$

with $\Phi = \Phi(X)$ and $A = \sigma_n^{-2}\Phi\Phi^\top + \Sigma_p^{-1}$. To make predictions using this equation we need to invert the A matrix of size $N \times N$ which may not be convenient if N, the dimension of the feature space, is large. However, we can **alternative formulation** rewrite the equation in the following way

$$
\begin{aligned}
f_* | \mathbf{x}_*, X, \mathbf{y} \sim \mathcal{N}\big(& \phi_*^\top \Sigma_p \Phi (K + \sigma_n^2 I)^{-1} \mathbf{y}, \\
& \phi_*^\top \Sigma_p \phi_* - \phi_*^\top \Sigma_p \Phi (K + \sigma_n^2 I)^{-1} \Phi^\top \Sigma_p \phi_* \big),
\end{aligned} \tag{2.12}
$$

where we have used the shorthand $\phi(\mathbf{x}_*) = \phi_*$ and defined $K = \Phi^\top \Sigma_p \Phi$. To show this for the mean, first note that using the definitions of A and K we have $\sigma_n^{-2}\Phi(K + \sigma_n^2 I) = \sigma_n^{-2}\Phi(\Phi^\top \Sigma_p \Phi + \sigma_n^2 I) = A\Sigma_p\Phi$. Now multiplying through by A^{-1} from left and $(K + \sigma_n^2 I)^{-1}$ from the right gives $\sigma_n^{-2}A^{-1}\Phi = \Sigma_p\Phi(K + \sigma_n^2 I)^{-1}$, showing the equivalence of the mean expressions in eq. (2.11) and eq. (2.12). For the variance we use the matrix inversion lemma, eq. (A.9), setting $Z^{-1} = \Sigma_p$, $W^{-1} = \sigma_n^2 I$ and $V = U = \Phi$ therein. In eq. (2.12) we **computational load** need to invert matrices of size $n \times n$ which is more convenient when $n < N$. Geometrically, note that n datapoints can span at most n dimensions in the feature space.

Notice that in eq. (2.12) the feature space always enters in the form of $\Phi^\top \Sigma_p \Phi$, $\phi_*^\top \Sigma_p \Phi$, or $\phi_*^\top \Sigma_p \phi_*$; thus the entries of these matrices are invariably of the form $\phi(\mathbf{x})^\top \Sigma_p \phi(\mathbf{x}')$ where $\mathbf{x}$ and $\mathbf{x}'$ are in either the training or the test sets. Let us define $k(\mathbf{x}, \mathbf{x}') = \phi(\mathbf{x})^\top \Sigma_p \phi(\mathbf{x}')$. For reasons that will become clear later **kernel** we call $k(\cdot, \cdot)$ a *covariance function* or *kernel*. Notice that $\phi(\mathbf{x})^\top \Sigma_p \phi(\mathbf{x}')$ is an inner product (with respect to Σ_p). As Σ_p is positive definite we can define $\Sigma_p^{1/2}$ so that $(\Sigma_p^{1/2})^2 = \Sigma_p$; for example if the SVD (singular value decomposition) of $\Sigma_p = UDU^\top$, where D is diagonal, then one form for $\Sigma_p^{1/2}$ is $UD^{1/2}U^\top$. Then defining $\psi(\mathbf{x}) = \Sigma_p^{1/2} \phi(\mathbf{x})$ we obtain a simple dot product representation $k(\mathbf{x}, \mathbf{x}') = \psi(\mathbf{x}) \cdot \psi(\mathbf{x}')$.

If an algorithm is defined solely in terms of inner products in input space then it can be lifted into feature space by replacing occurrences of those inner **kernel trick** products by $k(\mathbf{x}, \mathbf{x}')$; this is sometimes called the *kernel trick*. This technique is particularly valuable in situations where it is more convenient to compute the kernel than the feature vectors themselves. As we will see in the coming sections, this often leads to considering the kernel as the object of primary interest, and its corresponding feature space as having secondary practical importance.

2.2   Function-space View

An alternative and equivalent way of reaching identical results to the previous section is possible by considering inference directly in function space. We use a Gaussian process (GP) to describe a distribution over functions. Formally:

Definition 2.1 *A Gaussian process is a collection of random variables, any finite number of which have a joint Gaussian distribution.*   □

Gaussian process

A Gaussian process is completely specified by its mean function and co-variance function. We define mean function $m(\mathbf{x})$ and the covariance function $k(\mathbf{x}, \mathbf{x}')$ of a real process $f(\mathbf{x})$ as

covariance and mean function

$$
\begin{aligned}
m(\mathbf{x}) &= \mathbb{E}[f(\mathbf{x})], \\
k(\mathbf{x}, \mathbf{x}') &= \mathbb{E}[(f(\mathbf{x}) - m(\mathbf{x}))(f(\mathbf{x}') - m(\mathbf{x}'))],
\end{aligned}
\tag{2.13}
$$

and will write the Gaussian process as

$$
f(\mathbf{x}) \sim \mathcal{GP}\big(m(\mathbf{x}), k(\mathbf{x}, \mathbf{x}')\big).
\tag{2.14}
$$

Usually, for notational simplicity we will take the mean function to be zero, although this need not be done, see section 2.7.

In our case the random variables represent the value of the function $f(\mathbf{x})$ at location $\mathbf{x}$. Often, Gaussian processes are defined over time, i.e. where the index set of the random variables is time. This is not (normally) the case in our use of GPs; here the index set $\mathcal{X}$ is the set of possible inputs, which could be more general, e.g. $\mathbb{R}^D$. For notational convenience we use the (arbitrary) enumeration of the cases in the training set to identify the random variables such that $f_i \triangleq f(\mathbf{x}_i)$ is the random variable corresponding to the case $(\mathbf{x}_i, y_i)$ as would be expected.

index set ≡ input domain

A Gaussian process is defined as a collection of random variables. Thus, the definition automatically implies a *consistency* requirement, which is also some-times known as the marginalization property. This property simply means that if the GP e.g. specifies $(y_1, y_2) \sim \mathcal{N}(\boldsymbol{\mu}, \Sigma)$, then it must also specify $y_1 \sim \mathcal{N}(\mu_1, \Sigma_{11})$ where Σ_{11} is the relevant submatrix of Σ, see eq. (A.6). In other words, examination of a larger set of variables does not change the distribution of the smaller set. Notice that the consistency requirement is automatically fulfilled if the covariance function specifies entries of the covariance matrix.[5] The definition does not exclude Gaussian processes with finite index sets (which would be simply Gaussian *distributions*), but these are not particularly interesting for our purposes.

marginalization property

finite index set

---

[5]Note, however, that if you instead specified e.g. a function for the entries of the *inverse* covariance matrix, then the marginalization property would no longer be fulfilled, and one could not think of this as a consistent collection of random variables—this would not qualify as a Gaussian process.

Bayesian linear model
is a Gaussian process

A simple example of a Gaussian process can be obtained from our Bayesian linear regression model $f(\mathbf{x}) = \phi(\mathbf{x})^\top \mathbf{w}$ with prior $\mathbf{w} \sim \mathcal{N}(\mathbf{0}, \Sigma_p)$. We have for the mean and covariance

$$
\begin{aligned}
\mathbb{E}[f(\mathbf{x})] &= \phi(\mathbf{x})^\top \mathbb{E}[\mathbf{w}] = 0, \\
\mathbb{E}[f(\mathbf{x})f(\mathbf{x}')] &= \phi(\mathbf{x})^\top \mathbb{E}[\mathbf{w}\mathbf{w}^\top]\phi(\mathbf{x}') = \phi(\mathbf{x})^\top \Sigma_p \phi(\mathbf{x}').
\end{aligned}
\tag{2.15}
$$

Thus $f(\mathbf{x})$ and $f(\mathbf{x}')$ are jointly Gaussian with zero mean and covariance given by $\phi(\mathbf{x})^\top \Sigma_p \phi(\mathbf{x}')$. Indeed, the function values $f(\mathbf{x}_1), \ldots, f(\mathbf{x}_n)$ corresponding to any number of input points n are jointly Gaussian, although if $N < n$ then this Gaussian is singular (as the joint covariance matrix will be of rank N).

In this chapter our running example of a covariance function will be the *squared exponential*[6] (SE) covariance function; other covariance functions are discussed in chapter 4. The covariance function specifies the covariance between pairs of random variables

$$
\operatorname{cov}\big(f(\mathbf{x}_p), f(\mathbf{x}_q)\big) = k(\mathbf{x}_p, \mathbf{x}_q) = \exp\big(-\tfrac{1}{2}|\mathbf{x}_p - \mathbf{x}_q|^2\big).
\tag{2.16}
$$

Note, that the covariance between the *outputs* is written as a function of the *inputs*. For this particular covariance function, we see that the covariance is almost unity between variables whose corresponding inputs are very close, and decreases as their distance in the input space increases.

basis functions

It can be shown (see section 4.3.1) that the squared exponential covariance function corresponds to a Bayesian linear regression model with an infinite number of basis functions. Indeed for every positive definite covariance function $k(\cdot, \cdot)$, there exists a (possibly infinite) expansion in terms of basis functions (see Mercer's theorem in section 4.3). We can also obtain the SE covariance function from the linear combination of an infinite number of Gaussian-shaped basis functions, see eq. (4.13) and eq. (4.30).

The specification of the covariance function implies a distribution over functions. To see this, we can draw samples from the distribution of functions evaluated at any number of points; in detail, we choose a number of input points,[7] X_* and write out the corresponding covariance matrix using eq. (2.16) elementwise. Then we generate a random Gaussian vector with this covariance matrix

$$
\mathbf{f}_* \sim \mathcal{N}\big(\mathbf{0}, K(X_*, X_*)\big),
\tag{2.17}
$$

and plot the generated values as a function of the inputs. Figure 2.2(a) shows three such samples. The generation of multivariate Gaussian samples is described in section A.2.

smoothness

characteristic
length-scale

In the example in Figure 2.2 the input values were equidistant, but this need not be the case. Notice that "informally" the functions look smooth. In fact the squared exponential covariance function is infinitely differentiable, leading to the process being infinitely mean-square differentiable (see section 4.1). We also see that the functions seem to have a characteristic length-scale,

---

[6] Sometimes this covariance function is called the Radial Basis Function (RBF) or Gaussian; here we prefer squared exponential.

[7] Technically, these input points play the rôle of *test inputs* and therefore carry a subscript asterisk; this will become clearer later when both training and test points are involved.

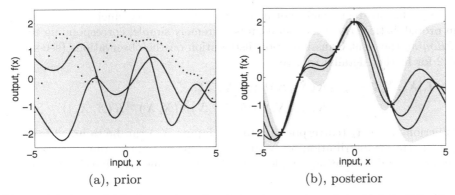

(a), prior   (b), posterior

Figure 2.2: Panel (a) shows three functions drawn at random from a GP prior; the dots indicate values of y actually generated; the two other functions have (less correctly) been drawn as lines by joining a large number of evaluated points. Panel (b) shows three random functions drawn from the posterior, i.e. the prior conditioned on the five noise free observations indicated. In both plots the shaded area represents the pointwise mean plus and minus two times the standard deviation for each input value (corresponding to the 95% confidence region), for the prior and posterior respectively.

which informally can be thought of as roughly the distance you have to move in input space before the function value can change significantly, see section 4.2.1. For eq. (2.16) the characteristic length-scale is around one unit. By replacing $|\mathbf{x}_p - \mathbf{x}_q|$ by $|\mathbf{x}_p - \mathbf{x}_q|/\ell$ in eq. (2.16) for some positive constant ℓ we could change the characteristic length-scale of the process. Also, the overall variance of the random function can be controlled by a positive pre-factor before the exp in eq. (2.16). We will discuss more about how such factors affect the predictions in section 2.3, and say more about how to set such scale parameters in chapter 5.

magnitude

Prediction with Noise-free Observations

We are usually not primarily interested in drawing random functions from the prior, but want to incorporate the knowledge that the training data provides about the function. Initially, we will consider the simple special case where the observations are noise free, that is we know $\{(\mathbf{x}_i, f_i)|i = 1,\ldots,n\}$. The joint distribution of the training outputs, $\mathbf{f}$, and the test outputs $\mathbf{f}_*$ according to the prior is

joint prior

$$\begin{bmatrix} \mathbf{f} \\ \mathbf{f}_* \end{bmatrix} \sim \mathcal{N}\left(\mathbf{0}, \begin{bmatrix} K(X,X) & K(X,X_*) \\ K(X_*,X) & K(X_*,X_*) \end{bmatrix}\right). \qquad (2.18)$$

If there are n training points and n_* test points then $K(X, X_*)$ denotes the $n \times n_*$ matrix of the covariances evaluated at all pairs of training and test points, and similarly for the other entries $K(X,X)$, $K(X_*,X_*)$ and $K(X_*,X)$. To get the posterior distribution over functions we need to restrict this joint prior distribution to contain only those functions which agree with the observed data points. Graphically in Figure 2.2 you may think of generating functions from the prior, and rejecting the ones that disagree with the observations, al-

graphical rejection

though this strategy would not be computationally very efficient. Fortunately, in probabilistic terms this operation is extremely simple, corresponding to *conditioning* the joint Gaussian prior distribution on the observations (see section A.2 for further details) to give

noise-free predictive distribution

$$\mathbf{f}_* | X_*, X, \mathbf{f} \sim \mathcal{N}\big(K(X_*, X)K(X, X)^{-1}\mathbf{f},$$
$$K(X_*, X_*) - K(X_*, X)K(X, X)^{-1}K(X, X_*)\big). \tag{2.19}$$

Function values $\mathbf{f}_*$ (corresponding to test inputs X_*) can be sampled from the joint posterior distribution by evaluating the mean and covariance matrix from eq. (2.19) and generating samples according to the method described in section A.2.

Figure 2.2(b) shows the results of these computations given the five data-points marked with + symbols. Notice that it is trivial to extend these computations to multidimensional inputs – one simply needs to change the evaluation of the covariance function in accordance with eq. (2.16), although the resulting functions may be harder to display graphically.

Prediction using Noisy Observations

It is typical for more realistic modelling situations that we do not have access to function values themselves, but only noisy versions thereof $y = f(\mathbf{x}) + \varepsilon$.[8] Assuming additive independent identically distributed Gaussian noise ε with variance σ_n^2, the prior on the noisy observations becomes

$$\text{cov}(y_p, y_q) = k(\mathbf{x}_p, \mathbf{x}_q) + \sigma_n^2 \delta_{pq} \quad \text{or} \quad \text{cov}(\mathbf{y}) = K(X, X) + \sigma_n^2 I, \tag{2.20}$$

where δ_{pq} is a Kronecker delta which is one iff $p = q$ and zero otherwise. It follows from the independence[9] assumption about the noise, that a diagonal matrix[10] is added, in comparison to the noise free case, eq. (2.16). Introducing the noise term in eq. (2.18) we can write the joint distribution of the observed target values and the function values at the test locations under the prior as

$$\begin{bmatrix} \mathbf{y} \\ \mathbf{f}_* \end{bmatrix} \sim \mathcal{N}\left(\mathbf{0}, \begin{bmatrix} K(X, X) + \sigma_n^2 I & K(X, X_*) \\ K(X_*, X) & K(X_*, X_*) \end{bmatrix}\right). \tag{2.21}$$

predictive distribution Deriving the conditional distribution corresponding to eq. (2.19) we arrive at the key predictive equations for Gaussian process regression

$$\mathbf{f}_* | X, \mathbf{y}, X_* \sim \mathcal{N}\big(\bar{\mathbf{f}}_*, \text{cov}(\mathbf{f}_*)\big), \quad \text{where} \tag{2.22}$$

$$\bar{\mathbf{f}}_* \triangleq \mathbb{E}[\mathbf{f}_* | X, \mathbf{y}, X_*] = K(X_*, X)[K(X, X) + \sigma_n^2 I]^{-1}\mathbf{y}, \tag{2.23}$$

$$\text{cov}(\mathbf{f}_*) = K(X_*, X_*) - K(X_*, X)[K(X, X) + \sigma_n^2 I]^{-1}K(X, X_*). \tag{2.24}$$

---

[8]There are some situations where it is reasonable to assume that the observations are noise-free, for example for computer simulations, see e.g. Sacks et al. [1989].

[9]More complicated noise models with non-trivial covariance structure can also be handled, see section 9.2.

[10]Notice that the Kronecker delta is on the index of the cases, not the value of the input; for the signal part of the covariance function the input *value* is the index set to the random variables describing the function, for the noise part it is the *identity* of the point.

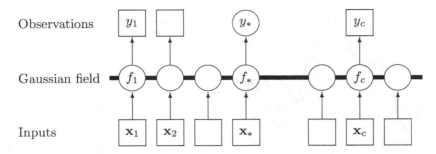

Figure 2.3: Graphical model (chain graph) for a GP for regression. Squares represent observed variables and circles represent unknowns. The thick horizontal bar represents a set of fully connected nodes. Note that an observation y_i is conditionally independent of all other nodes given the corresponding latent variable, f_i. Because of the marginalization property of GPs addition of further inputs, $\mathbf{x}$, latent variables, f, and *unobserved* targets, y_*, does not change the distribution of any other variables.

Notice that we now have exact correspondence with the weight space view in eq. (2.12) when identifying $K(C, D) = \Phi(C)^\top \Sigma_p \Phi(D)$, where C, D stand for either X or X_*. For any set of basis functions, we can compute the corresponding covariance function as $k(\mathbf{x}_p, \mathbf{x}_q) = \phi(\mathbf{x}_p)^\top \Sigma_p \phi(\mathbf{x}_q)$; conversely, for every (positive definite) covariance function k, there exists a (possibly infinite) expansion in terms of basis functions, see section 4.3. *(margin: correspondence with weight-space view)*

The expressions involving $K(X, X)$, $K(X, X_*)$ and $K(X_*, X_*)$ etc. can look rather unwieldy, so we now introduce a compact form of the notation setting $K = K(X, X)$ and $K_* = K(X, X_*)$. In the case that there is only one test point $\mathbf{x}_*$ we write $\mathbf{k}(\mathbf{x}_*) = \mathbf{k}_*$ to denote the vector of covariances between the test point and the n training points. Using this compact notation and for a single test point $\mathbf{x}_*$, equations 2.23 and 2.24 reduce to *(margin: compact notation)*

$$\bar{f}_* = \mathbf{k}_*^\top (K + \sigma_n^2 I)^{-1} \mathbf{y}, \tag{2.25}$$

$$\mathbb{V}[f_*] = k(\mathbf{x}_*, \mathbf{x}_*) - \mathbf{k}_*^\top (K + \sigma_n^2 I)^{-1} \mathbf{k}_*. \tag{2.26}$$

Let us examine the predictive distribution as given by equations 2.25 and 2.26. Note first that the mean prediction eq. (2.25) is a linear combination of observations $\mathbf{y}$; this is sometimes referred to as a *linear predictor*. Another way to look at this equation is to see it as a linear combination of n kernel functions, each one centered on a training point, by writing *(margin: predictive distribution; linear predictor)*

$$\bar{f}(\mathbf{x}_*) = \sum_{i=1}^{n} \alpha_i k(\mathbf{x}_i, \mathbf{x}_*) \tag{2.27}$$

where $\boldsymbol{\alpha} = (K + \sigma_n^2 I)^{-1} \mathbf{y}$. The fact that the mean prediction for $f(\mathbf{x}_*)$ can be written as eq. (2.27) despite the fact that the GP can be represented in terms of a (possibly infinite) number of basis functions is one manifestation of the *representer theorem*; see section 6.2 for more on this point. We can understand this result intuitively because although the GP defines a joint Gaussian distribution over all of the y variables, one for each point in the index set $\mathcal{X}$, for *(margin: representer theorem)*

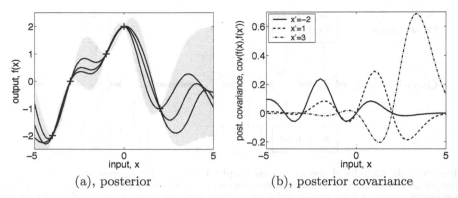

(a), posterior   (b), posterior covariance

Figure 2.4: Panel (a) is identical to Figure 2.2(b) showing three random functions drawn from the posterior. Panel (b) shows the posterior *co*-variance between $f(\mathbf{x})$ and $f(\mathbf{x}')$ for the same data for three different values of $\mathbf{x}'$. Note, that the covariance at close points is high, falling to zero at the training points (where there is no variance, since it is a noise-free process), then becomes negative, etc. This happens because if the smooth function happens to be less than the mean on one side of the data point, it tends to exceed the mean on the other side, causing a reversal of the sign of the covariance at the data points. Note for contrast that the *prior* covariance is simply of Gaussian shape and never negative.

making predictions at $\mathbf{x}_*$ we only care about the $(n+1)$-dimensional distribution defined by the n training points and the test point. As a Gaussian distribution is marginalized by just taking the relevant block of the joint covariance matrix (see section A.2) it is clear that conditioning this $(n+1)$-dimensional distribution on the observations gives us the desired result. A graphical model representation of a GP is given in Figure 2.3.

Note also that the variance in eq. (2.24) does not depend on the observed targets, but only on the inputs; this is a property of the Gaussian distribution. The variance is the difference between two terms: the first term $K(X_*, X_*)$ is simply the prior covariance; from that is subtracted a (positive) term, representing the information the observations gives us about the function. We can

noisy predictions
    very simply compute the predictive distribution of test targets $\mathbf{y}_*$ by adding $\sigma_n^2 I$ to the variance in the expression for $\text{cov}(\mathbf{f}_*)$.

joint predictions
    The predictive distribution for the GP model gives more than just pointwise errorbars of the simplified eq. (2.26). Although not stated explicitly, eq. (2.24) holds unchanged when X_* denotes multiple test inputs; in this case the *co*-variance of the test targets are computed (whose diagonal elements are the pointwise variances). In fact, eq. (2.23) is the mean function and eq. (2.24) the

posterior process
covariance function of the (Gaussian) posterior process; recall the definition of Gaussian process from page 13. The posterior covariance in illustrated in Figure 2.4(b).

marginal likelihood
    It will be useful (particularly for chapter 5) to introduce the *marginal likelihood* (or evidence) $p(\mathbf{y}|X)$ at this point. The marginal likelihood is the integral

---

input: X (inputs), $\mathbf{y}$ (targets), k (covariance function), σ_n^2 (noise level),
$\mathbf{x}_*$ (test input)

2:   $L := \text{cholesky}(K + \sigma_n^2 I)$

     $\boldsymbol{\alpha} := L^\top \backslash (L \backslash \mathbf{y})$ $\Big\}$ predictive mean eq. (2.25)

4:   $\bar{f}_* := \mathbf{k}_*^\top \boldsymbol{\alpha}$

     $\mathbf{v} := L \backslash \mathbf{k}_*$ $\Big\}$ predictive variance eq. (2.26)

6:   $\mathbb{V}[f_*] := k(\mathbf{x}_*, \mathbf{x}_*) - \mathbf{v}^\top \mathbf{v}$

     $\log p(\mathbf{y}|X) := -\frac{1}{2}\mathbf{y}^\top \boldsymbol{\alpha} - \sum_i \log L_{ii} - \frac{n}{2}\log 2\pi$ eq. (2.30)

8:   **return:** $\bar{f}_*$ (mean), $\mathbb{V}[f_*]$ (variance), $\log p(\mathbf{y}|X)$ (log marginal likelihood)

Algorithm 2.1: Predictions and log marginal likelihood for Gaussian process regression. The implementation addresses the matrix inversion required by eq. (2.25) and (2.26) using Cholesky factorization, see section A.4. For multiple test cases lines 4-6 are repeated. The log determinant required in eq. (2.30) is computed from the Cholesky factor (for large n it may not be possible to represent the determinant itself). The computational complexity is $n^3/6$ for the Cholesky decomposition in line 2, and $n^2/2$ for solving triangular systems in line 3 and (for each test case) in line 5.

of the likelihood times the prior

$$p(\mathbf{y}|X) \;=\; \int p(\mathbf{y}|\mathbf{f}, X) p(\mathbf{f}|X) \, d\mathbf{f}. \qquad (2.28)$$

The term *marginal* likelihood refers to the marginalization over the function values $\mathbf{f}$. Under the Gaussian process model the prior is Gaussian, $\mathbf{f}|X \sim \mathcal{N}(\mathbf{0}, K)$, or

$$\log p(\mathbf{f}|X) \;=\; -\tfrac{1}{2}\mathbf{f}^\top K^{-1}\mathbf{f} - \tfrac{1}{2}\log|K| - \tfrac{n}{2}\log 2\pi, \qquad (2.29)$$

and the likelihood is a factorized Gaussian $\mathbf{y}|\mathbf{f} \sim \mathcal{N}(\mathbf{f}, \sigma_n^2 I)$ so we can make use of equations A.7 and A.8 to perform the integration yielding the log marginal likelihood

$$\log p(\mathbf{y}|X) \;=\; -\tfrac{1}{2}\mathbf{y}^\top (K + \sigma_n^2 I)^{-1}\mathbf{y} - \tfrac{1}{2}\log|K + \sigma_n^2 I| - \tfrac{n}{2}\log 2\pi. \qquad (2.30)$$

This result can also be obtained directly by observing that $\mathbf{y} \sim \mathcal{N}(\mathbf{0}, K + \sigma_n^2 I)$.

A practical implementation of Gaussian process regression (GPR) is shown in Algorithm 2.1. The algorithm uses Cholesky decomposition, instead of directly inverting the matrix, since it is faster and numerically more stable, see section A.4. The algorithm returns the predictive mean and variance for noise free test data—to compute the predictive distribution for noisy test data y_*, simply add the noise variance σ_n^2 to the predictive variance of f_*.

2.3   Varying the Hyperparameters

Typically the covariance functions that we use will have some free parameters. For example, the squared-exponential covariance function in one dimension has the following form

$$k_y(x_p, x_q) \;=\; \sigma_f^2 \exp\left(-\frac{1}{2\ell^2}(x_p - x_q)^2\right) + \sigma_n^2 \delta_{pq}. \qquad (2.31)$$

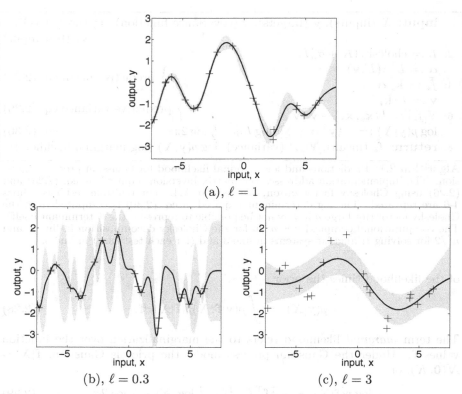

Figure 2.5: (a) Data is generated from a GP with hyperparameters $(\ell, \sigma_f, \sigma_n) = (1, 1, 0.1)$, as shown by the $+$ symbols. Using Gaussian process prediction with these hyperparameters we obtain a 95% confidence region for the underlying function f (shown in grey). Panels (b) and (c) again show the 95% confidence region, but this time for hyperparameter values $(0.3, 1.08, 0.00005)$ and $(3.0, 1.16, 0.89)$ respectively.

The covariance is denoted k_y as it is for the noisy targets y rather than for the underlying function f. Observe that the length-scale ℓ, the signal variance σ_f^2 and the noise variance σ_n^2 can be varied. In general we call the free parameters *hyperparameters*.[11]

hyperparameters

In chapter 5 we will consider various methods for determining the hyperparameters from training data. However, in this section our aim is more simply to explore the effects of varying the hyperparameters on GP prediction. Consider the data shown by $+$ signs in Figure 2.5(a). This was generated from a GP with the SE kernel with $(\ell, \sigma_f, \sigma_n) = (1, 1, 0.1)$. The figure also shows the 2 standard-deviation error bars for the predictions obtained using these values of the hyperparameters, as per eq. (2.24). Notice how the error bars get larger for input values that are distant from any training points. Indeed if the x-axis

---

[11]We refer to the parameters of the covariance function as hyperparameters to emphasize that they are parameters of a non-parametric model; in accordance with the weight-space view, section 2.1, the parameters (weights) of the underlying parametric model have been integrated out.

were extended one would see the error bars reflect the prior standard deviation of the process σ_f away from the data.

If we set the length-scale shorter so that $\ell = 0.3$ and kept the other parameters the same, then generating from this process we would expect to see plots like those in Figure 2.5(a) except that the x-axis should be rescaled by a factor of 0.3; equivalently if the same x-axis was kept as in Figure 2.5(a) then a sample function would look much more wiggly.

If we make predictions with a process with $\ell = 0.3$ on the data generated from the $\ell = 1$ process then we obtain the result in Figure 2.5(b). The remaining two parameters were set by optimizing the marginal likelihood, as explained in chapter 5. In this case the noise parameter is reduced to $\sigma_n = 0.00005$ as the greater flexibility of the "signal" means that the noise level can be reduced. This can be observed at the two datapoints near $x = 2.5$ in the plots. In Figure 2.5(a) ($\ell = 1$) these are essentially explained as a similar function value with differing noise. However, in Figure 2.5(b) ($\ell = 0.3$) the noise level is very low, so these two points have to be explained by a sharp variation in the value of the underlying function f. Notice also that the short length-scale means that the error bars in Figure 2.5(b) grow rapidly away from the datapoints.

too short length-scale

In contrast, we can set the length-scale longer, for example to $\ell = 3$, as shown in Figure 2.5(c). Again the remaining two parameters were set by optimizing the marginal likelihood. In this case the noise level has been increased to $\sigma_n = 0.89$ and we see that the data is now explained by a slowly varying function with a lot of noise.

too long length-scale

Of course we can take the position of a quickly-varying signal with low noise, or a slowly-varying signal with high noise to extremes; the former would give rise to a white-noise process model for the signal, while the latter would give rise to a constant signal with added white noise. Under both these models the datapoints produced should look like white noise. However, studying Figure 2.5(a) we see that white noise is not a convincing model of the data, as the sequence of y's does not alternate sufficiently quickly but has correlations due to the variability of the underlying function. Of course this is relatively easy to see in one dimension, but methods such as the marginal likelihood discussed in chapter 5 generalize to higher dimensions and allow us to score the various models. In this case the marginal likelihood gives a clear preference for $(\ell, \sigma_f, \sigma_n) = (1, 1, 0.1)$ over the other two alternatives.

model comparison

2.4   Decision Theory for Regression

In the previous sections we have shown how to compute predictive distributions for the outputs y_* corresponding to the novel test input $\mathbf{x}_*$. The predictive distribution is Gaussian with mean and variance given by eq. (2.25) and eq. (2.26). In practical applications, however, we are often forced to make a decision about how to act, i.e. we need a point-like prediction which is optimal in some sense. To this end we need a *loss function*, $\mathcal{L}(y_{\text{true}}, y_{\text{guess}})$, which specifies the loss (or

optimal predictions
loss function

penalty) incurred by guessing the value y_guess when the true value is y_true. For example, the loss function could equal the absolute deviation between the guess and the truth.

non-Bayesian paradigm
Bayesian paradigm

Notice that we computed the predictive distribution without reference to the loss function. In non-Bayesian paradigms, the model is typically trained by minimizing the empirical risk (or loss). In contrast, in the Bayesian setting there is a clear separation between the likelihood function (used for training, in addition to the prior) and the loss function. The likelihood function describes how the noisy measurements are assumed to deviate from the underlying noise-free function. The loss function, on the other hand, captures the consequences of making a specific choice, given an actual true state. The likelihood and loss function need not have anything in common.[12]

expected loss, risk

Our goal is to make the point prediction y_guess which incurs the smallest loss, but how can we achieve that when we don't know y_true? Instead, we minimize the *expected loss* or *risk*, by averaging w.r.t. our model's opinion as to what the truth might be

$$\tilde{R}_\mathcal{L}(y_\text{guess}|\mathbf{x}_*) = \int \mathcal{L}(y_*, y_\text{guess}) p(y_*|\mathbf{x}_*, \mathcal{D}) \, dy_*. \tag{2.32}$$

Thus our best guess, in the sense that it minimizes the expected loss, is

$$y_\text{optimal}|\mathbf{x}_* = \underset{y_\text{guess}}{\operatorname{argmin}} \tilde{R}_\mathcal{L}(y_\text{guess}|\mathbf{x}_*). \tag{2.33}$$

absolute error loss
squared error loss

In general the value of y_guess that minimizes the risk for the loss function $|y_\text{guess} - y_*|$ is the median of $p(y_*|\mathbf{x}_*, \mathcal{D})$, while for the squared loss $(y_\text{guess} - y_*)^2$ it is the mean of this distribution. When the predictive distribution is Gaussian the mean and the median coincide, and indeed for any symmetric loss function and symmetric predictive distribution we always get y_guess as the mean of the predictive distribution. However, in many practical problems the loss functions can be asymmetric, e.g. in safety critical applications, and point predictions may be computed directly from eq. (2.32) and eq. (2.33). A comprehensive treatment of decision theory can be found in Berger [1985].

2.5   An Example Application

robot arm

In this section we use Gaussian process regression to learn the inverse dynamics of a seven degrees-of-freedom SARCOS anthropomorphic robot arm. The task is to map from a 21-dimensional input space (7 joint positions, 7 joint velocities, 7 joint accelerations) to the corresponding 7 joint torques. This task has previously been used to study regression algorithms by Vijayakumar and Schaal [2000], Vijayakumar et al. [2002] and Vijayakumar et al. [2005].[13] Following

---

[12]Beware of fallacious arguments like: a Gaussian likelihood implies a squared error loss function.

[13]We thank Sethu Vijayakumar for providing us with the data.

this previous work we present results below on just one of the seven mappings, from the 21 input variables to the first of the seven torques.

One might ask why it is necessary to *learn* this mapping; indeed there exist physics-based rigid-body-dynamics models which allow us to obtain the torques from the position, velocity and acceleration variables. However, the real robot arm is actuated hydraulically and is rather lightweight and compliant, so the assumptions of the rigid-body-dynamics model are violated (as we see below). It is worth noting that the rigid-body-dynamics model is nonlinear, involving trigonometric functions and squares of the input variables.

why learning?

An inverse dynamics model can be used in the following manner: a planning module decides on a trajectory that takes the robot from its start to goal states, and this specifies the desired positions, velocities and accelerations at each time. The inverse dynamics model is used to compute the torques needed to achieve this trajectory and errors are corrected using a feedback controller.

The dataset consists of 48,933 input-output pairs, of which 44,484 were used as a training set and the remaining 4,449 were used as a test set. The inputs were linearly rescaled to have zero mean and unit variance on the training set. The outputs were centered so as to have zero mean on the training set.

Given a prediction method, we can evaluate the quality of predictions in several ways. Perhaps the simplest is the squared error loss, where we compute the squared residual $(y_* - \bar{f}(\mathbf{x}_*))^2$ between the mean prediction and the target at each test point. This can be summarized by the mean squared error (MSE), by averaging over the test set. However, this quantity is sensitive to the overall scale of the target values, so it makes sense to normalize by the variance of the targets of the test cases to obtain the *standardized mean squared error* (SMSE). This causes the trivial method of guessing the mean of the training targets to have a SMSE of approximately 1.

MSE

SMSE

Additionally if we produce a predictive distribution at each test input we can evaluate the negative log probability of the target under the model.[14] As GPR produces a Gaussian predictive density, one obtains

$$-\log p(y_*|\mathcal{D}, \mathbf{x}_*) \ = \ \frac{1}{2}\log(2\pi\sigma_*^2) + \frac{(y_* - \bar{f}(\mathbf{x}_*))^2}{2\sigma_*^2}, \qquad (2.34)$$

where the predictive variance σ_*^2 for GPR is computed as $\sigma_*^2 = \mathbb{V}(f_*) + \sigma_n^2$, where $\mathbb{V}(f_*)$ is given by eq. (2.26); we must include the noise variance σ_n^2 as we are predicting the noisy target y_*. This loss can be standardized by subtracting the loss that would be obtained under the trivial model which predicts using a Gaussian with the mean and variance of the training data. We denote this the standardized log loss (SLL). The mean SLL is denoted MSLL. Thus the MSLL will be approximately zero for simple methods and negative for better methods.

MSLL

A number of models were tested on the data. A linear regression (LR) model provides a simple baseline for the SMSE. By estimating the noise level from the

---

[14]It makes sense to use the *negative* log probability so as to obtain a loss, not a utility.

Method	SMSE	MSLL
LR	0.075	-1.29
RBD	0.104	–
LWPR	0.040	–
GPR	0.011	-2.25

Table 2.1: Test results on the inverse dynamics problem for a number of different methods. The "–" denotes a missing entry, caused by two methods not producing full predictive *distributions*, so MSLL could not be evaluated.

residuals on the training set one can also obtain a predictive variance and thus get a MSLL value for LR. The rigid-body-dynamics (RBD) model has a number of free parameters; these were estimated by Vijayakumar et al. [2005] using a least-squares fitting procedure. We also give results for the locally weighted projection regression (LWPR) method of Vijayakumar et al. [2005] which is an on-line method that cycles through the dataset multiple times. For the GP models it is computationally expensive to make use of all 44,484 training cases due to the $O(n^3)$ scaling of the basic algorithm. In chapter 8 we present several different approximate GP methods for large datasets. The result given in Table 2.1 was obtained with the subset of regressors (SR) approximation with a subset size of 4096. This result is taken from Table 8.1, which gives full results of the various approximation methods applied to the inverse dynamics problem. The squared exponential covariance function was used with a separate length-scale parameter for each of the 21 input dimensions, plus the signal and noise variance parameters σ_f^2 and σ_n^2. These parameters were set by optimizing the marginal likelihood eq. (2.30) on a subset of the data (see also chapter 5).

The results for the various methods are presented in Table 2.1. Notice that the problem is quite non-linear, so the linear regression model does poorly in comparison to non-linear methods.[15] The non-linear method LWPR improves over linear regression, but is outperformed by GPR.

2.6 Smoothing, Weight Functions and Equivalent Kernels

Gaussian process regression aims to reconstruct the underlying signal f by removing the contaminating noise ε. To do this it computes a weighted average of the noisy observations $\mathbf{y}$ as $\bar{f}(\mathbf{x}_*) = \mathbf{k}(\mathbf{x}_*)^\top (K + \sigma_n^2 I)^{-1} \mathbf{y}$; as $\bar{f}(\mathbf{x}_*)$ is a *linear* combination of the y values, Gaussian process regression is a *linear smoother* (see Hastie and Tibshirani [1990, sec. 2.8] for further details). In this section we study smoothing first in terms of a matrix analysis of the predictions at the training points, and then in terms of the equivalent kernel.

linear smoother

---

[15] It is perhaps surprising that RBD does worse than linear regression. However, Stefan Schaal (pers. comm., 2004) states that the RBD parameters were optimized on a very large dataset, of which the training data used here is subset, and if the RBD model were optimized w.r.t. this training set one might well expect it to outperform linear regression.

The predicted mean values $\bar{\mathbf{f}}$ at the training points are given by

$$\bar{\mathbf{f}} = K(K + \sigma_n^2 I)^{-1}\mathbf{y}. \tag{2.35}$$

Let K have the eigendecomposition $K = \sum_{i=1}^{n} \lambda_i \mathbf{u}_i \mathbf{u}_i^\top$, where λ_i is the ith eigenvalue and $\mathbf{u}_i$ is the corresponding eigenvector. As K is real and symmetric positive semidefinite, its eigenvalues are real and non-negative, and its eigenvectors are mutually orthogonal. Let $\mathbf{y} = \sum_{i=1}^{n} \gamma_i \mathbf{u}_i$ for some coefficients $\gamma_i = \mathbf{u}_i^\top \mathbf{y}$. Then

eigendecomposition

$$\bar{\mathbf{f}} = \sum_{i=1}^{n} \frac{\gamma_i \lambda_i}{\lambda_i + \sigma_n^2} \mathbf{u}_i. \tag{2.36}$$

Notice that if $\lambda_i/(\lambda_i + \sigma_n^2) \ll 1$ then the component in $\mathbf{y}$ along $\mathbf{u}_i$ is effectively eliminated. For most covariance functions that are used in practice the eigenvalues are larger for more slowly varying eigenvectors (e.g. fewer zero-crossings) so that this means that high-frequency components in $\mathbf{y}$ are smoothed out. The effective number of parameters or degrees of freedom of the smoother is defined as $\mathrm{tr}(K(K + \sigma_n^2 I)^{-1}) = \sum_{i=1}^{n} \lambda_i/(\lambda_i + \sigma_n^2)$, see Hastie and Tibshirani [1990, sec. 3.5]. Notice that this counts the number of eigenvectors which are not eliminated.

degrees of freedom

We can define a vector of functions $\mathbf{h}(\mathbf{x}_*) = (K + \sigma_n^2 I)^{-1}\mathbf{k}(\mathbf{x}_*)$. Thus we have $\bar{f}(\mathbf{x}_*) = \mathbf{h}(\mathbf{x}_*)^\top \mathbf{y}$, making it clear that the mean prediction at a point $\mathbf{x}_*$ is a linear combination of the target values $\mathbf{y}$. For a fixed test point $\mathbf{x}_*$, $\mathbf{h}(\mathbf{x}_*)$ gives the vector of weights applied to targets $\mathbf{y}$. $\mathbf{h}(\mathbf{x}_*)$ is called the *weight function* [Silverman, 1984]. As Gaussian process regression is a linear smoother, the weight function does not depend on $\mathbf{y}$. Note the difference between a linear *model*, where the prediction is a linear combination of the *inputs*, and a linear *smoother*, where the prediction is a linear combination of the training set targets.

weight function

Understanding the form of the weight function is made complicated by the matrix inversion of $K + \sigma_n^2 I$ and the fact that K depends on the specific locations of the n datapoints. Idealizing the situation one can consider the observations to be "smeared out" in $\mathbf{x}$-space at some density of observations. In this case analytic tools can be brought to bear on the problem, as shown in section 7.1. By analogy to kernel smoothing, Silverman [1984] called the idealized weight function the *equivalent kernel*; see also Girosi et al. [1995, sec. 2.1].

equivalent kernel

A kernel smoother centres a kernel function[16] κ on $\mathbf{x}_*$ and then computes $\kappa_i = \kappa(|\mathbf{x}_i - \mathbf{x}_*|/\ell)$ for each data point $(\mathbf{x}_i, y_i)$, where ℓ is a length-scale. The Gaussian is a commonly used kernel function. The prediction for $f(\mathbf{x}_*)$ is computed as $\hat{f}(\mathbf{x}_*) = \sum_{i=1}^{n} w_i y_i$ where $w_i = \kappa_i/\sum_{j=1}^{n} \kappa_j$. This is also known as the Nadaraya-Watson estimator, see e.g. Scott [1992, sec. 8.1].

kernel smoother

The weight function and equivalent kernel for a Gaussian process are illustrated in Figure 2.6 for a one-dimensional input variable x. We have used the squared exponential covariance function and have set the length-scale $\ell = 0.0632$ (so that $\ell^2 = 0.004$). There are $n = 50$ training points spaced randomly along

---

[16]Note that this kernel function does not need to be a valid covariance function.

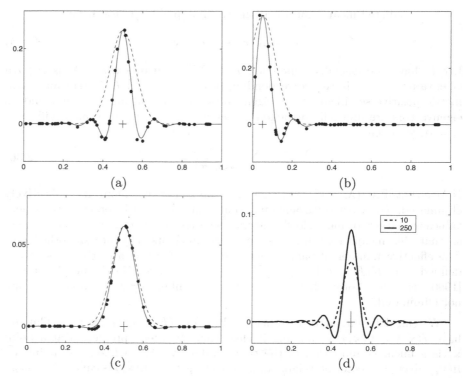

Figure 2.6: Panels (a)-(c) show the weight function $\mathbf{h}(x_*)$ (dots) corresponding to the $n = 50$ training points, the equivalent kernel (solid) and the original squared exponential kernel (dashed). Panel (d) shows the equivalent kernels for two different data densities. See text for further details. The small cross at the test point is to scale in all four plots.

the x-axis. Figures 2.6(a) and 2.6(b) show the weight function and equivalent kernel for $x_* = 0.5$ and $x_* = 0.05$ respectively, for $\sigma_n^2 = 0.1$. Figure 2.6(c) is also for $x_* = 0.5$ but uses $\sigma_n^2 = 10$. In each case the dots correspond to the weight function $\mathbf{h}(x_*)$ and the solid line is the equivalent kernel, whose construction is explained below. The dashed line shows a squared exponential kernel centered on the test point, scaled to have the same height as the maximum value in the equivalent kernel. Figure 2.6(d) shows the variation in the equivalent kernel as a function of n, the number of datapoints in the unit interval.

Many interesting observations can be made from these plots. Observe that the equivalent kernel has (in general) a shape quite different to the original SE kernel. In Figure 2.6(a) the equivalent kernel is clearly oscillatory (with negative sidelobes) and has a higher spatial frequency than the original kernel. Figure 2.6(b) shows similar behaviour although due to edge effects the equivalent kernel is truncated relative to that in Figure 2.6(a). In Figure 2.6(c) we see that at higher noise levels the negative sidelobes are reduced and the width of the equivalent kernel is similar to the original kernel. Also note that the overall height of the equivalent kernel in (c) is reduced compared to that in (a) and (b)—it averages over a wider area. The more oscillatory equivalent kernel for lower noise levels can be understood in terms of the eigenanalysis above; at higher noise levels only the large λ (slowly varying) components of $\mathbf{y}$ remain, while for smaller noise levels the more oscillatory components are also retained.

In Figure 2.6(d) we have plotted the equivalent kernel for $n = 10$ and $n = 250$ datapoints in $[0, 1]$; notice how the width of the equivalent kernel decreases as n increases. We discuss this behaviour further in section 7.1.

The plots of equivalent kernels in Figure 2.6 were made by using a dense grid of n_{grid} points on $[0, 1]$ and then computing the smoother matrix $K(K + \sigma_{\text{grid}}^2 I)^{-1}$. Each row of this matrix is the equivalent kernel at the appropriate location. However, in order to get the scaling right one has to set $\sigma_{\text{grid}}^2 = \sigma_n^2 n_{\text{grid}}/n$; for $n_{\text{grid}} > n$ this means that the effective variance at each of the n_{grid} points is larger, but as there are correspondingly more points this effect cancels out. This can be understood by imagining the situation if there were n_{grid}/n independent Gaussian observations with variance σ_{grid}^2 at a single x-position; this would be equivalent to one Gaussian observation with variance σ_n^2. In effect the n observations have been smoothed out uniformly along the interval. The form of the equivalent kernel can be obtained analytically if we go to the continuum limit and look to smooth a noisy function. The relevant theory and some example equivalent kernels are given in section 7.1.

2.7 Incorporating Explicit Basis Functions *

It is common but by no means necessary to consider GPs with a zero mean function. Note that this is not necessarily a drastic limitation, since the mean of the *posterior* process is not confined to be zero. Yet there are several reasons why one might wish to explicitly model a mean function, including interpretability of the model, convenience of expressing prior information and a number of analytical limits which we will need in subsequent chapters. The use of explicit basis functions is a way to specify a non-zero mean over functions, but as we will see in this section, one can also use them to achieve other interesting effects.

Using a *fixed* (deterministic) mean function $m(\mathbf{x})$ is trivial: Simply apply   *fixed mean function*
the usual zero mean GP to the *difference* between the observations and the fixed mean function. With

$$f(\mathbf{x}) \sim \mathcal{GP}\big(m(\mathbf{x}),\ k(\mathbf{x}, \mathbf{x}')\big), \tag{2.37}$$

the predictive mean becomes

$$\bar{\mathbf{f}}_* = \mathbf{m}(X_*) + K(X_*, X)K_y^{-1}(\mathbf{y} - \mathbf{m}(X)), \tag{2.38}$$

where $K_y = K + \sigma_n^2 I$, and the predictive variance remains unchanged from eq. (2.24).

However, in practice it can often be difficult to specify a fixed mean function. In many cases it may be more convenient to specify a few fixed basis functions,

stochastic mean
function

whose coefficients, β, are to be inferred from the data. Consider

$$g(\mathbf{x}) = f(\mathbf{x}) + \mathbf{h}(\mathbf{x})^\top \beta, \quad \text{where} \quad f(\mathbf{x}) \sim \mathcal{GP}\big(0, k(\mathbf{x}, \mathbf{x}')\big), \qquad (2.39)$$

here $f(\mathbf{x})$ is a zero mean GP, $\mathbf{h}(\mathbf{x})$ are a set of fixed basis functions, and β are additional parameters. This formulation expresses that the data is close to a global linear model with the residuals being modelled by a GP. This idea was explored explicitly as early as 1975 by Blight and Ott [1975], who used the GP to model the residuals from a polynomial regression, i.e. $\mathbf{h}(x) = (1, x, x^2, \dots)$.

polynomial regression

When fitting the model, one could optimize over the parameters β jointly with the hyperparameters of the covariance function. Alternatively, if we take the prior on β to be Gaussian, $\beta \sim \mathcal{N}(\mathbf{b}, B)$, we can also integrate out these parameters. Following O'Hagan [1978] we obtain another GP

$$g(\mathbf{x}) \sim \mathcal{GP}\big(\mathbf{h}(\mathbf{x})^\top \mathbf{b}, \ k(\mathbf{x}, \mathbf{x}') + \mathbf{h}(\mathbf{x})^\top B \mathbf{h}(\mathbf{x}')\big), \qquad (2.40)$$

now with an added contribution in the covariance function caused by the uncertainty in the parameters of the mean. Predictions are made by plugging the mean and covariance functions of $g(\mathbf{x})$ into eq. (2.39) and eq. (2.24). After rearranging, we obtain

$$\begin{aligned}
\bar{\mathbf{g}}(X_*) &= H_*^\top \bar{\beta} + K_*^\top K_y^{-1}(\mathbf{y} - H^\top \bar{\beta}) = \bar{\mathbf{f}}(X_*) + R^\top \bar{\beta}, \\
\operatorname{cov}(\mathbf{g}_*) &= \operatorname{cov}(\mathbf{f}_*) + R^\top (B^{-1} + H K_y^{-1} H^\top)^{-1} R,
\end{aligned} \qquad (2.41)$$

where the H matrix collects the $\mathbf{h}(\mathbf{x})$ vectors for all training (and H_* all test) cases, $\bar{\beta} = (B^{-1} + H K_y^{-1} H^\top)^{-1}(H K_y^{-1} \mathbf{y} + B^{-1} \mathbf{b})$, and $R = H_* - H K_y^{-1} K_*$. Notice the nice interpretation of the mean expression, eq. (2.41) top line: $\bar{\beta}$ is the mean of the global linear model parameters, being a compromise between the data term and prior, and the predictive mean is simply the mean linear output plus what the GP model predicts from the residuals. The covariance is the sum of the usual covariance term and a new non-negative contribution.

Exploring the limit of the above expressions as the prior on the β parameter becomes vague, $B^{-1} \to O$ (where O is the matrix of zeros), we obtain a predictive distribution which is independent of $\mathbf{b}$

$$\begin{aligned}
\bar{\mathbf{g}}(X_*) &= \bar{\mathbf{f}}(X_*) + R^\top \bar{\beta}, \\
\operatorname{cov}(\mathbf{g}_*) &= \operatorname{cov}(\mathbf{f}_*) + R^\top (H K_y^{-1} H^\top)^{-1} R,
\end{aligned} \qquad (2.42)$$

where the limiting $\bar{\beta} = (H K_y^{-1} H^\top)^{-1} H K_y^{-1} \mathbf{y}$. Notice that predictions under the limit $B^{-1} \to O$ should not be implemented naïvely by plugging the modified covariance function from eq. (2.40) into the standard prediction equations, since the entries of the covariance function tend to infinity, thus making it unsuitable for numerical implementation. Instead eq. (2.42) must be used. Even if the non-limiting case is of interest, eq. (2.41) is numerically preferable to a direct implementation based on eq. (2.40), since the global linear part will often add some very large eigenvalues to the covariance matrix, affecting its condition number.

2.7.1 Marginal Likelihood

In this short section we briefly discuss the marginal likelihood for the model with a Gaussian prior $\boldsymbol{\beta} \sim \mathcal{N}(\mathbf{b}, B)$ on the explicit parameters from eq. (2.40), as this will be useful later, particularly in section 6.3.1. We can express the marginal likelihood from eq. (2.30) as

$$
\begin{aligned}
\log p(\mathbf{y}|X, \mathbf{b}, B) = {} & -\tfrac{1}{2}(H^\top \mathbf{b} - \mathbf{y})^\top (K_y + H^\top B H)^{-1}(H^\top \mathbf{b} - \mathbf{y}) \\
& -\tfrac{1}{2}\log|K_y + H^\top B H| - \tfrac{n}{2}\log 2\pi,
\end{aligned} \tag{2.43}
$$

where we have included the explicit mean. We are interested in exploring the limit where $B^{-1} \to O$, i.e. when the prior is vague. In this limit the mean of the prior is irrelevant (as was the case in eq. (2.42)), so without loss of generality (for the limiting case) we assume for now that the mean is zero, $\mathbf{b} = \mathbf{0}$, giving

$$
\begin{aligned}
\log p(\mathbf{y}|X, \mathbf{b} {=} \mathbf{0}, B) = {} & -\tfrac{1}{2}\mathbf{y}^\top K_y^{-1}\mathbf{y} + \tfrac{1}{2}\mathbf{y}^\top C\mathbf{y} \\
& -\tfrac{1}{2}\log|K_y| - \tfrac{1}{2}\log|B| - \tfrac{1}{2}\log|A| - \tfrac{n}{2}\log 2\pi,
\end{aligned} \tag{2.44}
$$

where $A = B^{-1} + H K_y^{-1} H^\top$ and $C = K_y^{-1} H^\top A^{-1} H K_y^{-1}$ and we have used the matrix inversion lemma, eq. (A.9) and eq. (A.10).

We now explore the behaviour of the log marginal likelihood in the limit of vague priors on $\boldsymbol{\beta}$. In this limit the variances of the Gaussian in the directions spanned by columns of $H^\top$ will become infinite, and it is clear that this will require special treatment. The log marginal likelihood consists of three terms: a quadratic form in $\mathbf{y}$, a log determinant term, and a term involving $\log 2\pi$. Performing an eigendecomposition of the covariance matrix we see that the contributions to quadratic form term from the infinite-variance directions will be zero. However, the log determinant term will tend to minus infinity. The standard solution [Wahba, 1985, Ansley and Kohn, 1985] in this case is to project $\mathbf{y}$ onto the directions orthogonal to the span of $H^\top$ and compute the marginal likelihood in this subspace. Let the rank of $H^\top$ be m. Then as shown in Ansley and Kohn [1985] this means that we must discard the terms $-\tfrac{1}{2}\log|B| - \tfrac{m}{2}\log 2\pi$ from eq. (2.44) to give

$$
\log p(\mathbf{y}|X) = -\tfrac{1}{2}\mathbf{y}^\top K_y^{-1}\mathbf{y} + \tfrac{1}{2}\mathbf{y}^\top C\mathbf{y} - \tfrac{1}{2}\log|K_y| - \tfrac{1}{2}\log|A| - \tfrac{n-m}{2}\log 2\pi, \tag{2.45}
$$

where $A = H K_y^{-1} H^\top$ and $C = K_y^{-1} H^\top A^{-1} H K_y^{-1}$.

2.8 History and Related Work

Prediction with Gaussian processes is certainly not a very recent topic, especially for time series analysis; the basic theory goes back at least as far as the work of Wiener [1949] and Kolmogorov [1941] in the 1940's. Indeed Lauritzen [1981] discusses relevant work by the Danish astronomer T. N. Thiele dating from 1880.

time series

geostatistics

kriging

Gaussian process prediction is also well known in the geostatistics field (see, e.g. Matheron, 1973; Journel and Huijbregts, 1978) where it is known as *kriging*,[17] and in meteorology [Thompson, 1956, Daley, 1991] although this literature naturally has focussed mostly on two- and three-dimensional input spaces. Whittle [1963, sec. 5.4] also suggests the use of such methods for spatial prediction. Ripley [1981] and Cressie [1993] provide useful overviews of Gaussian process prediction in spatial statistics.

Gradually it was realized that Gaussian process prediction could be used in a general regression context. For example O'Hagan [1978] presents the general theory as given in our equations 2.23 and 2.24, and applies it to a number of one-dimensional regression problems. Sacks et al. [1989] describe GPR in the

computer experiments

context of computer experiments (where the observations y are noise free) and discuss a number of interesting directions such as the optimization of parameters in the covariance function (see our chapter 5) and experimental design (i.e. the choice of **x**-points that provide most information on f). The authors describe a number of computer simulations that were modelled, including an example where the response variable was the clock asynchronization in a circuit and the inputs were six transistor widths. Santner et al. [2003] is a recent book on the use of GPs for the design and analysis of computer experiments.

machine learning

Williams and Rasmussen [1996] described Gaussian process regression in a machine learning context, and described optimization of the parameters in the covariance function, see also Rasmussen [1996]. They were inspired to use Gaussian process by the connection to infinite neural networks as described in section 4.2.3 and in Neal [1996]. The "kernelization" of linear ridge regression described above is also known as *kernel ridge regression* see e.g. Saunders et al. [1998].

Relationships between Gaussian process prediction and regularization theory, splines, support vector machines (SVMs) and relevance vector machines (RVMs) are discussed in chapter 6.

2.9   Exercises

1. Replicate the generation of random functions from Figure 2.2. Use a regular (or random) grid of scalar inputs and the covariance function from eq. (2.16). Hints on how to generate random samples from multi-variate Gaussian distributions are given in section A.2. Invent some training data points, and make random draws from the resulting GP posterior using eq. (2.19).

2. In eq. (2.11) we saw that the predictive variance at $\mathbf{x}_*$ under the feature space regression model was $\text{var}(f(\mathbf{x}_*)) = \boldsymbol{\phi}(\mathbf{x}_*)^\top A^{-1} \boldsymbol{\phi}(\mathbf{x}_*)$. Show that $\text{cov}(f(\mathbf{x}_*), f(\mathbf{x}'_*)) = \boldsymbol{\phi}(\mathbf{x}_*)^\top A^{-1} \boldsymbol{\phi}(\mathbf{x}'_*)$. Check that this is compatible with the expression given in eq. (2.24).

---

[17]Matheron named the method after the South African mining engineer D. G. Krige.

3. The Wiener process is defined for $x \geq 0$ and has $f(0) = 0$. (See section B.2.1 for further details.) It has mean zero and a non-stationary covariance function $k(x, x') = \min(x, x')$. If we condition on the Wiener process passing through $f(1) = 0$ we obtain a process known as the Brownian bridge (or *tied-down* Wiener process). Show that this process has covariance $k(x, x') = \min(x, x') - xx'$ for $0 \leq x, x' \leq 1$ and mean 0. Write a computer program to draw samples from this process at a finite grid of x points in $[0, 1]$.

4. Let $\text{var}_n(f(\mathbf{x}_*))$ be the predictive variance of a Gaussian process regression model at $\mathbf{x}_*$ given a dataset of size n. The corresponding predictive variance using a dataset of only the first $n - 1$ training points is denoted $\text{var}_{n-1}(f(\mathbf{x}_*))$. Show that $\text{var}_n(f(\mathbf{x}_*)) \leq \text{var}_{n-1}(f(\mathbf{x}_*))$, i.e. that the predictive variance at $\mathbf{x}_*$ cannot increase as more training data is obtained. One way to approach this problem is to use the partitioned matrix equations given in section A.3 to decompose $\text{var}_n(f(\mathbf{x}_*)) = k(\mathbf{x}_*, \mathbf{x}_*) - \mathbf{k}_*^\top (K + \sigma_n^2 I)^{-1} \mathbf{k}_*$. An alternative information theoretic argument is given in Williams and Vivarelli [2000]. Note that while this conclusion is true for Gaussian process priors and Gaussian noise models it does not hold generally, see Barber and Saad [1996].

Chapter 3

Classification

In chapter 2 we have considered *regression* problems, where the targets are real valued. Another important class of problems is *classification*[1] problems, where we wish to assign an input pattern $\mathbf{x}$ to one of C classes, $\mathcal{C}_1, \ldots, \mathcal{C}_C$. Practical examples of classification problems are handwritten digit recognition (where we wish to classify a digitized image of a handwritten digit into one of ten classes 0-9), and the classification of objects detected in astronomical sky surveys into stars or galaxies. (Information on the distribution of galaxies in the universe is important for theories of the early universe.) These examples nicely illustrate that classification problems can either be binary (or two-class, $C = 2$) or multi-class ($C > 2$).

binary, multi-class

We will focus attention on *probabilistic classification*, where test predictions take the form of class probabilities; this contrasts with methods which provide only a *guess* at the class label, and this distinction is analogous to the difference between predictive distributions and point predictions in the regression setting. Since generalization to test cases inherently involves some level of uncertainty, it seems natural to attempt to make predictions in a way that reflects these uncertainties. In a practical application one may well seek a class guess, which can be obtained as the solution to a *decision problem*, involving the predictive probabilities as well as a specification of the consequences of making specific predictions (the loss function).

probabilistic classification

Both classification and regression can be viewed as *function approximation* problems. Unfortunately, the solution of classification problems using Gaussian processes is rather more demanding than for the regression problems considered in chapter 2. This is because we assumed in the previous chapter that the likelihood function was Gaussian; a Gaussian process prior combined with a Gaussian likelihood gives rise to a posterior Gaussian process over functions, and everything remains analytically tractable. For classification models, where the targets are discrete class labels, the Gaussian likelihood is inappropriate;[2]

non-Gaussian likelihood

---

[1] In the statistics literature classification is often called discrimination.

[2] One may choose to ignore the discreteness of the target values, and use a regression treatment, where all targets happen to be say ± 1 for binary classification. This is known as

in this chapter we treat methods of approximate inference for classification, where exact inference is not feasible.[3]

Section 3.1 provides a general discussion of classification problems, and describes the *generative* and *discriminative* approaches to these problems. In section 2.1 we saw how Gaussian process regression (GPR) can be obtained by generalizing linear regression. In section 3.2 we describe an analogue of linear regression in the classification case, logistic regression. In section 3.3 logistic regression is generalized to yield Gaussian process classification (GPC) using again the ideas behind the generalization of linear regression to GPR. For GPR the combination of a GP prior with a Gaussian likelihood gives rise to a posterior which is again a Gaussian process. In the classification case the likelihood is non-Gaussian but the posterior process can be *approximated* by a GP. The Laplace approximation for GPC is described in section 3.4 (for binary classification) and in section 3.5 (for multi-class classification), and the expectation propagation algorithm (for binary classification) is described in section 3.6. Both of these methods make use of a Gaussian approximation to the posterior. Experimental results for GPC are given in section 3.7, and a discussion of these results is provided in section 3.8.

3.1   Classification Problems

The natural starting point for discussing approaches to classification is the joint probability $p(y, \mathbf{x})$, where y denotes the class label. Using Bayes' theorem this joint probability can be decomposed either as $p(y)p(\mathbf{x}|y)$ or as $p(\mathbf{x})p(y|\mathbf{x})$. This gives rise to two different approaches to classification problems. The first, which we call the *generative* approach, models the class-conditional distributions $p(\mathbf{x}|y)$ for $y = \mathcal{C}_1, \ldots, \mathcal{C}_C$ and also the prior probabilities of each class, and then computes the posterior probability for each class using

generative approach

$$p(y|\mathbf{x}) = \frac{p(y)p(\mathbf{x}|y)}{\sum_{c=1}^{C} p(\mathcal{C}_c)p(\mathbf{x}|\mathcal{C}_c)}. \tag{3.1}$$

discriminative approach

The alternative approach, which we call the *discriminative* approach, focusses on modelling $p(y|\mathbf{x})$ directly. Dawid [1976] calls the generative and discriminative approaches the sampling and diagnostic paradigms, respectively.

To turn both the generative and discriminative approaches into practical methods we will need to create *models* for either $p(\mathbf{x}|y)$, or $p(y|\mathbf{x})$ respectively.[4] These could either be of parametric form, or non-parametric models such as those based on nearest neighbours. For the generative case a simple, com-

generative model example

---

least-squares classification, see section 6.5.

[3]Note, that the important distinction is between Gaussian and non-Gaussian likelihoods; regression with a non-Gaussian likelihood requires a similar treatment, but since classification defines an important conceptual and application area, we have chosen to treat it in a separate chapter; for non-Gaussian likelihoods in general, see section 9.3.

[4]For the generative approach inference for $p(y)$ is generally straightforward, being estimation of a binomial probability in the binary case, or a multinomial probability in the multi-class case.

mon choice would be to model the class-conditional densities with Gaussians: $p(\mathbf{x}|\mathcal{C}_c) = \mathcal{N}(\boldsymbol{\mu}_c, \Sigma_c)$. A Bayesian treatment can be obtained by placing appropriate priors on the mean and covariance of each of the Gaussians. However, note that this Gaussian model makes a strong assumption on the form of class-conditional density and if this is inappropriate the model may perform poorly.

For the binary discriminative case one simple idea is to turn the output of a regression model into a class probability using a *response function* (the inverse of a *link function*), which "squashes" its argument, which can lie in the domain $(-\infty, \infty)$, into the range $[0, 1]$, guaranteeing a valid probabilistic interpretation.

discriminative model example

One example is the *linear logistic regression* model

$$p(\mathcal{C}_1|\mathbf{x}) = \lambda(\mathbf{x}^\top \mathbf{w}), \quad \text{where} \quad \lambda(z) = \frac{1}{1 + \exp(-z)}, \tag{3.2}$$

which combines the linear model with the logistic response function. Another common choice of response function is the cumulative density function of a standard normal distribution $\Phi(z) = \int_{-\infty}^{z} \mathcal{N}(x|0, 1)dx$. This approach is known as *probit regression*. Just as we gave a Bayesian approach to linear regression in chapter 2 we can take a parallel approach to logistic regression, as discussed in section 3.2. As in the regression case, this model is an important step towards the Gaussian process classifier.

response function

probit regression

Given that there are the generative and discriminative approaches, which one should we prefer? This is perhaps the biggest question in classification, and we do not believe that there is a right answer, as both ways of writing the joint $p(y, \mathbf{x})$ are correct. However, it is possible to identify some strengths and weaknesses of the two approaches. The discriminative approach is appealing in that it is directly modelling what we want, $p(y|\mathbf{x})$. Also, density estimation for the class-conditional distributions is a hard problem, particularly when $\mathbf{x}$ is high dimensional, so if we are just interested in classification then the generative approach may mean that we are trying to solve a harder problem than we need to. However, to deal with missing input values, outliers and unlabelled data points in a principled fashion it is very helpful to have access to $p(\mathbf{x})$, and this can be obtained from marginalizing out the class label y from the joint as $p(\mathbf{x}) = \sum_y p(y)p(\mathbf{x}|y)$ in the generative approach. A further factor in the choice of a generative or discriminative approach could also be which one is most conducive to the incorporation of any prior information which is available. See Ripley [1996, sec. 2.1] for further discussion of these issues. The Gaussian process classifiers developed in this chapter are discriminative.

generative or discriminative?

missing values

3.1.1 Decision Theory for Classification

The classifiers described above provide predictive probabilities $p(y_*|\mathbf{x}_*)$ for a test input $\mathbf{x}_*$. However, sometimes one actually needs to make a decision and to do this we need to consider decision theory. Decision theory for the regression problem was considered in section 2.4; here we discuss decision theory for classification problems. A comprehensive treatment of decision theory can be found in Berger [1985].

loss, risk

zero-one loss

asymmetric loss

Bayes classifier

decision regions

reject option

risk minimization

Let $\mathcal{L}(c, c')$ be the loss incurred by making decision c' if the true class is $\mathcal{C}_c$. Usually $\mathcal{L}(c, c) = 0$ for all c. The expected loss[5] (or risk) of taking decision c' given $\mathbf{x}$ is $R_{\mathcal{L}}(c'|\mathbf{x}) = \sum_c \mathcal{L}(c, c')p(\mathcal{C}_c|\mathbf{x})$ and the optimal decision c^* is the one that minimizes $R_{\mathcal{L}}(c'|\mathbf{x})$. One common choice of loss function is the zero-one loss, where a penalty of one unit is paid for an incorrect classification, and 0 for a correct one. In this case the optimal decision rule is to choose the class $\mathcal{C}_c$ that maximizes[6] $p(\mathcal{C}_c|\mathbf{x})$, as this minimizes the expected error at $\mathbf{x}$. However, the zero-one loss is not always appropriate. A classic example of this is the difference in loss of failing to spot a disease when carrying out a medical test compared to the cost of a false positive on the test, so that $\mathcal{L}(c, c') \neq \mathcal{L}(c', c)$.

The optimal classifier (using zero-one loss) is known as the *Bayes classifier*. By this construction the feature space is divided into *decision regions* $\mathcal{R}_1, \ldots, \mathcal{R}_C$ such that a pattern falling in decision region $\mathcal{R}_c$ is assigned to class $\mathcal{C}_c$. (There can be more than one decision region corresponding to a single class.) The boundaries between the decision regions are known as *decision surfaces* or decision boundaries.

One would expect misclassification errors to occur in regions where the maximum class probability $\max_j p(\mathcal{C}_j|\mathbf{x})$ is relatively low. This could be due to either a region of strong overlap between classes, or lack of training examples within this region. Thus one sensible strategy is to add a *reject option* so that if $\max_j p(\mathcal{C}_j|\mathbf{x}) \geq \theta$ for a threshold θ in $(0, 1)$ then we go ahead and classify the pattern, otherwise we reject it and leave the classification task to a more sophisticated system. For multi-class classification we could alternatively require the gap between the most probable and the second most probable class to exceed θ, and otherwise reject. As θ is varied from 0 to 1 one obtains an error-reject curve, plotting the percentage of patterns classified incorrectly against the percentage rejected. Typically the error rate will fall as the rejection rate increases. Hansen et al. [1997] provide an analysis of the error-reject trade-off.

We have focused above on the probabilistic approach to classification, which involves a two-stage approach of first computing a posterior distribution over functions and then combining this with the loss function to produce a decision. However, it is worth noting that some authors argue that if our goal is to eventually make a decision then we should aim to approximate the classification function that minimizes the risk (expected loss), which is defined as

$$R_{\mathcal{L}}(c) = \int \mathcal{L}\big(y, c(\mathbf{x})\big)p(y, \mathbf{x}) \, dy d\mathbf{x}, \qquad (3.3)$$

where $p(y, \mathbf{x})$ is the joint distribution of inputs and targets and $c(\mathbf{x})$ is a classification function that assigns an input pattern $\mathbf{x}$ to one of C classes (see e.g. Vapnik [1995, ch. 1]). As $p(y, \mathbf{x})$ is unknown, in this approach one often then seeks to minimize an objective function which includes the empirical risk $\sum_{i=1}^n \mathcal{L}(y_i, c(\mathbf{x}_i))$ as well as a regularization term. While this is a reasonable

---

[5]In Economics one usually talks of maximizing expected utility rather than minimizing expected loss; loss is negative utility. This suggests that statisticians are pessimists while economists are optimists.

[6]If more than one class has equal posterior probability then ties can be broken arbitrarily.

method, we note that the probabilistic approach allows the same inference stage to be re-used with different loss functions, it can help us to incorporate prior knowledge on the function and/or noise model, and has the advantage of giving probabilistic predictions which can be helpful e.g. for the reject option.

3.2 Linear Models for Classification

In this section we briefly review linear models for binary classification, which form the foundation of Gaussian process classification models in the next section. We follow the SVM literature and use the labels $y = +1$ and $y = -1$ to distinguish the two classes, although for the multi-class case in section 3.5 we use 0/1 labels. The likelihood is

$$p(y = +1|\mathbf{x}, \mathbf{w}) = \sigma(\mathbf{x}^\top \mathbf{w}), \tag{3.4}$$

given the weight vector $\mathbf{w}$ and $\sigma(z)$ can be any sigmoid[7] function. When using the logistic, $\sigma(z) = \lambda(z)$ from eq. (3.2), the model is usually called simply *logistic regression*, but to emphasize the parallels to linear regression we prefer the term *linear logistic regression*. When using the cumulative Gaussian $\sigma(z) = \Phi(z)$, we call the model *linear probit regression*. *linear logistic regression*

linear probit regression

As the probability of the two classes must sum to 1, we have $p(y = -1|\mathbf{x}, \mathbf{w}) = 1 - p(y = +1|\mathbf{x}, \mathbf{w})$. Thus for a data point $(\mathbf{x}_i, y_i)$ the likelihood is given by $\sigma(\mathbf{x}_i^\top \mathbf{w})$ if $y_i = +1$, and $1 - \sigma(\mathbf{x}_i^\top \mathbf{w})$ if $y_i = -1$. For symmetric likelihood functions, such as the logistic or probit where $\sigma(-z) = 1 - \sigma(z)$, this can be written more concisely as *concise notation*

$$p(y_i|\mathbf{x}_i, \mathbf{w}) = \sigma(y_i f_i), \tag{3.5}$$

where $f_i \triangleq f(\mathbf{x}_i) = \mathbf{x}_i^\top \mathbf{w}$. Defining the logit transformation as $\text{logit}(\mathbf{x}) = \log\left(p(y = +1|\mathbf{x})/p(y = -1|\mathbf{x})\right)$ we see that the logistic regression model can be written as $\text{logit}(\mathbf{x}) = \mathbf{x}^\top \mathbf{w}$. The $\text{logit}(\mathbf{x})$ function is also called the *log odds ratio*. Generalized linear modelling [McCullagh and Nelder, 1983] deals with the issue of extending linear models to non-Gaussian data scenarios; the logit transformation is the canonical link function for binary data and this choice simplifies the algebra and algorithms. *logit*

log odds ratio

Given a dataset $\mathcal{D} = \{(\mathbf{x}_i, y_i)|i = 1, \dots, n\}$, we assume that the labels are generated independently, conditional on $f(\mathbf{x})$. Using the same Gaussian prior $\mathbf{w} \sim \mathcal{N}(\mathbf{0}, \Sigma_p)$ as for regression in eq. (2.4) we then obtain the un-normalized log posterior

$$\log p(\mathbf{w}|X, \mathbf{y}) \overset{c}{=} -\frac{1}{2}\mathbf{w}^\top \Sigma_p^{-1} \mathbf{w} + \sum_{i=1}^{n} \log \sigma(y_i f_i). \tag{3.6}$$

In the linear regression case with Gaussian noise the posterior was Gaussian with mean and covariance as given in eq. (2.8). For classification the posterior

---

[7]A sigmoid function is a monotonically increasing function mapping from $\mathbb{R}$ to $[0, 1]$. It derives its name from being shaped like a letter S.

concavity

unique maximum

IRLS algorithm

properties of maximum
likelihood

predictions

softmax
multiple logistic

does not have a simple analytic form. However, it is easy to show that for some sigmoid functions, such as the logistic and cumulative Gaussian, the log likelihood is a concave function of $\mathbf{w}$ for fixed $\mathcal{D}$. As the quadratic penalty on $\mathbf{w}$ is also concave then the log posterior is a concave function, which means that it is relatively easy to find its unique maximum. The concavity can also be derived from the fact that the Hessian of $\log p(\mathbf{w}|X, \mathbf{y})$ is negative definite (see section A.9 for further details). The standard algorithm for finding the maximum is Newton's method, which in this context is usually called the *iteratively reweighted least squares* (IRLS) algorithm, as described e.g. in McCullagh and Nelder [1983]. However, note that Minka [2003] provides evidence that other optimization methods (e.g. conjugate gradient ascent) may be faster than IRLS.

Notice that a maximum likelihood treatment (corresponding to an unpenalized version of eq. (3.6)) may result in some undesirable outcomes. If the dataset is linearly separable (i.e. if there exists a hyperplane which separates the positive and negative examples) then maximizing the (unpenalized) likelihood will cause $|\mathbf{w}|$ to tend to infinity, However, this will still give predictions in $[0, 1]$ for $p(y = +1|\mathbf{x}, \mathbf{w})$, although these predictions will be "hard" (i.e. zero or one). If the problem is ill-conditioned, e.g. due to duplicate (or linearly dependent) input dimensions, there will be no unique solution.

As an example, consider linear logistic regression in the case where $\mathbf{x}$-space is two dimensional and there is no bias weight so that $\mathbf{w}$ is also two-dimensional. The prior in weight space is Gaussian and for simplicity we have set $\Sigma_p = I$. Contours of the prior $p(\mathbf{w})$ are illustrated in Figure 3.1(a). If we have a data set $\mathcal{D}$ as shown in Figure 3.1(b) then this induces a posterior distribution in weight space as shown in Figure 3.1(c). Notice that the posterior is non-Gaussian and unimodal, as expected. The dataset is not linearly separable but a weight vector in the direction $(1, 1)^\top$ is clearly a reasonable choice, as the posterior distribution shows. To make predictions based the training set $\mathcal{D}$ for a test point $\mathbf{x}_*$ we have

$$p(y_* = +1|\mathbf{x}_*, \mathcal{D}) = \int p(y_* = +1|\mathbf{w}, \mathbf{x}_*) p(\mathbf{w}|\mathcal{D})\, d\mathbf{w}, \qquad (3.7)$$

integrating the prediction $p(y_* = +1|\mathbf{w}, \mathbf{x}_*) = \sigma(\mathbf{x}_*^\top \mathbf{w})$ over the posterior distribution of weights. This leads to contours of the predictive distribution as shown in Figure 3.1(d). Notice how the contours are bent, reflecting the integration of many different but plausible $\mathbf{w}$'s.

In the multi-class case we use the multiple logistic (or softmax) function

$$p(y = \mathcal{C}_c|\mathbf{x}, W) = \frac{\exp(\mathbf{x}^\top \mathbf{w}_c)}{\sum_{c'} \exp(\mathbf{x}^\top \mathbf{w}_{c'})}, \qquad (3.8)$$

where $\mathbf{w}_c$ is the weight vector for class c, and all weight vectors are collected into the matrix W. The corresponding log likelihood is of the form $\sum_{i=1}^n \sum_{c=1}^C \delta_{c,y_i}[\mathbf{x}_i^\top \mathbf{w}_c - \log(\sum_{c'} \exp(\mathbf{x}_i^\top \mathbf{w}_{c'}))]$. As in the binary case the log likelihood is a concave function of W.

It is interesting to note that in a generative approach where the class-conditional distributions $p(\mathbf{x}|y)$ are Gaussian with the same covariance matrix,

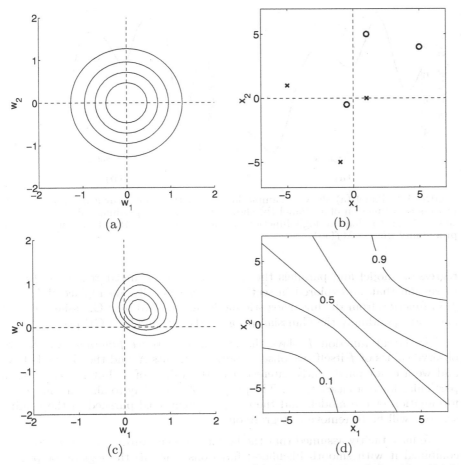

Figure 3.1: Linear logistic regression: Panel (a) shows contours of the prior distribution $p(\mathbf{w}) = \mathcal{N}(\mathbf{0}, I)$. Panel (b) shows the dataset, with circles indicating class $+1$ and crosses denoting class -1. Panel (c) shows contours of the posterior distribution $p(\mathbf{w}|\mathcal{D})$. Panel (d) shows contours of the predictive distribution $p(y_* = +1|\mathbf{x}_*)$.

$p(y|\mathbf{x})$ has the form given by eq. (3.4) and eq. (3.8) for the two- and multi-class cases respectively (when the constant function 1 is included in $\mathbf{x}$).

3.3 Gaussian Process Classification

For binary classification the basic idea behind Gaussian process prediction is very simple—we place a GP prior over the *latent function* $f(\mathbf{x})$ and then "squash" this through the logistic function to obtain a prior on $\pi(\mathbf{x}) \triangleq p(y = +1|\mathbf{x}) = \sigma(f(\mathbf{x}))$. Note that π is a deterministic function of f, and since f is stochastic, so is π. This construction is illustrated in Figure 3.2 for a one-dimensional input space. It is a natural generalization of the linear logistic

latent function

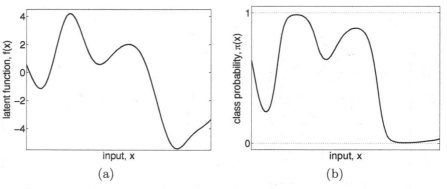

Figure 3.2: Panel (a) shows a sample latent function $f(x)$ drawn from a Gaussian process as a function of x. Panel (b) shows the result of squashing this sample function through the logistic logit function, $\lambda(z) = (1 + \exp(-z))^{-1}$ to obtain the class probability $\pi(x) = \lambda(f(x))$.

regression model and parallels the development from linear regression to GP regression that we explored in section 2.1. Specifically, we replace the linear $f(\mathbf{x})$ function from the linear logistic model in eq. (3.6) by a Gaussian process, and correspondingly the Gaussian prior on the weights by a GP prior.

nuisance function   The latent function f plays the rôle of a *nuisance function*: we do not observe values of f itself (we observe only the inputs X and the class labels $\mathbf{y}$) and we are not particularly interested in the values of f, but rather in π, in particular for test cases $\pi(\mathbf{x}_*)$. The purpose of f is solely to allow a convenient formulation of the model, and the computational goal pursued in the coming sections will be to remove (integrate out) f.

noise-free latent process   We have tacitly assumed that the latent Gaussian process is *noise-free*, and combined it with smooth likelihood functions, such as the logistic or probit. However, one can equivalently think of adding independent noise to the latent process in combination with a step-function likelihood. In particular, assuming Gaussian noise and a step-function likelihood is exactly equivalent to a noise-free[8] latent process and probit likelihood, see exercise 3.10.1.

Inference is naturally divided into two steps: first computing the distribution of the latent variable corresponding to a test case

$$p(f_*|X, \mathbf{y}, \mathbf{x}_*) = \int p(f_*|X, \mathbf{x}_*, \mathbf{f})p(\mathbf{f}|X, \mathbf{y}) \, d\mathbf{f}, \qquad (3.9)$$

where $p(\mathbf{f}|X, \mathbf{y}) = p(\mathbf{y}|\mathbf{f})p(\mathbf{f}|X)/p(\mathbf{y}|X)$ is the posterior over the latent variables, and subsequently using this distribution over the latent f_* to produce a probabilistic prediction

$$\bar{\pi}_* \triangleq p(y_* = +1|X, \mathbf{y}, \mathbf{x}_*) = \int \sigma(f_*)p(f_*|X, \mathbf{y}, \mathbf{x}_*) \, df_*. \qquad (3.10)$$

---

[8]This equivalence explains why no numerical problems arise from considering a noise-free process if care is taken with the implementation, see also comment at the end of section 3.4.3.

In the regression case (with Gaussian likelihood) computation of predictions was straightforward as the relevant integrals were Gaussian and could be computed analytically. In classification the non-Gaussian likelihood in eq. (3.9) makes the integral analytically intractable. Similarly, eq. (3.10) can be intractable analytically for certain sigmoid functions, although in the binary case it is only a one-dimensional integral so simple numerical techniques are generally adequate.

Thus we need to use either analytic approximations of integrals, or solutions based on Monte Carlo sampling. In the coming sections, we describe two analytic approximations which both approximate the non-Gaussian joint posterior with a Gaussian one: the first is the straightforward *Laplace approximation* method [Williams and Barber, 1998], and the second is the more sophisticated *expectation propagation* (EP) method due to Minka [2001]. (The cavity TAP approximation of Opper and Winther [2000] is closely related to the EP method.) A number of other approximations have also been suggested, see e.g. Gibbs and MacKay [2000], Jaakkola and Haussler [1999], and Seeger [2000]. Neal [1999] describes the use of Markov chain Monte Carlo (MCMC) approximations. All of these methods will typically scale as $\mathcal{O}(n^3)$; for large datasets there has been much work on further approximations to reduce computation time, as discussed in chapter 8.

The Laplace approximation for the binary case is described in section 3.4, and for the multi-class case in section 3.5. The EP method for binary classification is described in section 3.6. Relationships between Gaussian process classifiers and other techniques such as spline classifiers, support vector machines and least-squares classification are discussed in sections 6.3, 6.4 and 6.5 respectively.

3.4 The Laplace Approximation for the Binary GP Classifier

Laplace's method utilizes a Gaussian approximation $q(\mathbf{f}|X,\mathbf{y})$ to the posterior $p(\mathbf{f}|X,\mathbf{y})$ in the integral (3.9). Doing a second order Taylor expansion of $\log p(\mathbf{f}|X,\mathbf{y})$ around the maximum of the posterior, we obtain a Gaussian approximation

$$q(\mathbf{f}|X,\mathbf{y}) = \mathcal{N}(\mathbf{f}|\hat{\mathbf{f}}, A^{-1}) \propto \exp\big(-\tfrac{1}{2}(\mathbf{f}-\hat{\mathbf{f}})^\top A(\mathbf{f}-\hat{\mathbf{f}})\big), \qquad (3.11)$$

where $\hat{\mathbf{f}} = \operatorname{argmax}_\mathbf{f} p(\mathbf{f}|X,\mathbf{y})$ and $A = -\nabla\nabla \log p(\mathbf{f}|X,\mathbf{y})|_{\mathbf{f}=\hat{\mathbf{f}}}$ is the Hessian of the negative log posterior at that point.

The structure of the rest of this section is as follows: In section 3.4.1 we describe how to find $\hat{\mathbf{f}}$ and A. Section 3.4.2 explains how to make predictions having obtained $q(\mathbf{f}|\mathbf{y})$, and section 3.4.3 gives more implementation details for the Laplace GP classifier. The Laplace approximation for the marginal likelihood is described in section 3.4.4.

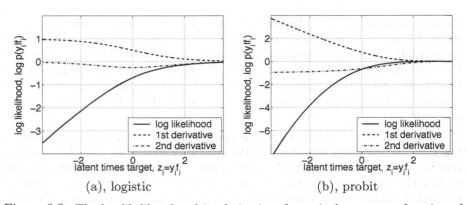

(a), logistic   (b), probit

Figure 3.3: The log likelihood and its derivatives for a single case as a function of $z_i = y_i f_i$, for (a) the logistic, and (b) the cumulative Gaussian likelihood. The two likelihood functions are fairly similar, the main qualitative difference being that for large negative arguments the log logistic behaves linearly whereas the log cumulative Gaussian has a quadratic penalty. Both likelihoods are log concave.

3.4.1 Posterior

By Bayes' rule the posterior over the latent variables is given by $p(\mathbf{f}|X,\mathbf{y}) = p(\mathbf{y}|\mathbf{f})p(\mathbf{f}|X)/p(\mathbf{y}|X)$, but as $p(\mathbf{y}|X)$ is independent of $\mathbf{f}$, we need only consider *un-normalized posterior* the un-normalized posterior when maximizing w.r.t. $\mathbf{f}$. Taking the logarithm and introducing expression eq. (2.29) for the GP prior gives

$$\Psi(\mathbf{f}) \triangleq \log p(\mathbf{y}|\mathbf{f}) + \log p(\mathbf{f}|X)$$
$$= \log p(\mathbf{y}|\mathbf{f}) - \frac{1}{2}\mathbf{f}^\top K^{-1}\mathbf{f} - \frac{1}{2}\log|K| - \frac{n}{2}\log 2\pi. \tag{3.12}$$

Differentiating eq. (3.12) w.r.t. $\mathbf{f}$ we obtain

$$\nabla\Psi(\mathbf{f}) = \nabla \log p(\mathbf{y}|\mathbf{f}) - K^{-1}\mathbf{f}, \tag{3.13}$$
$$\nabla\nabla\Psi(\mathbf{f}) = \nabla\nabla \log p(\mathbf{y}|\mathbf{f}) - K^{-1} = -W - K^{-1}, \tag{3.14}$$

where $W \triangleq -\nabla\nabla \log p(\mathbf{y}|\mathbf{f})$ is diagonal, since the likelihood factorizes over cases (the distribution for y_i depends only on f_i, not on $f_{j\neq i}$). Note, that if the likelihood $p(\mathbf{y}|\mathbf{f})$ is log concave, the diagonal elements of W are non-negative, and the Hessian in eq. (3.14) is negative definite, so that $\Psi(\mathbf{f})$ is concave and has a unique maximum (see section A.9 for further details).

There are many possible functional forms of the likelihood, which gives the target class probability as a function of the latent variable f. Two commonly *log likelihoods* used likelihood functions are the logistic, and the cumulative Gaussian, see *and their derivatives* Figure 3.3. The expressions for the log likelihood for these likelihood functions and their first and second derivatives w.r.t. the latent variable are given in the following table:

$\log p(y_i\vert f_i)$	$\dfrac{\partial}{\partial f_i}\log p(y_i\vert f_i)$	$\dfrac{\partial^2}{\partial f_i^2}\log p(y_i\vert f_i)$	
$-\log\big(1+\exp(-y_i f_i)\big)$	$t_i-\pi_i$	$-\pi_i(1-\pi_i)$	(3.15)
$\log\Phi(y_i f_i)$	$\dfrac{y_i\mathcal{N}(f_i)}{\Phi(y_i f_i)}$	$-\dfrac{\mathcal{N}(f_i)^2}{\Phi(y_i f_i)^2}-\dfrac{y_i f_i\mathcal{N}(f_i)}{\Phi(y_i f_i)}$	(3.16)

where we have defined $\pi_i = p(y_i = 1\vert f_i)$ and $\mathbf{t} = (\mathbf{y}+\mathbf{1})/2$. At the maximum of $\Psi(\mathbf{f})$ we have

$$\nabla\Psi = \mathbf{0} \implies \hat{\mathbf{f}} = K\big(\nabla\log p(\mathbf{y}\vert\hat{\mathbf{f}})\big), \tag{3.17}$$

as a self-consistent equation for $\hat{\mathbf{f}}$ (but since $\nabla\log p(\mathbf{y}\vert\hat{\mathbf{f}})$ is a non-linear function of $\hat{\mathbf{f}}$, eq. (3.17) cannot be solved directly). To find the maximum of Ψ we use Newton's method, with the iteration

Newton's method

$$\begin{aligned}
\mathbf{f}^{\text{new}} &= \mathbf{f} - (\nabla\nabla\Psi)^{-1}\nabla\Psi = \mathbf{f} + (K^{-1}+W)^{-1}\big(\nabla\log p(\mathbf{y}\vert\mathbf{f}) - K^{-1}\mathbf{f}\big) \\
&= (K^{-1}+W)^{-1}\big(W\mathbf{f} + \nabla\log p(\mathbf{y}\vert\mathbf{f})\big).
\end{aligned} \tag{3.18}$$

To gain more intuition about this update, let us consider what happens to datapoints that are well-explained under $\mathbf{f}$ so that $\partial\log p(y_i\vert f_i)/\partial f_i$ and W_{ii} are close to zero for these points. As an approximation, break $\mathbf{f}$ into two subvectors, $\mathbf{f}_1$ that corresponds to points that are *not* well-explained, and $\mathbf{f}_2$ to those that are. Then it is easy to show (see exercise 3.10.4) that

$$\begin{aligned}
\mathbf{f}_1^{\text{new}} &= K_{11}(I_{11} + W_{11}K_{11})^{-1}\big(W_{11}\mathbf{f}_1 + \nabla\log p(\mathbf{y}_1\vert\mathbf{f}_1)\big), \\
\mathbf{f}_2^{\text{new}} &= K_{21}K_{11}^{-1}\mathbf{f}_1^{\text{new}},
\end{aligned} \tag{3.19}$$

where K_{21} denotes the $n_2 \times n_1$ block of K containing the covariance between the two groups of points, etc. This means that $\mathbf{f}_1^{\text{new}}$ is computed by ignoring entirely the well-explained points, and $\mathbf{f}_2^{\text{new}}$ is predicted from $\mathbf{f}_1^{\text{new}}$ using the usual GP prediction methods (i.e. treating these points like test points). Of course, if the predictions of $\mathbf{f}_2^{\text{new}}$ fail to match the targets correctly they would cease to be well-explained and so be updated on the next iteration.

intuition on influence of well-explained points

Having found the maximum posterior $\hat{\mathbf{f}}$, we can now specify the Laplace approximation to the posterior as a Gaussian with mean $\hat{\mathbf{f}}$ and covariance matrix given by the negative inverse Hessian of Ψ from eq. (3.14)

$$q(\mathbf{f}\vert X,\mathbf{y}) = \mathcal{N}\big(\hat{\mathbf{f}},\, (K^{-1}+W)^{-1}\big). \tag{3.20}$$

One problem with the Laplace approximation is that it is essentially uncontrolled, in that the Hessian (evaluated at $\hat{\mathbf{f}}$) may give a poor approximation to the true shape of the posterior. The peak could be much broader or narrower than the Hessian indicates, or it could be a skew peak, while the Laplace approximation assumes it has elliptical contours.

3.4.2   Predictions

latent mean

The posterior mean for f_* under the Laplace approximation can be expressed by combining the GP predictive mean eq. (2.25) with eq. (3.17) into

$$\mathbb{E}_q[f_*|X,\mathbf{y},\mathbf{x}_*] = \mathbf{k}(\mathbf{x}_*)^\top K^{-1}\hat{\mathbf{f}} = \mathbf{k}(\mathbf{x}_*)^\top \nabla \log p(\mathbf{y}|\hat{\mathbf{f}}). \tag{3.21}$$

Compare this with the exact mean, given by Opper and Winther [2000] as

$$\mathbb{E}_p[f_*|X,\mathbf{y},\mathbf{x}_*] = \int \mathbb{E}[f_*|\mathbf{f},X,\mathbf{x}_*]p(\mathbf{f}|X,\mathbf{y})d\mathbf{f} \tag{3.22}$$

$$= \int \mathbf{k}(\mathbf{x}_*)^\top K^{-1}\mathbf{f}\, p(\mathbf{f}|X,\mathbf{y})d\mathbf{f} = \mathbf{k}(\mathbf{x}_*)^\top K^{-1}\mathbb{E}[\mathbf{f}|X,\mathbf{y}],$$

where we have used the fact that for a GP $\mathbb{E}[f_*|\mathbf{f},X,\mathbf{x}_*] = \mathbf{k}(\mathbf{x}_*)^\top K^{-1}\mathbf{f}$ and have let $\mathbb{E}[\mathbf{f}|X,\mathbf{y}]$ denote the posterior mean of $\mathbf{f}$ given X and $\mathbf{y}$. Notice the similarity between the middle expression of eq. (3.21) and eq. (3.22), where the exact (intractable) average $\mathbb{E}[\mathbf{f}|X,\mathbf{y}]$ has been replaced with the modal value $\hat{\mathbf{f}} = \mathbb{E}_q[\mathbf{f}|X,\mathbf{y}]$.

sign of kernel coefficients

A simple observation from eq. (3.21) is that positive training examples will give rise to a positive coefficient for their kernel function (as $\nabla_i \log p(y_i|f_i) > 0$ in this case), while negative examples will give rise to a negative coefficient; this is analogous to the solution to the support vector machine, see eq. (6.34). Also note that training points which have $\nabla_i \log p(y_i|f_i) \simeq 0$ (i.e. that are well-explained under $\hat{\mathbf{f}}$) do not contribute strongly to predictions at novel test points; this is similar to the behaviour of non-support vectors in the support vector machine (see section 6.4).

We can also compute $\mathbb{V}_q[f_*|X,\mathbf{y}]$, the variance of $f_*|X,\mathbf{y}$ under the Gaussian approximation. This comprises of two terms, i.e.

$$\mathbb{V}_q[f_*|X,\mathbf{y},\mathbf{x}_*] = \mathbb{E}_{p(f_*|X,\mathbf{x}_*,\mathbf{f})}[(f_* - \mathbb{E}[f_*|X,\mathbf{x}_*,\mathbf{f}])^2]$$
$$+ \mathbb{E}_{q(\mathbf{f}|X,\mathbf{y})}[(\mathbb{E}[f_*|X,\mathbf{x}_*,\mathbf{f}] - \mathbb{E}[f_*|X,\mathbf{y},\mathbf{x}_*])^2]. \tag{3.23}$$

The first term is due to the variance of f_* if we condition on a particular value of $\mathbf{f}$, and is given by $k(\mathbf{x}_*,\mathbf{x}_*) - \mathbf{k}(\mathbf{x}_*)^\top K^{-1}\mathbf{k}(\mathbf{x}_*)$, cf. eq. (2.19). The second term in eq. (3.23) is due to the fact that $\mathbb{E}[f_*|X,\mathbf{x}_*,\mathbf{f}] = \mathbf{k}(\mathbf{x}_*)^\top K^{-1}\mathbf{f}$ depends on $\mathbf{f}$ and thus there is an additional term of $\mathbf{k}(\mathbf{x}_*)^\top K^{-1}\operatorname{cov}(\mathbf{f}|X,\mathbf{y})K^{-1}\mathbf{k}(\mathbf{x}_*)$.

latent variance

Under the Gaussian approximation $\operatorname{cov}(\mathbf{f}|X,\mathbf{y}) = (K^{-1} + W)^{-1}$, and thus

$$\mathbb{V}_q[f_*|X,\mathbf{y},\mathbf{x}_*] = k(\mathbf{x}_*,\mathbf{x}_*) - \mathbf{k}_*^\top K^{-1}\mathbf{k}_* + \mathbf{k}_*^\top K^{-1}(K^{-1} + W)^{-1}K^{-1}\mathbf{k}_*$$
$$= k(\mathbf{x}_*,\mathbf{x}_*) - \mathbf{k}_*^\top (K + W^{-1})^{-1}\mathbf{k}_*, \tag{3.24}$$

where the last line is obtained using the matrix inversion lemma eq. (A.9).

averaged predictive probability

Given the mean and variance of f_*, we make predictions by computing

$$\bar{\pi}_* \simeq \mathbb{E}_q[\pi_*|X,\mathbf{y},\mathbf{x}_*] = \int \sigma(f_*)q(f_*|X,\mathbf{y},\mathbf{x}_*)\, df_*, \tag{3.25}$$

where $q(f_*|X, \mathbf{y}, \mathbf{x}_*)$ is Gaussian with mean and variance given by equations 3.21 and 3.24 respectively. Notice that because of the non-linear form of the sigmoid the predictive probability from eq. (3.25) is different from the sigmoid of the expectation of $\mathbf{f}$: $\hat{\pi}_* = \sigma(\mathbb{E}_q[f_*|\mathbf{y}])$. We will call the latter the *MAP prediction* to distinguish it from the *averaged predictions* from eq. (3.25).

MAP prediction

identical binary decisions

In fact, as shown in Bishop [1995, sec. 10.3], the predicted test labels given by choosing the class of highest probability obtained by averaged and MAP predictions are identical for *binary*[9] classification. To see this, note that the decision boundary using the the MAP value $\mathbb{E}_q[f_*|X, \mathbf{y}, \mathbf{x}_*]$ corresponds to $\sigma(\mathbb{E}_q[f_*|X, \mathbf{y}, \mathbf{x}_*]) = 1/2$ or $\mathbb{E}_q[f_*|X, \mathbf{y}, \mathbf{x}_*] = 0$. The decision boundary of the averaged prediction, $\mathbb{E}_q[\pi_*|X, \mathbf{y}, \mathbf{x}_*] = 1/2$, also corresponds to $\mathbb{E}_q[f_*|X, \mathbf{y}, \mathbf{x}_*] = 0$. This follows from the fact that $\sigma(f_*) - 1/2$ is antisymmetric while $q(f_*|X, \mathbf{y}, \mathbf{x}_*)$ is symmetric.

Thus if we are concerned only about the most probable classification, it is not necessary to compute predictions using eq. (3.25). However, as soon as we also need a confidence in the prediction (e.g. if we are concerned about a reject option) we need $\mathbb{E}_q[\pi_*|X, \mathbf{y}, \mathbf{x}_*]$. If $\sigma(z)$ is the cumulative Gaussian function then eq. (3.25) can be computed analytically, as shown in section 3.9. On the other hand if σ is the logistic function then we need to resort to sampling methods or analytical approximations to compute this one-dimensional integral. One attractive method is to note that the logistic function $\lambda(z)$ is the c.d.f. (cumulative density function) corresponding to the p.d.f. (probability density function) $p(z) = \text{sech}^2(z/2)/4$; this is known as the logistic or sech-squared distribution, see Johnson et al. [1995, ch. 23]. Then by approximating $p(z)$ as a mixture of Gaussians, one can approximate $\lambda(z)$ by a linear combination of error functions. This approximation was used by Williams and Barber [1998, app. A] and Wood and Kohn [1998]. Another approximation suggested in MacKay [1992d] is $\bar{\pi}_* \simeq \lambda(\kappa(f_*|\mathbf{y})\bar{f}_*)$, where $\kappa^2(f_*|\mathbf{y}) = (1 + \pi\mathbb{V}_q[f_*|X, \mathbf{y}, \mathbf{x}_*]/8)^{-1}$. The effect of the latent predictive variance is, as the approximation suggests, to "soften" the prediction that would be obtained using the MAP prediction $\hat{\pi}_* = \lambda(\bar{f}_*)$, i.e. to move it towards $1/2$.

3.4.3 Implementation

We give implementations for finding the Laplace approximation in Algorithm 3.1 and for making predictions in Algorithm 3.2. Care is taken to avoid numerically unstable computations while minimizing the computational effort; both can be achieved simultaneously. It turns out that several of the desired terms can be expressed in terms of the symmetric positive definite matrix

$$B = I + W^{\frac{1}{2}}KW^{\frac{1}{2}}, \tag{3.26}$$

computation of which costs only $\mathcal{O}(n^2)$, since W is diagonal. The B matrix has eigenvalues bounded below by 1 and bounded above by $1 + n\max_{ij}(K_{ij})/4$, so for many covariance functions B is guaranteed to be well-conditioned, and it is

---

[9]For multi-class predictions discussed in section 3.5 the situation is more complicated.

---

input: K (covariance matrix), $\mathbf{y}$ (± 1 targets), $p(\mathbf{y}|\mathbf{f})$ (likelihood function)

2:   $\mathbf{f} := \mathbf{0}$ initialization

    repeat   Newton iteration

4:     $W := -\nabla\nabla \log p(\mathbf{y}|\mathbf{f})$ eval. W e.g. using eq. (3.15) or (3.16)

      $L := \mathrm{cholesky}(I + W^{\frac{1}{2}}KW^{\frac{1}{2}})$ $B = I + W^{\frac{1}{2}}KW^{\frac{1}{2}}$

6:     $\mathbf{b} := W\mathbf{f} + \nabla \log p(\mathbf{y}|\mathbf{f})$ ⎫

      $\mathbf{a} := \mathbf{b} - W^{\frac{1}{2}}L^\top\backslash(L\backslash(W^{\frac{1}{2}}K\mathbf{b}))$ ⎬ eq. (3.18) using eq. (3.27)

8:     $\mathbf{f} := K\mathbf{a}$ ⎭

    until convergence   objective: $-\frac{1}{2}\mathbf{a}^\top\mathbf{f} + \log p(\mathbf{y}|\mathbf{f})$

10: $\log q(\mathbf{y}|X,\theta) := -\frac{1}{2}\mathbf{a}^\top\mathbf{f} + \log p(\mathbf{y}|\mathbf{f}) - \sum_i \log L_{ii}$ eq. (3.32)

    return: $\hat{\mathbf{f}} := \mathbf{f}$ (post. mode), $\log q(\mathbf{y}|X,\theta)$ (approx. log marg. likelihood)

Algorithm 3.1: Mode-finding for binary Laplace GPC. Commonly used convergence criteria depend on the difference in successive values of the objective function $\Psi(\mathbf{f})$ from eq. (3.12), the magnitude of the gradient vector $\nabla\Psi(\mathbf{f})$ from eq. (3.13) and/or the magnitude of the difference in successive values of $\mathbf{f}$. In a practical implementation one needs to secure against divergence by checking that each iteration leads to an increase in the objective (and trying a smaller step size if not). The computational complexity is dominated by the Cholesky decomposition in line 5 which takes $n^3/6$ operations (times the number of Newton iterations), all other operations are at most quadratic in n.

thus numerically safe to compute its Cholesky decomposition $LL^\top = B$, which is useful in computing terms involving B^{-1} and $|B|$.

The mode-finding procedure uses the Newton iteration given in eq. (3.18), involving the matrix $(K^{-1}+W)^{-1}$. Using the matrix inversion lemma eq. (A.9) we get

$$(K^{-1} + W)^{-1} = K - KW^{\frac{1}{2}}B^{-1}W^{\frac{1}{2}}K, \qquad (3.27)$$

where B is given in eq. (3.26). The advantage is that whereas K may have eigenvalues arbitrarily close to zero (and thus be numerically unstable to invert), we can safely work with B. In addition, Algorithm 3.1 keeps the vector $\mathbf{a} = K^{-1}\mathbf{f}$ in addition to $\mathbf{f}$, as this allows evaluation of the part of the objective $\Psi(\mathbf{f})$ in eq. (3.12) which depends on $\mathbf{f}$ without explicit reference to K^{-1} (again to avoid possible numerical problems).

Similarly, for the computation of the predictive variance $\mathbb{V}_q[f_*|\mathbf{y}]$ from eq. (3.24) we need to evaluate a quadratic form involving the matrix $(K + W^{-1})^{-1}$. Rewriting this as

$$(K + W^{-1})^{-1} = W^{\frac{1}{2}}W^{-\frac{1}{2}}(K + W^{-1})^{-1}W^{-\frac{1}{2}}W^{\frac{1}{2}} = W^{\frac{1}{2}}B^{-1}W^{\frac{1}{2}} \qquad (3.28)$$

achieves numerical stability (as opposed to inverting W itself, which may have arbitrarily small eigenvalues). Thus the predictive variance from eq. (3.24) can be computed as

$$
\begin{aligned}
\mathbb{V}_q[f_*|\mathbf{y}] &= k(\mathbf{x}_*, \mathbf{x}_*) - \mathbf{k}(\mathbf{x}_*)^\top W^{\frac{1}{2}}(LL^\top)^{-1}W^{\frac{1}{2}}\mathbf{k}(\mathbf{x}_*) \\
&= k(\mathbf{x}_*, \mathbf{x}_*) - \mathbf{v}^\top\mathbf{v}, \quad \text{where} \quad \mathbf{v} = L\backslash(W^{\frac{1}{2}}\mathbf{k}(\mathbf{x}_*)),
\end{aligned}
\qquad (3.29)
$$

which was also used by Seeger [2003, p. 27].

---

input: $\hat{\mathbf{f}}$ (mode), X (inputs), $\mathbf{y}$ (± 1 targets), k (covariance function),

$\qquad\qquad\qquad\qquad\qquad\qquad p(\mathbf{y}|\mathbf{f})$ (likelihood function), $\mathbf{x}_*$ test input

2: $W := -\nabla\nabla \log p(\mathbf{y}|\hat{\mathbf{f}})$

$\quad L := \text{cholesky}(I + W^{\frac{1}{2}} K W^{\frac{1}{2}})$ $\qquad\qquad\qquad\qquad B = I + W^{\frac{1}{2}} K W^{\frac{1}{2}}$

4: $\bar{f}_* := \mathbf{k}(\mathbf{x}_*)^\top \nabla \log p(\mathbf{y}|\hat{\mathbf{f}})$ $\qquad\qquad\qquad\qquad\qquad$ eq. (3.21)

$\quad \mathbf{v} := L\backslash\left(W^{\frac{1}{2}}\mathbf{k}(\mathbf{x}_*)\right)$

6: $\mathbb{V}[f_*] := k(\mathbf{x}_*, \mathbf{x}_*) - \mathbf{v}^\top \mathbf{v}$ $\qquad\qquad\left.\vphantom{\begin{array}{c}a\\a\end{array}}\right\}$ eq. (3.24) using eq. (3.29)

$\quad \bar{\pi}_* := \int \sigma(z) \mathcal{N}(z|\bar{f}_*, \mathbb{V}[f_*]) dz$ $\qquad\qquad\qquad\qquad$ eq. (3.25)

8: **return:** $\bar{\pi}_*$ (predictive class probability (for class 1))

Algorithm 3.2: Predictions for binary Laplace GPC. The posterior mode $\hat{\mathbf{f}}$ (which can be computed using Algorithm 3.1) is input. For multiple test inputs lines $4-7$ are applied to each test input. Computational complexity is $n^3/6$ operations once (line 3) plus n^2 operations per test case (line 5). The one-dimensional integral in line 7 can be done analytically for cumulative Gaussian likelihood, otherwise it is computed using an approximation or numerical quadrature.

In practice we compute the Cholesky decomposition $LL^\top = B$ during the Newton steps in Algorithm 3.1, which can be re-used to compute the predictive variance by doing backsubstitution with L as discussed above. In addition, L may again be re-used to compute $|I_n + W^{\frac{1}{2}} K W^{\frac{1}{2}}| = |B|$ (needed for the computation of the marginal likelihood eq. (3.32)) as $\log|B| = 2\sum \log L_{ii}$. To save computation, one could use an incomplete Cholesky factorization in the Newton steps, as suggested by Fine and Scheinberg [2002].

incomplete Cholesky factorization

Sometimes it is suggested that it can be useful to replace K by $K + \epsilon I$ where ϵ is a small constant, to improve the numerical conditioning[10] of K. However, by taking care with the implementation details as above this should not be necessary.

3.4.4 Marginal Likelihood

It will also be useful (particularly for chapter 5) to compute the Laplace approximation of the marginal likelihood $p(\mathbf{y}|X)$. (For the regression case with Gaussian noise the marginal likelihood can again be calculated analytically, see eq. (2.30).) We have

$$p(\mathbf{y}|X) = \int p(\mathbf{y}|\mathbf{f}) p(\mathbf{f}|X) \, d\mathbf{f} = \int \exp\left(\Psi(\mathbf{f})\right) d\mathbf{f}. \qquad (3.30)$$

Using a Taylor expansion of $\Psi(\mathbf{f})$ locally around $\hat{\mathbf{f}}$ we obtain $\Psi(\mathbf{f}) \simeq \Psi(\hat{\mathbf{f}}) - \frac{1}{2}(\mathbf{f} - \hat{\mathbf{f}})^\top A(\mathbf{f} - \hat{\mathbf{f}})$ and thus an approximation $q(\mathbf{y}|X)$ to the marginal likelihood as

$$p(\mathbf{y}|X) \simeq q(\mathbf{y}|X) = \exp\left(\Psi(\hat{\mathbf{f}})\right) \int \exp\left(-\tfrac{1}{2}(\mathbf{f} - \hat{\mathbf{f}})^\top A(\mathbf{f} - \hat{\mathbf{f}})\right) d\mathbf{f}. \qquad (3.31)$$

---

[10]Neal [1999] refers to this as adding "jitter" in the context of Markov chain Monte Carlo (MCMC) based inference; in his work the latent variables $\mathbf{f}$ are explicitly represented in the Markov chain which makes addition of jitter difficult to avoid. Within the analytical approximations of the *distribution* of $\mathbf{f}$ considered here, jitter is unnecessary.

This Gaussian integral can be evaluated analytically to obtain an approximation to the log marginal likelihood

$$\log q(\mathbf{y}|X, \boldsymbol{\theta}) \;=\; -\tfrac{1}{2}\hat{\mathbf{f}}^\top K^{-1}\hat{\mathbf{f}} + \log p(\mathbf{y}|\hat{\mathbf{f}}) - \tfrac{1}{2}\log|B|, \tag{3.32}$$

where $|B| = |K| \cdot |K^{-1} + W| = |I_n + W^{\frac{1}{2}} K W^{\frac{1}{2}}|$, and $\boldsymbol{\theta}$ is a vector of hyperparameters of the covariance function (which have previously been suppressed from the notation for brevity).

∗ 3.5 Multi-class Laplace Approximation

Our presentation follows Williams and Barber [1998]. We first introduce the vector of latent function values at all n training points and for all C classes

$$\mathbf{f} \;=\; \left(f_1^1, \ldots, f_n^1, f_1^2, \ldots, f_n^2, \ldots, f_1^C, \ldots, f_n^C\right)^\top. \tag{3.33}$$

Thus $\mathbf{f}$ has length Cn. In the following we will generally refer to quantities pertaining to a particular class with superscript c, and a particular case by subscript i (as usual); thus e.g. the vector of C latents for a particular case is $\mathbf{f}_i$. However, as an exception, vectors or matrices formed from the covariance function for class c will have a subscript c. The prior over $\mathbf{f}$ has the form $\mathbf{f} \sim \mathcal{N}(\mathbf{0}, K)$. As we have assumed that the C latent processes are uncorrelated, the covariance matrix K is block diagonal in the matrices $K_1, \ldots, K_C$. Each individual matrix K_c expresses the correlations of the latent function values within the class c. Note that the covariance functions pertaining to the different classes can be different. Let $\mathbf{y}$ be a vector of the same length as $\mathbf{f}$ which for each $i = 1, \ldots, n$ has an entry of 1 for the class which is the label for example i and 0 for the other $C - 1$ entries.

softmax

Let π_i^c denote output of the softmax at training point i, i.e.

$$p(y_i^c|\mathbf{f}_i) \;=\; \pi_i^c \;=\; \frac{\exp(f_i^c)}{\sum_{c'} \exp(f_i^{c'})}. \tag{3.34}$$

un-normalized posterior

Then $\boldsymbol{\pi}$ is a vector of the same length as $\mathbf{f}$ with entries π_i^c. The multi-class analogue of eq. (3.12) is the log of the un-normalized posterior

$$\Psi(\mathbf{f}) \;\triangleq\; -\tfrac{1}{2}\mathbf{f}^\top K^{-1}\mathbf{f} + \mathbf{y}^\top\mathbf{f} - \sum_{i=1}^n \log\Big(\sum_{c=1}^C \exp f_i^c\Big) - \tfrac{1}{2}\log|K| - \tfrac{Cn}{2}\log 2\pi. \tag{3.35}$$

As in the binary case we seek the MAP value $\hat{\mathbf{f}}$ of $p(\mathbf{f}|X, \mathbf{y})$. By differentiating eq. (3.35) w.r.t. $\mathbf{f}$ we obtain

$$\nabla\Psi \;=\; -K^{-1}\mathbf{f} + \mathbf{y} - \boldsymbol{\pi}. \tag{3.36}$$

Thus at the maximum we have $\hat{\mathbf{f}} = K(\mathbf{y} - \hat{\boldsymbol{\pi}})$. Differentiating again, and using

$$-\frac{\partial^2}{\partial f_i^c \partial f_i^{c'}} \log \sum_j \exp(f_i^j) \;=\; \pi_i^c \delta_{cc'} + \pi_i^c \pi_i^{c'}, \tag{3.37}$$

we obtain[11]

$$\nabla\nabla\Psi = -K^{-1} - W, \quad \text{where} \quad W \triangleq \text{diag}(\boldsymbol{\pi}) - \Pi\Pi^{\top}, \qquad (3.38)$$

where Π is a $Cn \times n$ matrix obtained by stacking vertically the diagonal matrices $\text{diag}(\boldsymbol{\pi}^c)$, and $\boldsymbol{\pi}^c$ is the subvector of $\boldsymbol{\pi}$ pertaining to class c. As in the binary case notice that $-\nabla\nabla\Psi$ is positive definite, thus $\Psi(\mathbf{f})$ is concave and the maximum is unique (see also exercise 3.10.2).

As in the binary case we use Newton's method to search for the mode of Ψ, giving

$$\mathbf{f}^{\text{new}} = (K^{-1} + W)^{-1}(W\mathbf{f} + \mathbf{y} - \boldsymbol{\pi}). \qquad (3.39)$$

This update if coded naïvely would take $\mathcal{O}(C^3 n^3)$ as matrices of size Cn have to be inverted. However, as described in section 3.5.1, we can utilize the structure of W to bring down the computational load to $\mathcal{O}(Cn^3)$.

The Laplace approximation gives us a Gaussian approximation $q(\mathbf{f}|X, \mathbf{y})$ to the posterior $p(\mathbf{f}|X, \mathbf{y})$. To make predictions at a test point $\mathbf{x}_*$ we need to compute the posterior distribution $q(\mathbf{f}_*|X, \mathbf{y}, \mathbf{x}_*)$ where $\mathbf{f}(\mathbf{x}_*) \triangleq \mathbf{f}_* = (f_*^1, \ldots, f_*^C)^{\top}$. In general we have

predictive
distribution for f_*

$$q(\mathbf{f}_*|X, \mathbf{y}, \mathbf{x}_*) = \int p(\mathbf{f}_*|X, \mathbf{x}_*, \mathbf{f}) q(\mathbf{f}|X, \mathbf{y}) \, d\mathbf{f}. \qquad (3.40)$$

As $p(\mathbf{f}_*|X, \mathbf{x}_*, \mathbf{f})$ and $q(\mathbf{f}|X, \mathbf{y})$ are both Gaussian, $q(\mathbf{f}_*|X, \mathbf{y}, \mathbf{x}_*)$ will also be Gaussian and we need only compute its mean and covariance. The predictive mean for class c is given by

$$\mathbb{E}_q[f^c(\mathbf{x}_*)|X, \mathbf{y}, \mathbf{x}_*] = \mathbf{k}_c(\mathbf{x}_*)^{\top} K_c^{-1} \hat{\mathbf{f}}^c = \mathbf{k}_c(\mathbf{x}_*)^{\top}(\mathbf{y}^c - \hat{\boldsymbol{\pi}}^c), \qquad (3.41)$$

where $\mathbf{k}_c(\mathbf{x}_*)$ is the vector of covariances between the test point and each of the training points for the cth covariance function, and $\hat{\mathbf{f}}^c$ is the subvector of $\hat{\mathbf{f}}$ pertaining to class c. The last equality comes from using eq. (3.36) at the maximum $\hat{\mathbf{f}}$. Note the close correspondence to eq. (3.21). This can be put into a vector form $\mathbb{E}_q[\mathbf{f}_*|\mathbf{y}] = Q_*^{\top}(\mathbf{y} - \hat{\boldsymbol{\pi}})$ by defining the $Cn \times C$ matrix

$$Q_* = \begin{pmatrix} \mathbf{k}_1(\mathbf{x}_*) & \mathbf{0} & \ldots & \mathbf{0} \\ \mathbf{0} & \mathbf{k}_2(\mathbf{x}_*) & \ldots & \mathbf{0} \\ \vdots & \vdots & \ddots & \vdots \\ \mathbf{0} & \mathbf{0} & \ldots & \mathbf{k}_C(\mathbf{x}_*) \end{pmatrix}. \qquad (3.42)$$

Using a similar argument to eq. (3.23) we obtain

$$\begin{aligned} \text{cov}_q(\mathbf{f}_*|X, \mathbf{y}, \mathbf{x}_*) &= \Sigma + Q_*^{\top} K^{-1}(K^{-1} + W)^{-1} K^{-1} Q_* \\ &= \text{diag}(\mathbf{k}(\mathbf{x}_*, \mathbf{x}_*)) - Q_*^{\top}(K + W^{-1})^{-1} Q_*, \end{aligned} \qquad (3.43)$$

where Σ is a diagonal $C \times C$ matrix with $\Sigma_{cc} = k_c(\mathbf{x}_*, \mathbf{x}_*) - \mathbf{k}_c^{\top}(\mathbf{x}_*) K_c^{-1} \mathbf{k}_c(\mathbf{x}_*)$, and $\mathbf{k}(\mathbf{x}_*, \mathbf{x}_*)$ is a vector of covariances, whose c'th element is $k_c(\mathbf{x}_*, \mathbf{x}_*)$.

---

[11]There is a sign error in equation 23 of Williams and Barber [1998] but not in their implementation.

> **input:** K (covariance matrix), $\mathbf{y}$ (0/1 targets)
> 2: $\mathbf{f} := \mathbf{0}$ initialization
>   **repeat**   Newton iteration
> 4:   compute $\boldsymbol{\pi}$ and Π from $\mathbf{f}$ with eq. (3.34) and defn. of Π under eq. (3.38)
>   **for** $c := 1 \ldots C$ **do**
> 6: $L := \mathrm{cholesky}(I_n + D_c^{\frac{1}{2}} K_c D_c^{\frac{1}{2}})$
> $E_c := D_c^{\frac{1}{2}} L^\top \backslash (L \backslash D_c^{\frac{1}{2}})$ E is block diag. $D^{\frac{1}{2}}(I_{Cn} + D^{\frac{1}{2}} K D^{\frac{1}{2}})^{-1} D^{\frac{1}{2}}$
> 8: $z_c := \sum_i \log L_{ii}$ compute $\frac{1}{2}$ log determinant
>   **end for**
> 10: $M := \mathrm{cholesky}(\sum_c E_c)$
> $\mathbf{b} := (D - \Pi\Pi^\top)\mathbf{f} + \mathbf{y} - \boldsymbol{\pi}$ $\mathbf{b} = W\mathbf{f} + \mathbf{y} - \boldsymbol{\pi}$ from eq. (3.39)
> 12: $\mathbf{c} := EK\mathbf{b}$
> $\left. \begin{array}{l} \mathbf{a} := \mathbf{b} - \mathbf{c} + ERM^\top \backslash (M \backslash (R^\top \mathbf{c})) \end{array} \right\}$ eq. (3.39) using eq. (3.45) and (3.47)
> 14: $\mathbf{f} := K\mathbf{a}$
>   **until** convergence   objective: $-\frac{1}{2}\mathbf{a}^\top \mathbf{f} + \mathbf{y}^\top \mathbf{f} + \sum_i \log \left(\sum_c \exp(f_c^i) \right)$
> 16: $\log q(\mathbf{y}|X,\theta) := -\frac{1}{2}\mathbf{a}^\top \mathbf{f} + \mathbf{y}^\top \mathbf{f} + \sum_i \log \left(\sum_c \exp(f_c^i) \right) - \sum_c z_c$ eq. (3.44)
>   **return:** $\hat{\mathbf{f}} := \mathbf{f}$ (post. mode), $\log q(\mathbf{y}|X,\theta)$ (approx. log marg. likelihood)

Algorithm 3.3: Mode-finding for multi-class Laplace GPC, where $D = \mathrm{diag}(\boldsymbol{\pi})$, R is a matrix of stacked identity matrices and a subscript c on a block diagonal matrix indicates the $n \times n$ submatrix pertaining to class c. The computational complexity is dominated by the Cholesky decomposition in lines 6 and 10 and the forward and backward substitutions in line 7 with total complexity $\mathcal{O}((C+1)n^3)$ (times the number of Newton iterations), all other operations are at most $\mathcal{O}(Cn^2)$ when exploiting diagonal and block diagonal structures. The memory requirement is $\mathcal{O}(Cn^2)$. For comments on convergence criteria for line 15 and avoiding divergence, refer to the caption of Algorithm 3.1 on page 46.

We now need to consider the predictive distribution $q(\boldsymbol{\pi}_*|\mathbf{y})$ which is obtained by softmaxing the Gaussian $q(\mathbf{f}_*|\mathbf{y})$. In the binary case we saw that the predicted classification could be obtained by thresholding the mean value of the Gaussian. In the multi-class case one *does* need to take the variability around the mean into account as it can affect the overall classification (see exercise 3.10.3). One simple way (which will be used in Algorithm 3.4) to estimate the mean prediction $\mathbb{E}_q[\boldsymbol{\pi}_*|\mathbf{y}]$ is to draw samples from the Gaussian $q(\mathbf{f}_*|\mathbf{y})$, softmax them and then average.

marginal likelihood

The Laplace approximation to the marginal likelihood can be obtained in the same way as for the binary case, yielding

$$\log p(\mathbf{y}|X,\boldsymbol{\theta}) \simeq \log q(\mathbf{y}|X,\boldsymbol{\theta}) \tag{3.44}$$

$$= -\tfrac{1}{2}\hat{\mathbf{f}}^\top K^{-1}\hat{\mathbf{f}} + \mathbf{y}^\top\hat{\mathbf{f}} - \sum_{i=1}^{n} \log \left(\sum_{c=1}^{C} \exp \hat{f}_i^c \right) - \tfrac{1}{2}\log|I_{Cn} + W^{\frac{1}{2}}KW^{\frac{1}{2}}|.$$

As for the inversion of $K^{-1} + W$, the determinant term can be computed efficiently by exploiting the structure of W, see section 3.5.1.

In this section we have described the Laplace approximation for multi-class classification. However, there has also been some work on EP-type methods for the multi-class case, see Seeger and Jordan [2004].

---

input: K (covariance matrix), $\hat{\mathbf{f}}$ (posterior mode), $\mathbf{x}_*$ (test input)

2: compute $\boldsymbol{\pi}$ and Π from $\hat{\mathbf{f}}$ using eq. (3.34) and defn. of Π under eq. (3.38)

    for $c := 1 \ldots C$ **do**

4:     $L := \text{cholesky}(I_n + D_c^{\frac{1}{2}} K_c D_c^{\frac{1}{2}})$

     $E_c := D_c^{\frac{1}{2}} L^\top \backslash (L \backslash D_c^{\frac{1}{2}})$ E is block diag. $D^{\frac{1}{2}}(I_{Cn} + D^{\frac{1}{2}} K D^{\frac{1}{2}})^{-1} D^{\frac{1}{2}}$

6: **end for**

    $M := \text{cholesky}(\sum_c E_c)$

8: **for** $c := 1 \ldots C$ **do**

     $\boldsymbol{\mu}_*^c := (\mathbf{y}^c - \boldsymbol{\pi}^c)^\top \mathbf{k}_*^c$ latent test mean from eq. (3.41)

10:    $\mathbf{b} := E_c \mathbf{k}_*^c$

     $\mathbf{c} := E_c(R(M^\top \backslash (M \backslash (R^\top \mathbf{b}))))$

12:    **for** $c' := 1 \ldots C$ **do**

       $\Sigma_{cc'} := \mathbf{c}^\top \mathbf{k}_*^{c'}$ $\Big\}$ latent test covariance from eq. (3.43)

14:    **end for**

     $\Sigma_{cc} := \Sigma_{cc} + k_c(\mathbf{x}_*, \mathbf{x}_*) - \mathbf{b}^\top \mathbf{k}_*^c$

16: **end for**

    $\boldsymbol{\pi}_* := \mathbf{0}$ initialize Monte Carlo loop to estimate

18: **for** $i := 1 : S$ **do**   predictive class probabilities using S samples

     $\mathbf{f}_* \sim \mathcal{N}(\boldsymbol{\mu}_*, \Sigma)$ sample latent values from joint Gaussian posterior

20:    $\boldsymbol{\pi}_* := \boldsymbol{\pi}_* + \exp(f_*^c)/\sum_{c'} \exp(f_*^{c'})$ accumulate probability eq. (3.34)

    end for

22: $\bar{\boldsymbol{\pi}}_* := \boldsymbol{\pi}_*/S$ normalize MC estimate of prediction vector

    return: $\mathbb{E}_{q(\mathbf{f})}[\boldsymbol{\pi}(\mathbf{f}(\mathbf{x}_*))|\mathbf{x}_*, X, \mathbf{y}] := \bar{\boldsymbol{\pi}}_*$ (predicted class probability vector)

Algorithm 3.4: Predictions for multi-class Laplace GPC, where $D = \text{diag}(\boldsymbol{\pi})$, R is a matrix of stacked identity matrices and a subscript c on a block diagonal matrix indicates the $n \times n$ submatrix pertaining to class c. The computational complexity is dominated by the Cholesky decomposition in lines 4 and 7 with a total complexity $\mathcal{O}((C+1)n^3)$, the memory requirement is $\mathcal{O}(Cn^2)$. For multiple test cases repeat from line 8 for each test case (in practice, for multiple test cases one may reorder the computations in lines 8-16 to avoid referring to all E_c matrices repeatedly).

3.5.1 Implementation

The implementation follows closely the implementation for the binary case detailed in section 3.4.3, with the slight complications that K is now a block diagonal matrix of size $Cn \times Cn$ and the W matrix is no longer diagonal, see eq. (3.38). Care has to be taken to exploit the structure of these matrices to reduce the computational burden.

The Newton iteration from eq. (3.39) requires the inversion of $K^{-1} + W$, which we first re-write as

$$(K^{-1} + W)^{-1} = K - K(K + W^{-1})^{-1}K, \qquad (3.45)$$

using the matrix inversion lemma, eq. (A.9). In the following the inversion of the above matrix $K + W^{-1}$ is our main concern. First, however, we apply the matrix inversion lemma, eq. (A.9) to the W matrix:[12]

$$
\begin{aligned}
W^{-1} = (D - \Pi\Pi^\top)^{-1} &= D^{-1} - R(I - R^\top DR)^{-1}R^\top \\
&= D^{-1} - RO^{-1}R^\top,
\end{aligned}
\tag{3.46}
$$

where $D = \mathrm{diag}(\boldsymbol{\pi})$, $R = D^{-1}\Pi$ is a $Cn \times n$ matrix of stacked I_n unit matrices, we use the fact that $\boldsymbol{\pi}$ normalizes over classes: $R^\top DR = \sum_c D_c = I_n$ and O is the zero matrix. Introducing the above in $K + W^{-1}$ and applying the matrix inversion lemma, eq. (A.9) again we have

$$
\begin{aligned}
(K + W^{-1})^{-1} &= (K + D^{-1} - RO^{-1}R^\top)^{-1} \\
&= E - ER(O + R^\top ER)^{-1}R^\top E = E - ER(\textstyle\sum_c E_c)^{-1}R^\top E.
\end{aligned}
\tag{3.47}
$$

where $E = (K + D^{-1})^{-1} = D^{\frac{1}{2}}(I + D^{\frac{1}{2}}KD^{\frac{1}{2}})^{-1}D^{\frac{1}{2}}$ is a block diagonal matrix and $R^\top ER = \sum_c E_c$. The Newton iterations can now be computed by inserting eq. (3.47) and (3.45) in eq. (3.39), as detailed in Algorithm 3.3. The predictions use an equivalent route to compute the Gaussian posterior, and the final step of deriving predictive class probabilities is done by Monte Carlo, as shown in Algorithm 3.4.

3.6   Expectation Propagation

The expectation propagation (EP) algorithm [Minka, 2001] is a general approximation tool with a wide range of applications. In this section we present only its application to the specific case of a GP model for binary classification. We note that Opper and Winther [2000] presented a similar method for binary GPC based on the fixed-point equations of the Thouless-Anderson-Palmer (TAP) type of mean-field approximation from statistical physics. The fixed points for the two methods are the same, although the precise details of the two algorithms are different. The EP algorithm naturally lends itself to sparse approximations, which will not be discussed in detail here, but touched upon in section 8.4.

The object of central importance is the posterior distribution over the latent variables, $p(\mathbf{f}|X, \mathbf{y})$. In the following notation we suppress the explicit dependence on hyperparameters, see section 3.6.2 for their treatment. The posterior is given by Bayes' rule, as the product of a normalization term, the prior and the likelihood

$$
p(\mathbf{f}|X, \mathbf{y}) = \frac{1}{Z}p(\mathbf{f}|X)\prod_{i=1}^{n}p(y_i|f_i),
\tag{3.48}
$$

where the prior $p(\mathbf{f}|X)$ is Gaussian and we have utilized the fact that the likelihood factorizes over the training cases. The normalization term is the marginal likelihood

$$
Z = p(\mathbf{y}|X) = \int p(\mathbf{f}|X)\prod_{i=1}^{n}p(y_i|f_i)\,d\mathbf{f}.
\tag{3.49}
$$

---

[12]Readers who are disturbed by our sloppy treatment of the inverse of singular matrices are invited to insert the matrix $(1 - \varepsilon)I_n$ between Π and $\Pi^\top$ in eq. (3.46) and verify that eq. (3.47) coincides with the limit $\varepsilon \to 0$.

So far, everything is exactly as in the regression case discussed in chapter 2. However, in the case of classification the likelihood $p(y_i|f_i)$ is not Gaussian, a property that was used heavily in arriving at analytical solutions for the regression framework. In this section we use the probit likelihood (see page 35) for binary classification

$$p(y_i|f_i) = \Phi(f_i y_i), \tag{3.50}$$

and this makes the posterior in eq. (3.48) analytically intractable. To overcome this hurdle in the EP framework we approximate the likelihood by a *local likelihood approximation*[13] in the form of an un-normalized Gaussian function in the latent variable f_i

$$p(y_i|f_i) \simeq t_i(f_i|\tilde{Z}_i, \tilde{\mu}_i, \tilde{\sigma}_i^2) \triangleq \tilde{Z}_i \mathcal{N}(f_i|\tilde{\mu}_i, \tilde{\sigma}_i^2), \tag{3.51}$$

which defines the *site parameters* $\tilde{Z}_i$, $\tilde{\mu}_i$ and $\tilde{\sigma}_i^2$. Remember that the notation $\mathcal{N}$ is used for a normalized Gaussian distribution. Notice that we are approximating the likelihood, i.e. a probability distribution which normalizes over the *targets* y_i, by an un-normalized Gaussian distribution over the *latent* variables f_i. This is reasonable, because we are interested in how the likelihood behaves as a function of the latent f_i. In the regression setting we utilized the Gaussian shape of the likelihood, but more to the point, the Gaussian distribution for the outputs y_i also implied a Gaussian shape as a function of the latent variable f_i. In order to compute the posterior we are of course primarily interested in how the likelihood behaves as a function of f_i.[14] The property that the likelihood should normalize over y_i (for any value of f_i) is not simultaneously achievable with the desideratum of Gaussian dependence on f_i; in the EP approximation we abandon exact normalization for tractability. The product of the (independent) local likelihoods t_i is

$$\prod_{i=1}^{n} t_i(f_i|\tilde{Z}_i, \tilde{\mu}_i, \tilde{\sigma}_i^2) = \mathcal{N}(\tilde{\boldsymbol{\mu}}, \tilde{\Sigma}) \prod_i \tilde{Z}_i, \tag{3.52}$$

where $\tilde{\boldsymbol{\mu}}$ is the vector of $\tilde{\mu}_i$ and $\tilde{\Sigma}$ is diagonal with $\tilde{\Sigma}_{ii} = \tilde{\sigma}_i^2$. We approximate the posterior $p(\mathbf{f}|X, \mathbf{y})$ by $q(\mathbf{f}|X, \mathbf{y})$

$$q(\mathbf{f}|X, \mathbf{y}) \triangleq \frac{1}{Z_{\text{EP}}} p(\mathbf{f}|X) \prod_{i=1}^{n} t_i(f_i|\tilde{Z}_i, \tilde{\mu}_i, \tilde{\sigma}_i^2) = \mathcal{N}(\boldsymbol{\mu}, \Sigma),$$

$$\text{with } \boldsymbol{\mu} = \Sigma \tilde{\Sigma}^{-1} \tilde{\boldsymbol{\mu}}, \text{ and } \Sigma = (K^{-1} + \tilde{\Sigma}^{-1})^{-1}, \tag{3.53}$$

where we have used eq. (A.7) to compute the product (and by definition, we know that the distribution must normalize correctly over $\mathbf{f}$). Notice, that we use the tilde-parameters $\tilde{\boldsymbol{\mu}}$ and $\tilde{\Sigma}$ (and $\tilde{Z}$) for the *local likelihood approximations*,

margin note: *site parameters*

---

[13]Note, that although each likelihood approximation is *local*, the posterior approximation produced by the EP algorithm is *global* because the latent variables are coupled through the prior.

[14]However, for computing the *marginal likelihood* normalization becomes crucial, see section 3.6.2.

and plain $\boldsymbol{\mu}$ and Σ for the parameters of the *approximate posterior*. The normalizing term of eq. (3.53), $Z_{\text{EP}} = q(\mathbf{y}|X)$, is the EP algorithm's approximation to the normalizing term Z from eq. (3.48) and eq. (3.49).

How do we choose the parameters of the local approximating distributions t_i? One of the most obvious ideas would be to minimize the Kullback-Leibler
KL divergence
(KL) divergence (see section A.5) between the posterior and its approximation: $\text{KL}\big(p(\mathbf{f}|X,\mathbf{y})\|q(\mathbf{f}|X,\mathbf{y})\big)$. Direct minimization of this KL divergence for the joint distribution on $\mathbf{f}$ turns out to be intractable. (One can alternatively choose to minimize the reversed KL divergence $\text{KL}\big(q(\mathbf{f}|X,\mathbf{y})\|p(\mathbf{f}|X,\mathbf{y})\big)$ with respect to the distribution $q(\mathbf{f}|X,\mathbf{y})$; this has been used to carry out variational inference for GPC, see, e.g. Seeger [2000].)

Instead, the key idea in the EP algorithm is to update the individual t_i approximations sequentially. Conceptually this is done by iterating the following four steps: we start from some current approximate posterior, from which we leave out the current t_i, giving rise to a marginal *cavity distribution*. Secondly, we combine the cavity distribution with the exact likelihood $p(y_i|f_i)$ to get the desired (non-Gaussian) marginal. Thirdly, we choose a Gaussian approximation to the non-Gaussian marginal, and in the final step we compute the t_i which makes the posterior have the desired marginal from step three. These four steps are iterated until convergence.

In more detail, we optimize the t_i approximations sequentially, using the approximation so far for all the other variables. In particular the approximate posterior for f_i contains three kinds of terms:

1. the prior $p(\mathbf{f}|X)$

2. the local approximate likelihoods t_j for all cases $j \neq i$

3. the exact likelihood for case i, $p(y_i|f_i) = \Phi(y_i f_i)$

Our goal is to combine these sources of information and choose parameters of t_i such that the marginal posterior is as accurate as possible. We will first combine the prior and the local likelihood approximations into the *cavity distribution*

$$q_{-i}(f_i) \;\propto\; \int p(\mathbf{f}|X) \prod_{j \neq i} t_j(f_j|\tilde{Z}_j, \tilde{\mu}_j, \tilde{\sigma}_j^2) df_j, \tag{3.54}$$

and subsequently combine this with the exact likelihood for case i. Conceptually, one can think of the combination of prior and the $n-1$ approximate likelihoods in eq. (3.54) in two ways, either by explicitly multiplying out the terms, or (equivalently) by removing approximate likelihood i from the approximate posterior in eq. (3.53). Here we will follow the latter approach. The marginal for f_i from $q(\mathbf{f}|X,\mathbf{y})$ is obtained by using eq. (A.6) in eq. (3.53) to give

$$q(f_i|X,\mathbf{y}) \;=\; \mathcal{N}(f_i|\mu_i, \sigma_i^2), \tag{3.55}$$

where $\sigma_i^2 = \Sigma_{ii}$. This marginal eq. (3.55) contains one approximate term

(namely t_i) "too many", so we need to divide it by t_i to get the cavity dis-   cavity distribution
tribution

$$q_{-i}(f_i) \triangleq \mathcal{N}(f_i|\mu_{-i}, \sigma^2_{-i}), \tag{3.56}$$

where $\mu_{-i} = \sigma^2_{-i}(\sigma_i^{-2}\mu_i - \tilde{\sigma}_i^{-2}\tilde{\mu}_i)$, and $\sigma^2_{-i} = (\sigma_i^{-2} - \tilde{\sigma}_i^{-2})^{-1}$.

Note that the cavity distribution and its parameters carry the subscript $-i$, indicating that they include all cases except number i. The easiest way to verify eq. (3.56) is to multiply the cavity distribution by the local likelihood approximation t_i from eq. (3.51) using eq. (A.7) to recover the marginal in eq. (3.55). Notice that despite the appearance of eq. (3.56), the cavity mean and variance are (of course) not dependent on $\tilde{\mu}_i$ and $\tilde{\sigma}_i^2$, see exercise 3.10.5.

To proceed, we need to find the new (un-normalized) Gaussian marginal which best approximates the product of the cavity distribution and the exact likelihood

$$\hat{q}(f_i) \triangleq \hat{Z}_i \mathcal{N}(\hat{\mu}_i, \hat{\sigma}_i^2) \simeq q_{-i}(f_i)p(y_i|f_i). \tag{3.57}$$

It is well known that when $q(x)$ is Gaussian, the distribution $q(x)$ which min-imizes $\text{KL}(p(x)\|q(x))$ is the one whose first and second moments match that of $p(x)$, see eq. (A.24). As $\hat{q}(f_i)$ is un-normalized we choose additionally to impose the condition that the zero-th moments (normalizing constants) should match when choosing the parameters of $\hat{q}(f_i)$ to match the right hand side of eq. (3.57). This process is illustrated in Figure 3.4.

The derivation of the moments is somewhat lengthy, so we have moved the details to section 3.9. The desired posterior marginal moments are

$$\hat{Z}_i = \Phi(z_i), \qquad \hat{\mu}_i = \mu_{-i} + \frac{y_i\sigma^2_{-i}\mathcal{N}(z_i)}{\Phi(z_i)\sqrt{1+\sigma^2_{-i}}}, \tag{3.58}$$

$$\hat{\sigma}_i^2 = \sigma^2_{-i} - \frac{\sigma^4_{-i}\mathcal{N}(z_i)}{(1+\sigma^2_{-i})\Phi(z_i)}\Big(z_i + \frac{\mathcal{N}(z_i)}{\Phi(z_i)}\Big), \quad \text{where} \quad z_i = \frac{y_i\mu_{-i}}{\sqrt{1+\sigma^2_{-i}}}.$$

The final step is to compute the parameters of the approximation t_i which achieves a match with the desired moments. In particular, the product of the cavity distribution and the local approximation must have the desired moments, leading to

$$\tilde{\mu}_i = \tilde{\sigma}_i^2(\hat{\sigma}_i^{-2}\hat{\mu}_i - \sigma^{-2}_{-i}\mu_{-i}), \qquad \tilde{\sigma}_i^2 = (\hat{\sigma}_i^{-2} - \sigma^{-2}_{-i})^{-1},$$
$$\tilde{Z}_i = \hat{Z}_i\sqrt{2\pi}\sqrt{\sigma^2_{-i} + \tilde{\sigma}_i^2}\exp\big(\tfrac{1}{2}(\mu_{-i} - \tilde{\mu}_i)^2/(\sigma^2_{-i} + \tilde{\sigma}_i^2)\big), \tag{3.59}$$

which is easily verified by multiplying the cavity distribution by the local ap-proximation using eq. (A.7) to obtain eq. (3.58). Note that the desired marginal posterior variance $\hat{\sigma}_i^2$ given by eq. (3.58) is guaranteed to be smaller than the cavity variance, such that $\tilde{\sigma}_i^2 > 0$ is always satisfied.[15]

This completes the update for a local likelihood approximation t_i. We then have to update the approximate posterior using eq. (3.53), but since only a

---

[15]In cases where the likelihood is log concave, one can show that $\tilde{\sigma}_i^2 > 0$, but for a general likelihood there may be no such guarantee.

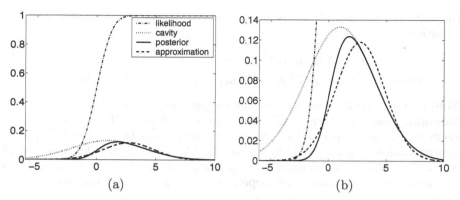

Figure 3.4: Approximating a single likelihood term by a Gaussian. Panel (a) dash-dotted: the exact likelihood, $\Phi(f_i)$ (the corresponding target being $y_i = 1$) as a function of the latent f_i, dotted: Gaussian cavity distribution $\mathcal{N}(f_i|\mu_{-i}=1,\ \sigma^2_{-i}=9)$, solid: posterior, dashed: posterior approximation. Panel (b) shows an enlargement of panel (a).

single site has changed one can do this with a computationally efficient rank-one update, see section 3.6.3. The EP algorithm is used iteratively, updating each local approximation in turn. It is clear that several passes over the data are required, since an update of one local approximation potentially influences all of the approximate marginal posteriors.

3.6.1 Predictions

The procedure for making predictions in the EP framework closely resembles the algorithm for the Laplace approximation in section 3.4.2. EP gives a Gaussian approximation to the posterior distribution, eq. (3.53). The approximate predictive mean for the latent variable f_* becomes

$$
\mathbb{E}_q[f_*|X,\mathbf{y},\mathbf{x}_*] = \mathbf{k}_*^\top K^{-1}\boldsymbol{\mu} = \mathbf{k}_*^\top K^{-1}(K^{-1}+\tilde{\Sigma}^{-1})^{-1}\tilde{\Sigma}^{-1}\tilde{\boldsymbol{\mu}}
$$
$$
= \mathbf{k}_*^\top (K+\tilde{\Sigma})^{-1}\tilde{\boldsymbol{\mu}}. \tag{3.60}
$$

The approximate latent predictive variance is analogous to the derivation from eq. (3.23) and eq. (3.24), with $\tilde{\Sigma}$ playing the rôle of W

$$
\mathbb{V}_q[f_*|X,\mathbf{y},\mathbf{x}_*] = k(\mathbf{x}_*,\mathbf{x}_*) - \mathbf{k}_*^\top (K+\tilde{\Sigma})^{-1}\mathbf{k}_*. \tag{3.61}
$$

The approximate predictive distribution for the binary target becomes

$$
q(y_* = 1|X,\mathbf{y},\mathbf{x}_*) = \mathbb{E}_q[\pi_*|X,\mathbf{y},\mathbf{x}_*] = \int \Phi(f_*)q(f_*|X,\mathbf{y},\mathbf{x}_*)\,df_*, \tag{3.62}
$$

where $q(f_*|X,\mathbf{y},\mathbf{x}_*)$ is the approximate latent predictive Gaussian with mean and variance given by eq. (3.60) and eq. (3.61). This integral is readily evaluated using eq. (3.80), giving the predictive probability

$$
q(y_* = 1|X,\mathbf{y},\mathbf{x}_*) = \Phi\Big(\frac{\mathbf{k}_*^\top (K+\tilde{\Sigma})^{-1}\tilde{\boldsymbol{\mu}}}{\sqrt{1+k(\mathbf{x}_*,\mathbf{x}_*)-\mathbf{k}_*^\top (K+\tilde{\Sigma})^{-1}\mathbf{k}_*}}\Big). \tag{3.63}
$$

3.6.2 Marginal Likelihood

The EP approximation to the marginal likelihood can be found from the normalization of eq. (3.53)

$$Z_{\mathrm{EP}} = q(\mathbf{y}|X) = \int p(\mathbf{f}|X) \prod_{i=1}^{n} t_i(f_i|\tilde{Z}_i, \tilde{\mu}_i, \tilde{\sigma}_i^2) \, d\mathbf{f}. \tag{3.64}$$

Using eq. (A.7) and eq. (A.8) in an analogous way to the treatment of the regression setting in equations (2.28) and (2.30) we arrive at

$$\log(Z_{\mathrm{EP}}|\boldsymbol{\theta}) = -\frac{1}{2} \log|K + \tilde{\Sigma}| - \frac{1}{2} \tilde{\boldsymbol{\mu}}^\top (K + \tilde{\Sigma})^{-1} \tilde{\boldsymbol{\mu}} \tag{3.65}$$

$$+ \sum_{i=1}^{n} \log \Phi\Big(\frac{y_i \mu_{-i}}{\sqrt{1 + \sigma_{-i}^2}}\Big) + \frac{1}{2} \sum_{i=1}^{n} \log(\sigma_{-i}^2 + \tilde{\sigma}_i^2) + \sum_{i=1}^{n} \frac{(\mu_{-i} - \tilde{\mu}_i)^2}{2(\sigma_{-i}^2 + \tilde{\sigma}_i^2)},$$

where $\boldsymbol{\theta}$ denotes the hyperparameters of the covariance function. This expression has a nice intuitive interpretation: the first two terms are the marginal likelihood for a regression model for $\tilde{\boldsymbol{\mu}}$, each component of which has independent Gaussian noise of variance $\tilde{\Sigma}_{ii}$ (as $\tilde{\Sigma}$ is diagonal), cf. eq. (2.30). The remaining three terms come from the normalization constants $\tilde{Z}_i$. The first of these penalizes the cavity (or leave-one-out) distributions for not agreeing with the classification labels, see eq. (3.82). In other words, we can see that the marginal likelihood combines two desiderata, (1) the means of the local likelihood approximations should be well predicted by a GP, and (2) the corresponding latent function, when ignoring a particular training example, should be able to predict the corresponding classification label well.

3.6.3 Implementation

The implementation for the EP algorithm follows the derivation in the previous section closely, except that care has to be taken to achieve numerical stability, in similar ways to the considerations for Laplace's method in section 3.4.3. In addition, we wish to be able to specifically handle the case were some site variances $\tilde{\sigma}_i^2$ may tend to infinity; this corresponds to ignoring the corresponding likelihood terms, and can form the basis of *sparse* approximations, touched upon in section 8.4. In this limit, everything remains well-defined, although this is not obvious e.g. from looking at eq. (3.65). It turns out to be slightly more convenient to use natural parameters $\tilde{\tau}_i$, $\tilde{\nu}_i$ and τ_{-i}, ν_{-i} for the site and cavity parameters   *natural parameters*

$$\tilde{\tau}_i = \tilde{\sigma}_i^{-2}, \quad \tilde{S} = \mathrm{diag}(\tilde{\boldsymbol{\tau}}), \quad \tilde{\boldsymbol{\nu}} = \tilde{S}\tilde{\boldsymbol{\mu}}, \quad \tau_{-i} = \sigma_{-i}^{-2}, \quad \nu_{-i} = \tau_{-i}\mu_{-i} \tag{3.66}$$

rather than $\tilde{\sigma}_i^2$, $\tilde{\mu}_i$ and σ_{-i}^2, μ_{-i} themselves. The symmetric matrix of central importance is

$$B = I + \tilde{S}^{\frac{1}{2}} K \tilde{S}^{\frac{1}{2}}, \tag{3.67}$$

which plays a rôle equivalent to eq. (3.26). Expressions involving the inverse of B are computed via Cholesky factorization, which is numerically stable since

input: K (covariance matrix), $\mathbf{y}$ (± 1 targets)
2: $\tilde{\boldsymbol{\nu}} := \mathbf{0}$, $\tilde{\boldsymbol{\tau}} := \mathbf{0}$, $\Sigma := K$, $\boldsymbol{\mu} := \mathbf{0}$ initialization and eq. (3.53)
    repeat
4:    for $i := 1$ to n do
        $\tau_{-i} := \sigma_i^{-2} - \tilde{\tau}_i$ $\left.\begin{array}{l}\\\end{array}\right\}$ compute approximate cavity para-
6:      $\nu_{-i} := \sigma_i^{-2}\mu_i - \tilde{\nu}_i$ meters ν_{-i} and τ_{-i} using eq. (3.56)
        compute the marginal moments $\hat{\mu}_i$ and $\hat{\sigma}_i^2$ using eq. (3.58)
8:      $\Delta\tilde{\tau} := \hat{\sigma}_i^{-2} - \tau_{-i} - \tilde{\tau}_i$ and $\tilde{\tau}_i := \tilde{\tau}_i + \Delta\tilde{\tau}$ $\left.\begin{array}{l}\\\end{array}\right\}$ update site parameters
        $\tilde{\nu}_i := \hat{\sigma}_i^{-2}\hat{\mu}_i - \nu_{-i}$ $\left.\begin{array}{l}\\\end{array}\right\}$ $\tilde{\tau}_i$ and $\tilde{\nu}_i$ using eq. (3.59)
10:     $\Sigma := \Sigma - \left((\Delta\tilde{\tau})^{-1} + \Sigma_{ii}\right)^{-1}\mathbf{s}_i\,\mathbf{s}_i^\top$ $\left.\begin{array}{l}\\\end{array}\right\}$update Σ and $\boldsymbol{\mu}$ by eq. (3.70) and
        $\boldsymbol{\mu} := \Sigma\tilde{\boldsymbol{\nu}}$ eq. (3.53). $\mathbf{s}_i$ is column i of Σ
12:   end for
        $L := \text{cholesky}(I_n + \tilde{S}^{\frac{1}{2}}K\tilde{S}^{\frac{1}{2}})$ $\left.\begin{array}{l}\\\end{array}\right\}$ re-compute the approximate
14:     $V := L^\top\backslash\tilde{S}^{\frac{1}{2}}K$ posterior parameters Σ and $\boldsymbol{\mu}$
        $\Sigma := K - V^\top V$ and $\boldsymbol{\mu} := \Sigma\tilde{\boldsymbol{\nu}}$ using eq. (3.53) and eq. (3.68)
16: until convergence
    compute $\log Z_{\text{EP}}$ using eq. (3.65), (3.73) and (3.74) and the existing L
18: return: $\tilde{\boldsymbol{\nu}}$, $\tilde{\boldsymbol{\tau}}$ (natural site param.), $\log Z_{\text{EP}}$ (approx. log marg. likelihood)

Algorithm 3.5: Expectation Propagation for binary classification. The targets $\mathbf{y}$ are used only in line 7. In lines 13-15 the parameters of the approximate posterior are re-computed (although they already exist); this is done because of the large number of rank-one updates in line 10 which would eventually cause loss of numerical precision in Σ. The computational complexity is dominated by the rank-one updates in line 10, which takes $\mathcal{O}(n^2)$ per variable, i.e. $\mathcal{O}(n^3)$ for an entire sweep over all variables. Similarly re-computing Σ in lines 13-15 is $\mathcal{O}(n^3)$.

the eigenvalues of B are bounded below by one. The parameters of the Gaussian approximate posterior from eq. (3.53) are computed as

$$\Sigma = (K^{-1} + \tilde{S})^{-1} = K - K(K + \tilde{S}^{-1})^{-1}K = K - K\tilde{S}^{\frac{1}{2}}B^{-1}\tilde{S}^{\frac{1}{2}}K. \quad (3.68)$$

After updating the parameters of a site, we need to update the approximate posterior eq. (3.53) taking the new site parameters into account. For the inverse covariance matrix of the approximate posterior we have from eq. (3.53)

$$\Sigma^{-1} = K^{-1} + \tilde{S}, \quad \text{and thus} \quad \Sigma_{\text{new}}^{-1} = K^{-1} + \tilde{S}_{\text{old}} + (\tilde{\tau}_i^{\text{new}} - \tilde{\tau}_i^{\text{old}})\mathbf{e}_i\mathbf{e}_i^\top, \quad (3.69)$$

where $\mathbf{e}_i$ is a unit vector in direction i, and we have used that $\tilde{S} = \text{diag}(\tilde{\boldsymbol{\tau}})$. Using the matrix inversion lemma eq. (A.9), on eq. (3.69) we obtain the new Σ

$$\Sigma^{\text{new}} = \Sigma^{\text{old}} - \frac{\tilde{\tau}_i^{\text{new}} - \tilde{\tau}_i^{\text{old}}}{1 + (\tilde{\tau}_i^{\text{new}} - \tilde{\tau}_i^{\text{old}})\Sigma_{ii}^{\text{old}}}\mathbf{s}_i\mathbf{s}_i^\top, \quad (3.70)$$

in time $\mathcal{O}(n^2)$, where $\mathbf{s}_i$ is the i'th column of Σ^{old}. The posterior mean is then calculated from eq. (3.53).

In the EP algorithm each site is updated in turn, and several passes over all sites are required. Pseudocode for the EP-GPC algorithm is given in Algorithm

---

> input: $\tilde{\boldsymbol{\nu}}$, $\tilde{\boldsymbol{\tau}}$ (natural site param.), X (inputs), $\mathbf{y}$ (± 1 targets),
> $\qquad\qquad\qquad\qquad$ k (covariance function), $\mathbf{x}_*$ test input
> 2: $\quad L := \text{cholesky}(I_n + \tilde{S}^{\frac{1}{2}} K \tilde{S}^{\frac{1}{2}})$ $\qquad\qquad B = I_n + \tilde{S}^{\frac{1}{2}} K \tilde{S}^{\frac{1}{2}}$
> $\quad\quad \mathbf{z} := \tilde{S}^{\frac{1}{2}} L^\top \backslash (L \backslash (\tilde{S}^{\frac{1}{2}} K \tilde{\boldsymbol{\nu}}))$ $\left.\begin{array}{c} \\ \\ \end{array}\right\}$ eq. (3.60) using eq. (3.71)
> 4: $\quad \bar{f}_* := \mathbf{k}(\mathbf{x}_*)^\top (\tilde{\boldsymbol{\nu}} - \mathbf{z})$
> $\quad\quad \mathbf{v} := L \backslash (\tilde{S}^{\frac{1}{2}} \mathbf{k}(\mathbf{x}_*))$ $\left.\begin{array}{c} \\ \\ \end{array}\right\}$ eq. (3.61) using eq. (3.72)
> 6: $\quad \mathbb{V}[f_*] := k(\mathbf{x}_*, \mathbf{x}_*) - \mathbf{v}^\top \mathbf{v}$
> $\quad\quad \bar{\pi}_* := \Phi(\bar{f}_* / \sqrt{1 + \mathbb{V}[f_*]})$ $\qquad\qquad\qquad$ eq. (3.63)
> 8: **return:** $\bar{\pi}_*$ (predictive class probability (for class 1))

Algorithm 3.6: Predictions for expectation propagation. The natural site parameters $\tilde{\boldsymbol{\nu}}$ and $\tilde{\boldsymbol{\tau}}$ of the posterior (which can be computed using algorithm 3.5) are input. For multiple test inputs lines 4-7 are applied to each test input. Computational complexity is $n^3/6 + n^2$ operations once (line 2 and 3) plus n^2 operations per test case (line 5), although the Cholesky decomposition in line 2 could be avoided by storing it in Algorithm 3.5. Note the close similarity to Algorithm 3.2 on page 47.

3.5. There is no formal guarantee of convergence, but several authors have reported that EP for Gaussian process models works relatively well.[16]

For the predictive distribution, we get the mean from eq. (3.60) which is evaluated using

$$\mathbb{E}_q[f_*|X, \mathbf{y}, \mathbf{x}_*] = \mathbf{k}_*^\top (K + \tilde{S}^{-1})^{-1} \tilde{S}^{-1} \tilde{\boldsymbol{\nu}} = \mathbf{k}_*^\top (I - (K + \tilde{S}^{-1})^{-1} K) \tilde{\boldsymbol{\nu}}$$
$$= \mathbf{k}_*^\top (I - \tilde{S}^{\frac{1}{2}} B^{-1} \tilde{S}^{\frac{1}{2}} K) \tilde{\boldsymbol{\nu}}, \qquad (3.71)$$

and the predictive variance from eq. (3.61) similarly by

$$\mathbb{V}_q[f_*|X, \mathbf{y}, \mathbf{x}_*] = k(\mathbf{x}_*, \mathbf{x}_*) - \mathbf{k}_*^\top (K + \tilde{S}^{-1})^{-1} \mathbf{k}_*$$
$$= k(\mathbf{x}_*, \mathbf{x}_*) - \mathbf{k}_*^\top \tilde{S}^{\frac{1}{2}} B^{-1} \tilde{S}^{\frac{1}{2}} \mathbf{k}_*. \qquad (3.72)$$

Pseudocode for making predictions using EP is given in Algorithm 3.6.

Finally, we need to evaluate the approximate log marginal likelihood from eq. (3.65). There are several terms which need careful consideration, principally due to the fact the $\tilde{\tau}_i$ values may be arbitrarily small (and cannot safely be inverted). We start with the fourth and first terms of eq. (3.65)

$$\tfrac{1}{2} \log |T^{-1} + \tilde{S}^{-1}| - \tfrac{1}{2} \log |K + \tilde{\Sigma}| = \tfrac{1}{2} \log |\tilde{S}^{-1}(I + \tilde{S} T^{-1})| - \tfrac{1}{2} \log |\tilde{S}^{-1} B|$$
$$= \tfrac{1}{2} \sum_i \log(1 + \tilde{\tau}_i \tau_{-i}^{-1}) - \sum_i \log L_{ii}, \qquad (3.73)$$

where T is a diagonal matrix of cavity precisions $T_{ii} = \tau_{-i} = \sigma_{-i}^{-2}$ and L is the Cholesky factorization of B. In eq. (3.73) we have factored out the matrix $\tilde{S}^{-1}$ from both determinants, and the terms cancel. Continuing with the part of the

---

[16]It has been conjectured (but not proven) by L. Csató (personal communication) that EP is guaranteed to converge if the likelihood is log concave.

fifth term from eq. (3.65) which is quadratic in $\tilde{\boldsymbol{\mu}}$ together with the second term

$$
\frac{1}{2}\tilde{\boldsymbol{\mu}}^{\top}(T^{-1}+\tilde{S}^{-1})^{-1}\tilde{\boldsymbol{\mu}} - \frac{1}{2}\tilde{\boldsymbol{\mu}}^{\top}(K+\tilde{\Sigma})^{-1}\tilde{\boldsymbol{\mu}}
$$
$$
= \frac{1}{2}\tilde{\boldsymbol{\nu}}^{\top}\tilde{S}^{-1}\big((T^{-1}+\tilde{S}^{-1})^{-1} - (K+\tilde{S}^{-1})^{-1}\big)\tilde{S}^{-1}\tilde{\boldsymbol{\nu}} \quad (3.74)
$$
$$
= \frac{1}{2}\tilde{\boldsymbol{\nu}}^{\top}\big((K^{-1}+\tilde{S})^{-1} - (T+\tilde{S})^{-1}\big)\tilde{\boldsymbol{\nu}}
$$
$$
= \frac{1}{2}\tilde{\boldsymbol{\nu}}^{\top}\big(K - K\tilde{S}^{\frac{1}{2}}B^{-1}\tilde{S}^{\frac{1}{2}}K - (T+\tilde{S})^{-1}\big)\tilde{\boldsymbol{\nu}},
$$

where in eq. (3.74) we apply the matrix inversion lemma eq. (A.9) to both parenthesis to be inverted. The remainder of the fifth term in eq. (3.65) is evaluated using the identity

$$
\frac{1}{2}\boldsymbol{\mu}_{-i}^{\top}(T^{-1}+\tilde{S}^{-1})^{-1}(\boldsymbol{\mu}_{-i}-2\tilde{\boldsymbol{\mu}}) = \frac{1}{2}\boldsymbol{\mu}_{-i}^{\top}T(\tilde{S}+T)^{-1}(\tilde{S}\boldsymbol{\mu}_{-i}-2\tilde{\boldsymbol{\nu}}), \quad (3.75)
$$

where $\boldsymbol{\mu}_{-i}$ is the vector of cavity means μ_{-i}. The third term in eq. (3.65) requires in no special treatment and can be evaluated as written.

3.7 Experiments

In this section we present the results of applying the algorithms for GP classification discussed in the previous sections to several data sets. The purpose is firstly to illustrate the behaviour of the methods and secondly to gain some insights into how good the performance is compared to some other commonly-used machine learning methods for classification.

Section 3.7.1 illustrates the action of a GP classifier on a toy binary prediction problem with a 2-d input space, and shows the effect of varying the length-scale ℓ in the SE covariance function. In section 3.7.2 we illustrate and compare the behaviour of the two approximate GP methods on a simple one-dimensional binary task. In section 3.7.3 we present results for a binary GP classifier on a handwritten digit classification task, and study the effect of varying the kernel parameters. In section 3.7.4 we carry out a similar study using a multi-class GP classifier to classify digits from all ten classes 0-9. In section 3.8 we discuss the methods from both experimental and theoretical viewpoints.

3.7.1 A Toy Problem

Figure 3.5 illustrates the operation of a Gaussian process classifier on a binary problem using the squared exponential kernel with a variable length-scale and the logistic response function. The Laplace approximation was used to make the plots. The data points lie within the square $[0,1]^2$, as shown in panel (a). Notice in particular the lone white point amongst the black points in the NE corner, and the lone black point amongst the white points in the SW corner.

In panel (b) the length-scale is $\ell = 0.1$, a relatively short value. In this case the latent function is free to vary relatively quickly and so the classifications

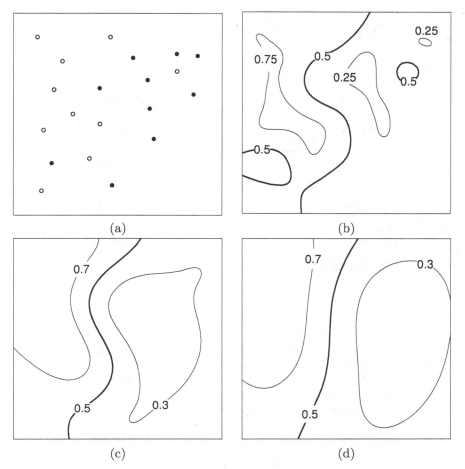

Figure 3.5: Panel (a) shows the location of the data points in the two-dimensional space $[0,1]^2$. The two classes are labelled as open circles (+1) and closed circles (-1). Panels (b)-(d) show contour plots of the predictive probability $\mathbb{E}_q[\pi(\mathbf{x}_*)|\mathbf{y}]$ for signal variance $\sigma_f^2 = 9$ and length-scales ℓ of 0.1, 0.2 and 0.3 respectively. The decision boundaries between the two classes are shown by the thicker black lines. The maximum value attained is 0.84, and the minimum is 0.19.

provided by thresholding the predictive probability $\mathbb{E}_q[\pi(\mathbf{x}_*)|\mathbf{y}]$ at 0.5 agrees with the training labels at all data points. In contrast, in panel (d) the length-scale is set to $\ell = 0.3$. Now the latent function must vary more smoothly, and so the two lone points are misclassified. Panel (c) was obtained with $\ell = 0.2$. As would be expected, the decision boundaries are more complex for shorter length-scales. Methods for setting the hyperparameters based on the data are discussed in chapter 5.

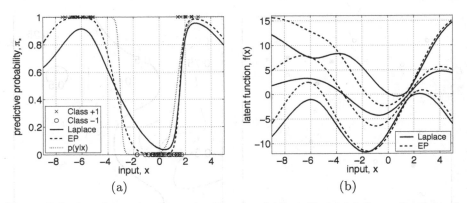

Figure 3.6: One-dimensional toy classification dataset: Panel (a) shows the dataset, where points from class +1 have been plotted at $\pi = 1$ and class -1 at $\pi = 0$, together with the predictive probability for Laplace's method and the EP approximation. Also shown is the probability $p(y=+1|x)$ of the data generating process. Panel (b) shows the corresponding distribution of the latent function $f(x)$, showing curves for the mean, and ± 2 standard deviations, corresponding to 95% confidence regions.

3.7.2   One-dimensional Example

Although Laplace's method and the EP approximation often give similar results, we here present a simple one-dimensional problem which highlights some of the differences between the methods. The data, shown in Figure 3.6(a), consists of 60 data points in three groups, generated from a mixture of three Gaussians, centered on -6 (20 points), 0 (30 points) and 2 (10 points), where the middle component has label -1 and the two other components label $+1$; all components have standard deviation 0.8; thus the two left-most components are well separated, whereas the two right-most components overlap.

Both approximation methods are shown with the same value of the hyperparameters, $\ell = 2.6$ and $\sigma_f = 7.0$, chosen to maximize the approximate marginal likelihood for Laplace's method. Notice in Figure 3.6 that there is a considerable difference in the value of the predictive probability for negative inputs. The Laplace approximation seems overly cautious, given the very clear separation of the data. This effect can be explained as a consequence of the intuition that the influence of "well-explained data points" is effectively reduced, see the discussion around eq. (3.19). Because the points in the left hand cluster are relatively well-explained by the model, they don't contribute as strongly to the posterior, and thus the predictive probability never gets very close to 1. Notice in Figure 3.6(b) the 95% confidence region for the latent function for Laplace's method actually includes functions that are negative at $x = -6$, which does not seem appropriate. For the positive examples centered around $x = 2$ on the right-hand side of Figure 3.6(b), this effect is not visible, because the points around the transition between the classes at $x=1$ are not so "well-explained"; this is because the points near the boundary are competing against the points from the other class, attempting to pull the latent function in opposite directions. Consequently, the datapoints in this region all contribute strongly.

Another sign of this effect is that the uncertainty in the latent function, which is closely related to the "effective" local density of the data, is very small in the region around $x = 1$; the small uncertainty reveals a high effective density, which is caused by all data points in the region contributing with full weight. It should be emphasized that the example was artificially constructed specifically to highlight this effect.

Finally, Figure 3.6 also shows clearly the effects of uncertainty in the latent function on $\mathbb{E}_q[\pi_*|\mathbf{y}]$. In the region between $x = 2$ to $x = 4$, the latent mean in panel (b) increases slightly, but the predictive probability *decreases* in this region in panel (a). This is caused by the increase in uncertainty for the latent function; when the widely varying functions are squashed through the non-linearity it is possible for both classes to get high probability, and the average prediction becomes less extreme.

3.7.3 Binary Handwritten Digit Classification Example

Handwritten digit and character recognition are popular real-world tasks for testing and benchmarking classifiers, with obvious application e.g. in postal services. In this section we consider the discrimination of images of the digit 3 from images of the digit 5 as an example of binary classification; the specific choice was guided by the experience that this is probably one of the most difficult binary subtasks. 10-class classification of the digits 0-9 is described in the following section.

We use the US Postal Service (USPS) database of handwritten digits which *USPS dataset* consists of 9298 segmented 16×16 greyscale images normalized so that the intensity of the pixels lies in $[-1, 1]$. The data was originally split into a training set of 7291 cases and a testset of the remaining 2007 cases, and has often been used in this configuration. Unfortunately, the data in the two partitions was collected in slightly different ways, such that the data in the two sets did not stem from the same distribution.[17] Since the basic underlying assumption for most machine learning algorithms is that the distribution of the training and test data should be identical, the original data partitions are not really suitable as a test bed for learning algorithms, the interpretation of the results being hampered by the change in distribution. Secondly, the original test set was rather small, sometimes making it difficult to differentiate the performance of different algorithms. To overcome these two problems, we decided to pool the *USPS repartitioned* two partitions and randomly split the data into two identically sized partitions of 4649 cases each. A side-effect is that it is not trivial to compare to results obtained using the original partitions. All experiments reported here use the repartitioned data. The binary 3s vs. 5s data has 767 training cases, divided 406/361 on 3s vs. 5s, while the test set has 773 cases split 418/355.

We present results of both Laplace's method and EP using identical ex- *squared exponential* perimental setups. The squared exponential covariance function $k(\mathbf{x}, \mathbf{x}') =$ *covariance function*

---

[17]It is well known e.g. that the original test partition had more difficult cases than the training set.

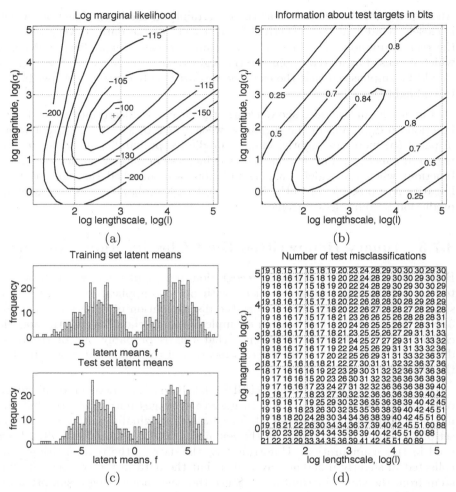

(a)

(b)

(c)

(d)

Figure 3.7: Binary Laplace approximation: 3s vs. 5s discrimination using the USPS data. Panel (a) shows a contour plot of the log marginal likelihood as a function of $\log(\ell)$ and $\log(\sigma_f)$. The marginal likelihood has an optimum at $\log(\ell) = 2.85$ and $\log(\sigma_f) = 2.35$, with an optimum value of $\log p(\mathbf{y}|X, \boldsymbol{\theta}) = -99$. Panel (b) shows a contour plot of the amount of information (in excess of a simple base-line model, see text) about the test cases in bits as a function of the same variables. The statistical uncertainty (because of the finite number of test cases) is about ± 0.03 bits (95% confidence interval). Panel (c) shows a histogram of the latent means for the training and test sets respectively at the values of the hyperparameters with optimal marginal likelihood (from panel (a)). Panel (d) shows the number of test errors (out of 773) when predicting using the sign of the latent mean.

hyperparameters

$\sigma_f^2 \exp(-|\mathbf{x} - \mathbf{x}'|^2/2\ell^2)$ was used, so there are two free parameters, namely σ_f (the process standard deviation, which controls its vertical scaling), and the length-scale ℓ (which controls the input length-scale). Let $\boldsymbol{\theta} = (\log(\ell), \log(\sigma_f))$ denote the vector of hyperparameters. We first present the results of Laplace's method in Figure 3.7 and discuss these at some length. We then briefly compare these with the results of the EP method in Figure 3.8.

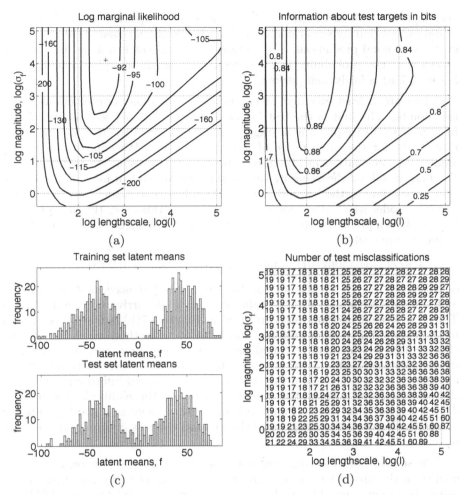

Figure 3.8: The EP algorithm on 3s vs. 5s digit discrimination task from the USPS data. Panel (a) shows a contour plot of the log marginal likelihood as a function of the hyperparameters $\log(\ell)$ and $\log(\sigma_f)$. The marginal likelihood has an optimum at $\log(\ell) = 2.6$ at the maximum value of $\log(\sigma_f)$, but the log marginal likelihood is essentially flat as a function of $\log(\sigma_f)$ in this region, so a good point is at $\log(\sigma_f) = 4.1$, where the log marginal likelihood has a value of -90. Panel (b) shows a contour plot of the amount of information (in excess of the baseline model) about the test cases in bits as a function of the same variables. Zero bits corresponds to no information and one bit to perfect binary generalization. The 773 test cases allows the information to be determined within ± 0.035 bits. Panel (c) shows a histogram of the latent means for the training and test sets respectively at the values of the hyperparameters with optimal marginal likelihood (from panel a). Panel (d) shows the number of test errors (out of 773) when predicting using the sign of the latent mean.

In Figure 3.7(a) we show a contour plot of the approximate log marginal likelihood (LML) $\log q(\mathbf{y}|X, \boldsymbol{\theta})$ as a function of $\log(\ell)$ and $\log(\sigma_f)$, obtained from runs on a grid of 17 evenly-spaced values of $\log(\ell)$ and 23 evenly-spaced values of $\log(\sigma_f)$. Notice that there is a maximum of the marginal likelihood

Laplace results

near $\log(\ell) = 2.85$ and $\log(\sigma_f) = 2.35$. As will be explained in chapter 5, we would expect that hyperparameters that yield a high marginal likelihood would give rise to good predictions. Notice that an increase of 1 unit on the log scale means that the probability is 2.7 times larger, so the marginal likelihood in Figure 3.7(a) is fairly well peaked.

test log predictive probability

There are at least two ways we can measure the quality of predictions at the test points. The first is the test log predictive probability $\log_2 p(y_*|\mathbf{x}_*, \mathcal{D}, \boldsymbol{\theta})$. In Figure 3.7(b) we plot the average over the test set of the test log predictive probability for the same range of hyperparameters. We express this as the amount of information in bits about the targets, by using log to the base 2. Further, we off-set the value by subtracting the amount of information that a simple base-line method would achieve. As a base-line model we use the best possible model which does not use the inputs; in this case, this model would just produce a predictive distribution reflecting the frequency of the two classes in the training set, i.e.

base-line method

$$-418/773 \log_2(406/767) - 355/773 \log_2(361/767) = 0.9956 \text{ bits}, \qquad (3.76)$$

essentially 1 bit. (If the classes had been perfectly balanced, and the training and test partitions also exactly balanced, we would arrive at exactly 1 bit.) Thus, our scaled information score used in Figure 3.7(b) would be zero for a method that did random guessing and 1 bit for a method which did perfect classification (with complete confidence). The information score measures how much information the model was able to extract from the inputs about the identity of the output. Note that this is *not* the mutual information between the model output and the test targets, but rather the Kullback-Leibler (KL) divergence between them. Figure 3.7 shows that there is a good qualitative agreement between the marginal likelihood and the test information, compare panels (a) and (b).

interpretation of information score

The second (and perhaps most commonly used) method for measuring the quality of the predictions is to compute the number of test errors made when using the predictions. This is done by computing $\mathbb{E}_q[\pi_*|\mathbf{y}]$ (see eq. (3.25)) for each test point, thresholding at $1/2$ to get "hard" predictions and counting the number of errors. Figure 3.7(d) shows the number of errors produced for each entry in the 17×23 grid of values for the hyperparameters. The general trend in this table is that the number of errors is lowest in the top left-hand corner and increases as one moves right and downwards. The number of errors rises dramatically in the far bottom righthand corner. However, note in general that the number of errors is quite small (there are 773 cases in the test set).

error rate

The qualitative differences between the two evaluation criteria depicted in Figure 3.7 panels (b) and (d) may at first sight seem alarming. And although panels (a) and (b) show similar trends, one may worry about using (a) to select the hyperparameters, if one is interested in minimizing the test misclassification rate. Indeed a full understanding of all aspects of these plots is quite involved, but as the following discussion suggests, we can explain the major trends.

First, bear in mind that the effect of increasing ℓ is to make the kernel function broader, so we might expect to observe effects like those in Figure 3.5

where large widths give rise to a lack of flexibility. Keeping ℓ constant, the effect of increasing σ_f is to increase the magnitude of the values obtained for $\hat{\mathbf{f}}$. By itself this would lead to "harder" predictions (i.e. predictive probabilities closer to 0 or 1), but we have to bear in mind that the variances associated will also increase and this increased uncertainty for the latent variables tends to "soften" the predictive probabilities, i.e. move them closer to $1/2$.

The most marked difference between Figure 3.7(b) and (d) is the behaviour in the the top left corner, where classification error rate remains small, but the test information and marginal likelihood are both poor. In the left hand side of the plots, the length scale ℓ is very short. This causes most points to be deemed "far away" from most other points. In this regime the prediction is dominated by the class-label of the nearest neighbours, and for the task at hand, this happens to give a low misclassification rate. In this parameter region the test latent variables $\mathbf{f}_*$ are very close to zero, corresponding to probabilities very close to $1/2$. Consequently, the predictive probabilities carry almost no information about the targets. In the top left corner, the predictive probabilities for all 773 test cases lie in the interval $[0.48, 0.53]$. Notice that a large amount of information implies a high degree of correct classification, but not vice versa. At the optimal marginal likelihood values of the hyperparameters, there are 21 misclassifications, which is slightly higher that the minimum number attained which is 15 errors.

In exercise 3.10.6 readers are encouraged to investigate further the behaviour of $\hat{\mathbf{f}}$ and the predictive probabilities etc. as functions of $\log(\ell)$ and $\log(\sigma_f)$ for themselves.

In Figure 3.8 we show the results on the same experiment, using the EP method. The findings are qualitatively similar, but there are significant differences. In panel (a) the approximate log marginal likelihood has a different shape than for Laplace's method, and the maximum of the log marginal likelihood is about 9 units on a natural log scale larger (i.e. the marginal probability is $\exp(9) \simeq 8000$ times higher). Also note that the marginal likelihood has a ridge (for $\log \ell = 2.6$) that extends into large values of $\log \sigma_f$. For these very large latent amplitudes (see also panel (c)) the probit likelihood function is well approximated by a step function (since it transitions from low to high values in the domain $[-3, 3]$). Once we are in this regime, it is of course irrelevant exactly how large the magnitude is, thus the ridge. Notice, however, that this does not imply that the prediction will always be "hard", since the variance of the latent function also grows.

Figure 3.8 shows a good qualitative agreement between the approximate log marginal likelihood and the test information, compare panels (a) and (b). The best value of the test information is significantly higher for EP than for Laplace's method. The classification error rates in panel (d) show a fairly similar behaviour to that of Laplace's method. In Figure 3.8(c) we show the latent means for training and test cases. These show a clear separation on the training set, and much larger magnitudes than for Laplace's method. The absolute values of the entries in $\mathbf{f}_*$ are quite large, often well in excess of 50, which may suggest very "hard" predictions (probabilities close to zero or one),

EP results

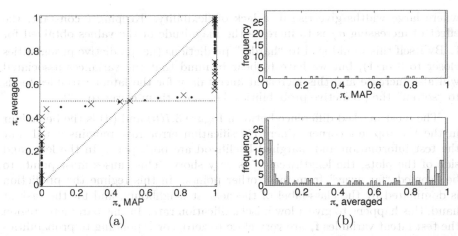

(a)   (b)

Figure 3.9: MAP vs. averaged predictions for the EP algorithm for the 3's vs. 5's digit discrimination using the USPS data. The optimal values of the hyperparameters from Figure 3.8(a) $\log(\ell) = 2.6$ and $\log(\sigma_f) = 4.1$ are used. The MAP predictions $\sigma(\mathbb{E}_q[f_*|\mathbf{y}])$ are "hard", mostly being very close to zero or one. On the other hand, the averaged predictions $\mathbb{E}_q[\pi_*|\mathbf{y}]$ from eq. (3.25) are a lot less extreme. In panel (a) the 21 cases that were misclassified are indicated by crosses (correctly classified cases are shown by points). Note that only 4 of the 21 misclassified points have confident predictions (i.e. outside $[0.1, 0.9]$). Notice that all points fall in the triangles below and above the horizontal line, confirming that averaging does not change the "most probable" class, and that it always makes the probabilities less extreme (i.e. closer to $1/2$). Panel (b) shows histograms of averaged and MAP predictions, where we have truncated values over 30.

since the sigmoid saturates for smaller arguments. However, when taking the uncertainties in the latent variables into account, and computing the predictions using averaging as in eq. (3.25) the predictive probabilities are "softened". In Figure 3.9 we can verify that the averaged predictive probabilities are much less extreme than the MAP predictions.

In order to evaluate the performance of the two approximate methods for GP classification, we compared to a linear probit model, a support vector machine, a least-squares classifier and a nearest neighbour approach, all of which are commonly used in the machine learning community. In Figure 3.10 we show *error-reject curve* error-reject curves for both misclassification rate and the test information measure. The error-reject curve shows how the performance develops as a function of the fraction of test cases that is being rejected. To compute these, we first modify the methods that do not naturally produce probabilistic predictions to do so, as described below. Based on the predictive probabilities, we reject test cases for which the maximum predictive probability is smaller than a threshold. Varying the threshold produces the error-reject curve.

The GP classifiers applied in Figure 3.10 used the hyperparameters which optimized the approximate marginal likelihood for each of the two methods. For the GP classifiers there were two free parameters σ_f and ℓ. The linear pro- *linear probit model* bit model (linear logistic models are probably more common, but we chose the probit here, since the other likelihood based methods all used probit) can be

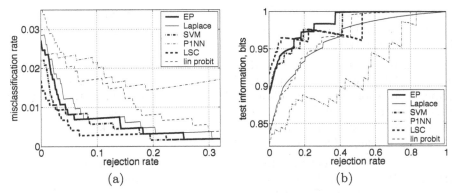

Figure 3.10: Panel (a) shows the error-reject curve and panel (b) the amount of information about the test cases as a function of the rejection rate. The probabilistic one nearest neighbour (P1NN) method has much worse performance than the other methods. Gaussian processes with EP behaves similarly to SVM's although the classification rate for SVM for low rejection rates seems to be a little better. Laplace's method is worse than EP and SVM. The GP least squares classifier (LSC) described in section 6.5 performs the best.

implemented as GP model using Laplace's method, which is equivalent to (although not computationally as efficient as) iteratively reweighted least squares (IRLS). The covariance function $k(\mathbf{x}, \mathbf{x}') = \theta^2 \mathbf{x}^\top \mathbf{x}'$ has a single hyperparameter, θ, which was set by maximizing the log marginal likelihood. This gives $\log p(\mathbf{y}|X, \theta) = -105$, at $\theta = 2.0$, thus the marginal likelihood for the linear covariance function is about 6 units on a natural log scale lower than the maximum log marginal likelihood for the Laplace approximation using the squared exponential covariance function.

The support vector machine (SVM) classifier (see section 6.4 for further details on the SVM) used the same SE kernel as the GP classifiers. For the SVM the rôle of ℓ is identical, and the trade-off parameter C in the SVM formulation (see eq. (6.37)) plays a similar rôle to σ_f^2. We carried out 5-fold cross validation on a grid in parameter space to identify the best combination of parameters w.r.t. the error rate; this turned out to be at $C = 1$, $\ell = 10$. Our experiments were conducted using the SVMTorch software [Collobert and Bengio, 2001]. In order to compute probabilistic predictions, we squashed the test-activities through a cumulative Gaussian, using the methods proposed by Platt [2000]: we made a parameterized linear transformation of the test-activities and fed this through the cumulative Gaussian.[18] The parameters of the linear transformation were chosen to maximize the log predictive probability, evaluated on the hold-out sets of the 5-fold cross validation.

support vector machine

The probabilistic one nearest neighbour (P1NN) method is a simple natural extension to the classical one nearest neighbour method which provides probabilistic predictions. It computes the leave-one-out (LOO) one nearest neighbour prediction on the training set, and records the fraction of cases π where the LOO predictions were correct. On test cases, the method then pre-

probabilistic one nearest neighbour

---

[18]Platt [2000] used a logistic whereas we use a cumulative Gaussian.

dicts the one nearest neighbour class with probability π, and the other class with probability $1 - \pi$. Rejections are based on thresholding on the distance to the nearest neighbour.

The least-squares classifier (LSC) is described in section 6.5. In order to produce probabilistic predictions, the method of Platt [2000] was used (as described above for the SVM) using the predictive means only (the predictive variances were ignored[19]), except that instead of the 5-fold cross validation, leave-one-out cross-validation (LOO-CV) was used, and the kernel parameters were also set using LOO-CV.

Figure 3.10 shows that the three best methods are the EP approximation for GPC, the SVM and the least-squares classifier (LSC). Presenting both the error rates and the test information helps to highlight differences which may not be apparent from a single plot alone. For example, Laplace's method and EP seem very similar on error rates, but quite different in test information. Notice also, that the error-reject curve itself reveals interesting differences, e.g. notice that although the P1NN method has an error rate comparable to other methods at zero rejections, things don't improve very much when rejections are allowed. Refer to section 3.8 for more discussion of the results.

3.7.4 10-class Handwritten Digit Classification Example

We apply the multi-class Laplace approximation developed in section 3.5 to the 10-class handwritten digit classification problem from the (repartitioned) USPS dataset, having $n = 4649$ training cases and $n_* = 4649$ cases for testing, see page 63. We used a squared exponential covariance function with two hyperparameters: a single signal amplitude σ_f, common to all 10 latent functions, and a single length-scale parameter ℓ, common to all 10 latent functions and common to all 256 input dimensions.

The behaviour of the method was investigated on a grid of values for the hyperparameters, see Figure 3.11. Note that the correspondence between the log marginal likelihood and the test information is not as close as for Laplace's method for binary classification in Figure 3.7 on page 64. The maximum value of the log marginal likelihood attained is -1018, and for the hyperparameters corresponding to this point the error rate is 3.1% and the test information 2.67 bits. As with the binary classification problem, the test information is standardized by subtracting off the negative entropy (information) of the targets which is -3.27 bits. The classification error rate in Figure 3.11(c) shows a clear minimum, and this is also attained at a shorter length-scale than where the marginal likelihood and test information have their maxima. This effect was also seen in the experiments on binary classification.

To gain some insight into the level of performance we compared these results with those obtained with the probabilistic one nearest neighbour method P1NN, a multiple logistic regression model and a SVM. The P1NN first uses an

---

[19]Of course, one could also have tried a variant where the full latent predictive distribution was averaged over, but we did not do that here.

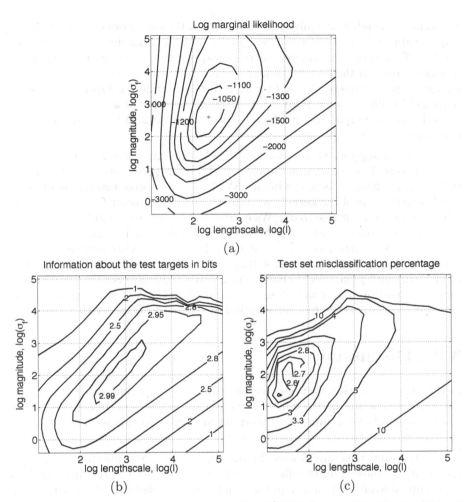

Figure 3.11: 10-way digit classification using the Laplace approximation. Panel (a) shows the approximate log marginal likelihood, reaching a maximum value of $\log p(\mathbf{y}|X, \boldsymbol{\theta}) = -1018$ at $\log \ell = 2.35$ and $\log \sigma_f = 2.6$. In panel (b) information about the test cases is shown. The maximum possible amount of information about the test targets, corresponding to perfect classification, would be 3.27 bits (the entropy of the targets). At the point of maximum marginal likelihood, the test information is 2.67 bits. In panel (c) the test set misclassification rate is shown in percent. At the point of maximum marginal likelihood the test error rate is 3.1%.

internal leave-one-out assessment on the training set to estimate its probability of being correct, π. For the test set it then predicts the nearest neighbour with probability π and all other classes with equal probability $(1 - \pi)/9$. We obtained $\pi = 0.967$, a test information of 2.98 bits and a test set classification error rate of 3.0%.

We also compare to multiple linear logistic regression. One way to implement this method is to view it as a Gaussian process with a linear covariance function, although it is equivalent and computationally more efficient to do the Laplace approximation over the "weights" of the linear model. In our case there are 10×257 weights (256 inputs and one bias), whereas there are 10×4696 latent function values in the GP. The linear covariance function $k(\mathbf{x}, \mathbf{x}') = \theta^2 \mathbf{x}^\top \mathbf{x}'$ has a single hyperparameter θ (used for all 10 latent functions). Optimizing the log marginal likelihood w.r.t. θ gives $\log p(\mathbf{y}|X, \theta) = -1339$ at $\theta = 1.45$. Using this value for the hyperparameter, the test information is 2.95 bits and the test set error rate is 5.7%.

Finally, a support vector machine (SVM) classifier was trained using the same SE kernel as the Gaussian process classifiers. (See section 6.4 for further details on the SVM.) As in the binary SVM case there were two free parameters ℓ (the length-scale of the kernel), and the trade-off parameter C (see eq. (6.37)), which plays a similar rôle to σ_f^2. We carried out 5-fold cross-validation on a grid in parameter space to identify the best combination of parameters w.r.t. the error rate; this turned out to be at $C = 1$, $\ell = 5$. Our experiments were conducted using the SVMTorch software [Collobert and Bengio, 2001], which implements multi-class SVM classification using the one-versus-rest method described in section 6.5. The test set error rate for the SVM is 2.2%; we did not attempt to evaluate the test information for the multi-class SVM.

3.8 Discussion

In the previous section we presented several sets of experiments comparing the two approximate methods for inference in GPC models, and comparing them to other commonly-used supervised learning methods. In this section we discuss the results and attempt to relate them to the properties of the models.

For the binary examples from Figures 3.7 and 3.8, we saw that the two approximations showed quite different qualitative behaviour of the approximated log marginal likelihood, although the exact marginal likelihood is of course identical. The EP approximation gave a higher maximum value of the log marginal likelihood (by about 9 units on the log scale) and the test information was somewhat better than for Laplace's method, although the test set error rates were comparable. However, although this experiment seems to favour the EP approximation, it is interesting to know how close these approximations are to the exact (analytically intractable) solutions. In Figure 3.12 we show the results of running a sophisticated Markov chain Monte Carlo method called Annealed Importance Sampling [Neal, 2001] carried out by Kuss and Rasmussen [2005]. The USPS dataset for these experiments was identical to the one used in Figures 3.7 and 3.8, so the results are directly comparable. It is seen that the MCMC results indicate that the EP method achieves a very high level of accuracy, i.e. that the difference between EP and Laplace's method is caused almost exclusively by approximation errors in Laplace's method.

The main reason for the inaccuracy of Laplace's method is that the high dimensional posterior is skew, and that the symmetric approximation centered on the mode is not characterizing the posterior volume very well. The posterior

Monte Carlo results

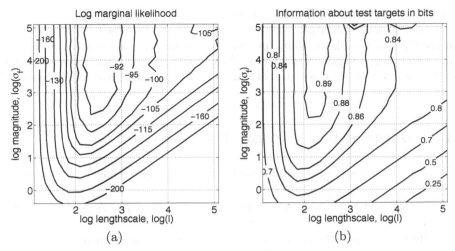

Figure 3.12: The log marginal likelihood, panel (a), and test information, panel (b), for the USPS 3's vs. 5's binary classification task computed using Markov chain Monte Carlo (MCMC). Comparing this to the Laplace approximation Figure 3.7 and Figure 3.8 shows that the EP approximation is surprisingly accurate. The slight wiggliness of the contour lines are caused by finite sample effects in the MCMC runs.

is a combination of the (correlated) Gaussian prior centered on the origin and the likelihood terms which (softly) cut off half-spaces which do not agree with the training set labels. Therefore the posterior looks like a correlated Gaussian restricted to the orthant which agrees with the labels. Its mode will be located close to the origin in that orthant, and it will decrease rapidly in the direction towards the origin due to conflicts from the likelihood terms, and decrease only slowly in the opposite direction (because of the prior). Seen in this light it is not surprising that the Laplace approximation is somewhat inaccurate. This explanation is corroborated further by Kuss and Rasmussen [2005].

It should be noted that all the methods compared on the binary digits classification task except for the linear probit model are using the squared distance between the digitized digit images measured directly in the image space as the sole input to the algorithm. This distance measure is not very well suited for the digit discrimination task—for example, two similar images that are slight translations of each other may have a huge squared distance, although of course identical labels. One of the strengths of the GP formalism is that one can use prior distributions over (latent, in this case) functions, and do inference based on these. If however, the prior over functions depends only on one particular aspect of the data (the squared distance in image space) which is not so well suited for discrimination, then the prior used is also not very appropriate. It would be more interesting to design covariance functions (parameterized by hyperparameters) which are more appropriate for the digit discrimination task, e.g. reflecting on the known invariances in the images, such as the "tangent-distance" ideas from Simard et al. [1992]; see also Schölkopf and Smola [2002, ch. 11] and section 9.10. The results shown here follow the common approach of using a generic

suitablility of the covariance function

covariance function with a minimum of hyperparameters, but this doesn't allow us to incorporate much prior information about the problem. For an example in the GP framework for doing inference about multiple hyperparameters with more complex covariance functions which provide clearly interpretable information about the data, see the carbon dioxide modelling problem discussed on page 118.

$*$ 3.9   Appendix: Moment Derivations

Consider the integral of a cumulative Gaussian, Φ, with respect to a Gaussian

$$
Z = \int_{-\infty}^{\infty} \Phi\left(\frac{x-m}{v}\right) \mathcal{N}(x|\mu, \sigma^2)\, dx, \quad \text{where} \quad \Phi(x) = \int_{-\infty}^{x} \mathcal{N}(y)\, dy, \quad (3.77)
$$

initially for the special case $v > 0$. Writing out in full, substituting $z = y - x + \mu - m$ and $w = x - \mu$ and interchanging the order of the integrals

$$
\begin{aligned}
Z_{v>0} &= \frac{1}{2\pi\sigma v} \int_{-\infty}^{\infty} \int_{-\infty}^{x} \exp\left(-\frac{(y-m)^2}{2v^2} - \frac{(x-\mu)^2}{2\sigma^2}\right) dy\, dx \\
&= \frac{1}{2\pi\sigma v} \int_{-\infty}^{\mu-m} \int_{-\infty}^{\infty} \exp\left(-\frac{(z+w)^2}{2v^2} - \frac{w^2}{2\sigma^2}\right) dw\, dz,
\end{aligned} \quad (3.78)
$$

or in matrix notation

$$
\begin{aligned}
Z_{v>0} &= \frac{1}{2\pi\sigma v} \int_{-\infty}^{\mu-m} \int_{-\infty}^{\infty} \exp\left(-\frac{1}{2}\begin{bmatrix} w \\ z \end{bmatrix}^{\top} \begin{bmatrix} \frac{1}{v^2}+\frac{1}{\sigma^2} & \frac{1}{v^2} \\ \frac{1}{v^2} & \frac{1}{v^2} \end{bmatrix} \begin{bmatrix} w \\ z \end{bmatrix}\right) dw\, dz \\
&= \int_{-\infty}^{\mu-m} \int_{-\infty}^{\infty} \mathcal{N}\left(\begin{bmatrix} w \\ z \end{bmatrix} \middle| \mathbf{0}, \begin{bmatrix} \sigma^2 & -\sigma^2 \\ -\sigma^2 & v^2+\sigma^2 \end{bmatrix}\right) dw\, dz, \quad (3.79)
\end{aligned}
$$

i.e. an (incomplete) integral over a joint Gaussian. The inner integral corresponds to marginalizing over w (see eq. (A.6)), yielding

$$
Z_{v>0} = \frac{1}{\sqrt{2\pi(v^2+\sigma^2)}} \int_{-\infty}^{\mu-m} \exp\left(-\frac{z^2}{2(v^2+\sigma^2)}\right) dz = \Phi\left(\frac{\mu-m}{\sqrt{v^2+\sigma^2}}\right), \quad (3.80)
$$

which assumed $v > 0$. If v is negative, we can substitute the symmetry $\Phi(-z) = 1 - \Phi(z)$ into eq. (3.77) to get

$$
Z_{v<0} = 1 - \Phi\left(\frac{\mu-m}{\sqrt{v^2+\sigma^2}}\right) = \Phi\left(-\frac{\mu-m}{\sqrt{v^2+\sigma^2}}\right). \quad (3.81)
$$

Collecting the two cases, eq. (3.80) and eq. (3.81) we arrive at

$$
Z = \int \Phi\left(\frac{x-m}{v}\right) \mathcal{N}(x|\mu, \sigma^2)\, dx = \Phi(z), \quad \text{where} \quad z = \frac{\mu-m}{v\sqrt{1+\sigma^2/v^2}}, \quad (3.82)
$$

for general $v \neq 0$. We wish to compute the moments of

$$
q(x) = Z^{-1} \Phi\left(\frac{x-m}{v}\right) \mathcal{N}(x|\mu, \sigma^2), \quad (3.83)
$$

where Z is given in eq. (3.82). Perhaps the easiest way to do this is to differentiate w.r.t. μ on both sides of eq. (3.82)

$$\frac{\partial Z}{\partial \mu} = \int \frac{x-\mu}{\sigma^2} \Phi\left(\frac{x-m}{v}\right) \mathcal{N}(x|\mu, \sigma^2)\, dx = \frac{\partial}{\partial \mu} \Phi(z) \iff \qquad (3.84)$$

$$\frac{1}{\sigma^2} \int x \Phi\left(\frac{x-m}{v}\right) \mathcal{N}(x|\mu, \sigma^2)\, dx - \frac{\mu Z}{\sigma^2} = \frac{\mathcal{N}(z)}{v\sqrt{1+\sigma^2/v^2}},$$

where we have used $\partial \Phi(z)/\partial \mu = \mathcal{N}(z)\partial z/\partial \mu$. We recognize the first term in the integral in the top line of eq. (3.84) as Z/σ^2 times the first moment of q which we are seeking. Multiplying through by σ^2/Z and rearranging we obtain

first moment

$$\mathbb{E}_q[x] = \mu + \frac{\sigma^2 \mathcal{N}(z)}{\Phi(z)v\sqrt{1+\sigma^2/v^2}}. \qquad (3.85)$$

Similarly, the second moment can be obtained by differentiating eq. (3.82) twice

$$\frac{\partial^2 Z}{\partial \mu^2} = \int \left[\frac{x^2}{\sigma^4} - \frac{2\mu x}{\sigma^4} + \frac{\mu^2}{\sigma^4} - \frac{1}{\sigma^2}\right] \Phi\left(\frac{x-m}{v}\right) \mathcal{N}(x|\mu, \sigma^2)\, dx = -\frac{z\mathcal{N}(z)}{v^2+\sigma^2}$$

$$\iff \mathbb{E}_q[x^2] = 2\mu \mathbb{E}_q[x] - \mu^2 + \sigma^2 - \frac{\sigma^4 z \mathcal{N}(z)}{\Phi(z)(v^2+\sigma^2)}, \qquad (3.86)$$

where the first and second terms of the integral in the top line of eq. (3.86) are multiples of the first and second moments. The second central moment after reintroducing eq. (3.85) into eq. (3.86) and simplifying is given by

second moment

$$\mathbb{E}_q\left[(x-\mathbb{E}_q[x])^2\right] = \mathbb{E}_q[x^2] - \mathbb{E}_q[x]^2 = \sigma^2 - \frac{\sigma^4 \mathcal{N}(z)}{(v^2+\sigma^2)\Phi(z)}\left(z + \frac{\mathcal{N}(z)}{\Phi(z)}\right). \qquad (3.87)$$

3.10 Exercises

1. For binary GPC, show the equivalence of using a noise-free latent process combined with a probit likelihood and a latent process with Gaussian noise combined with a step-function likelihood. Hint: introduce explicitly additional noisy latent variables $\tilde{f}_i$, which differ from f_i by Gaussian noise. Write down the step function likelihood for a single case as a function of $\tilde{f}_i$, integrate out the noisy variable, to arrive at the probit likelihood as a function of the noise-free process.

2. Consider a multinomial random variable $\mathbf{y}$ having C states, with $y_c = 1$ if the variable is in state c, and 0 otherwise. State c occurs with probability π_c. Show that $\text{cov}(\mathbf{y}) = \mathbb{E}[(\mathbf{y} - \boldsymbol{\pi})(\mathbf{y} - \boldsymbol{\pi})^\top] = \text{diag}(\boldsymbol{\pi}) - \boldsymbol{\pi}\boldsymbol{\pi}^\top$. Observe that $\text{cov}(\mathbf{y})$, being a covariance matrix, must necessarily be positive semidefinite. Using this fact show that the matrix $W = \text{diag}(\boldsymbol{\pi}) - \Pi\Pi^\top$ from eq. (3.38) is positive semidefinite. By showing that the vector of all ones is an eigenvector of $\text{cov}(\mathbf{y})$ with eigenvalue zero, verify that the matrix is indeed positive semidefinite, and not positive definite. (See section 4.1 for definitions of positive semidefinite and positive definite matrices.)

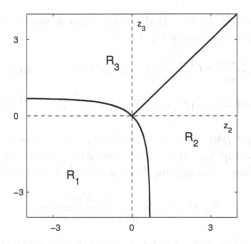

Figure 3.13: The decision regions for the three-class softmax function in z_2-z_3 space.

3. Consider the 3-class softmax function

$$p(\mathcal{C}_c) = \frac{\exp(f_c)}{\exp(f_1) + \exp(f_2) + \exp(f_3)},$$

where $c = 1, 2, 3$ and f_1, f_2, f_3 are the corresponding activations. To more easily visualize the decision boundaries, let $z_2 = f_2 - f_1$ and $z_3 = f_3 - f_1$. Thus

$$p(\mathcal{C}_1) = \frac{1}{1 + \exp(z_2) + \exp(z_3)}, \tag{3.88}$$

and similarly for the other classes. The decision boundary relating to $p(\mathcal{C}_1) > 1/3$ is the curve $\exp(z_2) + \exp(z_3) = 2$. The decision regions for the three classes are illustrated in Figure 3.13. Let $\mathbf{f} = (f_1, f_2, f_3)^\top$ have a Gaussian distribution centered on the origin, and let $\boldsymbol{\pi}(\mathbf{f}) = \text{softmax}(\mathbf{f})$. We now consider the effect of this distribution on $\bar{\boldsymbol{\pi}} = \int \boldsymbol{\pi}(\mathbf{f})p(\mathbf{f})\,d\mathbf{f}$. For a Gaussian with given covariance structure this integral is easily approximated by drawing samples from $p(\mathbf{f})$. Show that the classification can be made to fall into any of the three categories depending on the covariance matrix. Thus, by considering displacements of the mean of the Gaussian by ϵ from the origin into each of the three regions we have shown that overall classification depends not only on the mean of the Gaussian but also on its covariance. Show that this conclusion is still valid when it is recalled that $\mathbf{z}$ is derived from $\mathbf{f}$ as $\mathbf{z} = T\mathbf{f}$ where

$$T = \begin{pmatrix} 1 & 0 & -1 \\ 0 & 1 & -1 \end{pmatrix},$$

so that $\text{cov}(\mathbf{z}) = T\text{cov}(\mathbf{f})T^\top$.

4. Consider the update equation for $\mathbf{f}^{\text{new}}$ given by eq. (3.18) when some of the training points are well-explained under $\mathbf{f}$ so that $t_i \simeq \pi_i$ and $W_{ii} \simeq 0$

for these points. Break $\mathbf{f}$ into two subvectors, $\mathbf{f}_1$ that corresponds to points that are *not* well-explained, and $\mathbf{f}_2$ to those that are. Re-write $(K^{-1} + W)^{-1}$ from eq. (3.18) as $K(I + WK)^{-1}$ and let K be partitioned as K_{11}, K_{12}, K_{21}, K_{22} and similarly for the other matrices. Using the partitioned matrix inverse equations (see section A.3) show that

$$
\begin{aligned}
\mathbf{f}_1^{\text{new}} &= K_{11}(I_{11} + W_{11}K_{11})^{-1}\big(W_{11}\mathbf{f}_1 + \nabla \log p(\mathbf{y}_1|\mathbf{f}_1)\big), \\
\mathbf{f}_2^{\text{new}} &= K_{21}K_{11}^{-1}\mathbf{f}_1^{\text{new}}.
\end{aligned}
\tag{3.89}
$$

See section 3.4.1 for the consequences of this result.

5. Show that the expressions in eq. (3.56) for the cavity mean μ_{-i} and variance σ_{-i}^2 do not depend on the approximate likelihood terms $\tilde{\mu}_i$ and $\tilde{\sigma}_i^2$ for the corresponding case, despite the appearance of eq. (3.56).

6. Consider the USPS 3s vs. 5s prediction problem discussed in section 3.7.3. Use the implementation of the Laplace binary GPC provided to investigate how $\hat{\mathbf{f}}$ and the predictive probabilities etc. vary as functions of $\log(\ell)$ and $\log(\sigma_f)$.

Chapter 4

Covariance Functions

We have seen that a covariance function is the crucial ingredient in a Gaussian process predictor, as it encodes our assumptions about the function which we wish to learn. From a slightly different viewpoint it is clear that in supervised learning the notion of *similarity* between data points is crucial; it is a basic assumption that points with inputs $\mathbf{x}$ which are close are likely to have similar target values y, and thus training points that are near to a test point should be informative about the prediction at that point. Under the Gaussian process view it is the covariance function that defines nearness or similarity.

similarity

An arbitrary function of input pairs $\mathbf{x}$ and $\mathbf{x}'$ will not, in general, be a valid covariance function.[1] The purpose of this chapter is to give examples of some commonly-used covariance functions and to examine their properties. Section 4.1 defines a number of basic terms relating to covariance functions. Section 4.2 gives examples of stationary, dot-product, and other non-stationary covariance functions, and also gives some ways to make new ones from old. Section 4.3 introduces the important topic of eigenfunction analysis of covariance functions, and states Mercer's theorem which allows us to express the covariance function (under certain conditions) in terms of its eigenfunctions and eigenvalues. The covariance functions given in section 4.2 are valid when the input domain $\mathcal{X}$ is a subset of $\mathbb{R}^D$. In section 4.4 we describe ways to define covariance functions when the input domain is over structured objects such as strings and trees.

valid covariance functions

4.1 Preliminaries

A *stationary* covariance function is a function of $\mathbf{x} - \mathbf{x}'$. Thus it is invariant to translations in the input space.[2] For example the squared exponential co-

stationarity

---

[1]To be a valid covariance function it must be positive semidefinite, see eq. (4.2).

[2]In stochastic process theory a process which has constant mean and whose covariance function is invariant to translations is called *weakly stationary*. A process is *strictly stationary* if all of its finite dimensional distributions are invariant to translations [Papoulis, 1991, sec. 10.1].

isotropy

variance function given in equation 2.16 is stationary. If further the covariance function is a function only of $|\mathbf{x} - \mathbf{x}'|$ then it is called *isotropic*; it is thus invariant to all rigid motions. For example the squared exponential covariance function given in equation 2.16 is isotropic. As k is now only a function of $r = |\mathbf{x} - \mathbf{x}'|$ these are also known as *radial basis functions* (RBFs).

dot product covariance

If a covariance function depends only on $\mathbf{x}$ and $\mathbf{x}'$ through $\mathbf{x} \cdot \mathbf{x}'$ we call it a *dot product* covariance function. A simple example is the covariance function $k(\mathbf{x}, \mathbf{x}') = \sigma_0^2 + \mathbf{x} \cdot \mathbf{x}'$ which can be obtained from linear regression by putting $\mathcal{N}(0, 1)$ priors on the coefficients of x_d $(d = 1, \ldots, D)$ and a prior of $\mathcal{N}(0, \sigma_0^2)$ on the bias (or constant function) 1, see eq. (2.15). Another important example is the inhomogeneous polynomial kernel $k(\mathbf{x}, \mathbf{x}') = (\sigma_0^2 + \mathbf{x} \cdot \mathbf{x}')^p$ where p is a positive integer. Dot product covariance functions are invariant to a rotation of the coordinates about the origin, but not translations.

kernel

A general name for a function k of two arguments mapping a pair of inputs $\mathbf{x} \in \mathcal{X}$, $\mathbf{x}' \in \mathcal{X}$ into $\mathbb{R}$ is a *kernel*. This term arises in the theory of integral operators, where the operator T_k is defined as

$$(T_k f)(\mathbf{x}) = \int_{\mathcal{X}} k(\mathbf{x}, \mathbf{x}') f(\mathbf{x}') \, d\mu(\mathbf{x}'), \tag{4.1}$$

where μ denotes a measure; see section A.7 for further explanation of this point.[3] A real kernel is said to be *symmetric* if $k(\mathbf{x}, \mathbf{x}') = k(\mathbf{x}', \mathbf{x})$; clearly covariance functions must be symmetric from the definition.

Gram matrix
covariance matrix

Given a set of input points $\{\mathbf{x}_i | i = 1, \ldots, n\}$ we can compute the *Gram matrix* K whose entries are $K_{ij} = k(\mathbf{x}_i, \mathbf{x}_j)$. If k is a covariance function we call the matrix K the *covariance matrix*.

positive semidefinite

A real $n \times n$ matrix K which satisfies $Q(\mathbf{v}) = \mathbf{v}^\top K \mathbf{v} \geq 0$ for all vectors $\mathbf{v} \in \mathbb{R}^n$ is called positive semidefinite (PSD). If $Q(\mathbf{v}) = 0$ only when $\mathbf{v} = \mathbf{0}$ the matrix is positive definite. $Q(\mathbf{v})$ is called a *quadratic form*. A symmetric matrix is PSD if and only if all of its eigenvalues are non-negative. A Gram matrix corresponding to a general kernel function need not be PSD, but the Gram matrix corresponding to a covariance function is PSD.

A *kernel* is said to be positive semidefinite if

$$\int k(\mathbf{x}, \mathbf{x}') f(\mathbf{x}) f(\mathbf{x}') \, d\mu(\mathbf{x}) \, d\mu(\mathbf{x}') \geq 0, \tag{4.2}$$

for all $f \in L_2(\mathcal{X}, \mu)$. Equivalently a kernel function which gives rise to PSD Gram matrices for any choice of $n \in \mathbb{N}$ and $\mathcal{D}$ is positive semidefinite. To see this let f be the weighted sum of delta functions at each $\mathbf{x}_i$. Since such functions are limits of functions in $L_2(\mathcal{X}, \mu)$ eq. (4.2) implies that the Gram matrix corresponding to any $\mathcal{D}$ is PSD.

upcrossing rate

For a one-dimensional Gaussian process one way to understand the characteristic length-scale of the process (if this exists) is in terms of the number of upcrossings of a level u. Adler [1981, Theorem 4.1.1] states that the expected

---

[3]Informally speaking, readers will usually be able to substitute $d\mathbf{x}$ or $p(\mathbf{x})d\mathbf{x}$ for $d\mu(\mathbf{x})$.

number of upcrossings $\mathbb{E}[N_u]$ of the level u on the unit interval by a zero-mean, stationary, almost surely continuous Gaussian process is given by

$$\mathbb{E}[N_u] \;=\; \frac{1}{2\pi}\sqrt{\frac{-k''(0)}{k(0)}}\exp\left(-\frac{u^2}{2k(0)}\right). \qquad (4.3)$$

If $k''(0)$ does not exist (so that the process is not mean square differentiable) then if such a process has a zero at x_0 then it will almost surely have an infinite number of zeros in the arbitrarily small interval $(x_0, x_0 + \delta)$ [Blake and Lindsey, 1973, p. 303].

4.1.1   Mean Square Continuity and Differentiability   *

We now describe mean square continuity and differentiability of stochastic processes, following Adler [1981, sec. 2.2]. Let $\mathbf{x}_1, \mathbf{x}_2, \ldots$ be a sequence of points and $\mathbf{x}_*$ be a fixed point in $\mathbb{R}^D$ such that $|\mathbf{x}_k - \mathbf{x}_*| \to 0$ as $k \to \infty$. Then a process $f(\mathbf{x})$ is continuous in mean square at $\mathbf{x}_*$ if $\mathbb{E}[|f(\mathbf{x}_k) - f(\mathbf{x}_*)|^2] \to 0$ as $k \to \infty$. If this holds for all $\mathbf{x}_* \in A$ where A is a subset of $\mathbb{R}^D$ then $f(\mathbf{x})$ is said to be continuous in mean square (MS) over A. A random field is continuous in mean square at $\mathbf{x}_*$ if and only if its covariance function $k(\mathbf{x}, \mathbf{x}')$ is continuous at the point $\mathbf{x} = \mathbf{x}' = \mathbf{x}_*$. For stationary covariance functions this reduces to checking continuity at $k(\mathbf{0})$. Note that MS continuity does not necessarily imply sample function continuity; for a discussion of sample function continuity and differentiability see Adler [1981, ch. 3].

mean square continuity

The mean square derivative of $f(\mathbf{x})$ in the ith direction is defined as

$$\frac{\partial f(\mathbf{x})}{\partial x_i} \;=\; \underset{h \to 0}{\mathrm{l.\,i.\,m}}\,\frac{f(\mathbf{x} + h\mathbf{e}_i) - f(\mathbf{x})}{h}, \qquad (4.4)$$

when the limit exists, where l.i.m denotes the limit in mean square and $\mathbf{e}_i$ is the unit vector in the ith direction. The covariance function of $\partial f(\mathbf{x})/\partial x_i$ is given by $\partial^2 k(\mathbf{x}, \mathbf{x}')/\partial x_i \partial x_i'$. These definitions can be extended to higher order derivatives. For stationary processes, if the $2k$th-order partial derivative $\partial^{2k} k(\mathbf{x})/\partial^2 x_{i_1} \ldots \partial^2 x_{i_k}$ exists and is finite at $\mathbf{x} = \mathbf{0}$ then the kth order partial derivative $\partial^k f(\mathbf{x})/\partial x_{i_1} \ldots x_{i_k}$ exists for all $\mathbf{x} \in \mathbb{R}^D$ as a mean square limit. Notice that it is the properties of the kernel k around $\mathbf{0}$ that determine the smoothness properties (MS differentiability) of a stationary process.

mean square differentiability

4.2   Examples of Covariance Functions

In this section we consider covariance functions where the input domain $\mathcal{X}$ is a subset of the vector space $\mathbb{R}^D$. More general input spaces are considered in section 4.4. We start in section 4.2.1 with stationary covariance functions, then consider dot-product covariance functions in section 4.2.2 and other varieties of non-stationary covariance functions in section 4.2.3. We give an overview of some commonly used covariance functions in Table 4.1 and in section 4.2.4

we describe general methods for constructing new kernels from old. There exist several other good overviews of covariance functions, see e.g. Abrahamsen [1997].

4.2.1   Stationary Covariance Functions

In this section (and section 4.3) it will be convenient to allow kernels to be a map from $\mathbf{x} \in \mathcal{X}$, $\mathbf{x}' \in \mathcal{X}$ into $\mathbb{C}$ (rather than $\mathbb{R}$). If a zero-mean process f is complex-valued, then the covariance function is defined as $k(\mathbf{x}, \mathbf{x}') = \mathbb{E}[f(\mathbf{x})f^*(\mathbf{x}')]$, where $*$ denotes complex conjugation.

A stationary covariance function is a function of $\boldsymbol{\tau} = \mathbf{x} - \mathbf{x}'$. Sometimes in this case we will write k as a function of a single argument, i.e. $k(\boldsymbol{\tau})$.

The covariance function of a *stationary* process can be represented as the Fourier transform of a positive finite measure.

Bochner's theorem | **Theorem 4.1** *(Bochner's theorem) A complex-valued function k on $\mathbb{R}^D$ is the covariance function of a weakly stationary mean square continuous complex-valued random process on $\mathbb{R}^D$ if and only if it can be represented as*

$$k(\boldsymbol{\tau}) = \int_{\mathbb{R}^D} e^{2\pi i \mathbf{s} \cdot \boldsymbol{\tau}} \, d\mu(\mathbf{s}) \tag{4.5}$$

where μ is a positive finite measure.   □

The statement of Bochner's theorem is quoted from Stein [1999, p. 24]; a proof can be found in Gihman and Skorohod [1974, p. 208]. If μ has a density $S(\mathbf{s})$ then S is known as the *spectral density* or *power spectrum* corresponding to k.

spectral density
power spectrum

The construction given by eq. (4.5) puts non-negative power into each frequency $\mathbf{s}$; this is analogous to the requirement that the prior covariance matrix Σ_p on the weights in equation 2.4 be non-negative definite.

In the case that the spectral density $S(\mathbf{s})$ exists, the covariance function and the spectral density are Fourier duals of each other as shown in eq. (4.6);[4] this is known as the Wiener-Khintchine theorem, see, e.g. Chatfield [1989]

$$k(\boldsymbol{\tau}) = \int S(\mathbf{s}) e^{2\pi i \mathbf{s} \cdot \boldsymbol{\tau}} \, d\mathbf{s}, \qquad S(\mathbf{s}) = \int k(\boldsymbol{\tau}) e^{-2\pi i \mathbf{s} \cdot \boldsymbol{\tau}} \, d\boldsymbol{\tau}. \tag{4.6}$$

Notice that the variance of the process is $k(\mathbf{0}) = \int S(\mathbf{s}) \, d\mathbf{s}$ so the power spectrum must be integrable to define a valid Gaussian process.

To gain some intuition for the definition of the power spectrum given in eq. (4.6) it is important to realize that the complex exponentials $e^{2\pi i \mathbf{s} \cdot \mathbf{x}}$ are eigenfunctions of a stationary kernel with respect to Lebesgue measure (see section 4.3 for further details). Thus $S(\mathbf{s})$ is, loosely speaking, the amount of power allocated on average to the eigenfunction $e^{2\pi i \mathbf{s} \cdot \mathbf{x}}$ with frequency $\mathbf{s}$. $S(\mathbf{s})$ must eventually decay sufficiently fast as $|\mathbf{s}| \to \infty$ so that it is integrable; the

---

[4]See Appendix A.8 for details of Fourier transforms.

rate of this decay of the power spectrum gives important information about the smoothness of the associated stochastic process. For example it can determine the mean-square differentiability of the process (see section 4.3 for further details).

If the covariance function is isotropic (so that it is a function of r, where $r = |\boldsymbol{\tau}|$) then it can be shown that $S(\mathbf{s})$ is a function of $s \triangleq |\mathbf{s}|$ only [Adler, 1981, Theorem 2.5.2]. In this case the integrals in eq. (4.6) can be simplified by changing to spherical polar coordinates and integrating out the angular variables (see e.g. Bracewell, 1986, ch. 12) to obtain

$$k(r) = \frac{2\pi}{r^{D/2-1}} \int_0^\infty S(s) J_{D/2-1}(2\pi r s) s^{D/2}\, ds, \tag{4.7}$$

$$S(s) = \frac{2\pi}{s^{D/2-1}} \int_0^\infty k(r) J_{D/2-1}(2\pi r s) r^{D/2}\, dr, \tag{4.8}$$

where $J_{D/2-1}$ is a Bessel function of order $D/2-1$. Note that the dependence on the dimensionality D in equation 4.7 means that the same isotropic functional form of the spectral density can give rise to different isotropic covariance functions in different dimensions. Similarly, if we start with a particular isotropic covariance function $k(r)$ the form of spectral density will in general depend on D (see, e.g. the Matérn class spectral density given in eq. (4.15)) and in fact $k(r)$ may not be valid for all D. A necessary condition for the spectral density to exist is that $\int r^{D-1}|k(r)|\, dr < \infty$; see Stein [1999, sec. 2.10] for more details.

We now give some examples of commonly-used isotropic covariance functions. The covariance functions are given in a normalized form where $k(0) = 1$; we can multiply k by a (positive) constant σ_f^2 to get any desired process variance.

Squared Exponential Covariance Function

The *squared exponential* (SE) covariance function has already been introduced in chapter 2, eq. (2.16) and has the form

squared exponential

$$k_{\text{SE}}(r) = \exp\left(-\frac{r^2}{2\ell^2}\right), \tag{4.9}$$

with parameter ℓ defining the *characteristic length-scale*. Using eq. (4.3) we see that the mean number of level-zero upcrossings for a SE process in 1-d is $(2\pi\ell)^{-1}$, which confirms the rôle of ℓ as a length-scale. This covariance function is infinitely differentiable, which means that the GP with this covariance function has mean square derivatives of all orders, and is thus very smooth. The spectral density of the SE covariance function is $S(s) = (2\pi\ell^2)^{D/2} \exp(-2\pi^2\ell^2 s^2)$. Stein [1999] argues that such strong smoothness assumptions are unrealistic for modelling many physical processes, and recommends the Matérn class (see below). However, the squared exponential is probably the most widely-used kernel within the kernel machines field.

characteristic length-scale

infinitely divisible

The SE kernel is *infinitely divisible* in that $(k(r))^t$ is a valid kernel for all $t > 0$; the effect of raising k to the power of t is simply to rescale ℓ.

We now digress briefly, to show that the squared exponential covariance function can also be obtained by expanding the input $\mathbf{x}$ into a feature space defined by Gaussian-shaped basis functions centered densely in $\mathbf{x}$-space. For simplicity of exposition we consider scalar inputs with basis functions

infinite network
construction for SE
covariance function

$$\phi_c(x) = \exp\left(-\frac{(x-c)^2}{2\ell^2}\right), \tag{4.10}$$

where c denotes the centre of the basis function. From sections 2.1 and 2.2 we recall that with a Gaussian prior on the weights $\mathbf{w} \sim \mathcal{N}(\mathbf{0}, \sigma_p^2 I)$, this gives rise to a GP with covariance function

$$k(x_p, x_q) = \sigma_p^2 \sum_{c=1}^{N} \phi_c(x_p)\phi_c(x_q). \tag{4.11}$$

Now, allowing an infinite number of basis functions centered everywhere on an interval (and scaling down the variance of the prior on the weights with the number of basis functions) we obtain the limit

$$\lim_{N\to\infty} \frac{\sigma_p^2}{N} \sum_{c=1}^{N} \phi_c(x_p)\phi_c(x_q) = \sigma_p^2 \int_{c_{\min}}^{c_{\max}} \phi_c(x_p)\phi_c(x_q)dc. \tag{4.12}$$

Plugging in the Gaussian-shaped basis functions eq. (4.10) and letting the integration limits go to infinity we obtain

$$\begin{aligned}
k(x_p, x_q) &= \sigma_p^2 \int_{-\infty}^{\infty} \exp\left(-\frac{(x_p-c)^2}{2\ell^2}\right)\exp\left(-\frac{(x_q-c)^2}{2\ell^2}\right)dc \\
&= \sqrt{\pi}\ell\sigma_p^2 \exp\left(-\frac{(x_p-x_q)^2}{2(\sqrt{2}\ell)^2}\right),
\end{aligned} \tag{4.13}$$

which we recognize as a squared exponential covariance function with a $\sqrt{2}$ times longer length-scale. The derivation is adapted from MacKay [1998]. It is straightforward to generalize this construction to multivariate $\mathbf{x}$. See also eq. (4.30) for a similar construction where the centres of the basis functions are sampled from a Gaussian distribution; the constructions are equivalent when the variance of this Gaussian tends to infinity.

The Matérn Class of Covariance Functions

Matérn class

The *Matérn class* of covariance functions is given by

$$k_{\text{Matern}}(r) = \frac{2^{1-\nu}}{\Gamma(\nu)}\left(\frac{\sqrt{2\nu}r}{\ell}\right)^\nu K_\nu\left(\frac{\sqrt{2\nu}r}{\ell}\right), \tag{4.14}$$

with positive parameters ν and ℓ, where K_ν is a modified Bessel function [Abramowitz and Stegun, 1965, sec. 9.6]. This covariance function has a spectral density

$$S(s) = \frac{2^D \pi^{D/2}\Gamma(\nu+D/2)(2\nu)^\nu}{\Gamma(\nu)\ell^{2\nu}}\left(\frac{2\nu}{\ell^2} + 4\pi^2 s^2\right)^{-(\nu+D/2)} \tag{4.15}$$

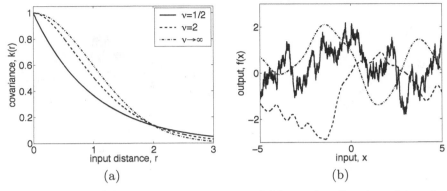

Figure 4.1: Panel (a): covariance functions, and (b): random functions drawn from Gaussian processes with Matérn covariance functions, eq. (4.14), for different values of ν, with $\ell = 1$. The sample functions on the right were obtained using a discretization of the x-axis of 2000 equally-spaced points.

in D dimensions. Note that the scaling is chosen so that for $\nu \to \infty$ we obtain the SE covariance function $e^{-r^2/2\ell^2}$, see eq. (A.25). Stein [1999] named this the Matérn class after the work of Matérn [1960]. For the Matérn class the process $f(\mathbf{x})$ is k-times MS differentiable if and only if $\nu > k$. The Matérn covariance functions become especially simple when ν is half-integer: $\nu = p + 1/2$, where p is a non-negative integer. In this case the covariance function is a product of an exponential and a polynomial of order p, the general expression can be derived from [Abramowitz and Stegun, 1965, eq. 10.2.15], giving

$$k_{\nu=p+1/2}(r) = \exp\left(-\frac{\sqrt{2\nu}r}{\ell}\right)\frac{\Gamma(p+1)}{\Gamma(2p+1)}\sum_{i=0}^{p}\frac{(p+i)!}{i!(p-i)!}\left(\frac{\sqrt{8\nu}r}{\ell}\right)^{p-i}. \quad (4.16)$$

It is possible that the most interesting cases for machine learning are $\nu = 3/2$ and $\nu = 5/2$, for which

$$\begin{aligned}
k_{\nu=3/2}(r) &= \left(1 + \frac{\sqrt{3}r}{\ell}\right)\exp\left(-\frac{\sqrt{3}r}{\ell}\right), \\
k_{\nu=5/2}(r) &= \left(1 + \frac{\sqrt{5}r}{\ell} + \frac{5r^2}{3\ell^2}\right)\exp\left(-\frac{\sqrt{5}r}{\ell}\right),
\end{aligned} \quad (4.17)$$

since for $\nu = 1/2$ the process becomes very rough (see below), and for $\nu \geq 7/2$, in the absence of explicit prior knowledge about the existence of higher order derivatives, it is probably very hard from finite noisy training examples to distinguish between values of $\nu \geq 7/2$ (or even to distinguish between finite values of ν and $\nu \to \infty$, the smooth squared exponential, in this case). For example a value of $\nu = 5/2$ was used in [Cornford et al., 2002].

Ornstein-Uhlenbeck Process and Exponential Covariance Function

The special case obtained by setting $\nu = 1/2$ in the Matérn class gives the exponential covariance function $k(r) = \exp(-r/\ell)$. The corresponding process

exponential

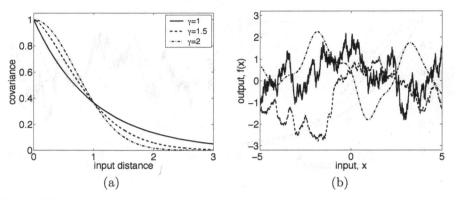

Figure 4.2: Panel (a) covariance functions, and (b) random functions drawn from Gaussian processes with the γ-exponential covariance function eq. (4.18), for different values of γ, with $\ell = 1$. The sample functions are only differentiable when $\gamma = 2$ (the SE case). The sample functions on the right were obtained using a discretization of the x-axis of 2000 equally-spaced points.

Ornstein-Uhlenbeck process

is MS continuous but not MS differentiable. In $D = 1$ this is the covariance function of the Ornstein-Uhlenbeck (OU) process. The OU process [Uhlenbeck and Ornstein, 1930] was introduced as a mathematical model of the velocity of a particle undergoing Brownian motion. More generally in $D = 1$ setting $\nu + 1/2 = p$ for integer p gives rise to a particular form of a continuous-time AR(p) Gaussian process; for further details see section B.2.1. The form of the Matérn covariance function and samples drawn from it for $\nu = 1/2$, $\nu = 2$ and $\nu \to \infty$ are illustrated in Figure 4.1.

The γ-exponential Covariance Function

γ-exponential

The γ-exponential family of covariance functions, which includes both the exponential and squared exponential, is given by

$$k(r) = \exp\left(-(r/\ell)^\gamma\right) \quad \text{for} \quad 0 < \gamma \le 2. \tag{4.18}$$

Although this function has a similar number of parameters to the Matérn class, it is (as Stein [1999] notes) in a sense less flexible. This is because the corresponding process is not MS differentiable except when $\gamma = 2$ (when it is infinitely MS differentiable). The covariance function and random samples from the process are shown in Figure 4.2. A proof of the positive definiteness of this covariance function can be found in Schoenberg [1938].

Rational Quadratic Covariance Function

rational quadratic

The *rational quadratic* (RQ) covariance function

$$k_{\text{RQ}}(r) = \left(1 + \frac{r^2}{2\alpha\ell^2}\right)^{-\alpha} \tag{4.19}$$

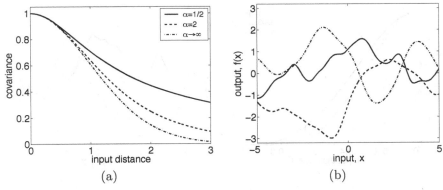

Figure 4.3: Panel (a) covariance functions, and (b) random functions drawn from Gaussian processes with rational quadratic covariance functions, eq. (4.20), for different values of α with $\ell = 1$. The sample functions on the right were obtained using a discretization of the x-axis of 2000 equally-spaced points.

with $\alpha,\ \ell > 0$ can be seen as a *scale mixture* (an infinite sum) of squared exponential (SE) covariance functions with different characteristic length-scales (sums of covariance functions are also a valid covariance, see section 4.2.4). Parameterizing now in terms of inverse squared length scales, $\tau = \ell^{-2}$, and putting a gamma distribution on $p(\tau | \alpha, \beta) \propto \tau^{\alpha-1} \exp(-\alpha\tau/\beta),$[5] we can add up the contributions through the following integral

$$
\begin{aligned}
k_{\mathrm{RQ}}(r) &= \int p(\tau | \alpha, \beta) k_{\mathrm{SE}}(r|\tau)\, d\tau \\
&\propto \int \tau^{\alpha-1} \exp\left(-\frac{\alpha\tau}{\beta}\right) \exp\left(-\frac{\tau r^2}{2}\right) d\tau \ \propto \ \left(1 + \frac{r^2}{2\alpha\ell^2}\right)^{-\alpha},
\end{aligned}
\tag{4.20}
$$

where we have set $\beta^{-1} = \ell^2$. The rational quadratic is also discussed by Matérn [1960, p. 17] using a slightly different parameterization; in our notation the limit of the RQ covariance for $\alpha \to \infty$ (see eq. (A.25)) is the SE covariance function with characteristic length-scale ℓ, eq. (4.9). Figure 4.3 illustrates the behaviour for different values of α; note that the process is infinitely MS differentiable for every α in contrast to the Matérn covariance function in Figure 4.1.

The previous example is a special case of kernels which can be written as superpositions of SE kernels with a distribution $p(\ell)$ of length-scales ℓ, $k(r) = \int \exp(-r^2/2\ell^2) p(\ell)\, d\ell$. This is in fact the most general representation for an isotropic kernel which defines a valid covariance function in any dimension D, see [Stein, 1999, sec. 2.10].

Piecewise Polynomial Covariance Functions with Compact Support

A family of piecewise polynomial functions with compact support provide another interesting class of covariance functions. Compact support means that

scale mixture

piecewise polynomial
covariance functions
with compact support

---

[5]Note that there are several common ways to parameterize the Gamma distribution—our choice is convenient here: α is the "shape" and β is the mean.

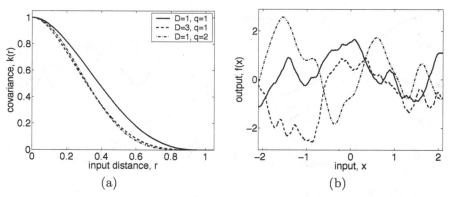

Figure 4.4: Panel (a): covariance functions, and (b): random functions drawn from Gaussian processes with piecewise polynomial covariance functions with compact support from eq. (4.21), with specified parameters.

the covariance between points become exactly zero when their distance exceeds a certain threshold. This means that the covariance matrix will become sparse by construction, leading to the possibility of computational advantages.[6] The **positive definiteness** challenge in designing these functions is how to guarantee positive definiteness. Multiple algorithms for deriving such covariance functions are discussed by Wendland [2005, ch. 9]. These functions are usually not positive definite **restricted dimension** for all input dimensions, but their validity is restricted up to some maximum dimension D. Below we give examples of covariance functions $k_{\mathrm{pp}D,q}(r)$ which are positive definite in $\mathbb{R}^D$

$$
\begin{aligned}
k_{\mathrm{pp}D,0}(r) &= (1-r)_+^j, && \text{where } j = \lfloor \tfrac{D}{2} \rfloor + q + 1, \\
k_{\mathrm{pp}D,1}(r) &= (1-r)_+^{j+1}\big((j+1)r+1\big), \\
k_{\mathrm{pp}D,2}(r) &= (1-r)_+^{j+2}\big((j^2+4j+3)r^2 + (3j+6)r+3\big)/3, && (4.21) \\
k_{\mathrm{pp}D,3}(r) &= (1-r)_+^{j+3}\big((j^3+9j^2+23j+15)r^3 + \\
&\qquad (6j^2+36j+45)r^2 + (15j+45)r+15\big)/15.
\end{aligned}
$$

The properties of three of these covariance functions are illustrated in Figure 4.4. These covariance functions are $2q$-times continuously differentiable, and thus the corresponding processes are q-times mean-square differentiable, see section 4.1.1. It is interesting to ask to what extent one could use the compactly-supported covariance functions described above in place of the other covariance functions mentioned in this section, while obtaining inferences that are similar. One advantage of the compact support is that it gives rise to sparsity of the Gram matrix which could be exploited, for example, when using iterative solutions to GPR problem, see section 8.3.6.

---

[6]If the product of the inverse covariance matrix with a vector (needed e.g. for prediction) is computed using a conjugate gradient algorithm, then products of the covariance matrix with vectors are the basic computational unit, and these can obviously be carried out much faster if the matrix is sparse.

Further Properties of Stationary Covariance Functions

The covariance functions given above decay monotonically with r and are always positive. However, this is not a necessary condition for a covariance function. For example Yaglom [1987] shows that $k(r) = c(\alpha r)^{-\nu} J_\nu(\alpha r)$ is a valid covariance function for $\nu \geq (D-2)/2$ and $\alpha > 0$; this function has the form of a damped oscillation.

Anisotropic versions of these isotropic covariance functions can be created   *anisotropy* by setting $r^2(\mathbf{x}, \mathbf{x}') = (\mathbf{x} - \mathbf{x}')^\top M(\mathbf{x} - \mathbf{x}')$ for some positive semidefinite M. If M is diagonal this implements the use of different length-scales on different dimensions—for further discussion of automatic relevance determination see section 5.1. General M's have been considered by Matérn [1960, p. 19], Poggio and Girosi [1990] and also in Vivarelli and Williams [1999]; in the latter work a low-rank M was used to implement a linear dimensionality reduction step from the input space to lower-dimensional feature space. More generally, one could assume the form

$$M = \Lambda \Lambda^\top + \Psi \qquad (4.22)$$

where Λ is a $D \times k$ matrix whose columns define k directions of high relevance, and Ψ is a diagonal matrix (with positive entries), capturing the (usual) axis-aligned relevances, see also Figure 5.1 on page 107. Thus M has a factor analysis   *factor analysis distance* form. For appropriate choices of k this may represent a good trade-off between flexibility and required number of parameters.

Stationary kernels can also be defined on a periodic domain, and can be readily constructed from stationary kernels on $\mathbb{R}$. Given a stationary kernel $k(x)$, the kernel $k_{\mathbb{T}}(x) = \sum_{m \in \mathbb{Z}} k(x + ml)$ is periodic with period l, as shown in   *periodization* section B.2.2 and Schölkopf and Smola [2002, eq. 4.42].

4.2.2   Dot Product Covariance Functions

As we have already mentioned above the kernel $k(\mathbf{x}, \mathbf{x}') = \sigma_0^2 + \mathbf{x} \cdot \mathbf{x}'$ can be obtained from linear regression. If $\sigma_0^2 = 0$ we call this the homogeneous linear kernel, otherwise it is inhomogeneous. Of course this can be generalized to $k(\mathbf{x}, \mathbf{x}') = \sigma_0^2 + \mathbf{x}^\top \Sigma_p \mathbf{x}'$ by using a general covariance matrix Σ_p on the components of $\mathbf{x}$, as described in eq. (2.4).[7] It is also the case that $k(\mathbf{x}, \mathbf{x}') = (\sigma_0^2 + \mathbf{x}^\top \Sigma_p \mathbf{x}')^p$ is a valid covariance function for positive integer p, because of the general result that a positive-integer power of a given covariance function is also a valid covariance function, as described in section 4.2.4. However, it is also interesting to show an explicit feature space construction for the polynomial covariance function. We consider the homogeneous polynomial case as the inhomogeneous case can simply be obtained by considering $\mathbf{x}$ to be extended

---

[7]Indeed the bias term could also be included in the general expression.

by concatenating a constant. We write

$$k(\mathbf{x}, \mathbf{x}') = (\mathbf{x} \cdot \mathbf{x}')^p = \Big(\sum_{d=1}^{D} x_d x_d'\Big)^p = \Big(\sum_{d_1=1}^{D} x_{d_1} x_{d_1}'\Big) \cdots \Big(\sum_{d_p=1}^{D} x_{d_p} x_{d_p}'\Big)$$

$$= \sum_{d_1=1}^{D} \cdots \sum_{d_p=1}^{D} (x_{d_1} \cdots x_{d_p})(x_{d_1}' \cdots x_{d_p}') \triangleq \boldsymbol{\phi}(\mathbf{x}) \cdot \boldsymbol{\phi}(\mathbf{x}'). \qquad (4.23)$$

Notice that this sum apparently contains D^p terms but in fact it is less than this as the order of the indices in the monomial $x_{d_1} \cdots x_{d_p}$ is unimportant, e.g. for $p = 2$, $x_1 x_2$ and $x_2 x_1$ are the same monomial. We can remove the redundancy by defining a vector $\mathbf{m}$ whose entry m_d specifies the number of times index d appears in the monomial, under the constraint that $\sum_{i=1}^{D} m_i = p$. Thus $\phi_{\mathbf{m}}(\mathbf{x})$, the feature corresponding to vector $\mathbf{m}$ is proportional to the monomial $x_1^{m_1} \ldots x_D^{m_D}$. The degeneracy of $\phi_{\mathbf{m}}(\mathbf{x})$ is $\frac{p!}{m_1! \ldots m_D!}$ (where as usual we define $0! = 1$), giving the feature map

$$\phi_{\mathbf{m}}(\mathbf{x}) = \sqrt{\frac{p!}{m_1! \cdots m_D!}} x_1^{m_1} \cdots x_D^{m_D}. \qquad (4.24)$$

For example, for $p = 2$ in $D = 2$, we have $\boldsymbol{\phi}(\mathbf{x}) = (x_1^2, x_2^2, \sqrt{2} x_1 x_2)^\top$. Dot-product kernels are sometimes used in a normalized form given by eq. (4.35).

For regression problems the polynomial kernel is a rather strange choice as the prior variance grows rapidly with $|\mathbf{x}|$ for $|\mathbf{x}| > 1$. However, such kernels have proved effective in high-dimensional classification problems (e.g. take $\mathbf{x}$ to be a vectorized binary image) where the input data are binary or greyscale normalized to $[-1, 1]$ on each dimension [Schölkopf and Smola, 2002, sec. 7.8].

4.2.3   Other Non-stationary Covariance Functions

Above we have seen examples of non-stationary dot product kernels. However, there are also other interesting kernels which are not of this form. In this section we first describe the covariance function belonging to a particular type of neural network; this construction is due to Neal [1996].

Consider a network which takes an input $\mathbf{x}$, has one hidden layer with N_H units and then linearly combines the outputs of the hidden units with a bias b to obtain $f(\mathbf{x})$. The mapping can be written

$$f(\mathbf{x}) = b + \sum_{j=1}^{N_H} v_j h(\mathbf{x}; \mathbf{u}_j), \qquad (4.25)$$

where the v_js are the hidden-to-output weights and $h(\mathbf{x}; \mathbf{u})$ is the hidden unit transfer function (which we shall assume is bounded) which depends on the input-to-hidden weights $\mathbf{u}$. For example, we could choose $h(\mathbf{x}; \mathbf{u}) = \tanh(\mathbf{x} \cdot \mathbf{u})$. This architecture is important because it has been shown by Hornik [1993] that networks with one hidden layer are universal approximators as the number of hidden units tends to infinity, for a wide class of transfer functions (but excluding polynomials). Let b and the v's have independent zero-mean distributions of variance σ_b^2 and σ_v^2, respectively, and let the weights $\mathbf{u}_j$ for each hidden unit be independently and identically distributed. Denoting all weights by $\mathbf{w}$, we obtain (following Neal [1996])

$$\mathbb{E}_{\mathbf{w}}[f(\mathbf{x})] = 0 \tag{4.26}$$

$$\mathbb{E}_{\mathbf{w}}[f(\mathbf{x})f(\mathbf{x}')] = \sigma_b^2 + \sum_j \sigma_v^2 \mathbb{E}_{\mathbf{u}}[h(\mathbf{x};\mathbf{u}_j)h(\mathbf{x}';\mathbf{u}_j)] \tag{4.27}$$

$$= \sigma_b^2 + N_H \sigma_v^2 \mathbb{E}_{\mathbf{u}}[h(\mathbf{x};\mathbf{u})h(\mathbf{x}';\mathbf{u})], \tag{4.28}$$

where eq. (4.28) follows because all of the hidden units are identically distributed. The final term in equation 4.28 becomes $\omega^2 \mathbb{E}_{\mathbf{u}}[h(\mathbf{x};\mathbf{u})h(\mathbf{x}';\mathbf{u})]$ by letting σ_v^2 scale as ω^2/N_H.

The sum in eq. (4.27) is over N_H identically and independently distributed random variables. As the transfer function is bounded, all moments of the distribution will be bounded and hence the central limit theorem can be applied, showing that the stochastic process will converge to a Gaussian process in the limit as $N_H \to \infty$.

By evaluating $\mathbb{E}_{\mathbf{u}}[h(\mathbf{x};\mathbf{u})h(\mathbf{x}';\mathbf{u})]$ we can obtain the covariance function of the neural network. For example if we choose the error function $h(z) = \mathrm{erf}(z) = 2/\sqrt{\pi}\int_0^z e^{-t^2} dt$ as the transfer function, let $h(\mathbf{x};\mathbf{u}) = \mathrm{erf}(u_0 + \sum_{j=1}^D u_j x_j)$ and choose $\mathbf{u} \sim \mathcal{N}(0,\Sigma)$ then we obtain [Williams, 1998]

neural network covariance function

$$k_{\mathrm{NN}}(\mathbf{x},\mathbf{x}') = \frac{2}{\pi}\sin^{-1}\left(\frac{2\tilde{\mathbf{x}}^\top\Sigma\tilde{\mathbf{x}}'}{\sqrt{(1+2\tilde{\mathbf{x}}^\top\Sigma\tilde{\mathbf{x}})(1+2\tilde{\mathbf{x}}'^\top\Sigma\tilde{\mathbf{x}}')}}\right), \tag{4.29}$$

where $\tilde{\mathbf{x}} = (1, x_1, \ldots, x_d)^\top$ is an augmented input vector. This is a true "neural network" covariance function. The "sigmoid" kernel $k(\mathbf{x},\mathbf{x}') = \tanh(a + b\mathbf{x}\cdot\mathbf{x}')$ has sometimes been proposed, but in fact this kernel is never positive definite and is thus not a valid covariance function, see, e.g. Schölkopf and Smola [2002, p. 113]. Figure 4.5 shows a plot of the neural network covariance function and samples from the prior. We have set $\Sigma = \mathrm{diag}(\sigma_0^2, \sigma^2)$. Samples from a GP with this covariance function can be viewed as superpositions of the functions $\mathrm{erf}(u_0 + ux)$, where σ_0^2 controls the variance of u_0 (and thus the amount of offset of these functions from the origin), and σ^2 controls u and thus the scaling on the x-axis. In Figure 4.5(b) we observe that the sample functions with larger σ vary more quickly. Notice that the samples display the non-stationarity of the covariance function in that for large values of $+x$ or $-x$ they should tend to a constant value, consistent with the construction as a superposition of sigmoid functions.

Another interesting construction is to set $h(\mathbf{x};\mathbf{u}) = \exp(-|\mathbf{x}-\mathbf{u}|^2/2\sigma_g^2)$, where σ_g sets the scale of this Gaussian basis function. With $\mathbf{u} \sim \mathcal{N}(\mathbf{0},\sigma_u^2 I)$

modulated squared exponential

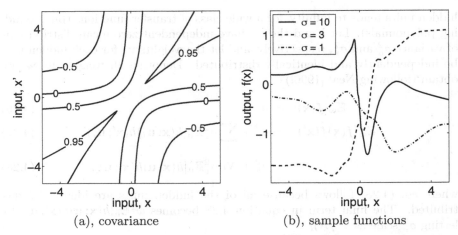

(a), covariance   (b), sample functions

Figure 4.5: Panel (a): a plot of the covariance function $k_{NN}(x, x')$ for $\sigma_0 = 10$, $\sigma = 10$. Panel (b): samples drawn from the neural network covariance function with $\sigma_0 = 2$ and σ as shown in the legend. The samples were obtained using a discretization of the x-axis of 500 equally-spaced points.

we obtain

$$k_G(\mathbf{x}, \mathbf{x}') = \frac{1}{(2\pi\sigma_u^2)^{d/2}} \int \exp\left(-\frac{|\mathbf{x} - \mathbf{u}|^2}{2\sigma_g^2} - \frac{|\mathbf{x}' - \mathbf{u}|^2}{2\sigma_g^2} - \frac{\mathbf{u}^\top \mathbf{u}}{2\sigma_u^2}\right) d\mathbf{u}$$
$$= \left(\frac{\sigma_e}{\sigma_u}\right)^d \exp\left(-\frac{\mathbf{x}^\top \mathbf{x}}{2\sigma_m^2}\right) \exp\left(-\frac{|\mathbf{x} - \mathbf{x}'|^2}{2\sigma_s^2}\right) \exp\left(-\frac{\mathbf{x}'^\top \mathbf{x}'}{2\sigma_m^2}\right), \quad (4.30)$$

where $1/\sigma_e^2 = 2/\sigma_g^2 + 1/\sigma_u^2$, $\sigma_s^2 = 2\sigma_g^2 + \sigma_g^4/\sigma_u^2$ and $\sigma_m^2 = 2\sigma_u^2 + \sigma_g^2$. This is in general a non-stationary covariance function, but if $\sigma_u^2 \to \infty$ (while scaling ω^2 appropriately) we recover the squared exponential $k_G(\mathbf{x}, \mathbf{x}') \propto \exp(-|\mathbf{x} - \mathbf{x}'|^2/4\sigma_g^2)$. For a finite value of σ_u^2, $k_G(\mathbf{x}, \mathbf{x}')$ comprises a squared exponential covariance function modulated by the Gaussian decay envelope function $\exp(-\mathbf{x}^\top \mathbf{x}/2\sigma_m^2)\exp(-\mathbf{x}'^\top \mathbf{x}'/2\sigma_m^2)$, cf. the vertical rescaling construction described in section 4.2.4.

warping

    One way to introduce non-stationarity is to introduce an arbitrary non-linear mapping (or warping) $\mathbf{u}(\mathbf{x})$ of the input $\mathbf{x}$ and then use a stationary covariance function in $\mathbf{u}$-space. Note that $\mathbf{x}$ and $\mathbf{u}$ need not have the same dimensionality as each other. This approach was used by Sampson and Guttorp [1992] to model patterns of solar radiation in southwestern British Columbia using Gaussian processes.

periodic random function

    Another interesting example of this warping construction is given in MacKay [1998] where the one-dimensional input variable x is mapped to the two-dimensional $\mathbf{u}(x) = (\cos(x), \sin(x))$ to give rise to a periodic random function of x. If we use the squared exponential kernel in $\mathbf{u}$-space, then

$$k(x, x') = \exp\left(-\frac{2\sin^2\left(\frac{x - x'}{2}\right)}{\ell^2}\right), \quad (4.31)$$

as $(\cos(x) - \cos(x'))^2 + (\sin(x) - \sin(x'))^2 = 4\sin^2(\frac{x - x'}{2})$.

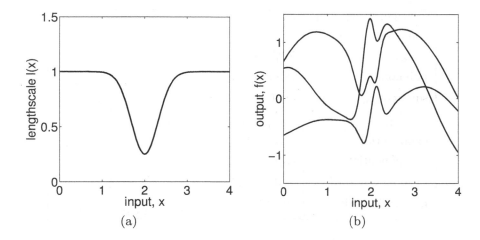

Figure 4.6: Panel (a) shows the chosen length-scale function $\ell(x)$. Panel (b) shows three samples from the GP prior using Gibbs' covariance function eq. (4.32). This figure is based on Fig. 3.9 in Gibbs [1997].

We have described above how to make an anisotropic covariance function by scaling different dimensions differently. However, we are not free to make these length-scales ℓ_d be functions of $\mathbf{x}$, as this will not in general produce a valid covariance function. Gibbs [1997] derived the covariance function $\qquad$ *varying length-scale*

$$k(\mathbf{x}, \mathbf{x}') = \prod_{d=1}^{D} \left(\frac{2\ell_d(\mathbf{x})\ell_d(\mathbf{x}')}{\ell_d^2(\mathbf{x}) + \ell_d^2(\mathbf{x}')} \right)^{1/2} \exp \left(-\sum_{d=1}^{D} \frac{(x_d - x_d')^2}{\ell_d^2(\mathbf{x}) + \ell_d^2(\mathbf{x}')} \right), \qquad (4.32)$$

where each $\ell_i(\mathbf{x})$ is an arbitrary positive function of $\mathbf{x}$. Note that $k(\mathbf{x}, \mathbf{x}) = 1$ for all $\mathbf{x}$. This covariance function is obtained by considering a grid of N Gaussian basis functions with centres $\mathbf{c}_j$ and a corresponding length-scale on input dimension d which varies as a positive function $\ell_d(\mathbf{c}_j)$. Taking the limit as $N \to \infty$ the sum turns into an integral and after some algebra eq. (4.32) is obtained.

An example of a variable length-scale function and samples from the prior corresponding to eq. (4.32) are shown in Figure 4.6. Notice that as the length-scale gets shorter the sample functions vary more rapidly as one would expect. The large length-scale regions on either side of the short length-scale region can be quite strongly correlated. If one tries the converse experiment by creating a length-scale function $\ell(x)$ which has a longer length-scale region between two shorter ones then the behaviour may not be quite what is expected; on initially transitioning into the long length-scale region the covariance drops off quite sharply due to the prefactor in eq. (4.32), before stabilizing to a slower variation. See Gibbs [1997, sec. 3.10.3] for further details. Exercises 4.5.4 and 4.5.5 invite you to investigate this further.

Paciorek and Schervish [2004] have generalized Gibbs' construction to obtain non-stationary versions of arbitrary isotropic covariance functions. Let k_S be a

covariance function	expression	S	ND
constant	σ_0^2	$\checkmark$	
linear	$\sum_{d=1}^{D} \sigma_d^2 x_d x_d'$		
polynomial	$(\mathbf{x} \cdot \mathbf{x}' + \sigma_0^2)^p$		
squared exponential	$\exp(-\frac{r^2}{2\ell^2})$	$\checkmark$	$\checkmark$
Matérn	$\frac{1}{2^{\nu-1}\Gamma(\nu)}\left(\frac{\sqrt{2\nu}}{\ell}r\right)^\nu K_\nu\left(\frac{\sqrt{2\nu}}{\ell}r\right)$	$\checkmark$	$\checkmark$
exponential	$\exp(-\frac{r}{\ell})$	$\checkmark$	$\checkmark$
γ-exponential	$\exp\left(-\left(\frac{r}{\ell}\right)^\gamma\right)$	$\checkmark$	$\checkmark$
rational quadratic	$(1 + \frac{r^2}{2\alpha\ell^2})^{-\alpha}$	$\checkmark$	$\checkmark$
neural network	$\sin^{-1}\left(\frac{2\tilde{\mathbf{x}}^\top\Sigma\tilde{\mathbf{x}}'}{\sqrt{(1+2\tilde{\mathbf{x}}^\top\Sigma\tilde{\mathbf{x}})(1+2\tilde{\mathbf{x}}'^\top\Sigma\tilde{\mathbf{x}}')}}\right)$		$\checkmark$

Table 4.1: Summary of several commonly-used covariance functions. The covariances are written either as a function of $\mathbf{x}$ and $\mathbf{x}'$, or as a function of $r = |\mathbf{x} - \mathbf{x}'|$. Two columns marked 'S' and 'ND' indicate whether the covariance functions are stationary and nondegenerate respectively. Degenerate covariance functions have finite rank, see section 4.3 for more discussion of this issue.

stationary, isotropic covariance function that is valid in every Euclidean space $\mathbb{R}^D$ for $D = 1, 2, \ldots$. Let $\Sigma(\mathbf{x})$ be a $D \times D$ matrix-valued function which is positive definite for all $\mathbf{x}$, and let $\Sigma_i \triangleq \Sigma(\mathbf{x}_i)$. (The set of Gibbs' $\ell_i(\mathbf{x})$ functions define a diagonal $\Sigma(\mathbf{x})$.) Then define the quadratic form

$$Q_{ij} = (\mathbf{x}_i - \mathbf{x}_j)^\top((\Sigma_i + \Sigma_j)/2)^{-1}(\mathbf{x}_i - \mathbf{x}_j). \tag{4.33}$$

Paciorek and Schervish [2004] show that

$$k_{\mathrm{NS}}(\mathbf{x}_i, \mathbf{x}_j) = 2^{D/2}|\Sigma_i|^{1/4}|\Sigma_j|^{1/4}|\Sigma_i + \Sigma_j|^{-1/2}k_{\mathrm{S}}(\sqrt{Q_{ij}}), \tag{4.34}$$

is a valid non-stationary covariance function.

In chapter 2 we described the linear regression model in feature space $f(\mathbf{x}) = \phi(\mathbf{x})^\top\mathbf{w}$. O'Hagan [1978] suggested making $\mathbf{w}$ a function of $\mathbf{x}$ to allow for different values of $\mathbf{w}$ to be appropriate in different regions. Thus he put a Gaussian process prior on $\mathbf{w}$ of the form $\mathrm{cov}(\mathbf{w}(\mathbf{x}), \mathbf{w}(\mathbf{x}')) = W_0 k_w(\mathbf{x}, \mathbf{x}')$ for some positive definite matrix W_0, giving rise to a prior on $f(\mathbf{x})$ with covariance $k_f(\mathbf{x}, \mathbf{x}') = \phi(\mathbf{x})^\top W_0 \phi(\mathbf{x}') k_w(\mathbf{x}, \mathbf{x}')$.

Wiener process

Finally we note that the Wiener process with covariance function $k(x, x') = \min(x, x')$ is a fundamental non-stationary process. See section B.2.1 and texts such as Grimmett and Stirzaker [1992, ch. 13] for further details.

4.2.4 Making New Kernels from Old

In the previous sections we have developed many covariance functions some of which are summarized in Table 4.1. In this section we show how to combine or modify existing covariance functions to make new ones.

The sum of two kernels is a kernel. Proof: consider the random process $f(\mathbf{x}) = f_1(\mathbf{x}) + f_2(\mathbf{x})$, where $f_1(\mathbf{x})$ and $f_2(\mathbf{x})$ are independent. Then $k(\mathbf{x}, \mathbf{x}') = k_1(\mathbf{x}, \mathbf{x}') + k_2(\mathbf{x}, \mathbf{x}')$. This construction can be used e.g. to add together kernels with different characteristic length-scales.

sum

The product of two kernels is a kernel. Proof: consider the random process $f(\mathbf{x}) = f_1(\mathbf{x}) f_2(\mathbf{x})$, where $f_1(\mathbf{x})$ and $f_2(\mathbf{x})$ are independent. Then $k(\mathbf{x}, \mathbf{x}') = k_1(\mathbf{x}, \mathbf{x}') k_2(\mathbf{x}, \mathbf{x}')$.[8] A simple extension of this argument means that $k^p(\mathbf{x}, \mathbf{x}')$ is a valid covariance function for $p \in \mathbb{N}$.

product

Let $a(\mathbf{x})$ be a given deterministic function and consider $g(\mathbf{x}) = a(\mathbf{x}) f(\mathbf{x})$ where $f(\mathbf{x})$ is a random process. Then $\mathrm{cov}(g(\mathbf{x}), g(\mathbf{x}')) = a(\mathbf{x}) k(\mathbf{x}, \mathbf{x}') a(\mathbf{x}')$. Such a construction can be used to normalize kernels by choosing $a(\mathbf{x}) = k^{-1/2}(\mathbf{x}, \mathbf{x})$ (assuming $k(\mathbf{x}, \mathbf{x}) > 0 \ \forall \mathbf{x}$), so that

vertical rescaling

$$\tilde{k}(\mathbf{x}, \mathbf{x}') = \frac{k(\mathbf{x}, \mathbf{x}')}{\sqrt{k(\mathbf{x}, \mathbf{x})} \sqrt{k(\mathbf{x}', \mathbf{x}')}}. \tag{4.35}$$

This ensures that $\tilde{k}(\mathbf{x}, \mathbf{x}) = 1$ for all $\mathbf{x}$.

We can also obtain a new process by convolution (or blurring). Consider an arbitrary fixed kernel $h(\mathbf{x}, \mathbf{z})$ and the map $g(\mathbf{x}) = \int h(\mathbf{x}, \mathbf{z}) f(\mathbf{z}) \, d\mathbf{z}$. Then clearly $\mathrm{cov}(g(\mathbf{x}), g(\mathbf{x}')) = \int h(\mathbf{x}, \mathbf{z}) k(\mathbf{z}, \mathbf{z}') h(\mathbf{x}', \mathbf{z}') \, d\mathbf{z} \, d\mathbf{z}'$.

convolution

If $k(\mathbf{x}_1, \mathbf{x}_1')$ and $k(\mathbf{x}_2, \mathbf{x}_2')$ are covariance functions over different spaces $\mathcal{X}_1$ and $\mathcal{X}_2$, then the direct sum $k(\mathbf{x}, \mathbf{x}') = k_1(\mathbf{x}_1, \mathbf{x}_1') + k_2(\mathbf{x}_2, \mathbf{x}_2')$ and the tensor product $k(\mathbf{x}, \mathbf{x}') = k_1(\mathbf{x}_1, \mathbf{x}_1') k_2(\mathbf{x}_2, \mathbf{x}_2')$ are also covariance functions (defined on the product space $\mathcal{X}_1 \times \mathcal{X}_2$), by virtue of the sum and product constructions.

direct sum
tensor product

The direct sum construction can be further generalized. Consider a function $f(\mathbf{x})$, where $\mathbf{x}$ is D-dimensional. An *additive* model [Hastie and Tibshirani, 1990] has the form $f(\mathbf{x}) = c + \sum_{i=1}^{D} f_i(x_i)$, i.e. a linear combination of functions of one variable. If the individual f_i's are taken to be independent stochastic processes, then the covariance function of f will have the form of a direct sum. If we now admit interactions of two variables, so that $f(\mathbf{x}) = c + \sum_{i=1}^{D} f_i(x_i) + \sum_{ij, j<i} f_{ij}(x_i, x_j)$ and the various f_i's and f_{ij}'s are independent stochastic processes, then the covariance function will have the form $k(\mathbf{x}, \mathbf{x}') = \sum_{i=1}^{D} k_i(x_i, x_i') + \sum_{i=2}^{D} \sum_{j=1}^{i-1} k_{ij}(x_i, x_j; x_i', x_j')$. Indeed this process can be extended further to provide a *functional ANOVA*[9] decomposition, ranging from a simple additive model up to full interaction of all D input variables. (The sum can also be truncated at some stage.) Wahba [1990, ch. 10] and Stitson et al. [1999] suggest using tensor products for kernels with interactions so that in the example above $k_{ij}(x_i, x_j; x_i', x_j')$ would have the form $k_i(x_i; x_i') k_j(x_j; x_j')$. Note that if D is large then the large number of pairwise (or higher-order) terms may be problematic; Plate [1999] has investigated using a combination of additive GP models plus a general covariance function that permits full interactions.

additive model

functional ANOVA

---

[8]If f_1 and f_2 are Gaussian processes then the product f will not in general be a Gaussian process, but there exists a GP with this covariance function.

[9]ANOVA stands for analysis of variance, a statistical technique that analyzes the interactions between various attributes.

4.3   Eigenfunction Analysis of Kernels

We first define eigenvalues and eigenfunctions and discuss Mercer's theorem which allows us to express the kernel (under certain conditions) in terms of these quantities. Section 4.3.1 gives the analytical solution of the eigenproblem for the SE kernel under a Gaussian measure. Section 4.3.2 discusses how to compute approximate eigenfunctions numerically for cases where the exact solution is not known.

It turns out that Gaussian process regression can be viewed as Bayesian linear regression with a possibly infinite number of basis functions, as discussed in chapter 2. One possible basis set is the *eigenfunctions* of the covariance function. A function $\phi(\cdot)$ that obeys the integral equation

$$\int k(\mathbf{x}, \mathbf{x}')\phi(\mathbf{x}) \, d\mu(\mathbf{x}) = \lambda\phi(\mathbf{x}'), \tag{4.36}$$

eigenvalue,
eigenfunction

is called an eigenfunction of kernel k with eigenvalue λ with respect to measure[10] μ. The two measures of particular interest to us will be (i) Lebesgue measure over a compact subset $\mathcal{C}$ of $\mathbb{R}^D$, or (ii) when there is a density $p(\mathbf{x})$ so that $d\mu(\mathbf{x})$ can be written $p(\mathbf{x})d\mathbf{x}$.

In general there are an infinite number of eigenfunctions, which we label $\phi_1(\mathbf{x})$, $\phi_2(\mathbf{x}),\ldots$ We assume the ordering is chosen such that $\lambda_1 \geq \lambda_2 \geq \ldots$. The eigenfunctions are orthogonal with respect to μ and can be chosen to be normalized so that $\int \phi_i(\mathbf{x})\phi_j(\mathbf{x}) \, d\mu(\mathbf{x}) = \delta_{ij}$ where δ_{ij} is the Kronecker delta.

Mercer's theorem

Mercer's theorem (see, e.g. König, 1986) allows us to express the kernel k in terms of the eigenvalues and eigenfunctions.

Theorem 4.2 *(Mercer's theorem).* *Let* $(\mathcal{X}, \mu)$ *be a finite measure space and* $k \in L_\infty(\mathcal{X}^2, \mu^2)$ *be a kernel such that* $T_k : L_2(\mathcal{X}, \mu) \to L_2(\mathcal{X}, \mu)$ *is positive definite (see eq. (4.2)). Let* $\phi_i \in L_2(\mathcal{X}, \mu)$ *be the normalized eigenfunctions of* T_k *associated with the eigenvalues* $\lambda_i > 0$. *Then:*

1. the eigenvalues $\{\lambda_i\}_{i=1}^\infty$ *are absolutely summable*

2.

$$k(\mathbf{x}, \mathbf{x}') = \sum_{i=1}^\infty \lambda_i\phi_i(\mathbf{x})\phi_i^*(\mathbf{x}'), \tag{4.37}$$

holds μ^2 *almost everywhere, where the series converges absolutely and uniformly* μ^2 *almost everywhere.* □

This decomposition is just the infinite-dimensional analogue of the diagonalization of a Hermitian matrix. Note that the sum may terminate at some value $N \in \mathbb{N}$ (i.e. the eigenvalues beyond N are zero), or the sum may be infinite. We have the following definition [Press et al., 1992, p. 794]

---

[10]For further explanation of measure see Appendix A.7.

Definition 4.1 *A degenerate kernel has only a finite number of non-zero eigenvalues.* □

A degenerate kernel is also said to have finite rank. If a kernel is not degenerate it is said to be *nondegenerate*. As an example a N-dimensional linear regression model in feature space (see eq. (2.10)) gives rise to a degenerate kernel with at most N non-zero eigenvalues. (Of course if the measure only puts weight on a finite number of points n in $\mathbf{x}$-space then the eigendecomposition is simply that of a $n \times n$ matrix, even if the kernel is nondegenerate.)

degenerate,
nondegenerate
kernel

The statement of Mercer's theorem above referred to a finite measure μ. If we replace this with Lebesgue measure and consider a stationary covariance function, then directly from Bochner's theorem eq. (4.5) we obtain

$$k(\mathbf{x} - \mathbf{x}') = \int_{\mathbb{R}^D} e^{2\pi i \mathbf{s} \cdot (\mathbf{x} - \mathbf{x}')} \, d\mu(\mathbf{s}) = \int_{\mathbb{R}^D} e^{2\pi i \mathbf{s} \cdot \mathbf{x}} \left(e^{2\pi i \mathbf{s} \cdot \mathbf{x}'} \right)^* d\mu(\mathbf{s}). \quad (4.38)$$

The complex exponentials $e^{2\pi i \mathbf{s} \cdot \mathbf{x}}$ are the eigenfunctions of a stationary kernel w.r.t. Lebesgue measure. Note the similarity to eq. (4.37) except that the summation has been replaced by an integral.

The rate of decay of the eigenvalues gives important information about the smoothness of the kernel. For example Ritter et al. [1995] showed that in 1-d with μ uniform on $[0, 1]$, processes which are r-times mean-square differentiable have $\lambda_i \propto i^{-(2r+2)}$ asymptotically. This makes sense as "rougher" processes have more power at high frequencies, and so their eigenvalue spectrum decays more slowly. The same phenomenon can be read off from the power spectrum of the Matérn class as given in eq. (4.15).

Hawkins [1989] gives the exact eigenvalue spectrum for the OU process on $[0, 1]$. Widom [1963; 1964] gives an asymptotic analysis of the eigenvalues of stationary kernels taking into account the effect of the density $d\mu(\mathbf{x}) = p(\mathbf{x})d\mathbf{x}$; Bach and Jordan [2002, Table 3] use these results to show the effect of varying $p(\mathbf{x})$ for the SE kernel. An exact eigenanalysis of the SE kernel under the Gaussian density is given in the next section.

4.3.1 An Analytic Example *

For the case that $p(x)$ is a Gaussian and for the squared-exponential kernel $k(x, x') = \exp(-(x - x')^2/2\ell^2)$, there are analytic results for the eigenvalues and eigenfunctions, as given by Zhu et al. [1998, sec. 4]. Putting $p(x) = \mathcal{N}(x|0, \sigma^2)$ we find that the eigenvalues λ_k and eigenfunctions ϕ_k (for convenience let $k = 0, 1, \dots$) are given by

$$\lambda_k = \sqrt{\frac{2a}{A}} B^k, \quad (4.39)$$

$$\phi_k(x) = \exp\left(-(c - a)x^2\right) H_k\left(\sqrt{2c}\,x\right), \quad (4.40)$$

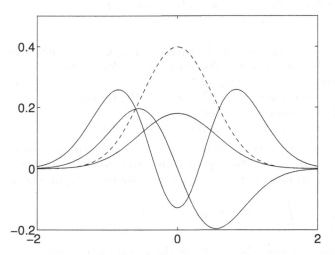

Figure 4.7: The first 3 eigenfunctions of the squared exponential kernel w.r.t. a Gaussian density. The value of $k = 0$, 1, 2 is equal to the number of zero-crossings of the function. The dashed line is proportional to the density $p(x)$.

where $H_k(x) = (-1)^k \exp(x^2) \frac{d^k}{dx^k} \exp(-x^2)$ is the kth order Hermite polynomial (see Gradshteyn and Ryzhik [1980, sec. 8.95]), $a^{-1} = 4\sigma^2$, $b^{-1} = 2\ell^2$ and

$$c = \sqrt{a^2 + 2ab}, \qquad A = a + b + c, \qquad B = b/A. \qquad (4.41)$$

Hints on the proof of this result are given in exercise 4.5.9. A plot of the first three eigenfunctions for $a = 1$ and $b = 3$ is shown in Figure 4.7.

The result for the eigenvalues and eigenfunctions is readily generalized to the multivariate case when the kernel and Gaussian density are products of the univariate expressions, as the eigenfunctions and eigenvalues will simply be products too. For the case that a and b are equal on all D dimensions, the degeneracy of the eigenvalue $\left(\frac{2a}{A}\right)^{D/2} B^k$ is $\binom{k+D-1}{D-1}$ which is $\mathcal{O}(k^{D-1})$. As $\sum_{j=0}^{k} \binom{j+D-1}{D-1} = \binom{k+D}{D}$ we see that the $\binom{k+D}{D}$'th eigenvalue has a value given by $\left(\frac{2a}{A}\right)^{D/2} B^k$, and this can be used to determine the rate of decay of the spectrum.

4.3.2   Numerical Approximation of Eigenfunctions

The standard numerical method for approximating the eigenfunctions and eigenvalues of eq. (4.36) is to use a numerical routine to approximate the integral (see, e.g. Baker [1977, ch. 3]). For example letting $d\mu(\mathbf{x}) = p(\mathbf{x})d\mathbf{x}$ in eq. (4.36) one could use the approximation

$$\lambda_i \phi_i(\mathbf{x}') = \int k(\mathbf{x}, \mathbf{x}') p(\mathbf{x}) \phi_i(\mathbf{x}) \, d\mathbf{x} \simeq \frac{1}{n} \sum_{l=1}^{n} k(\mathbf{x}_l, \mathbf{x}') \phi_i(\mathbf{x}_l), \qquad (4.42)$$

where the $\mathbf{x}_l$'s are sampled from $p(\mathbf{x})$. Plugging in $\mathbf{x}' = \mathbf{x}_l$ for $l = 1, \ldots, n$ into eq. (4.42) we obtain the matrix eigenproblem

$$K\mathbf{u}_i = \lambda_i^{\mathrm{mat}}\mathbf{u}_i, \qquad (4.43)$$

where K is the $n \times n$ Gram matrix with entries $K_{ij} = k(\mathbf{x}_i, \mathbf{x}_j)$, λ_i^{mat} is the ith matrix eigenvalue and $\mathbf{u}_i$ is the corresponding eigenvector (normalized so that $\mathbf{u}_i^\top \mathbf{u}_i = 1$). We have $\phi_i(\mathbf{x}_j) \sim \sqrt{n}(\mathbf{u}_i)_j$ where the $\sqrt{n}$ factor arises from the differing normalizations of the eigenvector and eigenfunction. Thus $\frac{1}{n}\lambda_i^{\mathrm{mat}}$ is an obvious estimator for λ_i for $i = 1, \ldots, n$. For fixed n one would expect that the larger eigenvalues would be better estimated than the smaller ones. The theory of the numerical solution of eigenvalue problems shows that for a fixed i, $\frac{1}{n}\lambda_i^{\mathrm{mat}}$ will converge to λ_i in the limit that $n \to \infty$ [Baker, 1977, Theorem 3.4]. It is also possible to study the convergence further; for example it is quite easy using the properties of principal components analysis (PCA) in feature space to show that for any l, $1 \le l \le n$, $\mathbb{E}_n[\frac{1}{n}\sum_{i=1}^{l}\lambda_i^{\mathrm{mat}}] \ge \sum_{i=1}^{l}\lambda_i$ and $\mathbb{E}_n[\frac{1}{n}\sum_{i=l+1}^{n}\lambda_i^{\mathrm{mat}}] \le \sum_{i=l+1}^{N}\lambda_i$, where $\mathbb{E}_n$ denotes expectation with respect to samples of size n drawn from $p(\mathbf{x})$. For further details see Shawe-Taylor and Williams [2003].

The Nyström method for approximating the ith eigenfunction (see Baker [1977] and Press et al. [1992, section 18.1]) is given by

$$\phi_i(\mathbf{x}') \simeq \frac{\sqrt{n}}{\lambda_i^{\mathrm{mat}}}\mathbf{k}(\mathbf{x}')^\top \mathbf{u}_i, \qquad (4.44)$$

Nyström method

where $\mathbf{k}(\mathbf{x}')^\top = (k(\mathbf{x}_1, \mathbf{x}'), \ldots, k(\mathbf{x}_n, \mathbf{x}'))$, which is obtained from eq. (4.42) by dividing both sides by λ_i. Equation 4.44 extends the approximation $\phi_i(\mathbf{x}_j) \simeq \sqrt{n}(\mathbf{u}_i)_j$ from the sample points $\mathbf{x}_1, \ldots, \mathbf{x}_n$ to all $\mathbf{x}$.

There is an interesting relationship between the kernel PCA method of Schölkopf et al. [1998] and the eigenfunction expansion discussed above. The eigenfunction expansion has (at least potentially) an infinite number of non-zero eigenvalues. In contrast, the kernel PCA algorithm operates on the $n \times n$ matrix K and yields n eigenvalues and eigenvectors. Eq. (4.42) clarifies the relationship between the two. However, note that eq. (4.44) is identical (up to scaling factors) to Schölkopf et al. [1998, eq. 4.1] which describes the projection of a new point $\mathbf{x}'$ onto the ith eigenvector in the kernel PCA feature space.

kernel PCA

4.4   Kernels for Non-vectorial Inputs

So far in this chapter we have assumed that the input $\mathbf{x}$ is a vector, measuring the values of a number of attributes (or features). However, for some learning problems the inputs are not vectors, but structured objects such as strings, trees or general graphs. For example, we may have a biological problem where we want to classify proteins (represented as strings of amino acid symbols).[11]

---

[11]Proteins are initially made up of 20 different amino acids, of which a few may later be modified bringing the total number up to 26 or 30.

Or our input may be parse-trees derived from a linguistic analysis. Or we may wish to represent chemical compounds as labelled graphs, with vertices denoting atoms and edges denoting bonds.

To follow the discriminative approach we need to extract some features from the input objects and build a predictor using these features. (For a classification problem, the alternative generative approach would construct class-conditional models over the objects themselves.) Below we describe two approaches to this feature extraction problem and the efficient computation of kernels from them: in section 4.4.1 we cover string kernels, and in section 4.4.2 we describe Fisher kernels. There exist other proposals for constructing kernels for strings, for example Watkins [2000] describes the use of pair hidden Markov models (HMMs that generate output symbols for two strings conditional on the hidden state) for this purpose.

4.4.1 String Kernels

We start by defining some notation for strings. Let $\mathcal{A}$ be a finite alphabet of characters. The concatenation of strings x and y is written xy and $|x|$ denotes the length of string x. The string s is a substring of x if we can write $x = usv$ for some (possibly empty) u, s and v.

Let $\phi_s(x)$ denote the number of times that substring s appears in string x. Then we define the kernel between two strings x and x' as

$$k(x, x') = \sum_{s \in \mathcal{A}^*} w_s \phi_s(x) \phi_s(x'), \qquad (4.45)$$

where w_s is a non-negative weight for substring s. For example, we could set $w_s = \lambda^{|s|}$, where $0 < \lambda < 1$, so that shorter substrings get more weight than longer ones.

A number of interesting special cases are contained in the definition 4.45:

bag-of-characters

- Setting $w_s = 0$ for $|s| > 1$ gives the bag-of-characters kernel. This takes the feature vector for a string x to be the number of times that each character in $\mathcal{A}$ appears in x.

bag-of-words

- In text analysis we may wish to consider the frequencies of word occurrence. If we require s to be bordered by whitespace then a "bag-of-words" representation is obtained. Although this is a very simple model of text (which ignores word order) it can be surprisingly effective for document classification and retrieval tasks, see e.g. Hand et al. [2001, sec. 14.3]. The weights can be set differently for different words, e.g. using the "term frequency inverse document frequency" (TF-IDF) weighting scheme developed in the information retrieval area [Salton and Buckley, 1988].

k-spectrum kernel

- If we only consider substrings of length k, then we obtain the k-spectrum kernel [Leslie et al., 2003].

Importantly, there are efficient methods using suffix trees that can compute a string kernel $k(x, x')$ in time linear in $|x| + |x'|$ (with some restrictions on the weights $\{w_s\}$) [Leslie et al., 2003, Vishwanathan and Smola, 2003].

Work on string kernels was started by Watkins [1999] and Haussler [1999]. There are many further developments of the methods we have described above; for example Lodhi et al. [2001] go beyond substrings to consider subsequences of x which are not necessarily contiguous, and Leslie et al. [2003] describe mismatch string kernels which allow substrings s and s' of x and x' respectively to match if there are at most m mismatches between them. We expect further developments in this area, tailoring (or engineering) the string kernels to have properties that make sense in a particular domain.

The idea of string kernels, where we consider matches of substrings, can easily be extended to trees, e.g. by looking at matches of subtrees [Collins and Duffy, 2002].

Leslie et al. [2003] have applied string kernels to the classification of protein domains into SCOP[12] superfamilies. The results obtained were significantly better than methods based on either PSI-BLAST[13] searches or a generative hidden Markov model classifier. Similar results were obtained by Jaakkola et al. [2000] using a Fisher kernel (described in the next section). Saunders et al. [2003] have also described the use of string kernels on the problem of classifying natural language newswire stories from the Reuters-21578[14] database into ten classes.

4.4.2 Fisher Kernels

As explained above, our problem is that the input x is a structured object of arbitrary size e.g. a string, and we wish to extract features from it. The *Fisher kernel* (introduced by Jaakkola et al., 2000) does this by taking a generative model $p(x|\boldsymbol{\theta})$, where $\boldsymbol{\theta}$ is a vector of parameters, and computing the feature vector $\boldsymbol{\phi_\theta}(x) = \nabla_\theta \log p(x|\boldsymbol{\theta})$. $\boldsymbol{\phi_\theta}(x)$ is sometimes called the *score vector*.

score vector

Take, for example, a Markov model for strings. Let x_k be the kth symbol in string x. Then a Markov model gives $p(x|\boldsymbol{\theta}) = p(x_1|\boldsymbol{\pi})\prod_{i=1}^{|x|-1} p(x_{i+1}|x_i, A)$, where $\boldsymbol{\theta} = (\boldsymbol{\pi}, A)$. Here $(\boldsymbol{\pi})_j$ gives the probability that x_1 will be the jth symbol in the alphabet $\mathcal{A}$, and A is a $|\mathcal{A}| \times |\mathcal{A}|$ stochastic matrix, with a_{jk} giving the probability that $p(x_{i+1} = k|x_i = j)$. Given such a model it is straightforward to compute the score vector for a given x.

It is also possible to consider other generative models $p(x|\boldsymbol{\theta})$. For example we might try a kth-order Markov model where x_i is predicted by the preceding k symbols. See Leslie et al. [2003] and Saunders et al. [2003] for an interesting discussion of the similarities of the features used in the k-spectrum kernel and the score vector derived from an order $k - 1$ Markov model; see also exercise

---

[12]Structural classification of proteins database, http://scop.mrc-lmb.cam.ac.uk/scop/.

[13]Position-Specific Iterative Basic Local Alignment Search Tool, see http://www.ncbi.nlm.nih.gov/Education/BLASTinfo/psi1.html.

[14]http://www.daviddlewis.com/resources/testcollections/reuters21578/.

4.5.12. Another interesting choice is to use a hidden Markov model (HMM) as the generative model, as discussed by Jaakkola et al. [2000]. See also exercise 4.5.11 for a linear kernel derived from an isotropic Gaussian model for $\mathbf{x} \in \mathbb{R}^D$.

We define a kernel $k(x, x')$ based on the score vectors for x and x'. One simple choice is to set

$$k(x, x') = \phi_{\boldsymbol{\theta}}^{\top}(x) M^{-1} \phi_{\boldsymbol{\theta}}(x'), \tag{4.46}$$

where M is a strictly positive definite matrix. Alternatively we might use the squared exponential kernel $k(x, x') = \exp(-\alpha |\phi_{\boldsymbol{\theta}}(x) - \phi_{\boldsymbol{\theta}}(x')|^2)$ for some $\alpha > 0$.

The structure of $p(x|\boldsymbol{\theta})$ as $\boldsymbol{\theta}$ varies has been studied extensively in information geometry (see, e.g. Amari, 1985). It can be shown that the manifold of $\log p(x|\boldsymbol{\theta})$ is Riemannian with a metric tensor which is the inverse of the *Fisher information matrix* F, where

Fisher information
matrix

$$F = \mathbb{E}_x[\phi_{\boldsymbol{\theta}}(x)\phi_{\boldsymbol{\theta}}^{\top}(x)]. \tag{4.47}$$

Fisher kernel

Setting $M = F$ in eq. (4.46) gives the *Fisher kernel*. If F is difficult to compute then one might resort to setting $M = I$. The advantage of using the Fisher information matrix is that it makes arc length on the manifold invariant to reparameterizations of $\boldsymbol{\theta}$.

TOP kernel

The Fisher kernel uses a class-independent model $p(x|\boldsymbol{\theta})$. Tsuda et al. [2002] have developed the *tangent of posterior odds* (TOP) kernel based on $\nabla_{\boldsymbol{\theta}}(\log p(y = +1|x, \boldsymbol{\theta}) - \log p(y = -1|x, \boldsymbol{\theta}))$, which makes use of class-conditional distributions for the $\mathcal{C}_+$ and $\mathcal{C}_-$ classes.

4.5   Exercises

1. The OU process with covariance function $k(x - x') = \exp(-|x - x'|/\ell)$ is the unique stationary first-order Markovian Gaussian process (see Appendix B for further details). Consider training inputs $x_1 < x_2 \ldots < x_{n-1} < x_n$ on $\mathbb{R}$ with corresponding function values $\mathbf{f} = (f(x_1), \ldots, f(x_n))^{\top}$. Let x_l denote the nearest training input to the left of a test point x_*, and similarly let x_u denote the nearest training input to the right of x_*. Then the Markovian property means that $p(f(x_*)|\mathbf{f}) = p(f(x_*)|f(x_l), f(x_u))$. Demonstrate this by choosing some x-points on the line and computing the predictive distribution $p(f(x_*)|\mathbf{f})$ using eq. (2.19), and observing that non-zero contributions only arise from x_l and x_u. Note that this only occurs in the noise-free case; if one allows the training points to be corrupted by noise (equations 2.23 and 2.24) then all points will contribute in general.

2. Computer exercise: write code to draw samples from the neural network covariance function, eq. (4.29) in 1-d and 2-d. Consider the cases when $\text{var}(u_0)$ is either 0 or non-zero. Explain the form of the plots obtained when $\text{var}(u_0) = 0$.

3. Consider the random process $f(\mathbf{x}) = \mathrm{erf}(u_0 + \sum_{i=1}^{D} u_j x_j)$, where $\mathbf{u} \sim \mathcal{N}(\mathbf{0}, \Sigma)$. Show that this non-linear transform of a process with an inhomogeneous linear covariance function has the same covariance function as the erf neural network. However, note that this process is not a Gaussian process. Draw samples from the given process and compare them to your results from exercise 4.5.2.

4. Derive Gibbs' non-stationary covariance function, eq. (4.32).

5. Computer exercise: write code to draw samples from Gibbs' non-stationary covariance function eq. (4.32) in 1-d and 2-d. Investigate various forms of length-scale function $\ell(\mathbf{x})$.

6. Show that the SE process is infinitely MS differentiable and that the OU process is not MS differentiable.

7. Prove that the eigenfunctions of a symmetric kernel are orthogonal w.r.t. the measure μ.

8. Let $\tilde{k}(\mathbf{x}, \mathbf{x}') = p^{1/2}(\mathbf{x}) k(\mathbf{x}, \mathbf{x}') p^{1/2}(\mathbf{x}')$, and assume $p(\mathbf{x}) > 0$ for all $\mathbf{x}$. Show that the eigenproblem $\int \tilde{k}(\mathbf{x}, \mathbf{x}') \tilde{\phi}_i(\mathbf{x}) d\mathbf{x} = \tilde{\lambda}_i \tilde{\phi}_i(\mathbf{x}')$ has the same eigenvalues as $\int k(\mathbf{x}, \mathbf{x}') p(\mathbf{x}) \phi_i(\mathbf{x}) d\mathbf{x} = \lambda_i \phi_i(\mathbf{x}')$, and that the eigenfunctions are related by $\tilde{\phi}_i(\mathbf{x}) = p^{1/2}(\mathbf{x}) \phi_i(\mathbf{x})$. Also give the matrix version of this problem (Hint: introduce a diagonal matrix P to take the rôle of $p(\mathbf{x})$). The significance of this connection is that it can be easier to find eigenvalues of symmetric matrices than general matrices.

9. Apply the construction in the previous exercise to the eigenproblem for the SE kernel and Gaussian density given in section 4.3.1, with $p(x) = \sqrt{2a/\pi} \exp(-2ax^2)$. Thus consider the modified kernel given by $\tilde{k}(x, x') = \exp(-ax^2) \exp(-b(x-x')^2) \exp(-a(x')^2)$. Using equation 7.374.8 in Gradshteyn and Ryzhik [1980]:

$$\int_{-\infty}^{\infty} \exp\left(-(x-y)^2\right) H_n(\alpha x) \, dx = \sqrt{\pi}(1 - \alpha^2)^{n/2} H_n\left(\frac{\alpha y}{(1 - \alpha^2)^{1/2}}\right),$$

verify that $\tilde{\phi}_k(x) = \exp(-cx^2) H_k(\sqrt{2c}\, x)$, and thus confirm equations 4.39 and 4.40.

10. Computer exercise: The analytic form of the eigenvalues and eigenfunctions for the SE kernel and Gaussian density are given in section 4.3.1. Compare these exact results to those obtained by the Nyström approximation for various values of n and choice of samples.

11. Let $\mathbf{x} \sim \mathcal{N}(\boldsymbol{\mu}, \sigma^2 I)$. Consider the Fisher kernel derived from this model with respect to variation of $\boldsymbol{\mu}$ (i.e. regard σ^2 as a constant). Show that:

$$\left. \frac{\partial \log p(\mathbf{x}|\boldsymbol{\mu})}{\partial \boldsymbol{\mu}} \right|_{\boldsymbol{\mu}=0} = \frac{\mathbf{x}}{\sigma^2}$$

and that $F = \sigma^{-2} I$. Thus the Fisher kernel for this model with $\boldsymbol{\mu} = \mathbf{0}$ is the linear kernel $k(\mathbf{x}, \mathbf{x}') = \frac{1}{\sigma^2} \mathbf{x} \cdot \mathbf{x}'$.

12. Consider a $k-1$ order Markov model for strings on a finite alphabet. Let this model have parameters $\theta_{t|s_1,\ldots,s_{k-1}}$ denoting the probability $p(x_i = t|x_{i-1} = s_1,\ldots,x_{k-1} = s_{k-1})$. Of course as these are probabilities they obey the constraint that $\sum_{t'} \theta_{t'|s_1,\ldots,s_{k-1}} = 1$. Enforcing this constraint can be achieved automatically by setting

$$\theta_{t|s_1,\ldots,s_{k-1}} = \frac{\theta_{t,s_1,\ldots,s_{k-1}}}{\sum_{t'} \theta_{t',s_1,\ldots,s_{k-1}}},$$

where the $\theta_{t,s_1,\ldots,s_{k-1}}$ parameters are now independent, as suggested in [Jaakkola et al., 2000]. The current parameter values are denoted $\boldsymbol{\theta}^0$. Let the current values of $\theta^0_{t,s_1,\ldots,s_{k-1}}$ be set so that $\sum_{t'} \theta^0_{t',s_1,\ldots,s_{k-1}} = 1$, i.e. that $\theta^0_{t,s_1,\ldots,s_{k-1}} = \theta^0_{t|s_1,\ldots,s_{k-1}}$.

Show that $\log p(x|\boldsymbol{\theta}) = \sum n_{t,s_1,\ldots,s_{k-1}} \log \theta_{t|s_1,\ldots,s_{k-1}}$ where $n_{t,s_1,\ldots,s_{k-1}}$ is the number of instances of the substring $s_{k-1}\ldots s_1 t$ in x. Thus, following Leslie et al. [2003], show that

$$\left.\frac{\partial \log p(x|\boldsymbol{\theta})}{\partial \theta_{t,s_1,\ldots,s_{k-1}}}\right|_{\boldsymbol{\theta}=\boldsymbol{\theta}^0} = \frac{n_{t,s_1,\ldots,s_{k-1}}}{\theta^0_{t|s_1,\ldots,s_{k-1}}} - n_{s_1,\ldots,s_{k-1}},$$

where $n_{s_1,\ldots,s_{k-1}}$ is the number of instances of the substring $s_{k-1}\ldots s_1$ in x. As $n_{s_1,\ldots,s_{k-1}}\theta^0_{t|s_1,\ldots,s_{k-1}}$ is the expected number of occurrences of the string $s_{k-1}\ldots s_1 t$ given the count $n_{s_1,\ldots,s_{k-1}}$, the Fisher score captures the degree to which this string is over- or under-represented relative to the model. For the k-spectrum kernel the relevant feature is $\phi_{s_{k-1}\ldots,s_1,t}(x) = n_{t,s_1,\ldots,s_{k-1}}$.

Chapter 5

Model Selection and Adaptation of Hyperparameters

In chapters 2 and 3 we have seen how to do regression and classification using a Gaussian process with a given fixed covariance function. However, in many practical applications, it may not be easy to specify all aspects of the covariance function with confidence. While some properties such as stationarity of the covariance function may be easy to determine from the context, we typically have only rather vague information about other properties, such as the value of free (hyper-) parameters, e.g. length-scales. In chapter 4 several examples of covariance functions were presented, many of which have large numbers of parameters. In addition, the exact form and possible free parameters of the likelihood function may also not be known in advance. Thus in order to turn Gaussian processes into powerful practical tools it is essential to develop methods that address the model selection problem. We interpret the model selection problem rather broadly, to include all aspects of the model including the discrete choice of the functional form for the covariance function as well as values for any hyperparameters.

model selection

In section 5.1 we outline the model selection problem. In the following sections different methodologies are presented: in section 5.2 Bayesian principles are covered, and in section 5.3 cross-validation is discussed, in particular the leave-one-out estimator. In the remaining two sections the different methodologies are applied specifically to learning in GP models, for regression in section 5.4 and classification in section 5.5.

5.1   The Model Selection Problem

In order for a model to be a practical tool in an application, one needs to make decisions about the details of its specification. Some properties may be easy to specify, while we typically have only vague information available about other aspects. We use the term model selection to cover both discrete choices and the setting of continuous (hyper-) parameters of the covariance functions. In fact, model selection can help both to refine the predictions of the model, and give a valuable interpretation to the user about the properties of the data, e.g. that a non-stationary covariance function may be preferred over a stationary one.

enable interpretation

A multitude of possible families of covariance functions exists, including squared exponential, polynomial, neural network, etc., see section 4.2 for an overview. Each of these families typically have a number of free *hyperparameters* whose values also need to be determined. Choosing a covariance function for a particular application thus comprises both setting of hyperparameters within a family, and comparing across different families. Both of these problems will be treated by the same methods, so there is no need to distinguish between them, and we will use the term "model selection" to cover both meanings. We will refer to the selection of a covariance function and its parameters as *training* of a Gaussian process.[1] In the following paragraphs we give example choices of parameterizations of distance measures for stationary covariance functions.

hyperparameters

training

Covariance functions such as the squared exponential can be parameterized in terms of hyperparameters. For example

$$k(\mathbf{x}_p, \mathbf{x}_q) \,=\, \sigma_f^2 \exp\big(-\frac{1}{2}(\mathbf{x}_p - \mathbf{x}_q)^\top M (\mathbf{x}_p - \mathbf{x}_q)\big) + \sigma_n^2 \delta_{pq}, \qquad (5.1)$$

where $\boldsymbol{\theta} = (\{M\}, \sigma_f^2, \sigma_n^2)^\top$ is a vector containing all the hyperparameters,[2] and $\{M\}$ denotes the parameters in the symmetric matrix M. Possible choices for the matrix M include

$$M_1 = \ell^{-2} I, \qquad M_2 = \mathrm{diag}(\boldsymbol{\ell})^{-2}, \qquad M_3 = \Lambda\Lambda^\top + \mathrm{diag}(\boldsymbol{\ell})^{-2}, \qquad (5.2)$$

where $\boldsymbol{\ell}$ is a vector of positive values, and Λ is a $D \times k$ matrix, $k < D$. The properties of functions with these covariance functions depend on the values of the hyperparameters. For many covariance functions it is easy to interpret the meaning of the hyperparameters, which is of great importance when trying to understand your data. For the squared exponential covariance function eq. (5.1) with distance measure M_2 from eq. (5.2), the $\ell_1, \ldots, \ell_D$ hyperparameters play the rôle of *characteristic length-scales*; loosely speaking, how far do you need to move (along a particular axis) in input space for the function values to become uncorrelated. Such a covariance function implements automatic relevance determination (ARD) [Neal, 1996], since the inverse of the length-scale determines how relevant an input is: if the length-scale has a very large value, the

characteristic length-scale

automatic relevance determination

---

[1] This contrasts the use of the word in the SVM literature, where "training" usually refers to finding the support vectors for a fixed kernel.

[2] Sometimes the noise level parameter, σ_n^2 is not considered a hyperparameter; however it plays an analogous role and is treated in the same way, so we simply consider it a hyperparameter.

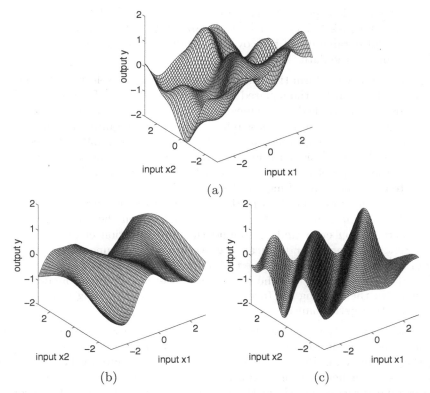

Figure 5.1: Functions with two dimensional input drawn at random from noise free squared exponential covariance function Gaussian processes, corresponding to the three different distance measures in eq. (5.2) respectively. The parameters were: (a) $\ell = 1$, (b) $\ell = (1,3)^\top$, and (c) $\Lambda = (1,-1)^\top$, $\ell = (6,6)^\top$. In panel (a) the two inputs are equally important, while in (b) the function varies less rapidly as a function of x_2 than x_1. In (c) the Λ column gives the direction of most rapid variation .

covariance will become almost independent of that input, effectively removing it from the inference. ARD has been used successfully for removing irrelevant input by several authors, e.g. Williams and Rasmussen [1996]. We call the parameterization of M_3 in eq. (5.2) the *factor analysis distance* due to the analogy with the (unsupervised) factor analysis model which seeks to explain the data through a low rank plus diagonal decomposition. For high dimensional datasets the k columns of the Λ matrix could identify a few directions in the input space with specially high "relevance", and their lengths give the inverse characteristic length-scale for those directions.

factor analysis distance

In Figure 5.1 we show functions drawn at random from squared exponential covariance function Gaussian processes, for different choices of M. In panel (a) we get an isotropic behaviour. In panel (b) the characteristic length-scale is different along the two input axes; the function varies rapidly as a function of x_1, but less rapidly as a function of x_2. In panel (c) the direction of most rapid variation is perpendicular to the direction $(1, 1)$. As this figure illustrates, there is plenty of scope for variation even inside a single family of covariance functions. Our task is, based on a set of training data, to make inferences about the form and parameters of the covariance function, or equivalently, about the relationships in the data.

It should be clear form the above example that model selection is essentially open ended. Even for the squared exponential covariance function, there is a huge variety of possible distance measures. However, this should not be a cause for despair, rather seen as a possibility to learn. It requires, however, a systematic and practical approach to model selection. In a nutshell we need to be able to compare two (or more) methods differing in values of particular parameters, or the shape of the covariance function, or compare a Gaussian process model to any other kind of model. Although there are endless variations in the suggestions for model selection in the literature three general principles cover most: (1) compute the probability of the model given the data, (2) estimate the generalization error and (3) bound the generalization error. We use the term *generalization error* to mean the average error on unseen test examples (from the same distribution as the training cases). Note that the training error is usually a poor proxy for the generalization error, since the model may fit the noise in the training set (over-fit), leading to low training error but poor generalization performance.

In the next section we describe the Bayesian view on model selection, which involves the computation of the probability of the model given the data, based on the marginal likelihood. In section 5.3 we cover cross-validation, which estimates the generalization performance. These two paradigms are applied to Gaussian process models in the remainder of this chapter. The probably approximately correct (PAC) framework is an example of a bound on the generalization error, and is covered in section 7.4.2.

5.2 Bayesian Model Selection

In this section we give a short outline description of the main ideas in Bayesian model selection. The discussion will be general, but focusses on issues which will be relevant for the specific treatment of Gaussian process models for regression in section 5.4 and classification in section 5.5.

hierarchical models   It is common to use a hierarchical specification of models. At the lowest level are the parameters, $\mathbf{w}$. For example, the parameters could be the parameters in a linear model, or the weights in a neural network model. At the second level are hyperparameters $\boldsymbol{\theta}$ which control the distribution of the parameters at the bottom level. For example the "weight decay" term in a neural network, or the "ridge" term in ridge regression are hyperparameters. At the top level we may have a (discrete) set of possible model structures, $\mathcal{H}_i$, under consideration.

We will first give a "mechanistic" description of the computations needed for Bayesian inference, and continue with a discussion providing the intuition about what is going on. Inference takes place one level at a time, by applying the rules of probability theory, see e.g. MacKay [1992b] for this framework and MacKay [1992a] for the context of neural networks. At the bottom level, the *posterior* over the parameters is given by Bayes' rule

level 1 inference

$$p(\mathbf{w}|\mathbf{y}, X, \boldsymbol{\theta}, \mathcal{H}_i) = \frac{p(\mathbf{y}|X, \mathbf{w}, \mathcal{H}_i)p(\mathbf{w}|\boldsymbol{\theta}, \mathcal{H}_i)}{p(\mathbf{y}|X, \boldsymbol{\theta}, \mathcal{H}_i)}, \tag{5.3}$$

where $p(\mathbf{y}|X, \mathbf{w}, \mathcal{H}_i)$ is the *likelihood* and $p(\mathbf{w}|\boldsymbol{\theta}, \mathcal{H}_i)$ is the parameter *prior*. The prior encodes as a probability distribution our knowledge about the parameters prior to seeing the data. If we have only vague prior information about the parameters, then the prior distribution is chosen to be broad to reflect this. The posterior combines the information from the prior and the data (through the likelihood). The normalizing constant in the denominator of eq. (5.3) $p(\mathbf{y}|X, \boldsymbol{\theta}, \mathcal{H}_i)$ is independent of the parameters, and called the *marginal likelihood* (or evidence), and is given by

$$p(\mathbf{y}|X, \boldsymbol{\theta}, \mathcal{H}_i) = \int p(\mathbf{y}|X, \mathbf{w}, \mathcal{H}_i)p(\mathbf{w}|\boldsymbol{\theta}, \mathcal{H}_i) \, d\mathbf{w}. \tag{5.4}$$

At the next level, we analogously express the posterior over the hyperparameters, where the marginal likelihood from the first level plays the rôle of the likelihood

level 2 inference

$$p(\boldsymbol{\theta}|\mathbf{y}, X, \mathcal{H}_i) = \frac{p(\mathbf{y}|X, \boldsymbol{\theta}, \mathcal{H}_i)p(\boldsymbol{\theta}|\mathcal{H}_i)}{p(\mathbf{y}|X, \mathcal{H}_i)}, \tag{5.5}$$

where $p(\boldsymbol{\theta}|\mathcal{H}_i)$ is the *hyper-prior* (the prior for the hyperparameters). The normalizing constant is given by

$$p(\mathbf{y}|X, \mathcal{H}_i) = \int p(\mathbf{y}|X, \boldsymbol{\theta}, \mathcal{H}_i)p(\boldsymbol{\theta}|\mathcal{H}_i)d\boldsymbol{\theta}. \tag{5.6}$$

At the top level, we compute the posterior for the model

level 3 inference

$$p(\mathcal{H}_i|\mathbf{y}, X) = \frac{p(\mathbf{y}|X, \mathcal{H}_i)p(\mathcal{H}_i)}{p(\mathbf{y}|X)}, \tag{5.7}$$

where $p(\mathbf{y}|X) = \sum_i p(\mathbf{y}|X, \mathcal{H}_i)p(\mathcal{H}_i)$. We note that the implementation of Bayesian inference calls for the evaluation of several integrals. Depending on the details of the models, these integrals may or may not be analytically tractable and in general one may have to resort to analytical approximations or Markov chain Monte Carlo (MCMC) methods. In practice, especially the evaluation of the integral in eq. (5.6) may be difficult, and as an approximation one may shy away from using the hyperparameter posterior in eq. (5.5), and instead maximize the marginal likelihood in eq. (5.4) w.r.t. the hyperparameters, $\boldsymbol{\theta}$. This approximation is known as type II maximum likelihood (ML-II). Of course, one should be careful with such an optimization step, since it opens up the possibility of overfitting, especially if there are many hyperparameters. The integral in eq. (5.6) can then be approximated using a local expansion around the maximum (the Laplace approximation). This approximation will be good if the posterior for $\boldsymbol{\theta}$ is fairly well peaked, which is more often the case for the

ML-II

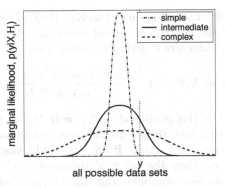

Figure 5.2: The marginal likelihood $p(\mathbf{y}|X, \mathcal{H}_i)$ is the probability of the data, given the model. The number of data points n and the inputs X are fixed, and not shown. The horizontal axis is an idealized representation of all possible vectors of targets $\mathbf{y}$. The marginal likelihood for models of three different complexities are shown. Note, that since the marginal likelihood is a probability distribution, it must normalize to unity. For a particular dataset indicated by $\mathbf{y}$ and a dotted line, the marginal likelihood prefers a model of intermediate complexity over too simple or too complex alternatives.

hyperparameters than for the parameters themselves, see MacKay [1999] for an illuminating discussion. The prior over models $\mathcal{H}_i$ in eq. (5.7) is often taken to be flat, so that a priori we do not favour one model over another. In this case, the probability for the model is proportional to the expression from eq. (5.6).

It is primarily the marginal likelihood from eq. (5.4) involving the integral over the parameter space which distinguishes the Bayesian scheme of inference from other schemes based on optimization. It is a property of the marginal likelihood that it automatically incorporates a trade-off between model fit and model complexity. This is the reason why the marginal likelihood is valuable in solving the model selection problem.

In Figure 5.2 we show a schematic of the behaviour of the marginal likelihood for three different model complexities. Let the number of data points n and the inputs X be fixed; the horizontal axis is an idealized representation of all possible vectors of targets $\mathbf{y}$, and the vertical axis plots the marginal likelihood $p(\mathbf{y}|X, \mathcal{H}_i)$. A simple model can only account for a limited range of possible sets of target values, but since the marginal likelihood is a probability distribution over $\mathbf{y}$ it must normalize to unity, and therefore the data sets which the model *does* account for have a large value of the marginal likelihood. Conversely for a complex model: it is capable of accounting for a wider range of data sets, and consequently the marginal likelihood doesn't attain such large values as for the simple model. For example, the simple model could be a linear model, and the complex model a large neural network. The figure illustrates why the marginal likelihood doesn't simply favour the models that fit the training data the best. This effect is called Occam's razor after William of Occam 1285-1349, whose principle: "plurality should not be assumed without necessity" he used to encourage simplicity in explanations. See also Rasmussen and Ghahramani [2001] for an investigation into Occam's razor in statistical models.

Occam's razor

Notice that the trade-off between data-fit and model complexity is automatic; there is no need to set a parameter externally to fix the trade-off. Do not confuse the automatic Occam's razor principle with the use of priors in the Bayesian method. Even if the priors are "flat" over complexity, the marginal likelihood will still tend to favour the least complex model able to explain the data. Thus, a model complexity which is well suited to the data can be selected using the marginal likelihood.

automatic trade-off

In the preceding paragraphs we have thought of the specification of a model as the model structure as well as the parameters of the priors, etc. If it is unclear how to set some of the parameters of the prior, one can treat these as hyperparameters, and do model selection to determine how to set them. At the same time it should be emphasized that the priors correspond to (probabilistic) assumptions about the data. If the priors are grossly at odds with the distribution of the data, inference will still take place under the assumptions encoded by the prior, see the step-function example in section 5.4.3. To avoid this situation, one should be careful not to employ priors which are too narrow, ruling out reasonable explanations of the data.[3]

5.3 Cross-validation

In this section we consider how to use methods of cross-validation (CV) for model selection. The basic idea is to split the training set into two disjoint sets, one which is actually used for training, and the other, the *validation* set, which is used to monitor performance. The performance on the validation set is used as a proxy for the generalization error and model selection is carried out using this measure.

cross-validation

In practice a drawback of hold-out method is that only a fraction of the full data set can be used for training, and that if the validation set it small, the performance estimate obtained may have large variance. To minimize these problems, CV is almost always used in the k-fold cross-validation setting: the data is split into k disjoint, equally sized subsets; validation is done on a single subset and training is done using the union of the remaining $k - 1$ subsets, the entire procedure being repeated k times, each time with a different subset for validation. Thus, a large fraction of the data can be used for training, and all cases appear as validation cases. The price is that k models must be trained instead of one. Typical values for k are in the range 3 to 10.

k-fold cross-validation

An extreme case of k-fold cross-validation is obtained for $k = n$, the number of training cases, also known as leave-one-out cross-validation (LOO-CV). Often the computational cost of LOO-CV ("training" n models) is prohibitive, but in certain cases, such as Gaussian process regression, there are computational shortcuts.

leave-one-out cross-validation (LOO-CV)

---

[3]This is known as Cromwell's dictum [Lindley, 1985] after Oliver Cromwell who on August 5th, 1650 wrote to the synod of the Church of Scotland: "I beseech you, in the bowels of Christ, consider it possible that you are mistaken."

other loss functions

Cross-validation can be used with any loss function. Although the squared error loss is by far the most common for regression, there is no reason not to allow other loss functions. For probabilistic models such as Gaussian processes it is natural to consider also cross-validation using the negative log probability loss. Craven and Wahba [1979] describe a variant of cross-validation using squared error known as generalized cross-validation which gives different weightings to different datapoints so as to achieve certain invariance properites. See Wahba [1990, sec. 4.3] for further details.

5.4   Model Selection for GP Regression

We apply Bayesian inference in section 5.4.1 and cross-validation in section 5.4.2 to Gaussian process regression with Gaussian noise. We conclude in section 5.4.3 with some more detailed examples of how one can use the model selection principles to tailor covariance functions.

5.4.1   Marginal Likelihood

Bayesian principles provide a persuasive and consistent framework for inference. Unfortunately, for most interesting models for machine learning, the required computations (integrals over parameter space) are analytically intractable, and good approximations are not easily derived. Gaussian process regression models with Gaussian noise are a rare exception: integrals over the parameters are analytically tractable and at the same time the models are very flexible. In this section we first apply the general Bayesian inference principles from section 5.2 to the specific Gaussian process model, in the simplified form where hyperparameters are optimized over. We derive the expressions for the marginal likelihood and interpret these.

model parameters

Since a Gaussian process model is a non-parametric model, it may not be immediately obvious what the parameters of the model are. Generally, one may regard the noise-free latent function values at the training inputs **f** as the parameters. The more training cases there are, the more parameters. Using the weight-space view, developed in section 2.1, one may equivalently think of the parameters as being the weights of the linear model which uses the basis-functions ϕ, which can be chosen as the eigenfunctions of the covariance function. Of course, we have seen that this view is inconvenient for nondegenerate covariance functions, since these would then have an infinite number of weights.

We proceed by applying eq. (5.3) and eq. (5.4) for the 1st level of inference—which we find that we have already done back in chapter 2! The predictive distribution from eq. (5.3) is given for the weight-space view in eq. (2.11) and eq. (2.12) and equivalently for the function-space view in eq. (2.22). The *marginal likelihood* (or evidence) from eq. (5.4) was computed in eq. (2.30),

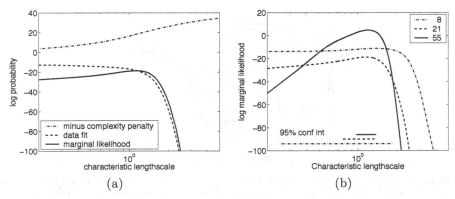

Figure 5.3: Panel (a) shows a decomposition of the log marginal likelihood into its constituents: data-fit and complexity penalty, as a function of the characteristic length-scale. The training data is drawn from a Gaussian process with SE covariance function and parameters $(\ell, \sigma_f, \sigma_n) = (1, 1, 0.1)$, the same as in Figure 2.5, and we are fitting only the length-scale parameter ℓ (the two other parameters have been set in accordance with the generating process). Panel (b) shows the log marginal likelihood as a function of the characteristic length-scale for different sizes of training sets. Also shown, are the 95% confidence intervals for the posterior length-scales.

and we re-state the result here

$$\log p(\mathbf{y}|X, \boldsymbol{\theta}) = -\frac{1}{2}\mathbf{y}^\top K_y^{-1}\mathbf{y} - \frac{1}{2}\log|K_y| - \frac{n}{2}\log 2\pi, \qquad (5.8)$$

where $K_y = K_f + \sigma_n^2 I$ is the covariance matrix for the noisy targets $\mathbf{y}$ (and K_f is the covariance matrix for the noise-free latent $\mathbf{f}$), and we now explicitly write the marginal likelihood conditioned on the hyperparameters (the parameters of the covariance function) $\boldsymbol{\theta}$. From this perspective it becomes clear why we call eq. (5.8) the log *marginal likelihood*, since it is obtained through marginaliza-   *marginal likelihood* tion over the latent function. Otherwise, if one thinks entirely in terms of the function-space view, the term "marginal" may appear a bit mysterious, and similarly the "hyper" from the $\boldsymbol{\theta}$ parameters of the covariance function.[4]

The three terms of the marginal likelihood in eq. (5.8) have readily inter-   *interpretation* pretable rôles: the only term involving the observed targets is the data-fit $-\mathbf{y}^\top K_y^{-1}\mathbf{y}/2$; $\log|K_y|/2$ is the complexity penalty depending only on the co- variance function and the inputs and $n\log(2\pi)/2$ is a normalization constant. In Figure 5.3(a) we illustrate this breakdown of the log marginal likelihood. The data-fit decreases monotonically with the length-scale, since the model be- comes less and less flexible. The negative complexity penalty increases with the length-scale, because the model gets less complex with growing length-scale. The marginal likelihood itself peaks at a value close to 1. For length-scales somewhat longer than 1, the marginal likelihood decreases rapidly (note the

---

[4]Another reason that we like to stick to the term "marginal likelihood" is that it is the likelihood of a non-parametric model, i.e. a model which requires access to all the training data when making predictions; this contrasts the situation for a parametric model, which "absorbs" the information from the training data into its (posterior) parameter (distribution). This difference makes the two "likelihoods" behave quite differently as a function of $\boldsymbol{\theta}$.

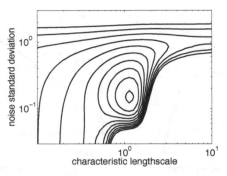

Figure 5.4: Contour plot showing the log marginal likelihood as a function of the characteristic length-scale and the noise level, for the same data as in Figure 2.5 and Figure 5.3. The signal variance hyperparameter was set to $\sigma_f^2 = 1$. The optimum is close to the parameters used when generating the data. Note, the two ridges, one for small noise and length-scale $\ell = 0.4$ and another for long length-scale and noise $\sigma_n^2 = 1$. The contour lines spaced 2 units apart in log probability density.

log scale!), due to the poor ability of the model to explain the data, compare to Figure 2.5(c). For smaller length-scales the marginal likelihood decreases somewhat more slowly, corresponding to models that do accommodate the data, but waste predictive mass at regions far away from the underlying function, compare to Figure 2.5(b).

In Figure 5.3(b) the dependence of the log marginal likelihood on the characteristic length-scale is shown for different numbers of training cases. Generally, the more data, the more peaked the marginal likelihood. For very small numbers of training data points the slope of the log marginal likelihood is very shallow as when only a little data has been observed, both very short and intermediate values of the length-scale are consistent with the data. With more data, the complexity term gets more severe, and discourages too short length-scales.

marginal likelihood gradient

To set the hyperparameters by maximizing the marginal likelihood, we seek the partial derivatives of the marginal likelihood w.r.t. the hyperparameters. Using eq. (5.8) and eq. (A.14-A.15) we obtain

$$
\begin{aligned}
\frac{\partial}{\partial \theta_j} \log p(\mathbf{y}|X, \boldsymbol{\theta}) &= \frac{1}{2} \mathbf{y}^\top K^{-1} \frac{\partial K}{\partial \theta_j} K^{-1} \mathbf{y} - \frac{1}{2} \operatorname{tr} \left(K^{-1} \frac{\partial K}{\partial \theta_j} \right) \\
&= \frac{1}{2} \operatorname{tr} \left((\boldsymbol{\alpha} \boldsymbol{\alpha}^\top - K^{-1}) \frac{\partial K}{\partial \theta_j} \right) \quad \text{where} \quad \boldsymbol{\alpha} = K^{-1} \mathbf{y}.
\end{aligned}
\tag{5.9}
$$

The complexity of computing the marginal likelihood in eq. (5.8) is dominated by the need to invert the K matrix (the log determinant of K is easily computed as a by-product of the inverse). Standard methods for matrix inversion of positive definite symmetric matrices require time $\mathcal{O}(n^3)$ for inversion of an n by n matrix. Once K^{-1} is known, the computation of the derivatives in eq. (5.9) requires only time $\mathcal{O}(n^2)$ per hyperparameter.[5] Thus, the computational over-

---

[5]Note that matrix-by-matrix products in eq. (5.9) should not be computed directly: in the first term, do the vector-by-matrix multiplications first; in the trace term, compute only the diagonal terms of the product.

head of computing derivatives is small, so using a gradient based optimizer is advantageous.

Estimation of $\boldsymbol{\theta}$ by optimzation of the marginal likelihood has a long history in spatial statistics, see e.g. Mardia and Marshall [1984]. As n increases, one would hope that the data becomes increasingly informative about $\boldsymbol{\theta}$. However, it is necessary to contrast what Stein [1999, sec. 3.3] calls fixed-domain asymptotics (where one gets increasingly dense observations within some region) with increasing-domain asymptotics (where the size of the observation region grows with n). Increasing-domain asymptotics are a natural choice in a time-series context but fixed-domain asymptotics seem more natural in spatial (and machine learning) settings. For further discussion see Stein [1999, sec. 6.4].

Figure 5.4 shows an example of the log marginal likelihood as a function of the characteristic length-scale and the noise standard deviation hyperparameters for the squared exponential covariance function, see eq. (5.1). The signal variance σ_f^2 was set to 1.0. The marginal likelihood has a clear maximum around the hyperparameter values which were used in the Gaussian process from which the data was generated. Note that for long length-scales and a noise level of $\sigma_n^2 = 1$, the marginal likelihood becomes almost independent of the length-scale; this is caused by the model explaining everything as noise, and no longer needing the signal covariance. Similarly, for small noise and a length-scale of $\ell = 0.4$, the marginal likelihood becomes almost independent of the noise level; this is caused by the ability of the model to exactly interpolate the data at this short length-scale. We note that although the model in this hyperparameter region explains all the data-points exactly, this model is still disfavoured by the marginal likelihood, see Figure 5.2.

There is no guarantee that the marginal likelihood does not suffer from multiple local optima. Practical experience with simple covariance functions seem to indicate that local maxima are not a devastating problem, but certainly they do exist. In fact, every local maximum corresponds to a particular interpretation of the data. In Figure 5.5 an example with two local optima is shown, together with the corresponding (noise free) predictions of the model at each of the two local optima. One optimum corresponds to a relatively complicated model with low noise, whereas the other corresponds to a much simpler model with more noise. With only 7 data points, it is not possible for the model to confidently reject either of the two possibilities. The numerical value of the marginal likelihood for the more complex model is about 60% higher than for the simple model. According to the Bayesian formalism, one ought to weight predictions from alternative explanations according to their posterior probabilities. In practice, with data sets of much larger sizes, one often finds that one local optimum is orders of magnitude more probable than other local optima, so averaging together alternative explanations may not be necessary. However, care should be taken that one doesn't end up in a bad local optimum.

multiple local maxima

Above we have described how to adapt the parameters of the covariance function given one dataset. However, it may happen that we are given several datasets all of which are assumed to share the same hyperparameters; this is known as *multi-task learning*, see e.g. Caruana [1997]. In this case one can

multi-task learning

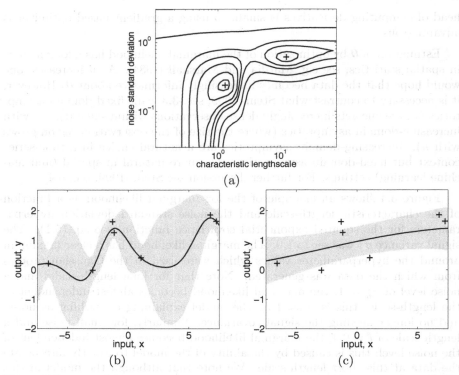

Figure 5.5: Panel (a) shows the marginal likelihood as a function of the hyperparameters ℓ (length-scale) and σ_n^2 (noise standard deviation), where $\sigma_f^2 = 1$ (signal standard deviation) for a data set of 7 observations (seen in panels (b) and (c)). There are two local optima, indicated with '+': the global optimum has low noise and a short length-scale; the local optimum has a high noise and a long length scale. In (b) and (c) the inferred underlying functions (and 95% confidence intervals) are shown for each of the two solutions. In fact, the data points were generated by a Gaussian process with $(\ell, \sigma_f^2, \sigma_n^2) = (1, 1, 0.1)$ in eq. (5.1).

simply sum the log marginal likelihoods of the individual problems and optimize this sum w.r.t. the hyperparameters [Minka and Picard, 1999].

5.4.2 Cross-validation

negative log validation density loss

The predictive log probability when leaving out training case i is

$$\log p(y_i | X, \mathbf{y}_{-i}, \boldsymbol{\theta}) = -\frac{1}{2} \log \sigma_i^2 - \frac{(y_i - \mu_i)^2}{2\sigma_i^2} - \frac{1}{2} \log 2\pi, \qquad (5.10)$$

where the notation $\mathbf{y}_{-i}$ means all targets *except* number i, and μ_i and σ_i^2 are computed according to eq. (2.23) and (2.24) respectively, in which the training sets are taken to be $(X_{-i}, \mathbf{y}_{-i})$. Accordingly, the LOO log predictive probability is

$$L_{\text{LOO}}(X, \mathbf{y}, \boldsymbol{\theta}) = \sum_{i=1}^{n} \log p(y_i | X, \mathbf{y}_{-i}, \boldsymbol{\theta}), \qquad (5.11)$$

see [Geisser and Eddy, 1979] for a discussion of this and related approaches. L_{LOO} in eq. (5.11) is sometimes called the log *pseudo*-likelihood. Notice, that in each of the n LOO-CV rotations, inference in the Gaussian process model (with fixed hyperparameters) essentially consists of computing the inverse covariance matrix, to allow predictive mean and variance in eq. (2.23) and (2.24) to be evaluated (i.e. there is no parameter-fitting, such as there would be in a parametric model). The key insight is that when repeatedly applying the prediction eq. (2.23) and (2.24), the expressions are almost identical: we need the inverses of covariance matrices with a single column and row removed in turn. This can be computed efficiently from the inverse of the complete covariance matrix using inversion by partitioning, see eq. (A.11-A.12). A similar insight has also been used for spline models, see e.g. Wahba [1990, sec. 4.2]. The approach was used for hyperparameter selection in Gaussian process models in Sundararajan and Keerthi [2001]. The expressions for the LOO-CV predictive mean and variance are

$$\mu_i = y_i - [K^{-1}\mathbf{y}]_i/[K^{-1}]_{ii}, \qquad \text{and} \qquad \sigma_i^2 = 1/[K^{-1}]_{ii}, \qquad (5.12)$$

where careful inspection reveals that the mean μ_i is in fact independent of y_i as indeed it should be. The computational expense of computing these quantities is $\mathcal{O}(n^3)$ once for computing the inverse of K plus $\mathcal{O}(n^2)$ for the entire LOO-CV procedure (when K^{-1} is known). Thus, the computational overhead for the LOO-CV quantities is negligible. Plugging these expressions into eq. (5.10) and (5.11) produces a performance estimator which we can optimize w.r.t. hyperparameters to do model selection. In particular, we can compute the partial derivatives of L_{LOO} w.r.t. the hyperparameters (using eq. (A.14)) and use conjugate gradient optimization. To this end, we need the partial derivatives of the LOO-CV predictive mean and variances from eq. (5.12) w.r.t. the hyperparameters

$$\frac{\partial \mu_i}{\partial \theta_j} = \frac{[Z_j \boldsymbol{\alpha}]_i}{[K^{-1}]_{ii}} - \frac{\alpha_i [Z_j K^{-1}]_{ii}}{[K^{-1}]_{ii}^2}, \qquad \frac{\partial \sigma_i^2}{\partial \theta_j} = \frac{[Z_j K^{-1}]_{ii}}{[K^{-1}]_{ii}^2}, \qquad (5.13)$$

where $\boldsymbol{\alpha} = K^{-1}\mathbf{y}$ and $Z_j = K^{-1}\frac{\partial K}{\partial \theta_j}$. The partial derivatives of eq. (5.11) are obtained by using the chain-rule and eq. (5.13) to give

$$\frac{\partial L_{\text{LOO}}}{\partial \theta_j} = \sum_{i=1}^{n} \frac{\partial \log p(y_i|X, \mathbf{y}_{-i}, \boldsymbol{\theta})}{\partial \mu_i} \frac{\partial \mu_i}{\partial \theta_j} + \frac{\partial \log p(y_i|X, \mathbf{y}_{-i}, \boldsymbol{\theta})}{\partial \sigma_i^2} \frac{\partial \sigma_i^2}{\partial \theta_j}$$

$$= \sum_{i=1}^{n} \left(\alpha_i [Z_j \boldsymbol{\alpha}]_i - \frac{1}{2}\left(1 + \frac{\alpha_i^2}{[K^{-1}]_{ii}}\right)[Z_j K^{-1}]_{ii} \right)/[K^{-1}]_{ii}. \qquad (5.14)$$

The computational complexity is $\mathcal{O}(n^3)$ for computing the inverse of K, and $\mathcal{O}(n^3)$ *per hyperparameter*[6] for the derivative eq. (5.14). Thus, the computational burden of the derivatives is greater for the LOO-CV method than for the method based on marginal likelihood, eq. (5.9).

---

[6]Computation of the matrix-by-matrix product $K^{-1}\frac{\partial K}{\partial \theta_j}$ for each hyperparameter is unavoidable.

LOO-CV with squared
error loss

In eq. (5.10) we have used the log of the validation density as a cross-validation measure of fit (or equivalently, the negative log validation density as a loss function). One could also envisage using other loss functions, such as the commonly used squared error. However, this loss function is only a function of the predicted mean and ignores the validation set variances. Further, since the mean prediction eq. (2.23) is independent of the scale of the covariances (i.e. you can multiply the covariance of the signal *and* noise by an arbitrary positive constant without changing the mean predictions), one degree of freedom is left undetermined[7] by a LOO-CV procedure based on squared error loss (or any other loss function which depends only on the mean predictions). But, of course, the full predictive distribution does depend on the scale of the covariance function. Also, computation of the derivatives based on the squared error loss has similar computational complexity as the negative log validation density loss. In conclusion, it seems unattractive to use LOO-CV based on squared error loss for hyperparameter selection.

Comparing the pseudo-likelihood for the LOO-CV methodology with the marginal likelihood from the previous section, it is interesting to ask under which circumstances each method might be preferable. Their computational demands are roughly identical. This issue has not been studied much empirically. However, it is interesting to note that the marginal likelihood tells us the probability of the observations *given the assumptions of the model*. This contrasts with the frequentist LOO-CV value, which gives an estimate for the (log) predictive probability, whether or not the assumptions of the model may be fulfilled. Thus Wahba [1990, sec. 4.8] has argued that CV procedures should be more robust against model mis-specification.

5.4.3 Examples and Discussion

In the following we give three examples of model selection for regression models. We first describe a 1-d modelling task which illustrates how special covariance functions can be designed to achieve various useful effects, and can be evaluated using the marginal likelihood. Secondly, we make a short reference to the model selection carried out for the robot arm problem discussed in chapter 2 and again in chapter 8. Finally, we discuss an example where we deliberately choose a covariance function that is not well-suited for the problem; this is the so-called mis-specified model scenario.

Mauna Loa Atmospheric Carbon Dioxide

We will use a modelling problem concerning the concentration of CO_2 in the atmosphere to illustrate how the marginal likelihood can be used to set multiple hyperparameters in hierarchical Gaussian process models. A complex covariance function is derived by combining several different kinds of simple covariance functions, and the resulting model provides an excellent fit to the data as well

---

[7]In the special case where we know either the signal or the noise variance there is no indeterminancy.

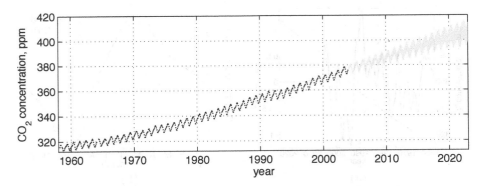

Figure 5.6: The 545 observations of monthly averages of the atmospheric concentration of CO_2 made between 1958 and the end of 2003, together with 95% predictive confidence region for a Gaussian process regression model, 20 years into the future. Rising trend and seasonal variations are clearly visible. Note also that the confidence interval gets wider the further the predictions are extrapolated.

as insights into its properties by interpretation of the adapted hyperparameters. Although the data is one-dimensional, and therefore easy to visualize, a total of 11 hyperparameters are used, which in practice rules out the use of cross-validation for setting parameters, except for the gradient-based LOO-CV procedure from the previous section.

The data [Keeling and Whorf, 2004] consists of monthly average atmospheric CO_2 concentrations (in parts per million by volume (ppmv)) derived from in situ air samples collected at the Mauna Loa Observatory, Hawaii, between 1958 and 2003 (with some missing values).[8] The data is shown in Figure 5.6. Our goal is the model the CO_2 concentration as a function of time x. Several features are immediately apparent: a long term rising trend, a pronounced seasonal variation and some smaller irregularities. In the following we suggest contributions to a combined covariance function which takes care of these individual properties. This is meant primarily to illustrate the power and flexibility of the Gaussian process framework—it is possible that other choices would be more appropriate for this data set.

To model the long term smooth rising trend we use a squared exponential (SE) covariance term, with two hyperparameters controlling the amplitude θ_1 and characteristic length-scale θ_2 *smooth trend*

$$k_1(x, x') = \theta_1^2 \exp\left(-\frac{(x - x')^2}{2\theta_2^2}\right). \tag{5.15}$$

Note that we just use a smooth trend; actually enforcing the trend a priori to be *increasing* is probably not so simple and (hopefully) not desirable. We can use the periodic covariance function from eq. (4.31) with a period of one year to model the seasonal variation. However, it is not clear that the seasonal trend is exactly periodic, so we modify eq. (4.31) by taking the product with a squared   *seasonal component*

---

[8]The data is available from `http://cdiac.esd.ornl.gov/ftp/trends/co2/maunaloa.co2`.

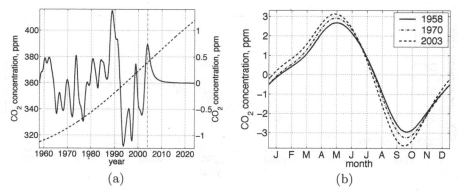

Figure 5.7: Panel (a): long term trend, dashed, left hand scale, predicted by the squared exponential contribution; superimposed is the medium term trend, full line, right hand scale, predicted by the rational quadratic contribution; the vertical dash-dotted line indicates the upper limit of the training data. Panel (b) shows the seasonal variation over the year for three different years. The concentration peaks in mid May and has a low in the beginning of October. The seasonal variation is smooth, but not of exactly sinusoidal shape. The peak-to-peak amplitude increases from about 5.5 ppm in 1958 to about 7 ppm in 2003, but the shape does not change very much. The characteristic decay length of the periodic component is inferred to be 90 years, so the seasonal trend changes rather slowly, as also suggested by the gradual progression between the three years shown.

exponential component (using the product construction from section 4.2.4), to allow a *decay* away from exact periodicity

$$k_2(x, x') = \theta_3^2 \exp\left(-\frac{(x - x')^2}{2\theta_4^2} - \frac{2\sin^2(\pi(x - x'))}{\theta_5^2}\right), \qquad (5.16)$$

where θ_3 gives the magnitude, θ_4 the *decay-time* for the periodic component, and θ_5 the smoothness of the periodic component; the period has been fixed to one (year). The seasonal component in the data is caused primarily by different rates of CO_2 uptake for plants depending on the season, and it is probably reasonable to assume that this pattern may itself change slowly over time, partially due to the elevation of the CO_2 level itself; if this effect turns out not to be relevant, then it can be effectively removed at the fitting stage by allowing θ_4 to become very large.

medium term irregularities

To model the (small) medium term irregularities a rational quadratic term is used, eq. (4.19)

$$k_3(x, x') = \theta_6^2 \left(1 + \frac{(x - x')^2}{2\theta_8 \theta_7^2}\right)^{-\theta_8}, \qquad (5.17)$$

where θ_6 is the magnitude, θ_7 is the typical length-scale and θ_8 is the shape parameter determining diffuseness of the length-scales, see the discussion on page 87. One could also have used a squared exponential form for this component, but it turns out that the rational quadratic works better (gives higher marginal likelihood), probably because it can accommodate several length-scales.

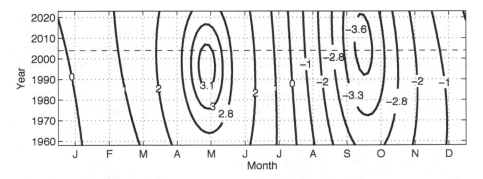

Figure 5.8: The time course of the seasonal effect, plotted in a months vs. year plot (with wrap-around continuity between the edges). The labels on the contours are in ppmv of CO_2. The training period extends up to the dashed line. Note the slow development: the height of the May peak may have started to recede, but the low in October may currently (2005) be deepening further. The seasonal effects from three particular years were also plotted in Figure 5.7(b).

Finally we specify a noise model as the sum of a squared exponential contribution and an independent component   *noise terms*

$$k_4(x_p, x_q) = \theta_9^2 \exp\left(-\frac{(x_p - x_q)^2}{2\theta_{10}^2}\right) + \theta_{11}^2 \delta_{pq}, \qquad (5.18)$$

where θ_9 is the magnitude of the correlated noise component, θ_{10} is its length-scale and θ_{11} is the magnitude of the independent noise component. Noise in the series could be caused by measurement inaccuracies, and by local short-term weather phenomena, so it is probably reasonable to assume at least a modest amount of correlation in time. Notice that the correlated noise component, the first term of eq. (5.18), has an identical expression to the long term component in eq. (5.15). When optimizing the hyperparameters, we will see that one of these components becomes large with a long length-scale (the long term trend), while the other remains small with a short length-scale (noise). The fact that we have chosen to call one of these components 'signal' and the other one 'noise' is only a question of interpretation. Presumably we are less interested in very short-term effect, and thus call it noise; if on the other hand we were interested in this effect, we would call it signal.

The final covariance function is

$$k(x, x') = k_1(x, x') + k_2(x, x') + k_3(x, x') + k_4(x, x'), \qquad (5.19)$$

with hyperparameters $\boldsymbol{\theta} = (\theta_1, \ldots, \theta_{11})^\top$. We first subtract the empirical mean of the data (341 ppm), and then fit the hyperparameters by optimizing the   *parameter estimation* marginal likelihood using a conjugate gradient optimizer. To avoid bad local minima (e.g. caused by swapping rôles of the rational quadratic and squared exponential terms) a few random restarts are tried, picking the run with the best marginal likelihood, which was $\log p(\mathbf{y}|X, \boldsymbol{\theta}) = -108.5$.

We now examine and interpret the hyperparameters which optimize the marginal likelihood. The long term trend has a magnitude of $\theta_1 = 66$ ppm and a length scale of $\theta_2 = 67$ years. The mean predictions inside the range of the training data and extending for 20 years into the future are depicted in Figure 5.7 (a). In the same plot (with right hand axis) we also show the medium term effects modelled by the rational quadratic component with magnitude $\theta_6 = 0.66$ ppm, typical length $\theta_7 = 1.2$ years and shape $\theta_8 = 0.78$. The very small shape value allows for covariance at many different length-scales, which is also evident in Figure 5.7 (a). Notice that beyond the edge of the training data the mean of this contribution smoothly decays to zero, but of course it still has a contribution to the uncertainty, see Figure 5.6.

The hyperparameter values for the decaying periodic contribution are: magnitude $\theta_3 = 2.4$ ppm, decay-time $\theta_4 = 90$ years, and the smoothness of the periodic component is $\theta_5 = 1.3$. The quite long decay-time shows that the data have a very close to periodic component in the short term. In Figure 5.7 (b) we show the mean periodic contribution for three years corresponding to the beginning, middle and end of the training data. This component is not exactly sinusoidal, and it changes its shape slowly over time, most notably the amplitude is increasing, see Figure 5.8.

For the noise components, we get the amplitude for the correlated component $\theta_9 = 0.18$ ppm, a length-scale of $\theta_{10} = 1.6$ months and an independent noise magnitude of $\theta_{11} = 0.19$ ppm. Thus, the correlation length for the noise component is indeed inferred to be short, and the total magnitude of the noise is just $\sqrt{\theta_9^2 + \theta_{11}^2} = 0.26$ ppm, indicating that the data can be explained very well by the model. Note also in Figure 5.6 that the model makes relatively confident predictions, the 95% confidence region being 16 ppm wide at a 20 year prediction horizon.

In conclusion, we have seen an example of how non-trivial structure can be inferred by using composite covariance functions, and that the ability to leave hyperparameters to be determined by the data is useful in practice. Of course a serious treatment of such data would probably require modelling of other effects, such as demographic and economic indicators too. Finally, one may want to use a real time-series approach (not just a regression from time to CO_2 level as we have done here), to accommodate causality, etc. Nevertheless, the ability of the Gaussian process to avoid simple parametric assumptions and still build in a lot of structure makes it, as we have seen, a very attractive model in many application domains.

Robot Arm Inverse Dynamics

We have discussed the use of GPR for the SARCOS robot arm inverse dynamics problem in section 2.5. This example is also further studied in section 8.3.7 where a variety of approximation methods are compared, because the size of the training set ($44,484$ examples) precludes the use of simple GPR due to its $\mathcal{O}(n^2)$ storage and $\mathcal{O}(n^3)$ time complexity.

One of the techniques considered in section 8.3.7 is the subset of datapoints (SD) method, where we simply discard some of the data and only make use

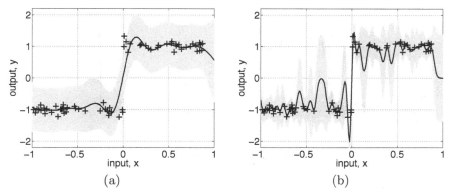

Figure 5.9: Mis-specification example. Fit to 64 datapoints drawn from a step function with Gaussian noise with standard deviation $\sigma_n = 0.1$. The Gaussian process models are using a squared exponential covariance function. Panel (a) shows the mean and 95% confidence interval for the noisy signal in grey, when the hyperparameters are chosen to maximize the marginal likelihood. Panel (b) shows the resulting model when the hyperparameters are chosen using leave-one-out cross-validation (LOO-CV). Note that the marginal likelihood chooses a high noise level and long length-scale, whereas LOO-CV chooses a smaller noise level and shorter length-scale. It is not immediately obvious which fit it worse.

of $m < n$ training examples. Given a subset of the training data of size m selected at random, we adjusted the hyperparameters by optimizing either the marginal likelihood or L_{LOO}. As ARD was used, this involved adjusting $D + 2 = 23$ hyperparameters. This process was repeated 10 times with different random subsets of the data selected for both $m = 1024$ and $m = 2048$. The results show that the predictive accuracy obtained from the two optimization methods is very similar on both standardized mean squared error (SMSE) and mean standardized log loss (MSLL) criteria, but that the marginal likelihood optimization is much quicker.

Step function example illustrating mis-specification

In this section we discuss the *mis-specified* model scenario, where we attempt to learn the hyperparameters for a covariance function which is not very well suited to the data. The mis-specification arises because the data comes from a function which has either zero or very low probability under the GP prior. One could ask why it is interesting to discuss this scenario, since one should surely simply avoid choosing such a model in practice. While this is true in theory, for practical reasons such as the convenience of using standard forms for the covariance function or because vague prior information, one inevitably ends up in a situation which resembles some level of mis-specification.

As an example, we use data from a noisy step function and fit a GP model with a squared exponential covariance function, Figure 5.9. There is mis-specification because it would be very unlikely that samples drawn from a GP with the stationary SE covariance function would look like a step function. For short length-scales samples can vary quite quickly, but they would tend to vary

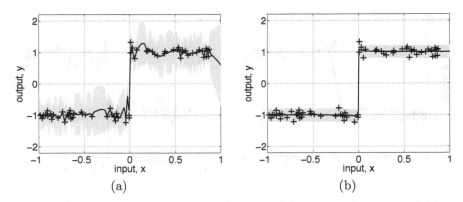

Figure 5.10: Same data as in Figure 5.9. Panel (a) shows the result of using a covariance function which is the sum of two squared-exponential terms. Although this is still a stationary covariance function, it gives rise to a higher marginal likelihood than for the squared-exponential covariance function in Figure 5.9(a), and probably also a better fit. In panel (b) the neural network covariance function eq. (4.29) was used, providing a much larger marginal likelihood and a very good fit.

rapidly all over, not just near the step. Conversely a stationary SE covariance function with a long length-scale could model the flat parts of the step function but not the rapid transition. Note that Gibbs' covariance function eq. (4.32) would be a one way to achieve the desired effect. It is interesting to note the differences between the model optimized with marginal likelihood in Figure 5.9(a), and one optimized with LOO-CV in panel (b) of the same figure. See exercise 5.6.2 for more on how these two criteria weight the influence of the prior.

For comparison, we show the predictive distribution for two other covariance functions in Figure 5.10. In panel (a) a sum of two squared exponential terms were used in the covariance. Notice that this covariance function is still stationary, but it is more flexible than a single squared exponential, since it has two magnitude and two length-scale parameters. The predictive distribution looks a little bit better, and the value of the log marginal likelihood improves from -37.7 in Figure 5.9(a) to -26.1 in Figure 5.10(a). We also tried the neural network covariance function from eq. (4.29), which is ideally suited to this case, since it allow saturation at different values in the positive and negative directions of x. As shown in Figure 5.10(b) the predictions are also near perfect, and the log marginal likelihood is much larger at 50.2.

5.5   Model Selection for GP Classification

In this section we compute the derivatives of the approximate marginal likelihood for the Laplace and EP methods for binary classification which are needed for training. We also give the detailed algorithms for these, and briefly discuss the possible use of cross-validation and other methods for training binary GP classifiers.

5.5.1 Derivatives of the Marginal Likelihood for Laplace's * Approximation

Recall from section 3.4.4 that the approximate log marginal likelihood was given in eq. (3.32) as

$$\log q(\mathbf{y}|X, \boldsymbol{\theta}) \;=\; -\frac{1}{2}\hat{\mathbf{f}}^{\top} K^{-1} \hat{\mathbf{f}} + \log p(\mathbf{y}|\hat{\mathbf{f}}) - \frac{1}{2}\log|B|, \qquad (5.20)$$

where $B = I + W^{\frac{1}{2}} K W^{\frac{1}{2}}$ and $\hat{\mathbf{f}}$ is the maximum of the posterior eq. (3.12) found by Newton's method in Algorithm 3.1, and W is the diagonal matrix $W = -\nabla\nabla \log p(\mathbf{y}|\hat{\mathbf{f}})$. We can now optimize the approximate marginal likelihood $q(\mathbf{y}|X, \boldsymbol{\theta})$ w.r.t. the hyperparameters, $\boldsymbol{\theta}$. To this end we seek the partial derivatives of $\partial q(\mathbf{y}|X, \boldsymbol{\theta})/\partial\theta_j$. The covariance matrix K is a function of the hyperparameters, but $\hat{\mathbf{f}}$ and therefore W are also implicitly functions of $\boldsymbol{\theta}$, since when $\boldsymbol{\theta}$ changes, the optimum of the posterior $\hat{\mathbf{f}}$ also changes. Thus

$$\frac{\partial \log q(\mathbf{y}|X, \boldsymbol{\theta})}{\partial\theta_j} \;=\; \frac{\partial \log q(\mathbf{y}|X, \boldsymbol{\theta})}{\partial\theta_j}\bigg|_{\text{explicit}} + \sum_{i=1}^{n} \frac{\partial \log q(\mathbf{y}|X, \boldsymbol{\theta})}{\partial \hat{f}_i} \frac{\partial \hat{f}_i}{\partial\theta_j}, \qquad (5.21)$$

by the chain rule. Using eq. (A.14) and eq. (A.15) the explicit term is given by

$$\frac{\partial \log q(\mathbf{y}|X, \boldsymbol{\theta})}{\partial\theta_j}\bigg|_{\text{explicit}} \;=\; \frac{1}{2}\hat{\mathbf{f}}^{\top} K^{-1} \frac{\partial K}{\partial\theta_j} K^{-1}\hat{\mathbf{f}} - \frac{1}{2}\operatorname{tr}\left((W^{-1} + K)^{-1}\frac{\partial K}{\partial\theta_j}\right). \qquad (5.22)$$

When evaluating the remaining term from eq. (5.21), we utilize the fact that $\hat{\mathbf{f}}$ is the maximum of the posterior, so that $\partial\Psi(\mathbf{f})/\partial\mathbf{f} = \mathbf{0}$ at $\mathbf{f} = \hat{\mathbf{f}}$, where the (un-normalized) log posterior $\Psi(\mathbf{f})$ is defined in eq. (3.12); thus the implicit derivatives of the two first terms of eq. (5.20) vanish, leaving only

$$\begin{aligned}
\frac{\partial \log q(\mathbf{y}|X, \boldsymbol{\theta})}{\partial \hat{f}_i} &\;=\; -\frac{1}{2}\frac{\partial \log|B|}{\partial \hat{f}_i} \;=\; -\frac{1}{2}\operatorname{tr}\left(B^{-1}K\frac{\partial W}{\partial \hat{f}_i}\right) \\
&\;=\; -\frac{1}{2}\big[(K^{-1} + W)^{-1}\big]_{ii}\frac{\partial^3}{\partial f_i^3}\log p(\mathbf{y}|\hat{\mathbf{f}}).
\end{aligned} \qquad (5.23)$$

In order to evaluate the derivative $\partial\hat{\mathbf{f}}/\partial\theta_j$, we differentiate the self-consistent eq. (3.17) $\hat{\mathbf{f}} = K\nabla \log p(\mathbf{y}|\hat{\mathbf{f}})$ to obtain

$$\frac{\partial\hat{\mathbf{f}}}{\partial\theta_j} \;=\; \frac{\partial K}{\partial\theta_j}\nabla \log p(\mathbf{y}|\hat{\mathbf{f}}) + K\frac{\partial\nabla \log p(\mathbf{y}|\hat{\mathbf{f}})}{\partial\hat{\mathbf{f}}}\frac{\partial\hat{\mathbf{f}}}{\partial\theta_j} \;=\; (I + KW)^{-1}\frac{\partial K}{\partial\theta_j}\nabla \log p(\mathbf{y}|\hat{\mathbf{f}}), \qquad (5.24)$$

where we have used the chain rule $\partial/\partial\theta_j = \partial\hat{\mathbf{f}}/\partial\theta_j \cdot \partial/\partial\hat{\mathbf{f}}$ and the identity $\partial\nabla \log p(\mathbf{y}|\hat{\mathbf{f}})/\partial\hat{\mathbf{f}} = -W$. The desired derivatives are obtained by plugging eq. (5.22-5.24) into eq. (5.21).

Details of the Implementation

The implementation of the log marginal likelihood and its partial derivatives w.r.t. the hyperparameters is shown in Algorithm 5.1. It is advantageous to re-

---

> **input:** X (inputs), $\mathbf{y}$ (± 1 targets), $\boldsymbol{\theta}$ (hypers), $p(\mathbf{y}|\mathbf{f})$ (likelihood function)
> 2:   compute K compute covariance matrix from X and $\boldsymbol{\theta}$
> $\mathbf{f} := \mathrm{mode}\big(K, \mathbf{y}, p(\mathbf{y}|\mathbf{f})\big)$ locate the posterior mode using Algorithm 3.1
> 4: $W := -\nabla\nabla \log p(\mathbf{y}|\mathbf{f})$
> $L := \mathrm{cholesky}(I + W^{\frac{1}{2}} K W^{\frac{1}{2}})$ solve $LL^\top = B = I + W^{\frac{1}{2}} K W^{\frac{1}{2}}$
> 6: $Z := -\frac{1}{2}\mathbf{a}^\top \mathbf{f} + \log p(\mathbf{y}|\mathbf{f}) - \sum \log(\mathrm{diag}(L))$ eq. (5.20)
> $R := W^{\frac{1}{2}} L^\top \backslash (L \backslash W^{\frac{1}{2}})$ $R = W^{\frac{1}{2}}(I + W^{\frac{1}{2}} K W^{\frac{1}{2}})^{-1} W^{\frac{1}{2}}$
> 8: $C := L \backslash (W^{\frac{1}{2}} K)$
> $\mathbf{s}_2 := -\frac{1}{2} \mathrm{diag}\big(\mathrm{diag}(K) - \mathrm{diag}(C^\top C)\big) \nabla^3 \log p(\mathbf{y}|\mathbf{f})$ $\Big\}$ eq. (5.23)
> 10:   **for** $j := 1 \ldots \dim(\boldsymbol{\theta})$ **do**
> $C := \partial K / \partial \theta_j$ compute derivative matrix from X and $\boldsymbol{\theta}$
> 12: $s_1 := \frac{1}{2}\mathbf{a}^\top C \mathbf{a} - \frac{1}{2}\mathrm{tr}(RC)$ eq. (5.22)
> $\mathbf{b} := C \nabla \log p(\mathbf{y}|\mathbf{f})$
> 14: $\mathbf{s}_3 := \mathbf{b} - KR\mathbf{b}$ $\Big\}$ eq. (5.24)
> $\nabla_j Z := s_1 + \mathbf{s}_2^\top \mathbf{s}_3$ eq. (5.21)
> 16:   **end for**
>   **return:** Z (log marginal likelihood), ∇Z (partial derivatives)

Algorithm 5.1: Compute the approximate log marginal likelihood and its derivatives w.r.t. the hyperparameters for binary Laplace GPC for use by an optimization routine, such as conjugate gradient optimization. In line 3 Algorithm 3.1 on page 46 is called to locate the posterior mode. In line 11 only the diagonal elements of the matrix product should be computed. In line 15 the notation ∇_j means the partial derivative w.r.t. the j'th hyperparameter. An actual implementation may also return the value of $\mathbf{f}$ to be used as an initial guess for the subsequent call (as an alternative the zero initialization in line 2 of Algorithm 3.1).

write the equations from the previous section in terms of well-conditioned symmetric positive definite matrices, whose solutions can be obtained by Cholesky factorization, combining numerical stability with computational speed.

In detail, the matrix of central importance turns out to be

$$R = (W^{-1} + K)^{-1} = W^{\frac{1}{2}}(I + W^{\frac{1}{2}} K W^{\frac{1}{2}})^{-1} W^{\frac{1}{2}}, \tag{5.25}$$

where the right hand side is suitable for numerical evaluation as in line 7 of Algorithm 5.1, reusing the Cholesky factor L from the Newton scheme above. Remember that W is diagonal so eq. (5.25) does not require any real matrix-by-matrix products. Rewriting eq. (5.22-5.23) is straightforward, and for eq. (5.24) we apply the matrix inversion lemma (eq. (A.9)) to $(I + KW)^{-1}$ to obtain $I - KR$, which is used in the implementation.

The computational complexity is dominated by the Cholesky factorization in line 5 which takes $n^3/6$ operations per iteration of the Newton scheme. In addition the computation of R in line 7 is also $\mathcal{O}(n^3)$, all other computations being at most $\mathcal{O}(n^2)$ per hyperparameter.

> **input**: X (inputs), $\mathbf{y}$ (± 1 targets), $\boldsymbol{\theta}$ (hyperparameters)
> 2: compute K compute covariance matrix from X and $\boldsymbol{\theta}$
> $(\tilde{\boldsymbol{\nu}}, \tilde{\boldsymbol{\tau}}, Z_{\text{EP}}) := \text{EP}(K, \mathbf{y})$ run the EP Algorithm 3.5
> 4: $L := \text{cholesky}(I + \tilde{S}^{\frac{1}{2}} K \tilde{S}^{\frac{1}{2}})$ solve $LL^{\top} = B = I + \tilde{S}^{\frac{1}{2}} K \tilde{S}^{\frac{1}{2}}$
> $\mathbf{b} := \tilde{\boldsymbol{\nu}} - \tilde{S}^{\frac{1}{2}} L \backslash (L^{\top} \backslash \tilde{S}^{\frac{1}{2}} K \tilde{\boldsymbol{\nu}})$ $\mathbf{b}$ from under eq. (5.27)
> 6: $R := \mathbf{b}\mathbf{b}^{\top} - \tilde{S}^{\frac{1}{2}} L^{\top} \backslash (L \backslash \tilde{S}^{\frac{1}{2}})$ $R = \mathbf{b}\mathbf{b}^{\top} - \tilde{S}^{\frac{1}{2}} B^{-1} \tilde{S}^{\frac{1}{2}}$
>   **for** $j := 1 \ldots \dim(\boldsymbol{\theta})$ **do**
> 8: $C := \partial K / \partial \theta_j$ compute derivative matrix from X and $\boldsymbol{\theta}$
> $\nabla_j Z_{\text{EP}} := \frac{1}{2} \text{tr}(RC)$ eq. (5.27)
> 10: **end for**
>   **return**: Z_{EP} (log marginal likelihood), ∇Z_{EP} (its partial derivatives)

Algorithm 5.2: Compute the log marginal likelihood and its derivatives w.r.t. the hyperparameters for EP binary GP classification for use by an optimization routine, such as conjugate gradient optimization. $\tilde{S}$ is a diagonal precision matrix with entries $\tilde{S}_{ii} = \tilde{\tau}_i$. In line 3 Algorithm 3.5 on page 58 is called to compute parameters of the EP approximation. In line 9 only the diagonal of the matrix product should be computed and the notation ∇_j means the partial derivative w.r.t. the j'th hyperparameter. The computational complexity is dominated by the Cholesky factorization in line 4 and the solution in line 6, both of which are $\mathcal{O}(n^3)$.

5.5.2 Derivatives of the Marginal Likelihood for EP   *

Optimization of the EP approximation to the marginal likelihood w.r.t. the hyperparameters of the covariance function requires evaluation of the partial derivatives from eq. (3.65). Luckily, it turns out that implicit terms in the derivatives caused by the solution of EP being a function of the hyperparameters is exactly zero. We will not present the proof here, see Seeger [2005]. Consequently, we only have to take account of the explicit dependencies

$$\frac{\partial Z_{\text{EP}}}{\partial \theta_j} = \frac{\partial}{\partial \theta_j}\left(-\frac{1}{2}\tilde{\boldsymbol{\mu}}^{\top}(K + \Sigma)^{-1}\tilde{\boldsymbol{\mu}} - \frac{1}{2}\log|K + \tilde{\Sigma}|\right) \tag{5.26}$$

$$= \frac{1}{2}\tilde{\boldsymbol{\mu}}^{\top}(K + \tilde{S}^{-1})^{-1}\frac{\partial K}{\partial \theta_j}(K + \tilde{S}^{-1})^{-1}\tilde{\boldsymbol{\mu}} - \frac{1}{2}\text{tr}\left((K + \tilde{S}^{-1})^{-1}\frac{\partial K}{\partial \theta_j}\right).$$

In Algorithm 5.2 the derivatives from eq. (5.26) are implemented using

$$\frac{\partial Z_{\text{EP}}}{\partial \theta_j} = \frac{1}{2}\text{tr}\left(\left(\mathbf{b}\mathbf{b}^{\top} - \tilde{S}^{\frac{1}{2}}B^{-1}S^{\frac{1}{2}}\right)\frac{\partial K}{\partial \theta_j}\right), \tag{5.27}$$

where $\mathbf{b} = (I - \tilde{S}^{\frac{1}{2}}B^{-1}\tilde{S}^{\frac{1}{2}}K)\tilde{\boldsymbol{\nu}}$.

5.5.3 Cross-validation

Whereas the LOO-CV estimates were easily computed for regression through the use of rank-one updates, it is not so obvious how to generalize this to classification. Opper and Winther [2000, sec. 5] use the cavity distributions of their mean-field approach as LOO-CV estimates, and one could similarly use the cavity distributions from the closely-related EP algorithm discussed in section 3.6. Although technically the cavity distribution for site i could depend on the label y_i (because the algorithm uses all cases when converging to its fixed point), this effect is probably very small and indeed Opper and Winther [2000, sec. 8] report very high precision for these LOO-CV estimates. As an alternative k-fold CV could be used explicitly for some moderate value of k.

Other Methods for Setting Hyperparameters

Above we have considered setting hyperparameters by optimizing the marginal likelihood or cross-validation criteria. However, some other criteria have been proposed in the literature. For example Cristianini et al. [2002] define the *alignment* between a Gram matrix K and the corresponding $+1/-1$ vector of targets $\mathbf{y}$ as

alignment

$$A(K, \mathbf{y}) = \frac{\mathbf{y}^\top K \mathbf{y}}{n\|K\|_F}, \tag{5.28}$$

where $\|K\|_F$ denotes the Frobenius norm of the matrix K, as defined in eq. (A.16). Lanckriet et al. [2004] show that if K is a convex combination of Gram matrices K_i so that $K = \sum_i \nu_i K_i$ with $\nu_i \geq 0$ for all i then the optimization of the alignment score w.r.t. the ν_i's can be achieved by solving a semidefinite programming problem.

5.5.4 Example

For an example of model selection, refer to section 3.7. Although the experiments there were done by exhaustively evaluating the marginal likelihood for a whole grid of hyperparameter values, the techniques described in this chapter could be used to locate the same solutions more efficiently.

5.6 Exercises

1. The optimization of the marginal likelihood w.r.t. the hyperparameters is generally not possible in closed form. Consider, however, the situation where one hyperparameter, θ_0 gives the overall scale of the covariance

$$k_y(\mathbf{x}, \mathbf{x}') = \theta_0 \tilde{k}_y(\mathbf{x}, \mathbf{x}'), \tag{5.29}$$

where k_y is the covariance function for the noisy targets (i.e. including noise contributions) and $\tilde{k}_y(\mathbf{x}, \mathbf{x}')$ may depend on further hyperparameters, $\theta_1, \theta_2, \ldots$. Show that the marginal likelihood can be optimized w.r.t. θ_0 in closed form.

2. Consider the difference between the log marginal likelihood given by: $\sum_i \log p(y_i|\{y_j, j < i\})$, and the LOO-CV using log probability which is given by $\sum_i \log p(y_i|\{y_j, j \neq i\})$. From the viewpoint of the marginal likelihood the LOO-CV conditions *too much* on the data. Show that the *expected* LOO-CV loss is greater than the expected marginal likelihood.

Chapter 6

Relationships between GPs and Other Models

In this chapter we discuss a number of concepts and models that are related to Gaussian process prediction. In section 6.1 we cover reproducing kernel Hilbert spaces (RKHSs), which define a Hilbert space of sufficiently-smooth functions corresponding to a given positive semidefinite kernel k.

As we discussed in chapter 1, there are many functions that are consistent with a given dataset $\mathcal{D}$. We have seen how the GP approach puts a prior over functions in order to deal with this issue. A related viewpoint is provided by *regularization* theory (described in section 6.2) where one seeks a trade-off between data-fit and the RKHS norm of function. This is closely related to the MAP estimator in GP prediction, and thus omits uncertainty in predictions and also the marginal likelihood. In section 6.3 we discuss splines, a special case of regularization which is obtained when the RKHS is defined in terms of differential operators of a given order.

There are a number of other families of kernel machines that are related to Gaussian process prediction. In section 6.4 we describe support vector machines, in section 6.5 we discuss least-squares classification (LSC), and in section 6.6 we cover relevance vector machines (RVMs).

6.1 Reproducing Kernel Hilbert Spaces

Here we present a brief introduction to reproducing kernel Hilbert spaces. The theory was developed by Aronszajn [1950]; a more recent treatise is Saitoh [1988]. Information can also be found in Wahba [1990], Schölkopf and Smola [2002] and Wegman [1982]. The collection of papers edited by Weinert [1982] provides an overview of the uses of RKHSs in statistical signal processing.

We start with a formal definition of a RKHS, and then describe two specific bases for a RKHS, firstly through Mercer's theorem and the eigenfunctions of k, and secondly through the reproducing kernel map.

Definition 6.1 *(Reproducing kernel Hilbert space). Let $\mathcal{H}$ be a Hilbert space of real functions f defined on an index set $\mathcal{X}$. Then $\mathcal{H}$ is called a reproducing kernel Hilbert space endowed with an inner product $\langle \cdot, \cdot \rangle_{\mathcal{H}}$ (and norm $\|f\|_{\mathcal{H}} = \sqrt{\langle f, f \rangle_{\mathcal{H}}}$) if there exists a function $k : \mathcal{X} \times \mathcal{X} \to \mathbb{R}$ with the following properties:*

1. for every $\mathbf{x}$, $k(\mathbf{x}, \mathbf{x}')$ as a function of $\mathbf{x}'$ belongs to $\mathcal{H}$, and

reproducing property

2. k has the reproducing property *$\langle f(\cdot), k(\cdot, \mathbf{x}) \rangle_{\mathcal{H}} = f(\mathbf{x})$.* $\square$

See e.g. Schölkopf and Smola [2002] and Wegman [1982]. Note also that as $k(\mathbf{x}, \cdot)$ and $k(\mathbf{x}', \cdot)$ are in $\mathcal{H}$ we have that $\langle k(\mathbf{x}, \cdot), k(\mathbf{x}', \cdot) \rangle_{\mathcal{H}} = k(\mathbf{x}, \mathbf{x}')$.

The RKHS uniquely determines k, and vice versa, as stated in the following theorem:

Theorem 6.1 *(Moore-Aronszajn theorem, Aronszajn [1950]). Let $\mathcal{X}$ be an index set. Then for every positive definite function $k(\cdot, \cdot)$ on $\mathcal{X} \times \mathcal{X}$ there exists a unique RKHS, and vice versa.* $\square$

The Hilbert space L_2 (which has the dot product $\langle f, g \rangle_{L_2} = \int f(\mathbf{x}) g(\mathbf{x}) d\mathbf{x}$) contains many non-smooth functions. In L_2 (which is not a RKHS) the delta function is the representer of evaluation, i.e. $f(\mathbf{x}) = \int f(\mathbf{x}') \delta(\mathbf{x} - \mathbf{x}') d\mathbf{x}'$. Kernels are the analogues of delta functions within the smoother RKHS. Note that the delta function is not itself in L_2; in contrast for a RKHS the kernel k is the representer of evaluation and is itself in the RKHS.

The above description is perhaps rather abstract. For our purposes the key intuition behind the RKHS formalism is that the squared norm $\|f\|_{\mathcal{H}}^2$ can be thought of as a generalization to functions of the n-dimensional quadratic form $\mathbf{f}^\top K^{-1} \mathbf{f}$ we have seen in earlier chapters.

Consider a real positive semidefinite kernel $k(\mathbf{x}, \mathbf{x}')$ with an eigenfunction expansion $k(\mathbf{x}, \mathbf{x}') = \sum_{i=1}^{N} \lambda_i \phi_i(\mathbf{x}) \phi_i(\mathbf{x}')$ relative to a measure μ. Recall from Mercer's theorem that the eigenfunctions are orthonormal w.r.t. μ, i.e. we have $\int \phi_i(\mathbf{x}) \phi_j(\mathbf{x}) \, d\mu(\mathbf{x}) = \delta_{ij}$. We now consider a Hilbert space comprised of linear combinations of the eigenfunctions, i.e. $f(\mathbf{x}) = \sum_{i=1}^{N} f_i \phi_i(\mathbf{x})$ with $\sum_{i=1}^{N} f_i^2/\lambda_i < \infty$. We assert that the inner product $\langle f, g \rangle_{\mathcal{H}}$ in the Hilbert space between

inner product
$\langle f, g \rangle_{\mathcal{H}}$

functions $f(\mathbf{x})$ and $g(\mathbf{x}) = \sum_{i=1}^{N} g_i \phi_i(\mathbf{x})$ is defined as

$$\langle f, g \rangle_{\mathcal{H}} = \sum_{i=1}^{N} \frac{f_i g_i}{\lambda_i}. \tag{6.1}$$

Thus this Hilbert space is equipped with a norm $\|f\|_{\mathcal{H}}$ where $\|f\|_{\mathcal{H}}^2 = \langle f, f \rangle_{\mathcal{H}} = \sum_{i=1}^{N} f_i^2/\lambda_i$. Note that for $\|f\|_{\mathcal{H}}$ to be finite the sequence of coefficients $\{f_i\}$ must decay quickly; effectively this imposes a smoothness condition on the space.

We now need to show that this Hilbert space is the RKHS corresponding to the kernel k, i.e. that it has the reproducing property. This is easily achieved as

$$\langle f(\cdot), k(\cdot, \mathbf{x})\rangle_{\mathcal{H}} = \sum_{i=1}^{N} \frac{f_i \lambda_i \phi_i(\mathbf{x})}{\lambda_i} = f(\mathbf{x}). \tag{6.2}$$

Similarly

$$\langle k(\mathbf{x}, \cdot), k(\mathbf{x}', \cdot)\rangle_{\mathcal{H}} = \sum_{i=1}^{N} \frac{\lambda_i \phi_i(\mathbf{x}) \lambda_i \phi_i(\mathbf{x}')}{\lambda_i} = k(\mathbf{x}, \mathbf{x}'). \tag{6.3}$$

Notice also that $k(\mathbf{x}, \cdot)$ is in the RKHS as it has norm $\sum_{i=1}^{N} (\lambda_i \phi_i(\mathbf{x}))^2/\lambda_i = k(\mathbf{x}, \mathbf{x}) < \infty$. We have now demonstrated that the Hilbert space comprised of linear combinations of the eigenfunctions with the restriction $\sum_{i=1}^{N} f_i^2/\lambda_i < \infty$ fulfils the two conditions given in Definition 6.1. As there is a unique RKHS associated with $k(\cdot, \cdot)$, this Hilbert space must be that RKHS.

The advantage of the abstract formulation of the RKHS is that the eigenbasis will change as we use different measures μ in Mercer's theorem. However, the RKHS norm is in fact solely a property of the kernel and is invariant under this change of measure. This can be seen from the fact that the proof of the RKHS properties above is not dependent on the measure; see also Kailath [1971, sec. II.B]. A finite-dimensional example of this measure invariance is explored in exercise 6.7.1.

Notice the analogy between the RKHS norm $\|f\|_{\mathcal{H}}^2 = \langle f, f\rangle_{\mathcal{H}} = \sum_{i=1}^{N} f_i^2/\lambda_i$ and the quadratic form $\mathbf{f}^\top K^{-1}\mathbf{f}$; if we express K and $\mathbf{f}$ in terms of the eigenvectors of K we obtain exactly the same form (but the sum has only n terms if $\mathbf{f}$ has length n).

If we sample the coefficients f_i in the eigenexpansion $f(\mathbf{x}) = \sum_{i=1}^{N} f_i \phi_i(\mathbf{x})$ from $\mathcal{N}(0, \lambda_i)$ then

$$\mathbb{E}[\|f\|_{\mathcal{H}}^2] = \sum_{i=1}^{N} \frac{\mathbb{E}[f_i^2]}{\lambda_i} = \sum_{i=1}^{N} 1. \tag{6.4}$$

Thus if N is infinite the sample functions are not in $\mathcal{H}$ (with probability 1) as the expected value of the RKHS norm is infinite; see Wahba [1990, p. 5] and Kailath [1971, sec. II.B] for further details. However, note that although sample functions of this Gaussian process are not in $\mathcal{H}$, the posterior mean after observing some data will lie in the RKHS, due to the smoothing properties of averaging.

Another view of the RKHS can be obtained from the *reproducing kernel map* construction. We consider the space of functions f defined as

$$\left\{ f(\mathbf{x}) = \sum_{i=1}^{n} \alpha_i k(\mathbf{x}, \mathbf{x}_i) : n \in \mathbb{N}, \mathbf{x}_i \in \mathcal{X}, \alpha_i \in \mathbb{R} \right\}. \tag{6.5}$$

Now let $g(\mathbf{x}) = \sum_{j=1}^{n'} \alpha'_j k(\mathbf{x}, \mathbf{x}'_j)$. Then we define the inner product

$$\langle f, g \rangle_{\mathcal{H}} = \sum_{i=1}^{n} \sum_{j=1}^{n'} \alpha_i \alpha'_j k(\mathbf{x}_i, \mathbf{x}'_j). \tag{6.6}$$

Clearly condition 1 of Definition 6.1 is fulfilled under the reproducing kernel map construction. We can also demonstrate the reproducing property, as

$$\langle k(\cdot, \mathbf{x}), f(\cdot) \rangle_{\mathcal{H}} = \sum_{i=1}^{n} \alpha_i k(\mathbf{x}, \mathbf{x}_i) = f(\mathbf{x}). \tag{6.7}$$

6.2 Regularization

The problem of inferring an underlying function $f(\mathbf{x})$ from a finite (and possibly noisy) dataset without any additional assumptions is clearly "ill posed". For example, in the noise-free case, *any* function that passes through the given data points is acceptable. Under a Bayesian approach our assumptions are characterized by a prior over functions, and given some data, we obtain a posterior over functions. The problem of bringing prior assumptions to bear has also been addressed under the *regularization* viewpoint, where these assumptions are encoded in terms of the smoothness of f.

We consider the functional

$$J[f] = \frac{\lambda}{2} \|f\|_{\mathcal{H}}^2 + Q(\mathbf{y}, \mathbf{f}), \tag{6.8}$$

regularizer

where $\mathbf{y}$ is the vector of targets we are predicting and $\mathbf{f} = (f(\mathbf{x}_1), \ldots, f(\mathbf{x}_n))^\top$ is the corresponding vector of function values, and λ is a scaling parameter that trades off the two terms. The first term is called the *regularizer* and represents smoothness assumptions on f as encoded by a suitable RKHS, and the second term is a data-fit term assessing the quality of the prediction $f(\mathbf{x}_i)$ for the observed datum y_i, e.g. the negative log likelihood.

(kernel) ridge regression

Ridge regression (described in section 2.1) can be seen as a particular case of regularization. Indeed, recalling that $\|f\|_{\mathcal{H}}^2 = \sum_{i=1}^{N} f_i^2 / \lambda_i$ where f_i is the coefficient of eigenfunction $\phi_i(\mathbf{x})$, we see that we are penalizing the weighted squared coefficients. This is taking place in feature space, rather than simply in input space, as per the standard formulation of ridge regression (see eq. (2.4)), so it corresponds to *kernel* ridge regression.

representer theorem

The *representer theorem* shows that each minimizer $f \in \mathcal{H}$ of $J[f]$ has the form $f(\mathbf{x}) = \sum_{i=1}^{n} \alpha_i k(\mathbf{x}, \mathbf{x}_i)$.[1] The representer theorem was first stated by Kimeldorf and Wahba [1971] for the case of squared error.[2] O'Sullivan et al. [1986] showed that the representer theorem could be extended to likelihood

---

[1] If the RKHS contains a null space of unpenalized functions then the given form is correct modulo a term that lies in this null space. This is explained further in section 6.3.

[2] Schoenberg [1964] proved the representer theorem for the special case of cubic splines and squared error. This was result extended to general RKHSs in Kimeldorf and Wahba [1971].

functions arising from generalized linear models. The representer theorem can be generalized still further, see e.g. Schölkopf and Smola [2002, sec. 4.2]. If the data-fit term is convex (see section A.9) then there will be a unique minimizer $\hat{f}$ of $J[f]$.

For Gaussian process prediction with likelihoods that involve the values of f at the n training points only (so that $Q(\mathbf{y}, \mathbf{f})$ is the negative log likelihood up to some terms not involving $\mathbf{f}$), the analogue of the representer theorem is obvious. This is because the predictive distribution of $f(\mathbf{x}_*) \triangleq f_*$ at test point $\mathbf{x}_*$ given the data $\mathbf{y}$ is $p(f_*|\mathbf{y}) = \int p(f_*|\mathbf{f})p(\mathbf{f}|\mathbf{y}) \, d\mathbf{f}$. As derived in eq. (3.22) we have

$$\mathbb{E}[f_*|\mathbf{y}] = \mathbf{k}(\mathbf{x}_*)^\top K^{-1}\mathbb{E}[\mathbf{f}|\mathbf{y}] \tag{6.9}$$

due to the formulae for the conditional distribution of a multivariate Gaussian. Thus $\mathbb{E}[f_*|\mathbf{y}] = \sum_{i=1}^n \alpha_i k(\mathbf{x}_*, \mathbf{x}_i)$, where $\boldsymbol{\alpha} = K^{-1}\mathbb{E}[\mathbf{f}|\mathbf{y}]$.

The regularization approach has a long tradition in inverse problems, dating back at least as far as Tikhonov [1963]; see also Tikhonov and Arsenin [1977]. For the application of this approach in the machine learning literature see e.g. Poggio and Girosi [1990].

In section 6.2.1 we consider RKHSs defined in terms of differential operators. In section 6.2.2 we demonstrate how to solve the regularization problem in the specific case of squared error, and in section 6.2.3 we compare and contrast the regularization approach with the Gaussian process viewpoint.

6.2.1 Regularization Defined by Differential Operators ∗

For $\mathbf{x} \in \mathbb{R}^D$ define

$$\|O^m f\|^2 = \int \sum_{j_1+\ldots+j_D=m} \left(\frac{\partial^m f(\mathbf{x})}{\partial x_1^{j_1}\ldots x_D^{j_D}}\right)^2 d\mathbf{x}. \tag{6.10}$$

For example for $m = 2$ and $D = 2$

$$\|O^2 f\|^2 = \int \left[\left(\frac{\partial^2 f}{\partial x_1^2}\right)^2 + 2\left(\frac{\partial^2 f}{\partial x_1 \partial x_2}\right)^2 + \left(\frac{\partial^2 f}{\partial x_2^2}\right)^2\right] dx_1 \, dx_2. \tag{6.11}$$

Now set $\|Pf\|^2 = \sum_{m=0}^M a_m \|O^m f\|^2$ with non-negative coefficients a_m. Notice that $\|Pf\|^2$ is translation and rotation invariant.

In this section we assume that $a_0 > 0$; if this is not the case and a_k is the first non-zero coefficient, then there is a *null space* of functions that are unpenalized. For example if $k = 2$ then constant and linear functions are in the null space. This case is dealt with in section 6.3.

$\|Pf\|^2$ penalizes f in terms of the variability of its function values and derivatives up to order M. How does this correspond to the RKHS formulation of section 6.1? The key is to recognize that the complex exponentials $\exp(2\pi i\mathbf{s} \cdot \mathbf{x})$ are eigenfunctions of the differential operator if $\mathcal{X} = \mathbb{R}^D$. In this case

$$\|Pf\|^2 = \int \sum_{m=0}^M a_m (4\pi^2 \mathbf{s} \cdot \mathbf{s})^m |\tilde{f}(\mathbf{s})|^2 d\mathbf{s}, \tag{6.12}$$

null space

where $\tilde{f}(\mathbf{s})$ is the Fourier transform of $f(\mathbf{x})$. Comparing eq. (6.12) with eq. (6.1) we see that the kernel has the power spectrum

$$S(\mathbf{s}) = \frac{1}{\sum_{m=0}^{M} a_m (4\pi^2 \mathbf{s} \cdot \mathbf{s})^m}, \qquad (6.13)$$

and thus by Fourier inversion we obtain the stationary kernel

$$k(\mathbf{x}) = \int \frac{e^{2\pi i \mathbf{s} \cdot \mathbf{x}}}{\sum_{m=0}^{M} a_m (4\pi^2 \mathbf{s} \cdot \mathbf{s})^m} \, d\mathbf{s}. \qquad (6.14)$$

A slightly different approach to obtaining the kernel is to use calculus of variations to minimize $J[f]$ with respect to f. The Euler-Lagrange equation leads to

$$f(\mathbf{x}) = \sum_{i=1}^{n} \alpha_i G(\mathbf{x} - \mathbf{x}_i), \qquad (6.15)$$

with

$$\sum_{m=0}^{M} (-1)^m a_m \nabla^{2m} G = \delta(\mathbf{x} - \mathbf{x}'), \qquad (6.16)$$

Green's function
$\equiv$ kernel

where $G(\mathbf{x}, \mathbf{x}')$ is known as a Green's function. Notice that the Green's function also depends on the boundary conditions. For the case of $\mathcal{X} = \mathbb{R}^D$ by Fourier transforming eq. (6.16) we recognize that G is in fact the kernel k. The differential operator $\sum_{m=0}^{M}(-1)^m a_m \nabla^{2m}$ and the integral operator $k(\cdot, \cdot)$ are in fact inverses, as shown by eq. (6.16). See Poggio and Girosi [1990] for further details. Arfken [1985] provides an introduction to calculus of variations and Green's functions. RKHSs for regularizers defined by differential operators are *Sobolev spaces*; see e.g. Adams [1975] for further details on Sobolev spaces.

We now give two specific examples of kernels derived from differential operators.

Example 1. Set $a_0 = \alpha^2$, $a_1 = 1$ and $a_m = 0$ for $m \geq 2$ in $D = 1$. Using the Fourier pair $e^{-\alpha|x|} \leftrightarrow 2\alpha/(\alpha^2 + 4\pi^2 s^2)$ we obtain $k(x - x') = \frac{1}{2\alpha} e^{-\alpha|x-x'|}$. Note that this is the covariance function of the Ornstein-Uhlenbeck process, see section 4.2.1.

Example 2. By setting $a_m = \frac{\sigma^{2m}}{m! 2^m}$ and using the power series $e^y = \sum_{k=0}^{\infty} y^k / k!$ we obtain

$$k(\mathbf{x} - \mathbf{x}') = \int \exp(2\pi i \mathbf{s} \cdot (\mathbf{x} - \mathbf{x}')) \exp(-\frac{\sigma^2}{2}(4\pi^2 \mathbf{s} \cdot \mathbf{s})) d\mathbf{s} \qquad (6.17)$$

$$= \frac{1}{(2\pi\sigma^2)^{D/2}} \exp(-\frac{1}{2\sigma^2}(\mathbf{x} - \mathbf{x}')^\top (\mathbf{x} - \mathbf{x}')), \qquad (6.18)$$

as shown by Yuille and Grzywacz [1989]. This is the squared exponential covariance function that we have seen earlier.

6.2.2 Obtaining the Regularized Solution

The representer theorem tells us the general form of the solution to eq. (6.8). We now consider a specific functional

$$J[f] = \frac{1}{2}\|f\|_{\mathcal{H}}^2 + \frac{1}{2\sigma_n^2}\sum_{i=1}^n (y_i - f(\mathbf{x}_i))^2, \tag{6.19}$$

which uses a squared error data-fit term (corresponding to the negative log likelihood of a Gaussian noise model with variance σ_n^2). Substituting $f(\mathbf{x}) = \sum_{i=1}^n \alpha_i k(\mathbf{x}, \mathbf{x}_i)$ and using $\langle k(\cdot, \mathbf{x}_i), k(\cdot, \mathbf{x}_j)\rangle_{\mathcal{H}} = k(\mathbf{x}_i, \mathbf{x}_j)$ we obtain

$$\begin{aligned} J[\boldsymbol{\alpha}] &= \frac{1}{2}\boldsymbol{\alpha}^\top K\boldsymbol{\alpha} + \frac{1}{2\sigma_n^2}|\mathbf{y} - K\boldsymbol{\alpha}|^2 \\ &= \frac{1}{2}\boldsymbol{\alpha}^\top (K + \frac{1}{\sigma_n^2}K^2)\boldsymbol{\alpha} - \frac{1}{\sigma_n^2}\mathbf{y}^\top K\boldsymbol{\alpha} + \frac{1}{2\sigma_n^2}\mathbf{y}^\top \mathbf{y}. \end{aligned} \tag{6.20}$$

Minimizing J by differentiating w.r.t. the vector of coefficients $\boldsymbol{\alpha}$ we obtain $\hat{\boldsymbol{\alpha}} = (K + \sigma_n^2 I)^{-1}\mathbf{y}$, so that the prediction for a test point $\mathbf{x}_*$ is $\hat{f}(\mathbf{x}_*) = \mathbf{k}(\mathbf{x}_*)^\top (K + \sigma_n^2 I)^{-1}\mathbf{y}$. This should look very familiar—it is exactly the form of the predictive mean obtained in eq. (2.23). In the next section we compare and contrast the regularization and GP views of the problem.

The solution $f(\mathbf{x}) = \sum_{i=1}^n \alpha_i k(\mathbf{x}, \mathbf{x}_i)$ that minimizes eq. (6.19) was called a *regularization network* in Poggio and Girosi [1990].   regularization network

6.2.3 The Relationship of the Regularization View to Gaussian Process Prediction

The regularization method returns $\hat{f} = \text{argmin}_f J[f]$. For a Gaussian process predictor we obtain a posterior distribution over functions. Can we make a connection between these two views? In fact we shall see in this section that $\hat{f}$ can be viewed as the *maximum a posteriori* (MAP) function under the posterior.

Following Szeliski [1987] and Poggio and Girosi [1990] we consider

$$\exp\left(-J[f]\right) = \exp\left(-\frac{\lambda}{2}\|Pf\|^2\right) \times \exp\left(-Q(\mathbf{y}, \mathbf{f})\right). \tag{6.21}$$

The first term on the RHS is a Gaussian process prior on f, and the second is proportional to the likelihood. As $\hat{f}$ is the minimizer of $J[f]$, it is the MAP function.

To get some intuition for the Gaussian process prior, imagine $f(\mathbf{x})$ being represented on a grid in $\mathbf{x}$-space, so that f is now an (infinite dimensional) vector $\mathbf{f}$. Thus we obtain $\|Pf\|^2 \simeq \sum_{m=0}^M a_m (D_m\mathbf{f})^\top (D_m\mathbf{f}) = \mathbf{f}^\top (\sum_m a_m D_m^\top D_m)\mathbf{f}$ where D_m is an appropriate finite-difference approximation of the differential operator O^m. Observe that this prior term is a quadratic form in $\mathbf{f}$.

To go into more detail concerning the MAP relationship we consider three cases: (i) when $Q(\mathbf{y}, \mathbf{f})$ is quadratic (corresponding to a Gaussian likelihood);

(ii) when $Q(\mathbf{y}, \mathbf{f})$ is not quadratic but convex and (iii) when $Q(\mathbf{y}, \mathbf{f})$ is not convex.

In case (i) we have seen in chapter 2 that the posterior mean function can be obtained exactly, and the posterior is Gaussian. As the mean of a Gaussian is also its mode this is the MAP solution. The correspondence between the GP posterior mean and the solution of the regularization problem $\hat{f}$ was made in Kimeldorf and Wahba [1970].

In case (ii) we have seen in chapter 3 for classification problems using the logistic, probit or softmax response functions that $Q(\mathbf{y}, \mathbf{f})$ is convex. Here the MAP solution can be found by finding $\hat{\mathbf{f}}$ (the MAP solution to the n-dimensional problem defined at the training points) and then extending it to other $\mathbf{x}$-values through the posterior mean conditioned on $\hat{\mathbf{f}}$.

In case (iii) there will be more than one local minimum of $J[f]$ under the regularization approach. One could check these minima to find the deepest one. However, in this case the argument for MAP is rather weak (especially if there are multiple optima of similar depth) and suggests the need for a fully Bayesian treatment.

While the regularization solution gives a part of the Gaussian process solution, there are the following limitations:

1. It does not characterize the uncertainty in the predictions, nor does it handle well multimodality in the posterior.

2. The analysis is focussed at approximating the first level of Bayesian inference, concerning predictions for f. It is not usually extended to the next level, e.g. to the computation of the marginal likelihood. The marginal likelihood is very useful for setting any parameters of the covariance function, and for model comparison (see chapter 5).

In addition, we find the specification of smoothness via the penalties on derivatives to be not very intuitive. The regularization viewpoint can be thought of as directly specifying the *inverse* covariance rather than the covariance. As marginalization is achieved for a Gaussian distribution directly from the covariance (and not the inverse covariance) it seems more natural to us to specify the covariance function. Also, while non-stationary covariance functions can be obtained from the regularization viewpoint, e.g. by replacing the Lebesgue measure in eq. (6.10) with a non-uniform measure $\mu(\mathbf{x})$, calculation of the corresponding covariance function can then be very difficult.

6.3 Spline Models

In section 6.2 we discussed regularizers which had $a_0 > 0$ in eq. (6.12). We now consider the case when $a_0 = 0$; in particular we consider the regularizer to be of the form $\|O^m f\|^2$, as defined in eq. (6.10). In this case polynomials of degree up to $m - 1$ are in the *null space* of the regularization operator, in that they are not penalized at all.

In the case that $\mathcal{X} = \mathbb{R}^D$ we can again use Fourier techniques to obtain the Green's function G corresponding to the Euler-Lagrange equation $(-1)^m \nabla^{2m} G(\mathbf{x}) = \delta(\mathbf{x})$. The result, as shown by Duchon [1977] and Meinguet [1979] is

$$G(\mathbf{x} - \mathbf{x}') = \begin{cases} c_{m,D} |\mathbf{x} - \mathbf{x}'|^{2m-D} \log |\mathbf{x} - \mathbf{x}'| & \text{if } 2m > D \text{ and } D \text{ even} \\ c_{m,D} |\mathbf{x} - \mathbf{x}'|^{2m-D} & \text{otherwise,} \end{cases} \qquad (6.22)$$

where $c_{m,D}$ is a constant (Wahba [1990, p. 31] gives the explicit form). Note that the constraint $2m > D$ has to be imposed to avoid having a Green's function that is singular at the origin. Explicit calculation of the Green's function for other domains $\mathcal{X}$ is sometimes possible; for example see Wahba [1990, sec. 2.2] for splines on the sphere.

Because of the null space, a minimizer of the regularization functional has the form

$$f(\mathbf{x}) = \sum_{i=1}^{n} \alpha_i G(\mathbf{x}, \mathbf{x}_i) + \sum_{j=1}^{k} \beta_j h_j(\mathbf{x}), \qquad (6.23)$$

where $h_1(\mathbf{x}), \ldots, h_k(\mathbf{x})$ are polynomials that span the null space. The exact values of the coefficients $\boldsymbol{\alpha}$ and $\boldsymbol{\beta}$ for a specific problem can be obtained in an analogous manner to the derivation in section 6.2.2; in fact the solution is equivalent to that given in eq. (2.42).

To gain some more insight into the form of the Green's function we consider the equation $(-1)^m \nabla^{2m} G(\mathbf{x}) = \delta(\mathbf{x})$ in Fourier space, leading to $\tilde{G}(\mathbf{s}) = (4\pi^2 \mathbf{s} \cdot \mathbf{s})^{-m}$. $\tilde{G}(\mathbf{s})$ plays a rôle like that of the power spectrum in eq. (6.13), but notice that $\int \tilde{G}(\mathbf{s}) d\mathbf{s}$ is infinite, which would imply that the corresponding process has infinite variance. The problem is of course that the null space is unpenalized; for example any arbitrary constant function can be added to f without changing the regularizer.

Because of the null space we have seen that one cannot obtain a simple connection between the spline solution and a corresponding Gaussian process problem. However, by introducing the notion of an *intrinsic random function* (IRF) one can define a *generalized covariance*; see Cressie [1993, sec. 5.4] and Stein [1999, section 2.9] for details. The basic idea is to consider linear combinations of $f(\mathbf{x})$ of the form $g(\mathbf{x}) = \sum_{i=1}^{k} a_i f(\mathbf{x} + \boldsymbol{\delta}_i)$ for which $g(\mathbf{x})$ is second-order stationary and where $(h_j(\boldsymbol{\delta}_1), \ldots, h_j(\boldsymbol{\delta}_k))\mathbf{a} = 0$ for $j = 1, \ldots, k$. A careful description of the equivalence of spline and IRF prediction is given in Kent and Mardia [1994].

IRF

The power-law form of $\tilde{G}(\mathbf{s}) = (4\pi^2 \mathbf{s} \cdot \mathbf{s})^{-m}$ means that there is no characteristic length-scale for random functions drawn from this (improper) prior. Thus we obtain the *self-similar* property characteristic of fractals; for further details see Szeliski [1987] and Mandelbrot [1982]. Some authors argue that the lack of a characteristic length-scale is appealing. This may sometimes be the case, but if we believe there is an appropriate length-scale (or set of length-scales) for a given problem but this is unknown in advance, we would argue that a hierarchical Bayesian formulation of the problem (as described in chapter 5) would be more appropriate.

Splines were originally introduced for one-dimensional interpolation and smoothing problems, and then generalized to the multivariate setting. Schoenberg [1964] considered the problem of finding the function that minimizes

spline interpolation

$$\int_a^b (f^{(m)}(x))^2 \, dx, \tag{6.24}$$

where $f^{(m)}$ denotes the m'th derivative of f, subject to the interpolation constraints $f(x_i) = f_i$, $x_i \in (a, b)$ for $i = 1, \ldots, n$ and for f in an appropriate Sobolev space. He showed that the solution is the natural polynomial spline, which is a piecewise polynomial of order $2m - 1$ in each interval $[x_i, x_{i+1}]$, $i = 1, \ldots, n - 1$, and of order $m - 1$ in the two outermost intervals. The pieces are joined so that the solution has $2m - 2$ continuous derivatives. Schoenberg also proved that the solution to the univariate smoothing problem (see eq. (6.19)) is a natural polynomial spline. A common choice is $m = 2$, leading to the cubic spline. One possible way of writing this solution is

natural polynomial spline

smoothing spline

$$f(x) = \sum_{j=0}^1 \beta_j x^j + \sum_{i=1}^n \alpha_i (x - x_i)_+^3, \quad \text{where } (x)_+ = \begin{cases} x & \text{if } x > 0 \\ 0 & \text{otherwise.} \end{cases} \tag{6.25}$$

It turns out that the coefficients $\boldsymbol{\alpha}$ and $\boldsymbol{\beta}$ can be computed in time $\mathcal{O}(n)$ using an algorithm due to Reinsch; see Green and Silverman [1994, sec. 2.3.3] for details.

Splines were first used in regression problems. However, by using generalized linear modelling [McCullagh and Nelder, 1983] they can be extended to classification problems and other non-Gaussian likelihoods, as we did for GP classification in section 3.3. Early references in this direction include Silverman [1978] and O'Sullivan et al. [1986].

There is a vast literature in relation to splines in both the statistics and numerical analysis literatures; for entry points see citations in Wahba [1990] and Green and Silverman [1994].

* 6.3.1   A 1-d Gaussian Process Spline Construction

In this section we will further clarify the relationship between splines and Gaussian processes by giving a GP construction for the solution of the univariate cubic spline smoothing problem whose cost functional is

$$\sum_{i=1}^n \big(f(x_i) - y_i\big)^2 + \lambda \int_0^1 \big(f''(x)\big)^2 \, dx, \tag{6.26}$$

where the observed data are $\{(x_i, y_i) | i = 1, \ldots, n, \ 0 < x_1 < \cdots < x_n < 1\}$ and λ is a *smoothing parameter* controlling the trade-off between the first term, the data-fit, and the second term, the regularizer, or complexity penalty. Recall that the solution is a piecewise polynomial as in eq. (6.25).

Following Wahba [1978], we consider the random function

$$g(x) = \sum_{j=0}^{1} \beta_j x^j + f(x) \tag{6.27}$$

where $\beta \sim \mathcal{N}(\mathbf{0}, \sigma_\beta^2 I)$ and $f(x)$ is a Gaussian process with covariance $\sigma_f^2 k_{\text{sp}}(x, x')$, where

$$k_{\text{sp}}(x, x') \triangleq \int_0^1 (x-u)_+ (x'-u)_+ \, du = \frac{|x-x'|v^2}{2} + \frac{v^3}{3}, \tag{6.28}$$

and $v = \min(x, x')$.

To complete the analogue of the regularizer in eq. (6.26), we need to remove any penalty on polynomial terms in the null space by making the prior vague, i.e. by taking the limit $\sigma_\beta^2 \to \infty$. Notice that the covariance has the form of contributions from explicit basis functions, $\mathbf{h}(x) = (1, x)^\top$ and a regular covariance function $k_{\text{sp}}(x, x')$, a problem which we have already studied in section 2.7. Indeed we have computed the limit where the prior becomes vague $\sigma_\beta^2 \to \infty$, the result is given in eq. (2.42).

Plugging into the mean equation from eq. (2.42), we get the predictive mean

$$\bar{f}(x_*) = \mathbf{k}(x_*)^\top K_y^{-1} (\mathbf{y} - H^\top \bar{\beta}) + \mathbf{h}(x_*)^\top \bar{\beta}, \tag{6.29}$$

where K_y is the covariance matrix corresponding to $\sigma_f^2 k_{\text{sp}}(x_i, x_j) + \sigma_n^2 \delta_{ij}$ evaluated at the training points, H is the matrix that collects the $\mathbf{h}(x_i)$ vectors at all training points, and $\bar{\beta} = (HK_y^{-1}H^\top)^{-1} HK_y^{-1} \mathbf{y}$ is given below eq. (2.42). It is not difficult to show that this predictive mean function is a piecewise cubic polynomial, since the elements of $\mathbf{k}(x_*)$ are piecewise[3] cubic polynomials. Showing that the mean function is a first order polynomial in the outer intervals $[0, x_1]$ and $[x_n, 1]$ is left as exercise 6.7.3.

So far k_{sp} has been produced rather mysteriously "from the hat"; we now provide some explanation. Shepp [1966] defined the l-fold integrated Wiener process as

$$W_l(x) = \int_0^1 \frac{(x-u)_+^l}{l!} Z(u) du, \qquad l = 0, 1, \dots \tag{6.30}$$

where $Z(u)$ denotes the Gaussian white noise process with covariance $\delta(u - u')$. Note that W_0 is the standard Wiener process. It is easy to show that $k_{\text{sp}}(x, x')$ is the covariance of the once-integrated Wiener process by writing $W_1(x)$ and $W_1(x')$ using eq. (6.30) and taking the expectation using the covariance of the white noise process. Note that W_l is the solution to the stochastic differential equation (SDE) $X^{(l+1)} = Z$; see Appendix B for further details on SDEs. Thus

---

[3]The pieces are joined at the datapoints, the points where the $\min(x, x')$ from the covariance function is non-differentiable.

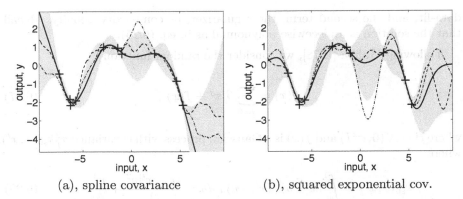

(a), spline covariance   (b), squared exponential cov.

Figure 6.1: Panel (a) shows the application of the spline covariance to a simple dataset. The full line shows the predictive mean, which is a piecewise cubic polynomial, and the grey area indicates the 95% confidence area. The two thin dashed and dash-dotted lines are samples from the posterior. Note that the posterior samples are not as smooth as the mean. For comparison a GP using the squared exponential covariance function is shown in panel (b). The hyperparameters in both cases were optimized using the marginal likelihood.

for the cubic spline we set $l = 1$ to obtain the SDE $X'' = Z$, corresponding to the regularizer $\int (f''(x))^2 dx$.

We can also give an explicit basis-function construction for the covariance function k_{sp}. Consider the family of random functions given by

$$f_N(x) = \frac{1}{\sqrt{N}} \sum_{i=0}^{N-1} \gamma_i (x - \frac{i}{N})_+, \tag{6.31}$$

where $\boldsymbol{\gamma}$ is a vector of parameters with $\boldsymbol{\gamma} \sim \mathcal{N}(\mathbf{0}, I)$. Note that the sum has the form of evenly spaced "ramps" whose magnitudes are given by the entries in the $\boldsymbol{\gamma}$ vector. Thus

$$\mathbb{E}[f_N(x)f_N(x')] = \frac{1}{N} \sum_{i=0}^{N-1} (x - \frac{i}{N})_+ (x' - \frac{i}{N})_+. \tag{6.32}$$

Taking the limit $N \to \infty$, we obtain eq. (6.28), a derivation which is also found in [Vapnik, 1998, sec. 11.6].

Notice that the covariance function k_{sp} given in eq. (6.28) corresponds to a Gaussian process which is MS continuous but only once MS differentiable. Thus samples from the prior will be quite "rough", although (as noted in section 6.1) the posterior mean, eq. (6.25), is smoother.

The constructions above can be generalized to the regularizer $\int (f^{(m)}(x))^2 \, dx$ by replacing $(x - u)_+$ with $(x - u)_+^{m-1}/(m - 1)!$ in eq. (6.28) and similarly in eq. (6.32), and setting $\mathbf{h}(x) = (1, x, \ldots, x^{m-1})^\top$.

Thus, we can use a Gaussian process formulation as an alternative to the usual spline fitting procedure. Note that the trade-off parameter λ from eq. (6.26)

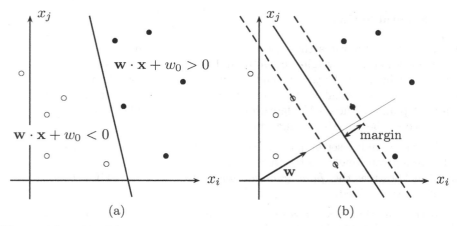

Figure 6.2: Panel (a) shows a linearly separable binary classification problem, and a separating hyperplane. Panel (b) shows the maximum margin hyperplane.

is now given as the ratio σ_n^2/σ_f^2. The hyperparameters σ_f^2 and σ_n^2 can be set using the techniques from section 5.4.1 by optimizing the marginal likelihood given in eq. (2.45). Kohn and Ansley [1987] give details of an $\mathcal{O}(n)$ algorithm (based on Kalman filtering) for the computation of the spline and the marginal likelihood. In addition to the predictive mean the GP treatment also yields an explicit estimate of the noise level and predictive error bars. Figure 6.1 shows a simple example. Notice that whereas the mean function is a piecewise cubic polynomial, samples from the posterior are not smooth. In contrast, for the squared exponential covariance functions shown in panel (b), both the mean and functions drawn from the posterior are infinitely differentiable.

6.4   Support Vector Machines   *

Since the mid 1990's there has been an explosion of interest in kernel machines, and in particular the support vector machine (SVM). The aim of this section is to provide a brief introduction to SVMs and in particular to compare them to Gaussian process predictors. We consider SVMs for classification and regression problems in sections 6.4.1 and 6.4.2 respectively. More comprehensive treatments can be found in Vapnik [1995], Cristianini and Shawe-Taylor [2000] and Schölkopf and Smola [2002].

6.4.1   Support Vector Classification

For support vector classifiers, the key notion that we need to introduce is that of the *maximum margin* hyperplane for a linear classifier. Then by using the "kernel trick" this can be lifted into feature space. We consider first the separable case and then the non-separable case. We conclude this section with a comparison between GP classifiers and SVMs.

The Separable Case

Figure 6.2(a) illustrates the case where the data is linearly separable. For a linear classifier with weight vector $\mathbf{w}$ and offset w_0, let the decision boundary be defined by $\mathbf{w} \cdot \mathbf{x} + w_0 = 0$, and let $\tilde{\mathbf{w}} = (\mathbf{w}, w_0)$. Clearly, there is a whole version space of weight vectors that give rise to the same classification of the training points. The SVM algorithm chooses a particular weight vector, that gives rise to the "maximum margin" of separation.

Let the training set be pairs of the form $(\mathbf{x}_i, y_i)$ for $i = 1, \ldots, n$, where $y_i = \pm 1$. For a given weight vector we can compute the quantity $\tilde{\gamma}_i = y_i(\mathbf{w} \cdot \mathbf{x} + w_0)$, which is known as the *functional margin*. Notice that $\tilde{\gamma}_i > 0$ if a training point is correctly classified.

functional margin

If the equation $f(\mathbf{x}) = \mathbf{w} \cdot \mathbf{x} + w_0$ defines a discriminant function (so that the output is $\text{sgn}(f(\mathbf{x}))$), then the hyperplane $c\mathbf{w} \cdot \mathbf{x} + cw_0$ defines the same discriminant function for any $c > 0$. Thus we have the freedom to choose the scaling of $\tilde{\mathbf{w}}$ so that $\min_i \tilde{\gamma}_i = 1$, and in this case $\tilde{\mathbf{w}}$ is known as the *canonical* form of the hyperplane.

geometrical margin

The *geometrical margin* is defined as $\gamma_i = \tilde{\gamma}_i/|\mathbf{w}|$. For a training point $\mathbf{x}_i$ that is correctly classified this is simply the distance from $\mathbf{x}_i$ to the hyperplane. To see this, let $c = 1/|\mathbf{w}|$ so that $\hat{\mathbf{w}} = \mathbf{w}/|\mathbf{w}|$ is a unit vector in the direction of $\mathbf{w}$, and $\hat{w}_0$ is the corresponding offset. Then $\hat{\mathbf{w}} \cdot \mathbf{x}$ computes the length of the projection of $\mathbf{x}$ onto the direction orthogonal to the hyperplane and $\hat{\mathbf{w}} \cdot \mathbf{x} + \hat{w}_0$ computes the distance to the hyperplane. For training points that are misclassified the geometrical margin is the negative distance to the hyperplane.

The geometrical margin for a dataset $\mathcal{D}$ is defined as $\gamma_\mathcal{D} = \min_i \gamma_i$. Thus for a canonical separating hyperplane the margin is $1/|\mathbf{w}|$. We wish to find the maximum margin hyperplane, i.e. the one that maximizes $\gamma_\mathcal{D}$.

optimization problem

By considering canonical hyperplanes, we are thus led to the following optimization problem to determine the maximum margin hyperplane:

$$\text{minimize } \frac{1}{2}|\mathbf{w}|^2 \quad \text{over } \mathbf{w}, w_0$$
$$\text{subject to } y_i(\mathbf{w} \cdot \mathbf{x}_i + w_0) \geq 1 \quad \text{for all } i = 1, \ldots, n. \tag{6.33}$$

It is clear by considering the geometry that for the maximum margin solution there will be at least one data point in each class for which $y_i(\mathbf{w} \cdot \mathbf{x}_i + w_0) = 1$, see Figure 6.2(b). Let the hyperplanes that pass through these points be denoted H_+ and H_- respectively.

This constrained optimization problem can be set up using Lagrange multipliers, and solved using numerical methods for quadratic programming[4] (QP) problems. The form of the solution is

$$\mathbf{w} = \sum_i \lambda_i y_i \mathbf{x}_i, \tag{6.34}$$

---

[4]A quadratic programming problem is an optimization problem where the objective function is quadratic and the constraints are linear in the unknowns.

where the λ_i's are non-negative Lagrange multipliers. Notice that the solution is a linear combination of the $\mathbf{x}_i$'s.

The key feature of equation 6.34 is that λ_i is zero for every $\mathbf{x}_i$ *except* those which lie on the hyperplanes H_+ or H_-; these points are called the *support vectors*. The fact that not all of the training points contribute to the final solution is referred to as the *sparsity* of the solution. The support vectors lie closest to the decision boundary. Note that if all of the other training points were removed (or moved around, but not crossing H_+ or H_-) the same maximum margin hyperplane would be found. The quadratic programming problem for finding the λ_i's is convex, i.e. there are no local minima. Notice the similarity of this to the convexity of the optimization problem for Gaussian process classifiers, as described in section 3.4.

support vectors

To make predictions for a new input $\mathbf{x}_*$ we compute

$$\mathrm{sgn}(\mathbf{w} \cdot \mathbf{x}_* + w_0) \; = \; \mathrm{sgn}\Big(\sum_{i=1}^{n} \lambda_i y_i (\mathbf{x}_i \cdot \mathbf{x}_*) + w_0 \Big). \qquad (6.35)$$

In the QP problem and in eq. (6.35) the training points $\{\mathbf{x}_i\}$ and the test point $\mathbf{x}_*$ enter the computations only in terms of inner products. Thus by using the kernel trick we can replace occurrences of the inner product by the kernel to obtain the equivalent result in feature space.

kernel trick

The Non-Separable Case

For linear classifiers in the original $\mathbf{x}$ space there will be some datasets that are not linearly separable. One way to generalize the SVM problem in this case is to allow violations of the constraint $y_i(\mathbf{w} \cdot \mathbf{x}_i + w_0) \geq 1$ but to impose a penalty when this occurs. This leads to the *soft margin* support vector machine problem, the minimization of

soft margin

$$\frac{1}{2}|\mathbf{w}|^2 + C \sum_{i=1}^{n} (1 - y_i f_i)_+ \qquad (6.36)$$

with respect to $\mathbf{w}$ and w_0, where $f_i = f(\mathbf{x}_i) = \mathbf{w} \cdot \mathbf{x}_i + w_0$ and $(z)_+ = z$ if $z > 0$ and 0 otherwise. Here $C > 0$ is a parameter that specifies the relative importance of the two terms. This convex optimization problem can again be solved using QP methods and yields a solution of the form given in eq. (6.34). In this case the support vectors (those with $\lambda_i \neq 0$) are not only those data points which lie on the separating hyperplanes, but also those that incur penalties. This can occur in two ways (i) the data point falls in between H_+ and H_- but on the correct side of the decision surface, or (ii) the data point falls on the wrong side of the decision surface.

In a feature space of dimension N, if $N > n$ then there will always be separating hyperplane. However, this hyperplane may not give rise to good generalization performance, especially if some of the labels are incorrect, and thus the soft margin SVM formulation is often used in practice.

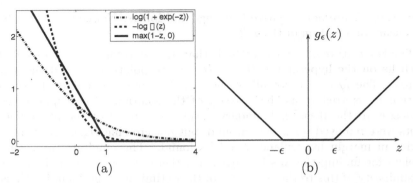

Figure 6.3: (a) A comparison of the hinge error, g_λ and g_Φ. (b) The ϵ-insensitive error function used in SVR.

For both the hard and soft margin SVM QP problems a wide variety of algorithms have been developed for their solution; see Schölkopf and Smola [2002, ch. 10] for details. Basic interior point methods involve inversions of $n \times n$ matrices and thus scale as $\mathcal{O}(n^3)$, as with Gaussian process prediction. However, there are other algorithms, such as the sequential minimal optimization (SMO) algorithm due to Platt [1999], which often have better scaling in practice.

Above we have described SVMs for the two-class (binary) classification problem. There are many ways of generalizing SVMs to the multi-class problem, see Schölkopf and Smola [2002, sec. 7.6] for further details.

Comparing Support Vector and Gaussian Process Classifiers

For the soft margin classifier we obtain a solution of the form $\mathbf{w} = \sum_i \alpha_i \mathbf{x}_i$ (with $\alpha_i = \lambda_i y_i$) and thus $|\mathbf{w}|^2 = \sum_{i,j} \alpha_i \alpha_j (\mathbf{x}_i \cdot \mathbf{x}_j)$. Kernelizing this we obtain $|\mathbf{w}|^2 = \boldsymbol{\alpha}^\top K \boldsymbol{\alpha} = \mathbf{f}^\top K^{-1} \mathbf{f}$, as[5] $K\boldsymbol{\alpha} = \mathbf{f}$. Thus the soft margin objective function can be written as

$$\frac{1}{2} \mathbf{f}^\top K^{-1} \mathbf{f} + C \sum_{i=1}^{n} (1 - y_i f_i)_+. \tag{6.37}$$

For the binary GP classifier, to obtain the MAP value $\hat{\mathbf{f}}$ of $p(\mathbf{f}|\mathbf{y})$ we minimize the quantity

$$\frac{1}{2} \mathbf{f}^\top K^{-1} \mathbf{f} - \sum_{i=1}^{n} \log p(y_i|f_i), \tag{6.38}$$

cf. eq. (3.12). (The final two terms in eq. (3.12) are constant if the kernel is fixed.)

For log-concave likelihoods (such as those derived from the logistic or probit response functions) there is a strong similarity between the two optimization problems in that they are both convex. Let $g_\lambda(z) \triangleq \log(1 + e^{-z})$, $g_\Phi = $

---

[5]Here the offset w_0 has been absorbed into the kernel so it is not an explicit extra parameter.

$-\log \Phi(z)$, and $g_{\text{hinge}}(z) \triangleq (1 - z)_+$ where $z = y_i f_i$. We refer to g_{hinge} as the *hinge* error function, due to its shape. As shown in Figure 6.3(a) all three data fit terms are monotonically decreasing functions of z. All three functions tend to infinity as $z \to -\infty$ and decay to zero as $z \to \infty$. The key difference is that the hinge function takes on the value 0 for $z \geq 1$, while the other two just decay slowly. It is this flat part of the hinge function that gives rise to the sparsity of the SVM solution.

hinge error function

Thus there is a close correspondence between the MAP solution of the GP classifier and the SVM solution. Can this correspondence be made closer by considering the hinge function as a negative log likelihood? The answer to this is no [Seeger, 2000, Sollich, 2002]. If $C g_{\text{hinge}}(z)$ defined a negative log likelihood, then $\exp(-C g_{\text{hinge}}(f)) + \exp(-C g_{\text{hinge}}(-f))$ should be a constant independent of f, but this is not the case. To see this, consider the quantity

$$\nu(f; C) = \kappa(C)[\exp(-C(1 - f)_+) + \exp(-C(1 + f)_+)]. \qquad (6.39)$$

$\kappa(C)$ cannot be chosen so as to make $\nu(f; C) = 1$ independent of the value of f for $C > 0$. By comparison, for the logistic and probit likelihoods the analogous expression is equal to 1. Sollich [2002] suggests choosing $\kappa(C) = 1/(1 + \exp(-2C))$ which ensures that $\nu(f, C) \leq 1$ (with equality only when $f = \pm 1$). He also gives an ingenious interpretation (involving a "don't know" class to soak up the unassigned probability mass) that does yield the SVM solution as the MAP solution to a certain Bayesian problem, although we find this construction rather contrived. Exercise 6.7.2 invites you to plot $\nu(f; C)$ as a function of f for various values of C.

One attraction of the GP classifier is that it produces an output with a clear probabilistic interpretation, a prediction for $p(y = +1|\mathbf{x})$. One can try to interpret the function value $f(\mathbf{x})$ output by the SVM probabilistically, and Platt [2000] suggested that probabilistic predictions can be generated from the SVM by computing $\sigma(a f(\mathbf{x}) + b)$ for some constants a, b that are fitted using some "unbiased version" of the training set (e.g. using cross-validation). One disadvantage of this rather *ad hoc* procedure is that unlike the GP classifiers it does not take into account the predictive variance of $f(\mathbf{x})$ (cf. eq. (3.25)). Seeger [2003, sec. 4.7.2] shows that better error-reject curves can be obtained on an experiment using the MNIST digit classification problem when the effect of this uncertainty is taken into account.

6.4.2 Support Vector Regression

The SVM was originally introduced for the classification problem, then extended to deal with the regression case. The key concept is that of the ϵ-insensitive error function. This is defined as

$$g_\epsilon(z) = \begin{cases} |z| - \epsilon & \text{if } |z| \geq \epsilon, \\ 0 & \text{otherwise.} \end{cases} \qquad (6.40)$$

This function is plotted in Figure 6.3(b). As in eq. (6.21) we can interpret $\exp(-g_\epsilon(z))$ as a likelihood model for the regression residuals (c.f. the squared error function corresponding to a Gaussian model). However, we note that this is quite an unusual choice of model for the distribution of residuals and is basically motivated by the desire to obtain a sparse solution (see below) as in support vector classifier. If $\epsilon = 0$ then the error model is a Laplacian distribution, which corresponds to least absolute values regression (Edgeworth [1887], cited in Rousseeuw [1984]); this is a heavier-tailed distribution than the Gaussian and provides some protection against outliers. Girosi [1991] showed that the Laplacian distribution can be viewed as a continuous mixture of zero-mean Gaussians with a certain distribution over their variances. Pontil et al. [1998] extended this result by allowing the means to uniformly shift in $[-\epsilon, \epsilon]$ in order to obtain a probabilistic model corresponding to the ϵ-insensitive error function. See also section 9.3 for work on robustification of the GP regression problem.

For the linear regression case with an ϵ-insensitive error function and a Gaussian prior on $\mathbf{w}$, the MAP value of $\mathbf{w}$ is obtained by minimizing

$$\frac{1}{2}|\mathbf{w}|^2 + C\sum_{i=1}^{n} g_\epsilon(y_i - f_i) \tag{6.41}$$

w.r.t. $\mathbf{w}$. The solution[6] is $f(\mathbf{x}_*) = \sum_{i=1}^{n} \alpha_i \mathbf{x}_i \cdot \mathbf{x}_*$ where the coefficients $\boldsymbol{\alpha}$ are obtained from a QP problem. The problem can also be kernelized to give the solution $f(\mathbf{x}_*) = \sum_{i=1}^{n} \alpha_i k(\mathbf{x}_i, \mathbf{x}_*)$.

As for support vector classification, many of the coefficients α_i are zero. The data points which lie inside the ϵ-"tube" have $\alpha_i = 0$, while those on the edge or outside have non-zero α_i.

* 6.5   Least-squares Classification

In chapter 3 we have argued that the use of logistic or probit likelihoods provides the natural route to develop a GP classifier, and that it is attractive in that the outputs can be interpreted probabilistically. However, there is an even simpler approach which treats classification as a regression problem.

Our starting point is binary classification using the linear predictor $f(\mathbf{x}) = \mathbf{w}^\top\mathbf{x}$. This is trained using linear regression with a target y_+ for patterns that have label $+1$, and target y_- for patterns that have label -1. (Targets y_+, y_- give slightly more flexibility than just using targets of ± 1.) As shown in Duda and Hart [1973, section 5.8], choosing y_+, y_- appropriately allows us to obtain the same solution as Fisher's linear discriminant using the decision criterion $f(\mathbf{x}) \gtrless 0$. Also, they show that using targets $y_+ = +1$, $y_- = -1$ with the least-squares error function gives a minimum squared-error approximation to the Bayes discriminant function $p(\mathcal{C}_+|\mathbf{x}) - p(\mathcal{C}_-|\mathbf{x})$ as $n \to \infty$. Following Rifkin and Klautau [2004] we call such methods least-squares classification (LSC). Note that under a probabilistic interpretation the squared-error criterion is rather an

---

[6]Here we have assumed that the constant 1 is included in the input vector $\mathbf{x}$.

odd choice as it implies a Gaussian noise model, yet only two values of the target (y_+ and y_-) are observed.

It is natural to extend the least-squares classifier using the kernel trick. This has been suggested by a number of authors including Poggio and Girosi [1990] and Suykens and Vanderwalle [1999]. Experimental results reported in Rifkin and Klautau [2004] indicate that performance comparable to SVMs can be obtained using kernel LSC (or as they call it the regularized least-squares classifier, RLSC).

Consider a single random variable y which takes on the value $+1$ with probability p and value -1 with probability $1-p$. Then the value of f which minimizes the squared error function $E = p(f-1)^2 + (1-p)(f+1)^2$ is $\hat{f} = 2p-1$, which is a linear rescaling of p to the interval $[-1, 1]$. (Equivalently if the targets are 1 and 0, we obtain $\hat{f} = p$.) Hence we observe that LSC will estimate p correctly in the large data limit. If we now consider not just a single random variable, but wish to estimate $p(\mathcal{C}_+|\mathbf{x})$ (or a linear rescaling of it), then as long as the approximating function $f(\mathbf{x})$ is sufficiently flexible, we would expect that in the limit $n \to \infty$ it would converge to $p(\mathcal{C}_+|\mathbf{x})$. (For more technical detail on this issue, see section 7.2.1 on consistency.) Hence LSC is quite a sensible procedure for classification, although note that there is no guarantee that $f(\mathbf{x})$ will be constrained to lie in the interval $[y_-, y_+]$. If we wish to guarantee a probabilistic interpretation, we could "squash" the predictions through a sigmoid, as suggested for SVMs by Platt [2000] and described on page 145.

When generalizing from the binary to multi-class situation there is some freedom as to how to set the problem up. Schölkopf and Smola [2002, sec. 7.6] identify four methods, namely one-versus-rest (where C binary classifiers are trained to classify each class against all the rest), all pairs (where $C(C-1)/2$ binary classifiers are trained), error-correcting output coding (where each class is assigned a binary codeword, and binary classifiers are trained on each bit separately), and multi-class objective functions (where the aim is to train C classifiers simultaneously rather than creating a number of binary classification problems). One also needs to specify how the outputs of the various classifiers that are trained are combined so as to produce an overall answer. For the one-versus-rest[7] method one simple criterion is to choose the classifier which produces the most positive output. Rifkin and Klautau [2004] performed extensive experiments and came to the conclusion that the one-versus-rest scheme using either SVMs or RLSC is as accurate as any other method overall, and has the merit of being conceptually simple and straightforward to implement.

6.5.1 Probabilistic Least-squares Classification

The LSC algorithm discussed above is attractive from a computational point of view, but to guarantee a valid probabilistic interpretation one may need to use a separate post-processing stage to "squash" the predictions through a sigmoid. However, it is not so easy to enforce a probabilistic interpretation

---

[7]This method is also sometimes called one-versus-all.

during the training stage. One possible solution is to combine the ideas of training using leave-one-out cross-validation, covered in section 5.4.2, with the use of a (parameterized) sigmoid function, as in Platt [2000]. We will call this method the probabilistic least-squares classifier (PLSC).

In section 5.4.2 we saw how to compute the Gaussian leave-one-out (LOO) predictive probabilities, and that training of hyperparameters can be based on the sum of the log LOO probabilities. Using this idea, we express the LOO probability by squashing a linear function of the Gaussian predictive probability through a cumulative Gaussian

$$
\begin{aligned}
p(y_i|X, \mathbf{y}_{-i}, \boldsymbol{\theta}) &= \int \Phi\big(y_i(\alpha f_i + \beta)\big)\mathcal{N}(f_i|\mu_i, \sigma_i^2)\, df_i \\
&= \Phi\Big(\frac{y_i(\alpha\mu_i + \beta)}{\sqrt{1 + \alpha^2\sigma_i^2}}\Big),
\end{aligned}
\tag{6.42}
$$

where the integral is given in eq. (3.82) and the leave-one-out predictive mean μ_i and variance σ_i^2 are given in eq. (5.12). The objective function is the sum of the log LOO probabilities, eq. (5.11) which can be used to set the hyperparameters as well as the two additional parameters of the linear transformation, α and β in eq. (6.42). Introducing the likelihood in eq. (6.42) into the objective eq. (5.11) and taking derivatives we obtain

$$
\begin{aligned}
\frac{\partial L_{\text{LOO}}}{\partial \theta_j} &= \sum_{i=1}^{n} \frac{\partial \log p(y_i|X, \mathbf{y}_{-i}, \boldsymbol{\theta})}{\partial \mu_i} \frac{\partial \mu_i}{\partial \theta_j} + \frac{\partial \log p(y_i|X, \mathbf{y}_{-i}, \boldsymbol{\theta})}{\partial \sigma_i^2} \frac{\partial \sigma_i^2}{\partial \theta_j} \\
&= \sum_{i=1}^{n} \frac{\mathcal{N}(r_i)}{\Phi(y_i r_i)} \frac{y_i\alpha}{\sqrt{1 + \alpha^2\sigma_i^2}}\Big(\frac{\partial \mu_i}{\partial \theta_j} - \frac{\alpha(\alpha\mu_i + \beta)}{2(1 + \alpha^2\sigma_i^2)} \frac{\partial \sigma_i^2}{\partial \theta_j}\Big),
\end{aligned}
\tag{6.43}
$$

where $r_i = (\alpha\mu_i + \beta)/\sqrt{1 + \alpha^2\sigma_i^2}$ and the partial derivatives of the Gaussian LOO parameters $\partial \mu_i/\partial \theta_j$ and $\partial \sigma_i^2/\partial \theta_j$ are given in eq. (5.13). Finally, for the linear transformation parameters we have

$$
\begin{aligned}
\frac{\partial L_{\text{LOO}}}{\partial \alpha} &= \sum_{i=1}^{n} \frac{\mathcal{N}(r_i)}{\Phi(y_i r_i)} \frac{y_i}{\sqrt{1 + \alpha^2\sigma_i^2}} \frac{\mu_i - \beta\alpha\sigma_i^2}{1 + \alpha^2\sigma_i^2}, \\
\frac{\partial L_{\text{LOO}}}{\partial \beta} &= \sum_{i=1}^{n} \frac{\mathcal{N}(r_i)}{\Phi(y_i r_i)} \frac{y_i}{\sqrt{1 + \alpha^2\sigma_i^2}}.
\end{aligned}
\tag{6.44}
$$

These partial derivatives can be used to train the parameters of the GP. There are several options on how to do predictions, but the most natural would seem to be to compute predictive mean and variance and squash it through the sigmoid, parallelling eq. (6.42). Applying this model to the USPS 3s vs. 5s binary classification task discussed in section 3.7.3, we get a test set error rate of $12/773 = 0.0155\%$, which compares favourably with the results reported for other methods in Figure 3.10. However, the test set information is only 0.77 bits,[8] which is very poor.

---

[8]The test information is dominated by a single test case, which is predicted confidently to belong to the wrong class. Visual inspection of the digit reveals that indeed it looks as though the testset label is wrong for this case. This observation highlights the danger of not explicitly allowing for data mislabelling in the model for this kind of data.

6.6   Relevance Vector Machines   *

Although usually not presented as such, the relevance vector machine (RVM) introduced by Tipping [2001] is actually a special case of a Gaussian process. The covariance function has the form

$$k(\mathbf{x}, \mathbf{x}') = \sum_{j=1}^{N} \frac{1}{\alpha_j} \phi_j(\mathbf{x}) \phi_j(\mathbf{x}'), \qquad (6.45)$$

where α_j are hyperparameters and the N *basis functions* $\phi_j(\mathbf{x})$ are usually, but not necessarily taken to be Gaussian-shaped basis functions centered on each of the n training data points

$$\phi_j(\mathbf{x}) = \exp\left(-\frac{|\mathbf{x} - \mathbf{x}_j|^2}{2\ell^2}\right), \qquad (6.46)$$

where ℓ is a length-scale hyperparameter controlling the width of the basis function. Notice that this is simply the construction for the covariance function corresponding to an N-dimensional set of basis functions given in section 2.1.2, with $\Sigma_p = \mathrm{diag}(\alpha_1^{-1}, \dots, \alpha_N^{-1})$.

The covariance function in eq. (6.45) has two interesting properties: firstly, it is clear that the feature space corresponding to the covariance function is finite dimensional, i.e. the covariance function is *degenerate*, and secondly the covariance function has the odd property that it *depends on the training data*. This dependency means that the prior over functions depends on the data, a property which is at odds with a strict Bayesian interpretation. Although the usual treatment of the model is still possible, this dependency of the prior on the data may lead to some surprising effects, as discussed below.

Training the RVM is analogous to other GP models: optimize the marginal likelihood w.r.t. the hyperparameters. This optimization often leads to a significant number of the α_j hyperparameters tending towards infinity, effectively removing, or *pruning*, the corresponding basis function from the covariance function in eq. (6.45). The basic idea is that basis functions that are not significantly contributing to explaining the data should be removed, resulting in a *sparse* model. The basis functions that survive are called *relevance vectors*. Empirically it is often observed that the number of relevance vectors is smaller than the number of support vectors on the same problem [Tipping, 2001].

relevance vectors

The original RVM algorithm [Tipping, 2001] was not able to exploit the sparsity very effectively during model fitting as it was initialized with all of the α_is set to finite values, meaning that all of the basis functions contributed to the model. However, careful analysis of the RVM marginal likelihood by Faul and Tipping [2002] showed that one can carry out optimization w.r.t. a single α_i analytically. This has led to the accelerated training algorithm described in Tipping and Faul [2003] which starts with an empty model (i.e. all α_is set to infinity) and adds basis functions sequentially. As the number of relevance vectors is (usually much) less than the number of training cases it will often be much faster to train and make predictions using a RVM than a non-sparse

GP. Also note that the basis functions can include additional hyperparameters, e.g. one could use an automatic relevance determination (ARD) form of basis function by using different length-scales on different dimensions in eq. (6.46). These additional hyperparameters could also be set by optimizing the marginal likelihood.

The use of a degenerate covariance function which depends on the data has some undesirable effects. Imagine a test point, $\mathbf{x}_*$, which lies far away from the relevance vectors. At $\mathbf{x}_*$ all basis functions will have values close to zero, and since no basis function can give any appreciable signal, the predictive distribution will be a Gaussian with a mean close to zero and *variance close to zero* (or to the inferred noise level). This behaviour is undesirable, and could lead to dangerously false conclusions. If the $\mathbf{x}_*$ is far from the relevance vectors, then the model shouldn't be able to draw strong conclusions about the output (we are extrapolating), but the predictive uncertainty becomes very small—this is the opposite behaviour of what we would expect from a reasonable model. Here, we have argued that for localized basis functions, the RVM has undesirable properties, but as argued in Rasmussen and Quiñonero-Candela [2005] it is actually the degeneracy of the covariance function which is the core of the problem. Although the work of Rasmussen and Quiñonero-Candela [2005] goes some way towards fixing the problem, there is an inherent conflict: degeneracy of the covariance function is good for computational reasons, but bad for modelling reasons.

6.7   Exercises

1. We motivate the fact that the RKHS norm does not depend on the density $p(\mathbf{x})$ using a finite-dimensional analogue. Consider the n-dimensional vector $\mathbf{f}$, and let the $n \times n$ matrix Φ be comprised of non-colinear columns $\phi_1, \ldots, \phi_n$. Then $\mathbf{f}$ can be expressed as a linear combination of these basis vectors $\mathbf{f} = \sum_{i=1}^n c_i \phi_i = \Phi \mathbf{c}$ for some coefficients $\{c_i\}$. Let the ϕs be eigenvectors of the covariance matrix K w.r.t. a diagonal matrix P with non-negative entries, so that $KP\Phi = \Phi\Lambda$, where Λ is a diagonal matrix containing the eigenvalues. Note that $\Phi^\top P\Phi = I_n$. Show that $\sum_{i=1}^n c_i^2/\lambda_i = \mathbf{c}^\top\Lambda^{-1}\mathbf{c} = \mathbf{f}^\top K^{-1}\mathbf{f}$, and thus observe that $\mathbf{f}^\top K^{-1}\mathbf{f}$ can be expressed as $\mathbf{c}^\top\Lambda^{-1}\mathbf{c}$ for any valid P and corresponding Φ. Hint: you may find it useful to set $\tilde{\Phi} = P^{1/2}\Phi$, $\tilde{K} = P^{1/2}KP^{1/2}$ etc.

2. Plot eq. (6.39) as a function of f for different values of C. Show that there is no value of C and $\kappa(C)$ which makes $\nu(f;C)$ equal to 1 for all values of f. Try setting $\kappa(C) = 1/(1 + \exp(-2C))$ as suggested in Sollich [2002] and observe what effect this has.

3. Show that the predictive mean for the spline covariance GP in eq. (6.29) is a linear function of x_* when x_* is located either to the left or to the right of all training points. Hint: consider the eigenvectors corresponding to the two largest eigenvalues of the training set covariance matrix from eq. (2.40) in the vague limit.

Chapter 7

Theoretical Perspectives

This chapter covers a number of more theoretical issues relating to Gaussian processes. In section 2.6 we saw how GPR carries out a linear smoothing of the datapoints using the weight function. The form of the weight function can be understood in terms of the equivalent kernel, which is discussed in section 7.1.

As one gets more and more data, one would hope that the GP predictions would converge to the true underlying predictive distribution. This question of consistency is reviewed in section 7.2, where we also discuss the concepts of equivalence and orthogonality of GPs.

When the generating process for the data is assumed to be a GP it is particularly easy to obtain results for *learning curves* which describe how the accuracy of the predictor increases as a function of n, as described in section 7.3. An alternative approach to the analysis of generalization error is provided by the PAC-Bayesian analysis discussed in section 7.4. Here we seek to relate (with high probability) the error observed on the training set to the generalization error of the GP predictor.

Gaussian processes are just one of the many methods that have been developed for supervised learning problems. In section 7.5 we compare and contrast GP predictors with other supervised learning methods.

7.1 The Equivalent Kernel

In this section we consider regression problems. We have seen in section 6.2 that the posterior mean for GP regression can be obtained as the function which minimizes the functional

$$J[f] = \frac{1}{2}\|f\|_{\mathcal{H}}^2 + \frac{1}{2\sigma_n^2}\sum_{i=1}^{n}\left(y_i - f(\mathbf{x}_i)\right)^2, \tag{7.1}$$

where $\|f\|_{\mathcal{H}}$ is the RKHS norm corresponding to kernel k. Our goal is now to understand the behaviour of this solution as $n \to \infty$.

Let $\mu(\mathbf{x}, y)$ be the probability measure from which the data pairs $(\mathbf{x}_i, y_i)$ are generated. Observe that

$$\mathbb{E}\Big[\sum_{i=1}^{n}\big(y_i - f(\mathbf{x}_i)\big)^2\Big] = n \int \big(y - f(\mathbf{x})\big)^2 d\mu(\mathbf{x}, y). \tag{7.2}$$

Let $\eta(\mathbf{x}) = \mathbb{E}[y|\mathbf{x}]$ be the *regression function* corresponding to the probability measure μ. The variance around $\eta(\mathbf{x})$ is denoted $\sigma^2(\mathbf{x}) = \int(y - \eta(\mathbf{x}))^2 d\mu(y|\mathbf{x})$. Then writing $y - f = (y - \eta) + (\eta - f)$ we obtain

$$\int \big(y - f(\mathbf{x})\big)^2 d\mu(\mathbf{x}, y) = \int \big(\eta(\mathbf{x}) - f(\mathbf{x})\big)^2 d\mu(\mathbf{x}) + \int \sigma^2(\mathbf{x}) \, d\mu(\mathbf{x}), \tag{7.3}$$

as the cross term vanishes due to the definition of $\eta(\mathbf{x})$.

As the second term on the right hand side of eq. (7.3) is independent of f, an idealization of the regression problem consists of minimizing the functional

$$J_\mu[f] = \frac{n}{2\sigma_n^2} \int \big(\eta(\mathbf{x}) - f(\mathbf{x})\big)^2 d\mu(\mathbf{x}) + \frac{1}{2}\|f\|_{\mathcal{H}}^2. \tag{7.4}$$

The form of the minimizing solution is most easily understood in terms of the eigenfunctions $\{\phi_i(\mathbf{x})\}$ of the kernel k w.r.t. to $\mu(\mathbf{x})$, where $\int \phi_i(\mathbf{x})\phi_j(\mathbf{x})d\mu(\mathbf{x}) = \delta_{ij}$, see section 4.3. Assuming that the kernel is nondegenerate so that the ϕs form a complete orthonormal basis, we write $f(\mathbf{x}) = \sum_{i=1}^{\infty} f_i \phi_i(\mathbf{x})$. Similarly, $\eta(\mathbf{x}) = \sum_{i=1}^{\infty} \eta_i \phi_i(\mathbf{x})$, where $\eta_i = \int \eta(\mathbf{x})\phi_i(\mathbf{x})d\mu(\mathbf{x})$. Thus

$$J_\mu[f] = \frac{n}{2\sigma_n^2} \sum_{i=1}^{\infty} (\eta_i - f_i)^2 + \frac{1}{2}\sum_{i=1}^{\infty} \frac{f_i^2}{\lambda_i}. \tag{7.5}$$

This is readily minimized by differentiation w.r.t. each f_i to obtain

$$f_i = \frac{\lambda_i}{\lambda_i + \sigma_n^2/n}\eta_i. \tag{7.6}$$

Notice that the term $\sigma_n^2/n \to 0$ as $n \to \infty$ so that in this limit we would expect that $f(\mathbf{x})$ will converge to $\eta(\mathbf{x})$. There are two caveats: (1) we have assumed that $\eta(\mathbf{x})$ is sufficiently well-behaved so that it can be represented by the generalized Fourier series $\sum_{i=1}^{\infty} \eta_i \phi_i(\mathbf{x})$, and (2) we assumed that the kernel is nondegenerate. If the kernel is degenerate (e.g. a polynomial kernel) then f should converge to the best μ-weighted L_2 approximation to η within the span of the ϕ's. In section 7.2.1 we will say more about rates of convergence of f to η; clearly in general this will depend on the smoothness of η, the kernel k and the measure $\mu(\mathbf{x}, y)$.

From a Bayesian perspective what is happening is that the prior on f is being overwhelmed by the data as $n \to \infty$. Looking at eq. (7.6) we also see that if $\sigma_n^2 \gg n\lambda_i$ then f_i is effectively zero. This means that we cannot find out about the coefficients of eigenfunctions with small eigenvalues until we get sufficient amounts of data. Ferrari Trecate et al. [1999] demonstrated this by showing that regression performance of a certain nondegenerate GP could be approximated by taking the first m eigenfunctions, where m was chosen so that $\lambda_m \simeq \sigma_n^2/n$. Of course as more data is obtained then m has to be increased.

Using the fact that $\eta_i = \int \eta(\mathbf{x}')\phi_i(\mathbf{x}')d\mu(\mathbf{x}')$ and defining $\sigma_{\mathrm{eff}}^2 \triangleq \sigma_n^2/n$ we obtain

$$f(\mathbf{x}) = \sum_{i=1}^{\infty} \frac{\lambda_i \eta_i}{\lambda_i + \sigma_{\mathrm{eff}}^2}\phi_i(\mathbf{x}) = \int \Big[\sum_{i=1}^{\infty} \frac{\lambda_i \phi_i(\mathbf{x})\phi_i(\mathbf{x}')}{\lambda_i + \sigma_{\mathrm{eff}}^2}\Big]\eta(\mathbf{x}')\,d\mu(\mathbf{x}'). \qquad (7.7)$$

The term in square brackets in eq. (7.7) is the *equivalent kernel* for the smoothing problem; we denote it by $h_n(\mathbf{x}, \mathbf{x}')$. Notice the similarity to the vector-valued weight function $\mathbf{h}(\mathbf{x})$ defined in section 2.6. The difference is that there the prediction was obtained as a linear combination of a finite number of observations y_i with weights given by $h_i(\mathbf{x})$ while here we have a noisy function $y(\mathbf{x})$ instead, with $\bar{f}(\mathbf{x}') = \int h_n(\mathbf{x}, \mathbf{x}')y(\mathbf{x})d\mu(\mathbf{x})$. Notice that in the limit $n \to \infty$ (so that $\sigma_{\mathrm{eff}}^2 \to 0$) the equivalent kernel tends towards the delta function. equivalent kernel

The form of the equivalent kernel given in eq. (7.7) is not very useful in practice as it requires knowledge of the eigenvalues/functions for the combination of k and μ. However, in the case of stationary kernels we can use Fourier methods to compute the equivalent kernel. Consider the functional

$$J_\rho[f] = \frac{\rho}{2\sigma_n^2}\int (y(\mathbf{x}) - f(\mathbf{x}))^2 \, d\mathbf{x} + \frac{1}{2}\|f\|_{\mathcal{H}}^2, \qquad (7.8)$$

where ρ has dimensions of the number of observations per unit of $\mathbf{x}$-space (length/area/volume etc. as appropriate). Using a derivation similar to eq. (7.6) we obtain

$$\tilde{h}(\mathbf{s}) = \frac{S_f(\mathbf{s})}{S_f(\mathbf{s}) + \sigma_n^2/\rho} = \frac{1}{1 + S_f^{-1}(\mathbf{s})\sigma_n^2/\rho}, \qquad (7.9)$$

where $S_f(\mathbf{s})$ is the power spectrum of the kernel k. The term σ_n^2/ρ corresponds to the power spectrum of a white noise process, as the delta function covariance function of white noise corresponds to a constant in the Fourier domain. This analysis is known as Wiener filtering; see, e.g. Papoulis [1991, sec. 14-1]. Equation (7.9) is the same as eq. (7.6) except that the discrete eigenspectrum has been replaced by a continuous one. Wiener filtering

As can be observed in Figure 2.6, the equivalent kernel essentially gives a weighting to the observations locally around $\mathbf{x}$. Thus identifying ρ with $np(\mathbf{x})$ we can obtain an approximation to the equivalent kernel for stationary kernels when the width of the kernel is smaller than the length-scale of variations in $p(\mathbf{x})$. This form of analysis was used by Silverman [1984] for splines in one dimension.

7.1.1 Some Specific Examples of Equivalent Kernels

We first consider the OU process in 1-d. This has $k(r) = \exp(-\alpha|r|)$ (setting $\alpha = 1/\ell$ relative to our previous notation and $r = x - x'$), and power spectrum

$S(s) = 2\alpha/(4\pi^2 s^2 + \alpha^2)$. Let $v_n \triangleq \sigma_n^2/\rho$. Using eq. (7.9) we obtain

$$\tilde{h}(s) = \frac{2\alpha}{v_n(4\pi^2 s^2 + \beta^2)}, \tag{7.10}$$

where $\beta^2 = \alpha^2 + 2\alpha/v_n$. This again has the form of Fourier transform of an OU covariance function[1] and can be inverted to obtain $h(r) = \frac{\alpha}{v_n\beta}e^{-\beta|r|}$. In particular notice that as n increases (and thus v_n decreases) the inverse length-scale β of $h(r)$ increases; asymptotically $\beta \sim n^{1/2}$ for large n. This shows that the width of equivalent kernel for the OU covariance function will scale as $n^{-1/2}$ asymptotically. Similarly the width will scale as $p(\mathbf{x})^{-1/2}$ asymptotically.

A similar analysis can be carried out for the AR(2) Gaussian process in 1-d (see section B.2) which has a power spectrum $\propto (4\pi^2 s^2 + \alpha^2)^{-2}$ (i.e. it is in the Matérn class with $\nu = 3/2$). In this case we can show (using the Fourier relationships given by Papoulis [1991, p. 326]) that the width of the equivalent kernel scales as $n^{-1/4}$ asymptotically.

Analysis of the equivalent kernel has also been carried out for spline models. Silverman [1984] gives the explicit form of the equivalent kernel in the case of a one-dimensional cubic spline (corresponding to the regularizer $\|Pf\|^2 = \int (f'')^2 dx$). Thomas-Agnan [1996] gives a general expression for the equivalent kernel for the spline regularizer $\|Pf\|^2 = \int (f^{(m)})^2 dx$ in one dimension and also analyzes end-effects if the domain of interest is a bounded open interval. For the regularizer $\|Pf\|^2 = \int (\nabla^2 f)^2 d\mathbf{x}$ in two dimensions, the equivalent kernel is given in terms of the Kelvin function kei (Poggio et al. 1985, Stein 1991).

Silverman [1984] has also shown that for splines of order m in 1-d (corresponding to a roughness penalty of $\int (f^{(m)})^2 dx$) the width of the equivalent kernel will scale as $n^{-1/2m}$ asymptotically. In fact it can be shown that this is true for splines in $D > 1$ dimensions too, see exercise 7.7.1.

Another interesting case to consider is the squared exponential kernel, where $S(\mathbf{s}) = (2\pi\ell^2)^{D/2}\exp(-2\pi^2\ell^2|\mathbf{s}|^2)$. Thus

$$\tilde{h}_{\text{SE}}(\mathbf{s}) = \frac{1}{1 + b\exp(2\pi^2\ell^2|\mathbf{s}|^2)}, \tag{7.11}$$

where $b = \sigma_n^2/\rho(2\pi\ell^2)^{D/2}$. We are unaware of an exact result in this case, but the following approximation due to Sollich and Williams [2005] is simple but effective. For large ρ (i.e. large n) b will be small. Thus for small $s = |\mathbf{s}|$ we have that $\tilde{h}_{\text{SE}} \simeq 1$, but for large s it is approximately 0. The change takes place around the point s_c where $b\exp(2\pi^2\ell^2 s_c^2) = 1$, i.e. $s_c^2 = \log(1/b)/2\pi^2\ell^2$. As $\exp(2\pi^2\ell^2 s^2)$ grows quickly with s, the transition of $\tilde{h}_{\text{SE}}$ between 1 and 0 can be expected to be rapid, and thus well-approximated by a step function. By using the standard result for the Fourier transform of the step function we obtain

$$h_{\text{SE}}(x) = 2s_c\text{sinc}(2\pi s_c x) \tag{7.12}$$

---

[1] The fact that $\tilde{h}(s)$ has the same form as $S_f(s)$ is particular to the OU covariance function and is not generally the case.

for $D = 1$, where $\text{sinc}(z) = \sin(z)/z$. A similar calculation in $D > 1$ using eq. (4.7) gives

$$h_{\text{SE}}(r) = \left(\frac{s_c}{r}\right)^{D/2} J_{D/2}(2\pi s_c r). \tag{7.13}$$

Notice that s_c scales as $(\log(n))^{1/2}$ so that the width of the equivalent kernel will decay very slowly as n increases. Notice that the plots in Figure 2.6 show the sinc-type shape, although the sidelobes are not quite as large as would be predicted by the sinc curve (because the transition is smoother than a step function in Fourier space so there is less "ringing").

7.2   Asymptotic Analysis   *

In this section we consider two asymptotic properties of Gaussian processes, consistency and equivalence/orthogonality.

7.2.1   Consistency

In section 7.1 we have analyzed the asymptotics of GP regression and have seen how the minimizer of the functional eq. (7.4) converges to the regression function as $n \to \infty$. We now broaden the focus by considering loss functions other than squared loss, and the case where we work directly with eq. (7.1) rather than the smoothed version eq. (7.4).

The set up is as follows: Let $\mathcal{L}(\cdot, \cdot)$ be a pointwise loss function. Consider a procedure that takes training data $\mathcal{D}$ and this loss function, and returns a function $f_{\mathcal{D}}(\mathbf{x})$. For a measurable function f, the risk (expected loss) is defined as

$$R_{\mathcal{L}}(f) = \int \mathcal{L}(y, f(\mathbf{x})) \, d\mu(\mathbf{x}, y). \tag{7.14}$$

Let $f_{\mathcal{L}}^*$ denote the function that minimizes this risk. For squared loss $f_{\mathcal{L}}^*(\mathbf{x}) = \mathbb{E}[y|\mathbf{x}]$. For 0/1 loss with classification problems, we choose $f_{\mathcal{L}}^*(\mathbf{x})$ to be the class c at $\mathbf{x}$ such that $p(\mathcal{C}_c|\mathbf{x}) > p(\mathcal{C}_j|\mathbf{x})$ for all $j \neq c$ (breaking ties arbitrarily).

Definition 7.1 *We will say that a procedure that returns $f_{\mathcal{D}}$ is* consistent *for*   consistency *a given measure $\mu(\mathbf{x}, y)$ and loss function $\mathcal{L}$ if*

$$R_{\mathcal{L}}(f_{\mathcal{D}}) \to R_{\mathcal{L}}(f_{\mathcal{L}}^*) \qquad \text{as } n \to \infty, \tag{7.15}$$

where convergence is assessed in a suitable manner, e.g. in probability. If $f_{\mathcal{D}}(\mathbf{x})$ is consistent for all Borel probability measures $\mu(\mathbf{x}, y)$ then it is said to be universally consistent. □

A simple example of a consistent procedure is the kernel regression method. As described in section 2.6 one obtains a prediction at test point $\mathbf{x}_*$ by computing $\hat{f}(\mathbf{x}_*) = \sum_{i=1}^{n} w_i y_i$ where $w_i = \kappa_i / \sum_{j=1}^{n} \kappa_j$ (the Nadaraya-Watson estimator). Let h be the width of the kernel κ and D be the dimension of the input space. It can be shown that under suitable regularity conditions if $h \to 0$ and $nh^D \to \infty$ as $n \to \infty$ then the procedure is consistent; see e.g. [Györfi et al., 2002, Theorem 5.1] for the regression case with squared loss and Devroye et al. [1996, Theorem 10.1] for the classification case using 0/1 loss. An intuitive understanding of this result can be obtained by noting that $h \to 0$ means that only datapoints very close to $\mathbf{x}_*$ will contribute to the prediction (eliminating bias), while the condition $nh^D \to \infty$ means that a large number of datapoints will contribute to the prediction (eliminating noise/variance).

It will first be useful to consider why we might hope that GPR and GPC should be universally consistent. As discussed in section 7.1, the key property is that a non-degenerate kernel will have an infinite number of eigenfunctions forming an orthonormal set. Thus from generalized Fourier analysis a linear combination of eigenfunctions $\sum_{i=1}^{\infty} c_i \phi_i(\mathbf{x})$ should be able to represent a sufficiently well-behaved target function $f_{\mathcal{L}}^*$. However, we have to estimate the infinite number of coefficients $\{c_i\}$ from the noisy observations. This makes it clear that we are playing a game involving infinities which needs to be played with care, and there are some results [Diaconis and Freedman, 1986, Freedman, 1999, Grünwald and Langford, 2004] which show that in certain circumstances Bayesian inference in infinite-dimensional objects can be inconsistent.

However, there are some positive recent results on the consistency of GPR and GPC. Choudhuri et al. [2005] show that for the binary classification case under certain assumptions GPC is consistent. The assumptions include smoothness on the mean and covariance function of the GP, smoothness on $\mathbb{E}[y|\mathbf{x}]$ and an assumption that the domain is a bounded subset of $\mathbb{R}^D$. Their result holds for the class of response functions which are c.d.f.s of a unimodal symmetric density; this includes the probit and logistic functions.

For GPR, Choi and Schervish [2004] show that for a one-dimensional input space of finite length under certain assumptions consistency holds. Here the assumptions again include smoothness of the mean and covariance function of the GP and smoothness of $\mathbb{E}[y|\mathbf{x}]$. An additional assumption is that the noise has a normal or Laplacian distribution (with an unknown variance which is inferred).

There are also some consistency results relating to the functional

$$J_{\lambda_n}[f] \;=\; \frac{\lambda_n}{2}\|f\|_{\mathcal{H}}^2 + \frac{1}{n}\sum_{i=1}^{n} \mathcal{L}\big(y_i, f(\mathbf{x}_i)\big), \qquad (7.16)$$

where $\lambda_n \to 0$ as $n \to \infty$. Note that to agree with our previous formulations we would set $\lambda_n = 1/n$, but other decay rates on λ_n are often considered.

In the splines literature, Cox [1984] showed that for regression problems using the regularizer $\|f\|_m^2 = \sum_{k=0}^{m} \|O^k f\|^2$ (using the definitions in eq. (6.10)) consistency can be obtained under certain technical conditions. Cox and O'Sullivan [1990] considered a wide range of problems (including regression problems with squared loss and classification using logistic loss) where the solution is obtained by minimizing the regularized risk using a spline smoothness term. They showed that if $f_{\mathcal{L}}^* \in \mathcal{H}$ (where $\mathcal{H}$ is the RKHS corresponding to the spline regularizer) then as $n \to \infty$ and $\lambda_n \to 0$ at an appropriate rate, one gets convergence of $f_{\mathcal{D}}$ to $f_{\mathcal{L}}^*$.

More recently, Zhang [2004, Theorem 4.4] has shown that for the classification problem with a number of different loss functions (including logistic loss, hinge loss and quadratic loss) and for general RKHSs with a nondegenerate kernel, that if $\lambda_n \to 0$, $\lambda_n n \to \infty$ and $\mu(\mathbf{x}, y)$ is sufficiently regular then the classification error of $f_{\mathcal{D}}$ will converge to the Bayes optimal error in probability as $n \to \infty$. Similar results have also been obtained by Steinwart [2005] with various rates on the decay of λ_n depending on the smoothness of the kernel. Bartlett et al. [2003] have characterized the loss functions that lead to universal consistency.

Above we have focussed on regression and classification problems. However, similar analyses can also be given for other problems such as density estimation and deconvolution; see Wahba [1990, chs. 8, 9] for references. Also we have discussed consistency using a fixed decay rate for λ_n. However, it is also possible to analyze the asymptotics of methods where λ_n is set in a data-dependent way, e.g. by cross-validation;[2] see Wahba [1990, sec. 4.5] and references therein for further details.

Consistency is evidently a desirable property of supervised learning procedures. However, it is an asymptotic property that does not say very much about how a given prediction procedure will perform on a particular problem with a given dataset. For instance, note that we only required rather general properties of the kernel function (e.g. non-degeneracy) for some of the consistency results. However, the choice of the kernel can make a huge difference to how a procedure performs in practice. Some analyses related to this issue are given in section 7.3.

7.2.2   Equivalence and Orthogonality

The presentation in this section is based mainly on Stein [1999, ch. 4]. For two probability measures μ_0 and μ_1 defined on a measurable space $(\Omega, \mathcal{F})$,[3] μ_0 is said to be *absolutely continuous* w.r.t. μ_1 if for all $A \in \mathcal{F}$, $\mu_1(A) = 0$ implies $\mu_0(A) = 0$. If μ_0 is absolutely continuous w.r.t. μ_1 and μ_1 is absolutely continuous w.r.t. μ_0 the two measures are said to be *equivalent*, written $\mu_0 \equiv \mu_1$. μ_0 and μ_1 are said to be *orthogonal*, written $\mu_0 \perp \mu_1$, if there exists an $A \in \mathcal{F}$ such that $\mu_0(A) = 1$ and $\mu_1(A) = 0$. (Note that in this case we have $\mu_0(A^c) = 0$ and $\mu_1(A^c) = 1$, where A^c is the complement of A.) The dichotomy theorem for Gaussian processes (due to Hajek [1958] and, independently, Feldman [1958]) states that two Gaussian processes are either equivalent or orthogonal.

Equivalence and orthogonality for Gaussian measures μ_0, μ_1 with corresponding probability densities p_0, p_1, can be characterized in terms of the

---

[2]Cross validation is discussed in section 5.3.
[3]See section A.7 for background on measurable spaces.

symmetrized Kullback-Leibler divergence KL_{sym} between them, given by

$$KL_{sym}(p_0, p_1) = \int (p_0(\mathbf{f}) - p_1(\mathbf{f})) \log \frac{p_0(\mathbf{f})}{p_1(\mathbf{f})} d\mathbf{f}. \qquad (7.17)$$

The measures are equivalent if $KL_{sym} < \infty$ and orthogonal otherwise. For two finite-dimensional Gaussian distributions $\mathcal{N}(\boldsymbol{\mu}_0, K_0)$ and $\mathcal{N}(\boldsymbol{\mu}_1, K_1)$ we have [Kullback, 1959, sec. 9.1]

$$\begin{aligned} KL_{sym} &= \tfrac{1}{2} \operatorname{tr}(K_0 - K_1)(K_1^{-1} - K_0^{-1}) \\ &+ \tfrac{1}{2} \operatorname{tr}(K_1^{-1} + K_0^{-1})(\boldsymbol{\mu}_0 - \boldsymbol{\mu}_1)(\boldsymbol{\mu}_0 - \boldsymbol{\mu}_1)^\top. \end{aligned} \qquad (7.18)$$

This expression can be simplified considerably by simultaneously diagonalizing K_0 and K_1. Two finite-dimensional Gaussian distributions are equivalent if the null spaces of their covariance matrices coincide, and are orthogonal otherwise.

Things can get more interesting if we consider infinite-dimensional distributions, i.e. Gaussian processes. Consider some closed subset $R \in \mathbb{R}^D$. Choose some finite number n of $\mathbf{x}$-points in R and let $\mathbf{f} = (f_1, \ldots, f_n)^\top$ denote the values corresponding to these inputs. We consider the KL_{sym}-divergence as above, but in the limit $n \to \infty$. KL_{sym} can now diverge if the rates of decay of the eigenvalues of the two processes are not the same. For example, consider zero-mean periodic processes with period 1 where the eigenvalue λ_j^i indicates the amount of power in the sin/cos terms of frequency $2\pi j$ for process $i = 0, 1$. Then using eq. (7.18) we have

$$KL_{sym} = \frac{(\lambda_0^0 - \lambda_0^1)^2}{\lambda_0^0 \lambda_0^1} + 2 \sum_{j=1}^{\infty} \frac{(\lambda_j^0 - \lambda_j^1)^2}{\lambda_j^0 \lambda_j^1} \qquad (7.19)$$

(see also [Stein, 1999, p. 119]). Some corresponding results for the equivalence or orthogonality of non-periodic Gaussian processes are given in Stein [1999, pp. 119-122]. Stein (p. 109) gives an example of two equivalent Gaussian processes on $\mathbb{R}$, those with covariance functions $\exp(-r)$ and $1/2\exp(-2r)$. (It is easy to check that for large s these have the same power spectrum.)

We now turn to the consequences of equivalence for the model selection problem. Suppose that we know that either $\mathcal{GP}_0$ or $\mathcal{GP}_1$ is the correct model. Then if $\mathcal{GP}_0 \equiv \mathcal{GP}_1$ then it is not possible to determine which model is correct with probability 1. However, under a Bayesian setting all this means is if we have prior probabilities π_0 and $\pi_1 = 1 - \pi_0$ on these two hypotheses, then after observing some data $\mathcal{D}$ the posterior probabilities $p(\mathcal{GP}_i|\mathcal{D})$ (for $i = 0, 1$) will not be 0 or 1, but could be heavily skewed to one model or the other.

The other important observation is to consider the predictions made by $\mathcal{GP}_0$ or $\mathcal{GP}_1$. Consider the case where $\mathcal{GP}_0$ is the correct model and $\mathcal{GP}_1 \equiv \mathcal{GP}_0$. Then Stein [1999, sec. 4.3] shows that the predictions of $\mathcal{GP}_1$ are asymptotically optimal, in the sense that the expected relative prediction error between $\mathcal{GP}_1$ and $\mathcal{GP}_0$ tends to 0 as $n \to \infty$ under some technical conditions. Stein's Corollary 9 (p. 132) shows that this conclusion remains true under additive noise if the un-noisy GPs are equivalent. One caveat about equivalence is although the predictions of $\mathcal{GP}_1$ are asymptotically optimal when $\mathcal{GP}_0$ is the correct model and $\mathcal{GP}_0 \equiv \mathcal{GP}_1$, one would see differing predictions for finite n.

7.3   Average-case Learning Curves   *

In section 7.2 we have discussed the asymptotic properties of Gaussian process predictors and related methods. In this section we will say more about the speed of convergence under certain specific assumptions. Our goal will be to obtain a *learning curve* describing the generalization error as a function of the training set size n. This is an average-case analysis, averaging over the choice of target functions (drawn from a GP) and over the **x** locations of the training points.

In more detail, we first consider a target function f drawn from a Gaussian process. n locations are chosen to make observations at, giving rise to the training set $\mathcal{D} = (X, \mathbf{y})$. The y_is are (possibly) noisy observations of the underlying function f. Given a loss function $\mathcal{L}(\cdot, \cdot)$ which measures the difference between the prediction for f and f itself, we obtain an estimator $f_{\mathcal{D}}$ for f. Below we will use the squared loss, so that the posterior mean $\bar{f}_{\mathcal{D}}(\mathbf{x})$ is the estimator. Then the *generalization error* (given f and $\mathcal{D}$) is given by

generalization error

$$E^g_{\mathcal{D}}(f) \;=\; \int \mathcal{L}(f(\mathbf{x}_*), \bar{f}_{\mathcal{D}}(\mathbf{x}_*)) p(\mathbf{x}_*) \, d\mathbf{x}_*. \tag{7.20}$$

As this is an expected loss it is technically a risk, but the term generalization error is commonly used.

$E^g_{\mathcal{D}}(f)$ depends on both the choice of f and on X. (Note that **y** depends on the choice of f, and also on the noise, if present.) The first level of averaging we consider is over functions f drawn from a GP prior, to obtain

$$E^g(X) \;=\; \int E^g_{\mathcal{D}}(f) p(f) \, df. \tag{7.21}$$

It will turn out that for regression problems with Gaussian process priors and predictors this average can be readily calculated. The second level of averaging assumes that the **x**-locations of the training set are drawn i.i.d. from $p(\mathbf{x})$ to give

$$E^g(n) \;=\; \int E^g(X) p(\mathbf{x}_1) \ldots p(\mathbf{x}_n) \, dx_1 \ldots dx_n. \tag{7.22}$$

A plot of $E^g(n)$ against n is known as a *learning curve*.

learning curve

Rather than averaging over X, an alternative is to minimize $E^g(X)$ w.r.t. X. This gives rise to the *optimal experimental design* problem. We will not say more about this problem here, but it has been subject to a large amount of investigation. An early paper on this subject is by Ylvisaker [1975]. These questions have been addressed both in the statistical literature and in theoretical numerical analysis; for the latter area the book by Ritter [2000] provides a useful overview.

We now proceed to develop the average-case analysis further for the specific case of GP predictors and GP priors for the regression case using squared loss. Let f be drawn from a zero-mean GP with covariance function k_0 and noise level σ_0^2. Similarly the predictor assumes a zero-mean process, but covariance function k_1 and noise level σ_1^2. At a particular test location $\mathbf{x}_*$, averaging over f we have

$$\mathbb{E}[(f(\mathbf{x}_*) - \mathbf{k}_1(\mathbf{x}_*)^\top K_{1,y}^{-1}\mathbf{y})^2] \tag{7.23}$$
$$= \mathbb{E}[f^2(\mathbf{x}_*)] - 2\mathbf{k}_1(\mathbf{x}_*)^\top K_{1,y}^{-1}\mathbb{E}[f(\mathbf{x}_*)\mathbf{y}] + \mathbf{k}_1(\mathbf{x}_*)^\top K_{1,y}^{-1}\mathbb{E}[\mathbf{y}\mathbf{y}^\top]K_{1,y}^{-1}\mathbf{k}_1(\mathbf{x}_*)$$
$$= k_0(\mathbf{x}_*,\mathbf{x}_*) - 2\mathbf{k}_1(\mathbf{x}_*)^\top K_{1,y}^{-1}\mathbf{k}_0(\mathbf{x}_*) + \mathbf{k}_1(\mathbf{x})^\top K_{1,y}^{-1}K_{0,y}K_{1,y}^{-1}\mathbf{k}_1(\mathbf{x}_*)$$

where $K_{i,y} = K_{i,f} + \sigma_i^2$ for $i = 0,\ 1$, i.e. the covariance matrix including the assumed noise. If $k_1 = k_0$ so that the predictor is correctly specified then the above expression reduces to $k_0(\mathbf{x}_*,\mathbf{x}_*) - \mathbf{k}_0(\mathbf{x}_*)^\top K_{0,y}^{-1}\mathbf{k}_0(\mathbf{x}_*)$, the predictive variance of the GP.

Averaging the error over $p(\mathbf{x}_*)$ we obtain

$$E^g(X) = \int \mathbb{E}[(f(\mathbf{x}_*) - \mathbf{k}_1(\mathbf{x}_*)^\top K_{1,y}^{-1}\mathbf{y})^2]p(\mathbf{x}_*)\,d\mathbf{x}_* \tag{7.24}$$
$$= \int k_0(\mathbf{x}_*,\mathbf{x}_*)p(\mathbf{x}_*)\,d\mathbf{x}_* - 2\operatorname{tr}\left(K_{1,y}^{-1}\int \mathbf{k}_0(\mathbf{x}_*)\mathbf{k}_1(\mathbf{x}_*)^\top p(\mathbf{x}_*)\,d\mathbf{x}_*\right)$$
$$+ \operatorname{tr}\left(K_{1,y}^{-1}K_{0,y}K_{1,y}^{-1}\int \mathbf{k}_1(\mathbf{x}_*)\mathbf{k}_1(\mathbf{x})^\top p(\mathbf{x}_*)\,d\mathbf{x}_*\right).$$

For some choices of $p(\mathbf{x}_*)$ and the covariance functions these integrals will be analytically tractable, reducing the computation of $E^g(X)$ to a $n \times n$ matrix computation.

To obtain $E^g(n)$ we need to perform a final level of averaging over X. In general this is difficult even if $E^g(X)$ can be computed exactly, but it is sometimes possible, e.g. for the noise-free OU process on the real line, see section 7.6.

The form of $E^g(X)$ can be simplified considerably if we express the covariance functions in terms of their eigenfunction expansions. In the case that $k_0 = k_1$ we use the definition $k(\mathbf{x},\mathbf{x}') = \sum_i \lambda_i\phi_i(\mathbf{x})\phi_i(\mathbf{x}')$ and $\int k(\mathbf{x},\mathbf{x}')\phi_i(\mathbf{x})p(\mathbf{x})\,d\mathbf{x} = \lambda_i\phi_i(\mathbf{x}')$. Let Λ be a diagonal matrix of the eigenvalues and Φ be the $N \times n$ design matrix, as defined in section 2.1.2. Then from eq. (7.24) we obtain

$$E^g(X) = \operatorname{tr}(\Lambda) - \operatorname{tr}((\sigma_n^2 I + \Phi^\top\Lambda\Phi)^{-1}\Phi^\top\Lambda^2\Phi)$$
$$= \operatorname{tr}(\Lambda^{-1} + \sigma_n^{-2}\Phi\Phi^\top)^{-1}, \tag{7.25}$$

where the second line follows through the use of the matrix inversion lemma eq. (A.9) (or directly if we use eq. (2.11)), as shown in Sollich [1999] or Opper and Vivarelli [1999]. Using the fact that $\mathbb{E}_X[\Phi\Phi^\top] = nI$, a naïve approximation would replace $\Phi\Phi^\top$ inside the trace with its expectation; in fact Opper and Vivarelli [1999] showed that this gives a lower bound, so that

$$E^g(n) \geq \operatorname{tr}(\Lambda^{-1} + n\sigma_n^{-2}I)^{-1} = \sigma^2 \sum_{i=1}^{N} \frac{\lambda_i}{\sigma_n^2 + n\lambda_i}. \tag{7.26}$$

Examining the asymptotics of eq. (7.26), we see that for each eigenvalue where $\lambda_i \gg \sigma_n^2/n$ we add σ_n^2/n onto the bound on the generalization error. As we saw in section 7.1, more eigenfunctions "come into play" as n increases, so the rate of decay of $E^g(n)$ is slower than $1/n$. Sollich [1999] derives a number of more accurate approximations to the learning curve than eq. (7.26).

For the noiseless case with $k_1 = k_0$, there is a simple lower bound $E^g(n) \geq \sum_{i=n+1}^{\infty} \lambda_i$ due to Micchelli and Wahba [1981]. This bound is obtained by demonstrating that the optimal n pieces of information are the projections of the random function f onto the first n eigenfunctions. As observations which simply consist of function evaluations will not in general provide such information this is a lower bound. Plaskota [1996] generalized this result to give a bound on the learning curve if the observations are noisy.

Some asymptotic results for the learning curves are known. For example, in Ritter [2000, sec. V.2] covariance functions obeying Sacks-Ylvisaker conditions[4] of order r in 1-d are considered. He shows that for an optimal sampling of the input space the generalization error goes as $\mathcal{O}(n^{-(2r+1)/(2r+2)})$ for the noisy problem. Similar rates can also be found in Sollich [2002] for random designs. For the noise-free case Ritter [2000, p. 103] gives the rate as $\mathcal{O}(n^{-(2r+1)})$.

One can examine the learning curve not only asymptotically but also for small n, where typically the curve has a roughly linear decrease with n. Williams and Vivarelli [2000] explained this behaviour by observing that the introduction of a datapoint $\mathbf{x}_1$ reduces the variance locally around $\mathbf{x}_1$ (assuming a stationary covariance function). The addition of another datapoint at $\mathbf{x}_2$ will also create a "hole" there, and so on. With only a small number of datapoints it is likely that these holes will be far apart so their contributions will add, thus explaining the initial linear trend.

Sollich [2002] has also investigated the mismatched case where $k_0 \neq k_1$. This can give rise to a rich variety of behaviours in the learning curves, including plateaux. Stein [1999, chs. 3, 4] has also carried out some analysis of the mismatched case.

Although we have focused on GP regression with squared loss, we note that Malzahn and Opper [2002] have developed more general techniques that can be used to analyze learning curves for other situations such as GP classification.

7.4   PAC-Bayesian Analysis   *

In section 7.3 we gave an *average-case* analysis of generalization, taking the average with respect to a GP prior over functions. In this section we present a different kind of analysis within the *probably approximately correct* (PAC) framework due to Valiant [1984]. Seeger [2002; 2003] has presented a PAC-Bayesian analysis of generalization in Gaussian process classifiers and we get to this in a number of stages; we first present an introduction to the PAC framework (section 7.4.1), then describe the PAC-Bayesian approach (section

PAC

---

[4]Roughly speaking, a stochastic process which possesses r MS derivatives but not $r+1$ is said to satisfy Sacks-Ylvisaker conditions of order r; in 1-d this gives rise to a spectrum $\lambda_i \propto i^{-(2r+2)}$ asymptotically. The OU process obeys Sacks-Ylvisaker conditions of order 0.

7.4.2) and then finally the application to GP classification (section 7.4.3). Our presentation is based mainly on Seeger [2003].

7.4.1   The PAC Framework

Consider a fixed measure $\mu(\mathbf{x}, y)$. Given a loss function $\mathcal{L}$ there exists a function $\eta(\mathbf{x})$ which minimizes the expected risk. By running a learning algorithm on a data set $\mathcal{D}$ of size n drawn i.i.d. from $\mu(\mathbf{x}, y)$ we obtain an estimate $f_{\mathcal{D}}$ of η which attains an expected risk $R_{\mathcal{L}}(f_{\mathcal{D}})$. We are not able to evaluate $R_{\mathcal{L}}(f_{\mathcal{D}})$ as we do not know μ. However, we do have access to the empirical distribution of the training set $\hat{\mu}(\mathbf{x}, y) = \frac{1}{n} \sum_i \delta(\mathbf{x} - \mathbf{x}_i)\delta(y - y_i)$ and can compute the empirical risk $\hat{R}_{\mathcal{L}}(f_{\mathcal{D}}) = \frac{1}{n} \sum_i \mathcal{L}(y_i, f_{\mathcal{D}}(\mathbf{x}_i))$. Because the training set had been used to compute $f_{\mathcal{D}}$ we would expect $\hat{R}_{\mathcal{L}}(f_{\mathcal{D}})$ to underestimate $R_{\mathcal{L}}(f_{\mathcal{D}})$,[5] and the aim of the PAC analysis is to provide a bound on $R_{\mathcal{L}}(f_{\mathcal{D}})$ based on $\hat{R}_{\mathcal{L}}(f_{\mathcal{D}})$.

A PAC bound has the following format

$$p_{\mathcal{D}}\{R_{\mathcal{L}}(f_{\mathcal{D}}) \leq \hat{R}_{\mathcal{L}}(f_{\mathcal{D}}) + \mathrm{gap}(f_{\mathcal{D}}, \mathcal{D}, \delta)\} \geq 1 - \delta, \qquad (7.27)$$

where $p_{\mathcal{D}}$ denotes the probability distribution of datasets drawn i.i.d. from $\mu(\mathbf{x}, y)$, and $\delta \in (0, 1)$ is called the confidence parameter. The bound states that, averaged over draws of the dataset $\mathcal{D}$ from $\mu(\mathbf{x}, y)$, $R_{\mathcal{L}}(f_{\mathcal{D}})$ does not exceed the sum of $\hat{R}_{\mathcal{L}}(f_{\mathcal{D}})$ and the gap term with probability of at least $1 - \delta$. The δ accounts for the "probably" in PAC, and the "approximately" derives from the fact that the gap term is positive for all n. It is important to note that PAC analyses are *distribution-free*, i.e. eq. (7.27) must hold for any measure μ.

There are two kinds of PAC bounds, depending on whether $\mathrm{gap}(f_{\mathcal{D}}, \mathcal{D}, \delta)$ actually depends on the particular sample $\mathcal{D}$ (rather than on simple statistics like n). Bounds that do depend on $\mathcal{D}$ are called data dependent, and those that do not are called data independent. The PAC-Bayesian bounds given below are data dependent.

It is important to understand the interpretation of a PAC bound and to clarify this we first consider a simpler case of statistical inference. We are given a dataset $\mathcal{D} = \{\mathbf{x}_1, \ldots, \mathbf{x}_n\}$ drawn i.i.d. from a distribution $\mu(\mathbf{x})$ that has mean $\mathbf{m}$. An estimate of $\mathbf{m}$ is given by the sample mean $\bar{\mathbf{x}} = \sum_i \mathbf{x}_i / n$. Under certain assumptions we can obtain (or put bounds on) the *sampling distribution* $p(\bar{\mathbf{x}}|\mathbf{m})$ which relates to the choice of dataset $\mathcal{D}$. However, if we wish to perform probabilistic inference for $\mathbf{m}$ we need to combine $p(\bar{\mathbf{x}}|\mathbf{m})$ with a prior distribution $p(\mathbf{m})$ and use Bayes' theorem to obtain the posterior.[6] The situation is similar (although somewhat more complex) for PAC bounds as these concern the sampling distribution of the expected and empirical risks of $f_{\mathcal{D}}$ w.r.t. $\mathcal{D}$.

---

[5] It is also possible to consider PAC analyses of other empirical quantities such as the cross-validation error (see section 5.3) which do not have this bias.

[6] In introductory treatments of frequentist statistics the logical hiatus of going from the sampling distribution to inference on the parameter of interest is often not well explained.

We might wish to make a conditional statement like

$$p_{\mathcal{D}}\{R_{\mathcal{L}}(f_{\mathcal{D}}) \leq r + \text{gap}(f_{\mathcal{D}}, \mathcal{D}, \delta) | \hat{R}_{\mathcal{L}}(f_{\mathcal{D}}) = r\} \geq 1 - \delta, \qquad (7.28)$$

where r is a small value, but such a statement cannot be inferred directly from the PAC bound. This is because the gap might be heavily anti-correlated with $\hat{R}_{\mathcal{L}}(f_{\mathcal{D}})$ so that the gap is large when the empirical risk is small.

PAC bounds are sometimes used to carry out model selection—given a learning machine which depends on a (discrete or continuous) parameter vector $\boldsymbol{\theta}$, one can seek to minimize the generalization bound as a function of $\boldsymbol{\theta}$. However, this procedure may not be well-justified if the generalization bounds are loose. Let the *slack* denote the difference between the value of the bound and the generalization error. The danger of choosing $\boldsymbol{\theta}$ to minimize the bound is that if the slack depends on $\boldsymbol{\theta}$ then the value of $\boldsymbol{\theta}$ that minimizes the bound may be very different from the value of $\boldsymbol{\theta}$ that minimizes the generalization error. See Seeger [2003, sec. 2.2.4] for further discussion.

7.4.2   PAC-Bayesian Analysis

We now consider a Bayesian set up, with a prior distribution $p(\mathbf{w})$ over the parameters $\mathbf{w}$, and a "posterior" distribution $q(\mathbf{w})$. (Strictly speaking the analysis does not require $q(\mathbf{w})$ to be the posterior distribution, just some other distribution, but in practice we will consider q to be an (approximate) posterior distribution.) We also limit our discussion to binary classification with labels $\{-1, 1\}$, although more general cases can be considered, see Seeger [2003, sec. 3.2.2].

The predictive distribution for f_* at a test point $\mathbf{x}_*$ given $q(\mathbf{w})$ is $q(f_*|\mathbf{x}_*) = \int q(f_*|\mathbf{w}, \mathbf{x}_*)q(\mathbf{w})d\mathbf{w}$, and the *predictive classifier* outputs $\text{sgn}(q(f_*|\mathbf{x}_*) - 1/2)$. The *Gibbs classifier* has also been studied in learning theory; given a test point $\mathbf{x}_*$ one draws a sample $\tilde{\mathbf{w}}$ from $q(\mathbf{w})$ and predicts the label using $\text{sgn}(f(\mathbf{x}_*; \tilde{\mathbf{w}}))$. The main reason for introducing the Gibbs classifier here is that the PAC-Bayesian theorems given below apply to Gibbs classifiers.

predictive classifier
Gibbs classifier

For a given parameter vector $\mathbf{w}$ giving rise to a classifier $c(\mathbf{x}; \mathbf{w})$, the expected risk and empirical risk are given by

$$R_{\mathcal{L}}(\mathbf{w}) = \int \mathcal{L}(y, c(\mathbf{x}; \mathbf{w})) \, d\mu(\mathbf{x}, y), \quad \hat{R}_{\mathcal{L}}(\mathbf{w}) = \frac{1}{n} \sum_{i=1}^{n} \mathcal{L}(y_i, c(\mathbf{x}_i; \mathbf{w})). \quad (7.29)$$

As the Gibbs classifier draws samples from $q(\mathbf{w})$ we consider the averaged risks

$$R_{\mathcal{L}}(q) = \int R_{\mathcal{L}}(\mathbf{w})q(\mathbf{w}) \, d\mathbf{w}, \qquad \hat{R}_{\mathcal{L}}(q) = \int \hat{R}_{\mathcal{L}}(\mathbf{w})q(\mathbf{w}) \, d\mathbf{w}. \qquad (7.30)$$

Theorem 7.1 *(McAllester's PAC-Bayesian theorem) For any probability measures p and q over $\mathbf{w}$ and for any bounded loss function $\mathcal{L}$ for which $\mathcal{L}(y, c(\mathbf{x})) \in [0, 1]$ for any classifier c and input $\mathbf{x}$ we have*

McAllester's
PAC-Bayesian theorem

$$p_{\mathcal{D}}\left\{ R_{\mathcal{L}}(q) \leq \hat{R}_{\mathcal{L}}(q) + \sqrt{\frac{\text{KL}(q||p) + \log\frac{1}{\delta} + \log n + 2}{2n - 1}} \; \forall \, q \right\} \geq 1 - \delta. \quad (7.31)$$

$\square$

The proof can be found in McAllester [2003]. The Kullback-Leibler (KL) divergence $\mathrm{KL}(q\|p)$ is defined in section A.5. An example of a loss function which obeys the conditions of the theorem is the 0/1 loss.

For the special case of 0/1 loss, Seeger [2002] gives the following tighter bound.

Theorem 7.2 *(Seeger's PAC-Bayesian theorem) For any distribution over $\mathcal{X} \times \{-1, +1\}$ and for any probability measures p and q over $\mathbf{w}$ the following bound holds for i.i.d. samples drawn from the data distribution*

$$p_{\mathcal{D}}\left\{ \mathrm{KL}_{\mathrm{Ber}}(\hat{R}_{\mathcal{L}}(q)\|R_{\mathcal{L}}(q)) \leq \frac{1}{n}(\mathrm{KL}(q\|p) + \log \frac{n+1}{\delta}) \; \forall \, q \right\} \geq 1 - \delta. \quad (7.32)$$

$\square$

Here $\mathrm{KL}_{\mathrm{Ber}}(\cdot\|\cdot)$ is the KL divergence between two Bernoulli distributions (defined in eq. (A.22)). Thus the theorem bounds (with high probability) the KL divergence between $\hat{R}_{\mathcal{L}}(q)$ and $R_{\mathcal{L}}(q)$.

The PAC-Bayesian theorems above refer to a Gibbs classifier. If we are interested in the predictive classifier $\mathrm{sgn}(q(f_*|\mathbf{x}_*) - 1/2)$ then Seeger [2002] shows that if $q(f_*|\mathbf{x}_*)$ is symmetric about its mean then the expected risk of the predictive classifier is less than twice the expected risk of the Gibbs classifier. However, this result is based on a simple bounding argument and in practice one would expect that the predictive classifier will usually give better performance than the Gibbs classifier. Recent work by Meir and Zhang [2003] provides some PAC bounds directly for Bayesian algorithms (like the predictive classifier) whose predictions are made on the basis of a data-dependent posterior distribution.

7.4.3 PAC-Bayesian Analysis of GP Classification

To apply this bound to the Gaussian process case we need to compute the KL divergence $\mathrm{KL}(q\|p)$ between the posterior distribution $q(\mathbf{w})$ and the prior distribution $p(\mathbf{w})$. Although this could be considered w.r.t. the weight vector $\mathbf{w}$ in the eigenfunction expansion, in fact it turns out to be more convenient to consider the latent function value $f(\mathbf{x})$ at every possible point in the input space $\mathcal{X}$ as the parameter. We divide this (possibly infinite) vector into two parts, (1) the values corresponding to the training points $\mathbf{x}_1, \ldots, \mathbf{x}_n$, denoted $\mathbf{f}$, and (2) those at the remaining points in $\mathbf{x}$-space (the test points) $\mathbf{f}_*$.

The key observation is that all methods we have described for dealing with GP classification problems produce a posterior approximation $q(\mathbf{f}|\mathbf{y})$ which is defined at the training points. (This is an approximation for Laplace's method and for EP; MCMC methods sample from the exact posterior.) This posterior over $\mathbf{f}$ is then extended to the test points by setting $q(\mathbf{f}, \mathbf{f}_*|\mathbf{y}) = q(\mathbf{f}|\mathbf{y})p(\mathbf{f}_*|\mathbf{f})$. Of course for the prior distribution we have a similar decomposition $p(\mathbf{f}, \mathbf{f}_*) =$

$p(\mathbf{f})p(\mathbf{f}_*|\mathbf{f})$. Thus the KL divergence is given by

$$
\begin{aligned}
\mathrm{KL}(q||p) &= \int q(\mathbf{f}|\mathbf{y})p(\mathbf{f}_*|\mathbf{f}) \log \frac{q(\mathbf{f}|\mathbf{y})p(\mathbf{f}_*|\mathbf{f})}{p(\mathbf{f})p(\mathbf{f}_*|\mathbf{f})} \, d\mathbf{f} d\mathbf{f}_* \\
&= \int q(\mathbf{f}|\mathbf{y}) \log \frac{q(\mathbf{f}|\mathbf{y})}{p(\mathbf{f})} d\mathbf{f},
\end{aligned}
\tag{7.33}
$$

as shown e.g. in Seeger [2002]. Notice that this has reduced a rather scary infinite-dimensional integration to a more manageable n-dimensional integration; in the case that $q(\mathbf{f}|\mathbf{y})$ is Gaussian (as for the Laplace and EP approximations), this KL divergence can be computed using eq. (A.23). For the Laplace approximation with $p(\mathbf{f}) = \mathcal{N}(\mathbf{0}, K)$ and $q(\mathbf{f}|\mathbf{y}) = \mathcal{N}(\hat{\mathbf{f}}, A^{-1})$ this gives

$$
\mathrm{KL}(q||p) = \tfrac{1}{2}\log|K| + \tfrac{1}{2}\log|A| + \tfrac{1}{2}\mathrm{tr}\left(A^{-1}(K^{-1} - A)\right) + \tfrac{1}{2}\hat{\mathbf{f}}^\top K^{-1}\hat{\mathbf{f}}.
\tag{7.34}
$$

Seeger [2002] has evaluated the quality of the bound produced by the PAC-Bayesian method for a Laplace GPC on the task of discriminating handwritten 2s and 3s from the MNIST handwritten digits database.[7] He reserved a test set of 1000 examples and used training sets of size 500, 1000, 2000, 5000 and 9000. The classifications were replicated ten times using draws of the training sets from a pool of 12089 examples. We quote example results for $n = 5000$ where the training error was 0.0187 ± 0.0016, the test error was 0.0195 ± 0.0011 and the PAC-Bayesian bound on the generalization error (evaluated for $\delta = 0.01$) was 0.076 ± 0.002. (The $\pm$ figures denote a 95% confidence interval.) The classification results are for the Gibbs classifier; for the predictive classifier the test error rate was 0.0171 ± 0.0016. Thus the generalization error is around 2%, while the PAC bound is 7.6%. Many PAC bounds struggle to predict error rates below 100%(!), so this is an impressive and highly non-trivial result. Further details and experiments can be found in Seeger [2002].

7.5 Comparison with Other Supervised Learning Methods

The focus of this book is on Gaussian process methods for supervised learning. However, there are many other techniques available for supervised learning such as linear regression, logistic regression, decision trees, neural networks, support vector machines, kernel smoothers, k-nearest neighbour classifiers, etc., and we need to consider the relative strengths and weaknesses of these approaches.

Supervised learning is an *inductive* process—given a finite training set we wish to infer a function f that makes predictions for all possible input values. The additional assumptions made by the learning algorithm are known as its *inductive bias* (see e.g. Mitchell [1997, p. 43]). Sometimes these assumptions are explicit, but for other algorithms (e.g. for decision tree induction) they can be rather more implicit.

inductive bias

---

[7]See http://yann.lecun.com/exdb/mnist.

However, for all their variety, supervised learning algorithms are based on the idea that similar input patterns will usually give rise to similar outputs (or output distributions), and it is the precise notion of similarity that differentiates the algorithms. For example some algorithms may do feature selection and decide that there are input dimensions that are irrelevant to the predictive task. Some algorithms may construct new features out of those provided and measure similarity in this derived space. As we have seen, many regression techniques can be seen as linear smoothers (see section 2.6) and these techniques vary in the definition of the weight function that is used.

One important distinction between different learning algorithms is how they relate to the question of universal consistency (see section 7.2.1). For example a linear regression model will be inconsistent if the function that minimizes the risk cannot be represented by a linear function of the inputs. In general a model with a finite-dimensional parameter vector will not be universally consistent. Examples of such models are linear regression and logistic regression with a finite-dimensional feature vector, and neural networks with a fixed number of hidden units. In contrast to these *parametric* models we have *non-parametric* models (such as k-nearest neighbour classifiers, kernel smoothers and Gaussian processes and SVMs with nondegenerate kernels) which do not compress the training data into a finite-dimensional parameter vector. An intermediate position is taken by *semi-parametric* models such as neural networks where the number of hidden units k is allowed to increase as n increases. In this case universal consistency results can be obtained [Devroye et al., 1996, ch. 30] under certain technical conditions and growth rates on k.

Although universal consistency is a "good thing", it does not necessarily mean that we should only consider procedures that have this property; for example if on a specific problem we knew that a linear regression model was consistent for that problem then it would be very natural to use it.

neural networks

In the 1980's there was a large surge in interest in artificial neural networks (ANNs), which are feedforward networks consisting of an input layer, followed by one or more layers of non-linear transformations of weighted combinations of the activity from previous layers, and an output layer. One reason for this surge of interest was the use of the backpropagation algorithm for training ANNs. Initial excitement centered around that fact that training non-linear networks was possible, but later the focus came onto the generalization performance of ANNs, and how to deal with questions such as how many layers of hidden units to use, how many units there should be in each layer, and what type of non-linearities should be used, etc.

For a particular ANN the search for a good set of weights for a given training set is complicated by the fact that there can be local optima in the optimization problem; this can cause significant difficulties in practice. In contrast for Gaussian process regression and classification the posterior for the latent variables is convex.

Bayesian neural networks

One approach to the problems raised above was to put ANNs in a Bayesian framework, as developed by MacKay [1992a] and Neal [1996]. This gives rise to posterior distributions over weights for a given architecture, and the use of the marginal likelihood (see section 5.2) for model comparison and selection. In contrast to Gaussian process regression the marginal likelihood for a given ANN model is not analytically tractable, and thus approximation techniques such as the Laplace approximation [MacKay, 1992a] and Markov chain Monte Carlo methods [Neal, 1996] have to be used. Neal's observation [1996] that certain ANNs with one hidden layer converge to a Gaussian process prior over functions (see section 4.2.3) led us to consider GPs as alternatives to ANNs.

MacKay [2003, sec. 45.7] raises an interesting question whether in moving from neural networks to Gaussian processes we have "thrown the baby out with the bathwater?". This question arises from his statements that "neural networks were meant to be intelligent models that discovered features and patterns in data", while "Gaussian processes are simply smoothing devices". Our answer to this question is that GPs give us a computationally attractive method for dealing with the smoothing problem for a given kernel, and that issues of feature discovery etc. can be addressed through methods to select the kernel function (see chapter 5 for more details on how to do this). Note that using a distance function $r^2(\mathbf{x}, \mathbf{x}') = (\mathbf{x} - \mathbf{x}')^\top M(\mathbf{x} - \mathbf{x}')$ with M having a low-rank form $M = \Lambda\Lambda^\top + \Psi$ as in eq. (4.22), features are described by the columns of Λ. However, some of the non-convexity of the neural network optimization problem now returns, as optimizing the marginal likelihood in terms of the parameters of M may well have local optima.

As we have seen from chapters 2 and 3 linear regression and logistic regression with Gaussian priors on the parameters are a natural starting point for the development of Gaussian process regression and Gaussian process classification. However, we need to enhance the flexibility of these models, and the use of non-degenerate kernels opens up the possibility of universal consistency.

linear and logistic regression

Kernel smoothers and classifiers have been described in sections 2.6 and 7.2.1. At a high level there are similarities between GP prediction and these methods as a kernel is placed on every training example and the prediction is obtained through a weighted sum of the kernel functions, but the details of the prediction and the underlying logic differ. Note that the GP prediction view gives us much more, e.g. error bars on the predictions and the use of the marginal likelihood to set parameters in the kernel (see section 5.2). On the other hand the computational problem that needs to be solved to carry out GP prediction is more demanding than that for simple kernel-based methods.

kernel smoothers and classifiers

Kernel smoothers and classifiers are non-parametric methods, and consistency can often be obtained under conditions where the width h of the kernel tends to zero while $nh^D \to \infty$. The equivalent kernel analysis of GP regression (section 7.1) shows that there are quite close connections between the kernel regression method and GPR, but note that the equivalent kernel automatically reduces its width as n grows; in contrast the decay of h has to be imposed for kernel regression. Also, for some kernel smoothing and classification algorithms the width of the kernel is increased in areas of low observation density; for example this would occur in algorithms that consider the k nearest neighbours of a test point. Again notice from the equivalent kernel analysis that the width of the equivalent kernel is larger in regions of low density, although the exact dependence on the density will depend on the kernel used.

regularization networks, splines, SVMs and RVMs

The similarities and differences between GP prediction and regularization networks, splines, SVMs and RVMs have been discussed in chapter 6.

∗ 7.6 Appendix: Learning Curve for the Ornstein-Uhlenbeck Process

We now consider the calculation of the learning curve for the OU covariance function $k(r) = \exp(-\alpha|r|)$ on the interval $[0, 1]$, assuming that the training x's are drawn from the uniform distribution $U(0, 1)$. Our treatment is based on Williams and Vivarelli [2000].[8] We first calculate $E^g(X)$ for a fixed design, and then integrate over possible designs to obtain $E^g(n)$.

In the absence of noise the OU process is Markovian (as discussed in Appendix B and exercise 4.5.1). We consider the interval $[0, 1]$ with points $x_1 < x_2 \ldots < x_{n-1} < x_n$ placed on this interval. Also let $x_0 = 0$ and $x_{n+1} = 1$. Due to the Markovian nature of the process the prediction at a test point x depends only on the function values of the training points immediately to the left and right of x. Thus in the i-th interval (counting from 0) the bounding points are x_i and x_{i+1}. Let this interval have length δ_i.

Using eq. (7.24) we have

$$E^g(X) = \int_0^1 \sigma_f^2(x)\,dx = \sum_{i=0}^n \int_{x_i}^{x_{i+1}} \sigma_f^2(x)\,dx, \qquad (7.35)$$

where $\sigma_f^2(x)$ is the predictive variance at input x. Using the Markovian property we have in interval i (for $i = 1, \ldots, n-1$) that $\sigma_f^2(x) = k(0) - \mathbf{k}(x)^\top K^{-1} \mathbf{k}(x)$ where K is the 2×2 Gram matrix

$$K = \begin{pmatrix} k(0) & k(\delta_i) \\ k(\delta_i) & k(0) \end{pmatrix} \qquad (7.36)$$

and $\mathbf{k}(x)$ is the corresponding vector of length 2. Thus

$$K^{-1} = \frac{1}{\Delta_i} \begin{pmatrix} k(0) & -k(\delta_i) \\ -k(\delta_i) & k(0) \end{pmatrix}, \qquad (7.37)$$

where $\Delta_i = k^2(0) - k^2(\delta_i)$ and

$$\sigma_f^2(x) = k(0) - \frac{1}{\Delta_i}[k(0)(k^2(x_{i+1}-x)+k^2(x-x_i)) - 2k(\delta_i)k(x-x_i)k(x_{i+1}-x)]. \qquad (7.38)$$

Thus

$$\int_{x_i}^{x_{i+1}} \sigma_f^2(x)dx = \delta_i k(0) - \frac{2}{\Delta_i}(I_1(\delta_i) - I_2(\delta_i)) \qquad (7.39)$$

---

[8]CW thanks Manfred Opper for pointing out that the upper bound developed in Williams and Vivarelli [2000] is exact for the noise-free OU process.

where

$$I_1(\delta) \;=\; k(0) \int_0^\delta k^2(z)dz, \qquad I_2(\delta) \;=\; k(\delta) \int_0^\delta k(z)k(\delta - z)dz. \qquad (7.40)$$

For $k(r) = \exp(-\alpha|r|)$ these equations reduce to $I_1(\delta) = (1 - e^{-2\alpha\delta})/(2\alpha)$, $I_2(\delta) = \delta e^{-2\alpha\delta}$ and $\Delta = 1 - e^{-2\alpha\delta}$. Thus

$$\int_{x_i}^{x_{i+1}} \sigma_f^2(x)dx \;=\; \delta_i - \frac{1}{\alpha} + \frac{2\delta_i e^{-2\alpha\delta_i}}{1 - e^{-2\alpha\delta_i}}. \qquad (7.41)$$

This calculation is not correct in the first and last intervals where only x_1 and x_n are relevant (respectively). For the 0th interval we have that $\sigma_f^2(x) = k(0) - k^2(x_1 - x)/k(0)$ and thus

$$\int_0^{x_1} \sigma_f^2(x) \;=\; \delta_0 k(0) - \frac{1}{k(0)} \int_0^{x_1} k^2(x_1 - x)dx \qquad (7.42)$$

$$= \; \delta_0 - \frac{1}{2\alpha}(1 - e^{-2\alpha\delta_0}), \qquad (7.43)$$

and a similar result holds for $\int_{x_n}^1 \sigma_f^2(x)$.

Putting this all together we obtain

$$E^g(X) \;=\; 1 - \frac{n}{\alpha} + \frac{1}{2\alpha}(e^{-2\alpha\delta_0} + e^{-2\alpha\delta_n}) + \sum_{i=1}^{n-1} \frac{2\delta_i e^{-2\alpha\delta_i}}{1 - e^{-2\alpha\delta_i}}. \qquad (7.44)$$

Choosing a regular grid so that $\delta_0 = \delta_n = 1/2n$ and $\delta_i = 1/n$ for $i = 1, \ldots, n - 1$ it is straightforward to show (see exercise 7.7.4) that E^g scales as $\mathcal{O}(n^{-1})$, in agreement with the general Sacks-Ylvisaker result [Ritter, 2000, p. 103] when it is recalled that the OU process obeys Sacks-Ylvisaker conditions of order 0. A similar calculation is given in Plaskota [1996, sec. 3.8.2] for the Wiener process on $[0, 1]$ (note that this is also Markovian, but non-stationary).

We have now worked out the generalization error for a fixed design X. However to compute $E^g(n)$ we need to average $E^g(X)$ over draws of X from the uniform distribution. The theory of order statistics David [1970, eq. 2.3.4] tells us that $p(\delta) = n(1 - \delta)^{n-1}$ for all the δ_i, $i = 0, \ldots, n$. Taking the expectation of $E^g(X)$ then turns into the problem of evaluating the one-dimensional integrals $\int e^{-2\alpha\delta} p(\delta)d\delta$ and $\int \delta e^{-2\alpha\delta}(1 - e^{-2\alpha\delta})^{-1}p(\delta)d\delta$. Exercise 7.7.5 asks you to compute these integrals numerically.

7.7 Exercises

1. Consider a spline regularizer with $S_f(\mathbf{s}) = c^{-1}|\mathbf{s}|^{-2m}$. (As we noted in section 6.3 this is not strictly a power spectrum as the spline is an improper prior, but it can be used as a power spectrum in eq. (7.9) for the

purposes of this analysis.) The equivalent kernel corresponding to this spline is given by

$$h(\mathbf{x}) = \int \frac{\exp(2\pi i \mathbf{s} \cdot \mathbf{x})}{1 + \gamma |\mathbf{s}|^{2m}} \, d\mathbf{s}, \qquad (7.45)$$

where $\gamma = c\sigma_n^2/\rho$. By changing variables in the integration to $|\mathbf{t}| = \gamma^{1/2m}|\mathbf{s}|$ show that the width of $h(\mathbf{x})$ scales as $n^{-1/2m}$.

2. Equation 7.45 gives the form of the equivalent kernel for a spline regularizer. Show that $h(\mathbf{0})$ is only finite if $2m > D$. (Hint: transform the integration to polar coordinates.) This observation was made by P. Whittle in the discussion of Silverman [1985], and shows the need for the condition $2m > D$ for spline smoothing.

3. Computer exercise: Space $n + 1$ points out evenly along the interval $(-1/2, 1/2)$. (Take n to be even so that one of the sample points falls at 0.) Calculate the weight function (see section 2.6) corresponding to Gaussian process regression with a particular covariance function and noise level, and plot this for the point $x = 0$. Now compute the equivalent kernel corresponding to the covariance function (see, e.g. the examples in section 7.1.1), plot this on the same axes and compare results. Hint 1: Recall that the equivalent kernel is defined in terms of integration (see eq. (7.7)) so that there will be a scaling factor of $1/(n + 1)$. Hint 2: If you wish to use large n (say > 1000), use the n_{grid} method described in section 2.6.

4. Consider $E^g(X)$ as given in eq. (7.44) and choose a regular grid design X so that $\delta_0 = \delta_n = 1/2n$ and $\delta_i = 1/n$ for $i = 1, \ldots, n-1$. Show that $E^g(X)$ scales as $\mathcal{O}(n^{-1})$ asymptotically. Hint: when expanding $1 - \exp(-2\alpha\delta_i)$, be sure to extend the expansion to sufficient order.

5. Compute numerically the expectation of $E^g(X)$ eq. (7.44) over random designs for the OU process example discussed in section 7.6. Make use of the fact [David, 1970, eq. 2.3.4] that $p(\delta) = n(1 - \delta)^{n-1}$ for all the δ_i, $i = 0, \ldots, n$. Investigate the scaling behaviour of $E^g(n)$ w.r.t. n.

Chapter 8

Approximation Methods for Large Datasets

As we have seen in the preceding chapters a significant problem with Gaussian process prediction is that it typically scales as $\mathcal{O}(n^3)$. For large problems (e.g. $n > 10,000$) both storing the Gram matrix and solving the associated linear systems are prohibitive on modern workstations (although this boundary can be pushed further by using high-performance computers).

An extensive range of proposals have been suggested to deal with this problem. Below we divide these into five parts: in section 8.1 we consider reduced-rank approximations to the Gram matrix; in section 8.2 a general strategy for greedy approximations is described; in section 8.3 we discuss various methods for approximating the GP regression problem for fixed hyperparameters; in section 8.4 we describe various methods for approximating the GP classification problem for fixed hyperparameters; and in section 8.5 we describe methods to approximate the marginal likelihood and its derivatives. Many (although not all) of these methods use a subset of size $m < n$ of the training examples.

8.1 Reduced-rank Approximations of the Gram Matrix

In the GP regression problem we need to invert the matrix $K + \sigma_n^2 I$ (or at least to solve a linear system $(K + \sigma_n^2 I)\mathbf{v} = \mathbf{y}$ for $\mathbf{v}$). If the matrix K has rank q (so that it can be represented in the form $K = QQ^\top$ where Q is an $n \times q$ matrix) then this matrix inversion can be speeded up using the matrix inversion lemma eq. (A.9) as $(QQ^\top + \sigma_n^2 I_n)^{-1} = \sigma_n^{-2} I_n - \sigma_n^{-2} Q(\sigma_n^2 I_q + Q^\top Q)^{-1} Q^\top$. Notice that the inversion of an $n \times n$ matrix has now been transformed to the inversion of a $q \times q$ matrix.[1]

---

[1] For numerical reasons this is not the best way to solve such a linear system but it does illustrate the savings that can be obtained with reduced-rank representations.

In the case that the kernel is derived from an explicit feature expansion with N features, then the Gram matrix will have rank $\min(n, N)$ so that exploitation of this structure will be beneficial if $n > N$. Even if the kernel is non-degenerate it may happen that it has a fast-decaying eigenspectrum (see e.g. section 4.3.1) so that a reduced-rank approximation will be accurate.

If K is not of rank $< n$, we can still consider reduced-rank *approximations* to K. The optimal reduced-rank approximation of K w.r.t. the Frobenius norm (see eq. (A.16)) is $U_q \Lambda_q U_q^\top$, where Λ_q is the diagonal matrix of the leading q eigenvalues of K and U_q is the matrix of the corresponding orthonormal eigenvectors [Golub and Van Loan, 1989, Theorem 8.1.9]. Unfortunately, this is of limited interest in practice as computing the eigendecomposition is an $\mathcal{O}(n^3)$ operation. However, it does suggest that if we can more cheaply obtain an approximate eigendecomposition then this may give rise to a useful reduced-rank approximation to K.

We now consider selecting a subset I of the n datapoints; set I has size $m < n$. The remaining $n - m$ datapoints form the set R. (As a mnemonic, I is for the included datapoints and R is for the remaining points.) We sometimes call the included set the active set. Without loss of generality we assume that the datapoints are ordered so that set I comes first. Thus K can be partitioned as

$$K = \begin{pmatrix} K_{mm} & K_{m(n-m)} \\ K_{(n-m)m} & K_{(n-m)(n-m)} \end{pmatrix}. \tag{8.1}$$

The top $m \times n$ block will also be referred to as K_{mn} and its transpose as K_{nm}.

In section 4.3.2 we saw how to approximate the eigenfunctions of a kernel using the Nyström method. We can now apply the same idea to approximating the eigenvalues/vectors of K. We compute the eigenvectors and eigenvalues of K_{mm} and denote them $\{\lambda_i^{(m)}\}_{i=1}^m$ and $\{\mathbf{u}_i^{(m)}\}_{i=1}^m$. These are extended to all n points using eq. (4.44) to give

$$\tilde{\lambda}_i^{(n)} \triangleq \frac{n}{m} \lambda_i^{(m)}, \qquad\qquad i = 1, \ldots, m \tag{8.2}$$

$$\tilde{\mathbf{u}}_i^{(n)} \triangleq \sqrt{\frac{m}{n}} \frac{1}{\lambda_i^{(m)}} K_{nm} \mathbf{u}_i^{(m)}, \qquad\qquad i = 1, \ldots, m \tag{8.3}$$

where the scaling of $\tilde{\mathbf{u}}_i^{(n)}$ has been chosen so that $|\tilde{\mathbf{u}}_i^{(n)}| \simeq 1$. In general we have a choice of how many of the approximate eigenvalues/vectors to include in our approximation of K; choosing the first p we get $\tilde{K} = \sum_{i=1}^p \tilde{\lambda}_i^{(n)} \tilde{\mathbf{u}}_i^{(n)} (\tilde{\mathbf{u}}_i^{(n)})^\top$. Below we will set $p = m$ to obtain

$$\tilde{K} = K_{nm} K_{mm}^{-1} K_{mn} \tag{8.4}$$

Nyström approximation   using equations 8.2 and 8.3, which we call the Nyström approximation to K. Computation of $\tilde{K}$ takes time $\mathcal{O}(m^2 n)$ as the eigendecomposition of K_{mm} is $\mathcal{O}(m^3)$ and the computation of each $\tilde{\mathbf{u}}_i^{(n)}$ is $\mathcal{O}(mn)$. Fowlkes et al. [2001] have applied the Nyström method to approximate the top few eigenvectors in a computer vision problem where the matrices in question are larger than $10^6 \times 10^6$ in size.

The Nyström approximation has been applied above to approximate the elements of K. However, using the approximation for the ith eigenfunction $\tilde{\phi}_i(\mathbf{x}) = (\sqrt{m}/\lambda_i^{(m)})\mathbf{k}_m(\mathbf{x})^\top \mathbf{u}_i^{(m)}$, where $\mathbf{k}_m(\mathbf{x}) = (k(\mathbf{x}, \mathbf{x}_1), \ldots, k(\mathbf{x}, \mathbf{x}_m))^\top$ (a restatement of eq. (4.44) using the current notation) and $\lambda_i \simeq \lambda_i^{(m)}/m$ it is easy to see that in general we obtain an approximation for the kernel $k(\mathbf{x}, \mathbf{x}') = \sum_{i=1}^N \lambda_i \phi_i(\mathbf{x})\phi_i(\mathbf{x}')$ as

$$\tilde{k}(\mathbf{x}, \mathbf{x}') = \sum_{i=1}^m \frac{\lambda_i^{(m)}}{m}\tilde{\phi}_i(\mathbf{x})\tilde{\phi}_i(\mathbf{x}') \tag{8.5}$$

$$= \sum_{i=1}^m \frac{\lambda_i^{(m)}}{m}\frac{m}{(\lambda_i^{(m)})^2}\mathbf{k}_m(\mathbf{x})^\top \mathbf{u}_i^{(m)}(\mathbf{u}_i^{(m)})^\top \mathbf{k}_m(\mathbf{x}') \tag{8.6}$$

$$= \mathbf{k}_m(\mathbf{x})^\top K_{mm}^{-1}\mathbf{k}_m(\mathbf{x}'). \tag{8.7}$$

Clearly eq. (8.4) is obtained by evaluating eq. (8.7) for all pairs of datapoints in the training set.

By multiplying out eq. (8.4) using $K_{mn} = [K_{mm} K_{m(n-m)}]$ it is easy to show that $K_{mm} = \tilde{K}_{mm}$, $K_{m(n-m)} = \tilde{K}_{m(n-m)}$, $K_{(n-m)m} = \tilde{K}_{(n-m)m}$, but that $\tilde{K}_{(n-m)(n-m)} = K_{(n-m)m}K_{mm}^{-1}K_{m(n-m)}$. The difference $K_{(n-m)(n-m)} - \tilde{K}_{(n-m)(n-m)}$ is in fact the *Schur complement* of K_{mm} [Golub and Van Loan, 1989, p. 103]. It is easy to see that $K_{(n-m)(n-m)} - \tilde{K}_{(n-m)(n-m)}$ is positive semi-definite; if a vector $\mathbf{f}$ is partitioned as $\mathbf{f}^\top = (\mathbf{f}_m^\top, \mathbf{f}_{n-m}^\top)$ and $\mathbf{f}$ has a Gaussian distribution with zero mean and covariance K then $\mathbf{f}_{n-m}|\mathbf{f}_m$ has the Schur complement as its covariance matrix, see eq. (A.6).

The Nyström approximation was derived in the above fashion by Williams and Seeger [2001] for application to kernel machines. An alternative view which gives rise to the same approximation is due to Smola and Schölkopf [2000] (and also Schölkopf and Smola [2002, sec. 10.2]). Here the starting point is that we wish to approximate the kernel centered on point $\mathbf{x}_i$ as a linear combination of kernels from the active set, so that

$$k(\mathbf{x}_i, \mathbf{x}) \simeq \sum_{j \in I} c_{ij}k(\mathbf{x}_j, \mathbf{x}) \triangleq \hat{k}(\mathbf{x}_i, \mathbf{x}) \tag{8.8}$$

for some coefficients $\{c_{ij}\}$ that are to be determined so as to optimize the approximation. A reasonable criterion to minimize is

$$E(C) = \sum_{i=1}^n \|k(\mathbf{x}_i, \mathbf{x}) - \hat{k}(\mathbf{x}_i, \mathbf{x})\|_{\mathcal{H}}^2 \tag{8.9}$$

$$= \operatorname{tr} K - 2\operatorname{tr}(CK_{mn}) + \operatorname{tr}(CK_{mm}C^\top), \tag{8.10}$$

where the coefficients are arranged into a $n \times m$ matrix C. Minimizing $E(C)$ w.r.t. C gives $C_{\text{opt}} = K_{nm}K_{mm}^{-1}$; thus we obtain the approximation $\hat{K} = K_{nm}K_{mm}^{-1}K_{mn}$ in agreement with eq. (8.4). Also, it can be shown that $E(C_{\text{opt}}) = \operatorname{tr}(K - \hat{K})$.

Smola and Schölkopf [2000] suggest a greedy algorithm to choose points to include into the active set so as to minimize the error criterion. As it takes

$\mathcal{O}(mn)$ operations to evaluate the change in E due to including one new datapoint (see exercise 8.7.2) it is infeasible to consider all members of set R for inclusion on each iteration; instead Smola and Schölkopf [2000] suggest finding the best point to include from a randomly chosen subset of set R on each iteration.

Recent work by Drineas and Mahoney [2005] analyzes a similar algorithm to the Nyström approximation, except that they use biased sampling with replacement (choosing column i of K with probability $\propto k_{ii}^2$) and a pseudoinverse of the inner $m \times m$ matrix. For this algorithm they are able to provide probabilistic bounds on the quality of the approximation. Earlier work by Frieze et al. [1998] had developed an approximation to the singular value decomposition (SVD) of a rectangular matrix using a weighted random subsampling of its rows and columns, and probabilistic error bounds. However, this is rather different from the Nyström approximation; see Drineas and Mahoney [2005, sec. 5.2] for details.

Fine and Scheinberg [2002] suggest an alternative low-rank approximation to K using the incomplete Cholesky factorization (see Golub and Van Loan [1989, sec. 10.3.2]). The idea here is that when computing the Cholesky decomposition of K pivots below a certain threshold are skipped.[2] If the number of pivots greater than the threshold is k the incomplete Cholesky factorization takes time $\mathcal{O}(nk^2)$.

8.2   Greedy Approximation

Many of the methods described below use an active set of training points of size m selected from the training set of size $n > m$. We assume that it is impossible to search for the optimal subset of size m due to combinatorics. The points in the active set could be selected randomly, but in general we might expect better performance if the points are selected greedily w.r.t. some criterion. In the statistics literature greedy approaches are also known as forward selection strategies.

A general recipe for greedy approximation is given in Algorithm 8.1. The algorithm starts with the active set I being empty, and the set R containing the indices of all training examples. On each iteration one index is selected from R and added to I. This is achieved by evaluating some criterion Δ and selecting the data point that optimizes this criterion. For some algorithms it can be too expensive to evaluate Δ on all points in R, so some working set $J \subset R$ can be chosen instead, usually at random from R.

Greedy selection methods have been used with the subset of regressors (SR), subset of datapoints (SD) and the projected process (PP) methods described below.

---

[2]As a technical detail, symmetric permutations of the rows and columns are required to stabilize the computations.

```
      input: m, desired size of active set
 2:   Initialization I = ∅, R = {1, . . . , n}
      for j := 1 . . . m do
 4:       Create working set J ⊆ R
          Compute Δ_j for all j ∈ J
 6:       i = argmax_{j∈J} Δ_j
          Update model to include data from example i
 8:       I ← I ∪ {i}, R ← R\{i}
      end for
10:   return: I
```

Algorithm 8.1: General framework for greedy subset selection. Δ_j is the criterion function evaluated on data point j.

8.3 Approximations for GPR with Fixed Hyperparameters

We present six approximation schemes for GPR below, namely the subset of regressors (SR), the Nyström method, the subset of datapoints (SD), the projected process (PP) approximation, the Bayesian committee machine (BCM) and the iterative solution of linear systems. Section 8.3.7 provides a summary of these methods and a comparison of their performance on the SARCOS data which was introduced in section 2.5.

8.3.1 Subset of Regressors

Silverman [1985, sec. 6.1] showed that the *mean* GP predictor can be obtained from a finite-dimensional generalized linear regression model $f(\mathbf{x}_*) = \sum_{i=1}^{n} \alpha_i k(\mathbf{x}_*, \mathbf{x}_i)$ with a prior $\boldsymbol{\alpha} \sim \mathcal{N}(\mathbf{0}, K^{-1})$. To see this we use the mean prediction for linear regression model in feature space given by eq. (2.11), i.e. $\bar{f}(\mathbf{x}_*) = \sigma_n^{-2} \boldsymbol{\phi}(\mathbf{x}_*)^\top A^{-1} \Phi \mathbf{y}$ with $A = \Sigma_p^{-1} + \sigma_n^{-2} \Phi \Phi^\top$. Setting $\boldsymbol{\phi}(\mathbf{x}_*) = \mathbf{k}(\mathbf{x}_*)$, $\Phi = \Phi^\top = K$ and $\Sigma_p^{-1} = K$ we obtain

$$\bar{f}(\mathbf{x}_*) = \sigma_n^{-2} \mathbf{k}^\top(\mathbf{x}_*)[\sigma_n^{-2} K(K + \sigma_n^2 I)]^{-1} K \mathbf{y} \tag{8.11}$$

$$= \mathbf{k}^\top(\mathbf{x}_*)(K + \sigma_n^2 I)^{-1} \mathbf{y}, \tag{8.12}$$

in agreement with eq. (2.25). Note, however, that the predictive (co)variance of this model is different from full GPR.

A simple approximation to this model is to consider only a subset of regressors, so that

$$f_{\text{SR}}(\mathbf{x}_*) = \sum_{i=1}^{m} \alpha_i k(\mathbf{x}_*, \mathbf{x}_i), \qquad \text{with} \qquad \boldsymbol{\alpha}_m \sim \mathcal{N}(\mathbf{0}, K_{mm}^{-1}). \tag{8.13}$$

Again using eq. (2.11) we obtain

$$\bar{f}_{\mathrm{SR}}(\mathbf{x}_*) = \mathbf{k}_m(\mathbf{x}_*)^\top (K_{mn}K_{nm} + \sigma_n^2 K_{mm})^{-1} K_{mn}\mathbf{y}, \tag{8.14}$$

$$\mathbb{V}[f_{\mathrm{SR}}(\mathbf{x}_*)] = \sigma_n^2 \mathbf{k}_m(\mathbf{x}_*)^\top (K_{mn}K_{nm} + \sigma_n^2 K_{mm})^{-1} \mathbf{k}_m(\mathbf{x}_*). \tag{8.15}$$

Thus the posterior mean for $\boldsymbol{\alpha}_m$ is given by

$$\bar{\boldsymbol{\alpha}}_m = (K_{mn}K_{nm} + \sigma_n^2 K_{mm})^{-1} K_{mn}\mathbf{y}. \tag{8.16}$$

This method has been proposed, for example, in Wahba [1990, chapter 7], and in Poggio and Girosi [1990, eq. 25] via the regularization framework. The name "subset of regressors" (SR) was suggested to us by G. Wahba. The computations for equations 8.14 and 8.15 take time $\mathcal{O}(m^2 n)$ to carry out the necessary matrix computations. After this the prediction of the mean for a new test point takes time $\mathcal{O}(m)$, and the predictive variance takes $\mathcal{O}(m^2)$.

SR marginal likelihood   Under the subset of regressors model we have $\mathbf{f} \sim \mathcal{N}(\mathbf{0}, \tilde{K})$ where $\tilde{K}$ is defined as in eq. (8.4). Thus the log marginal likelihood under this model is

$$\log p_{\mathrm{SR}}(\mathbf{y}|X) = -\frac{1}{2}\log|\tilde{K} + \sigma_n^2 I_n| - \frac{1}{2}\mathbf{y}^\top(\tilde{K} + \sigma_n^2 I_n)^{-1}\mathbf{y} - \frac{n}{2}\log(2\pi). \tag{8.17}$$

Notice that the covariance function defined by the SR model has the form $\tilde{k}(\mathbf{x}, \mathbf{x}') = \mathbf{k}(\mathbf{x})^\top K_{mm}^{-1} \mathbf{k}(\mathbf{x}')$, which is exactly the same as that from the Nyström approximation for the covariance function eq. (8.7). In fact if the covariance function $k(\mathbf{x}, \mathbf{x}')$ in the predictive mean and variance equations 2.25 and 2.26 is replaced systematically with $\tilde{k}(\mathbf{x}, \mathbf{x}')$ we obtain equations 8.14 and 8.15, as shown in Appendix 8.6.

If the kernel function decays to zero for $|\mathbf{x}| \to \infty$ for fixed $\mathbf{x}'$, then $\tilde{k}(\mathbf{x}, \mathbf{x})$ will be near zero when $\mathbf{x}$ is distant from points in the set I. This will be the case even when the kernel is stationary so that $k(\mathbf{x}, \mathbf{x})$ is independent of $\mathbf{x}$. Thus we might expect that using the approximate kernel will give poor predictions, especially underestimates of the predictive variance, when $\mathbf{x}$ is far from points in the set I.

An interesting idea suggested by Rasmussen and Quiñonero-Candela [2005] to mitigate this problem is to define the SR model with $m + 1$ basis functions, where the extra basis function is centered on the test point $\mathbf{x}_*$, so that $y_{\mathrm{SR}*}(\mathbf{x}_*) = \sum_{i=1}^m \alpha_i k(\mathbf{x}_*, \mathbf{x}_i) + \alpha_* k(\mathbf{x}_*, \mathbf{x}_*)$. This model can then be used to make predictions, and it can be implemented efficiently using the partitioned matrix inverse equations A.11 and A.12. The effect of the extra basis function centered on $\mathbf{x}_*$ is to maintain predictive variance at the test point.

So far we have not said how the subset I should be chosen. One simple method is to choose it randomly from X, another is to run clustering on $\{\mathbf{x}_i\}_{i=1}^n$ to obtain centres. Alternatively, a number of greedy forward selection algorithms for I have been proposed. Luo and Wahba [1997] choose the next kernel so as to minimize the residual sum of squares (RSS) $|\mathbf{y} - K_{nm}\boldsymbol{\alpha}_m|^2$ after optimizing $\boldsymbol{\alpha}_m$. Smola and Bartlett [2001] take a similar approach, but choose as their criterion the quadratic form

$$\frac{1}{\sigma_n^2}|\mathbf{y} - K_{nm}\bar{\boldsymbol{\alpha}}_m|^2 + \bar{\boldsymbol{\alpha}}_m^\top K_{mm}\bar{\boldsymbol{\alpha}}_m = \mathbf{y}^\top(\tilde{K} + \sigma_n^2 I_n)^{-1}\mathbf{y}, \tag{8.18}$$

where the right hand side follows using eq. (8.16) and the matrix inversion lemma. Alternatively, Quiñonero-Candela [2004] suggests using the approximate log marginal likelihood $\log p_{\text{SR}}(\mathbf{y}|X)$ (see eq. (8.17)) as the selection criterion. In fact the quadratic term from eq. (8.18) is one of the terms comprising $\log p_{\text{SR}}(\mathbf{y}|X)$.

For all these suggestions the complexity of evaluating the criterion on a new example is $\mathcal{O}(mn)$, by making use of partitioned matrix equations. Thus it is likely to be too expensive to consider all points in R on each iteration, and we are likely to want to consider a smaller working set, as described in Algorithm 8.1.

Note that the SR model is obtained by selecting some subset of the datapoints of size m in a random or greedy manner. The relevance vector machine (RVM) described in section 6.6 has a similar flavour in that it automatically selects (in a greedy fashion) which datapoints to use in its expansion. However, note one important difference which is that the RVM uses a *diagonal* prior on the α's, while for the SR method we have $\boldsymbol{\alpha}_m \sim \mathcal{N}(\mathbf{0}, K_{mm}^{-1})$.

comparison with RVM

8.3.2 The Nyström Method

Williams and Seeger [2001] suggested approximating the GPR equations by replacing the matrix K by $\tilde{K}$ in the mean and variance prediction equations 2.25 and 2.26, and called this the *Nyström method* for approximate GPR. Notice that in this proposal the covariance function k is not systematically replaced by $\tilde{k}$, it is only occurrences of the matrix K that are replaced. As for the SR model the time complexity is $\mathcal{O}(m^2 n)$ to carry out the necessary matrix computations, and then $\mathcal{O}(n)$ for the predictive mean of a test point and $\mathcal{O}(mn)$ for the predictive variance.

Experimental evidence in Williams et al. [2002] suggests that for large m the SR and Nyström methods have similar performance, but for small m the Nyström method can be quite poor. Also the fact that k is not systematically replaced by $\tilde{k}$ means that embarrassments can occur like the approximated predictive variance being negative. For these reasons we do not recommend the Nyström method over the SR method. However, the Nyström method can be effective when λ_{m+1}, the $(m+1)$th eigenvalue of K, is much smaller than σ_n^2.

8.3.3 Subset of Datapoints

The subset of regressors method described above approximated the form of the predictive distribution, and particularly the predictive mean. Another simple approximation to the full-sample GP predictor is to keep the GP predictor, but only on a smaller subset of size m of the data. Although this is clearly wasteful of data, it can make sense if the predictions obtained with m points are sufficiently accurate for our needs.

Clearly it can make sense to select which points are taken into the active set I, and typically this is achieved by greedy algorithms. However, one has to be wary of the amount of computation that is needed, especially if one considers each member of R at each iteration.

Lawrence et al. [2003] suggest choosing as the next point (or site) for inclusion into the active set the one that maximizes the *differential entropy score* $\Delta_j \triangleq H[p(f_j)] - H[p^{\text{new}}(f_j)]$, where $H[p(f_j)]$ is the entropy of the Gaussian at site $j \in R$ (which is a function of the variance at site j as the posterior is Gaussian, see eq. (A.20)), and $H[p^{\text{new}}(f_j)]$ is the entropy at this site once the observation at site j has been included. Let the posterior variance of f_j before inclusion be v_j. As $p(f_j|\mathbf{y}_I, y_j) \propto p(f_j|\mathbf{y}_I)\mathcal{N}(y_j|f_j, \sigma^2)$ we have $(v_j^{\text{new}})^{-1} = v_j^{-1} + \sigma^{-2}$. Using the fact that the entropy of a Gaussian with variance v is $\log(2\pi e v)/2$ we obtain

$$\Delta_j = \tfrac{1}{2}\log(1 + v_j/\sigma^2). \tag{8.19}$$

Δ_j is a monotonic function of v_j so that it is maximized by choosing the site with the largest variance. Lawrence et al. [2003] call their method the *informative*
IVM *vector machine* (IVM)

If coded naïvely the complexity of computing the variance at all sites in R on a single iteration is $\mathcal{O}(m^3 + (n-m)m^2)$ as we need to evaluate eq. (2.26) at each site (and the matrix inversion of $K_{mm} + \sigma_n^2 I$ can be done once in $\mathcal{O}(m^3)$ then stored). However, as we are incrementally growing the matrices K_{mm} and $K_{m(n-m)}$ in fact the cost is $\mathcal{O}(mn)$ per inclusion, leading to an overall complexity of $\mathcal{O}(m^2 n)$ when using a subset of size m. For example, once a site has been chosen for inclusion the matrix $K_{mm} + \sigma_n^2 I$ is grown by including an extra row and column. The inverse of this expanded matrix can be found using eq. (A.12) although it would be better practice numerically to use a Cholesky decomposition approach as described in Lawrence et al. [2003]. The scheme evaluates Δ_j over all $j \in R$ at each step to choose the inclusion site. This makes sense when m is small, but as it gets larger it can make sense to select candidate inclusion sites from a subset of R. Lawrence et al. [2003] call this the randomized greedy selection method and give further ideas on how to choose the subset.

The differential entropy score Δ_j is not the only criterion that can be used for site selection. For example the *information gain* criterion $\text{KL}(p^{\text{new}}(f_j)\|p(f_j))$ can also be used (see Seeger et al., 2003). The use of greedy selection heuristics here is similar to the problem of *active learning*, see e.g. MacKay [1992c].

8.3.4 Projected Process Approximation

The SR method has the unattractive feature that it is based on a degenerate GP, the finite-dimensional model given in eq. (8.13). The SD method is a non-degenerate process model but it only makes use of m datapoints. The projected process (PP) approximation is also a non-degenerate process model but it can make use of all n datapoints. We call it a *projected* process approximation as it represents only $m < n$ latent function values, but computes a likelihood involving all n datapoints by projecting up the m latent points to n dimensions.

One problem with the basic GPR algorithm is the fact that the likelihood term requires us to have f-values for the n training points. However, say we only represent m of these values explicitly, and denote these as $\mathbf{f}_m$. Then the remaining f-values in R denoted $\mathbf{f}_{n-m}$ have a conditional distribution $p(\mathbf{f}_{n-m}|\mathbf{f}_m)$, the mean of which is given by $\mathbb{E}[\mathbf{f}_{n-m}|\mathbf{f}_m] = K_{(n-m)m}K_{mm}^{-1}\mathbf{f}_m$.[3] Say we replace the true likelihood term for the points in R by $\mathcal{N}(\mathbf{y}_{n-m}|\mathbb{E}[\mathbf{f}_{n-m}|\mathbf{f}_m], \sigma_n^2 I)$. Including also the likelihood contribution of the points in set I we have

$$q(\mathbf{y}|\mathbf{f}_m) \;=\; \mathcal{N}(\mathbf{y}|K_{nm}K_{mm}^{-1}\mathbf{f}_m, \sigma_n^2 I), \tag{8.20}$$

which can also be written as $q(\mathbf{y}|\mathbf{f}_m) = \mathcal{N}(\mathbf{y}|\mathbb{E}[\mathbf{f}|\mathbf{f}_m], \sigma_n^2 I)$. The key feature here is that we have absorbed the information in all n points of $\mathcal{D}$ into the m points in I.

The form of $q(\mathbf{y}|\mathbf{f}_m)$ in eq. (8.20) might seem rather arbitrary, but in fact it can be shown that if we consider minimizing $\mathrm{KL}(q(\mathbf{f}|\mathbf{y})\|p(\mathbf{f}|\mathbf{y}))$, the KL-divergence between the approximating distribution $q(\mathbf{f}|\mathbf{y})$ and the true posterior $p(\mathbf{f}|\mathbf{y})$ over all q distributions of the form $q(\mathbf{f}|\mathbf{y}) \propto p(\mathbf{f})R(\mathbf{f}_m)$ where R is positive and depends on $\mathbf{f}_m$ only, this is the form we obtain. See Seeger [2003, Lemma 4.1 and sec. C.2.1] for detailed derivations, and also Csató [2002, sec. 3.3].

To make predictions we first have to compute the posterior distribution $q(\mathbf{f}_m|\mathbf{y})$. Define the shorthand $P = K_{mm}^{-1}K_{mn}$ so that $\mathbb{E}[\mathbf{f}|\mathbf{f}_m] = P^\top \mathbf{f}_m$. Then we have

$$q(\mathbf{y}|\mathbf{f}_m) \;\propto\; \exp\big(-\frac{1}{2\sigma_n^2}(\mathbf{y} - P^\top\mathbf{f}_m)^\top(\mathbf{y} - P^\top\mathbf{f}_m)\big). \tag{8.21}$$

Combining this with the prior $p(\mathbf{f}_m) \propto \exp(-\mathbf{f}_m^\top K_{mm}^{-1}\mathbf{f}_m/2)$ we obtain

$$q(\mathbf{f}_m|\mathbf{y}) \;\propto\; \exp\big(-\frac{1}{2}\mathbf{f}_m^\top(K_{mm}^{-1} + \frac{1}{\sigma_n^2}PP^\top)\mathbf{f}_m + \frac{1}{\sigma_n^2}\mathbf{y}^\top P^\top\mathbf{f}_m\big), \tag{8.22}$$

which can be recognized as a Gaussian $\mathcal{N}(\boldsymbol{\mu}, A)$ with

$$A^{-1} = \sigma_n^{-2}(\sigma_n^2 K_{mm}^{-1} + PP^\top) = \sigma_n^{-2}K_{mm}^{-1}(\sigma_n^2 K_{mm} + K_{mn}K_{nm})K_{mm}^{-1}, \tag{8.23}$$

$$\boldsymbol{\mu} = \sigma_n^{-2}AP\mathbf{y} = K_{mm}(\sigma_n^2 K_{mm} + K_{mn}K_{nm})^{-1}K_{mn}\mathbf{y}. \tag{8.24}$$

Thus the predictive mean is given by

$$\mathbb{E}_q[f(\mathbf{x}_*)] = \mathbf{k}_m(\mathbf{x}_*)^\top K_{mm}^{-1}\boldsymbol{\mu} \tag{8.25}$$

$$= \mathbf{k}_m(\mathbf{x}_*)^\top(\sigma_n^2 K_{mm} + K_{mn}K_{nm})^{-1}K_{mn}\mathbf{y}, \tag{8.26}$$

which turns out to be just the same as the predictive mean under the SR model, as given in eq. (8.14). However, the predictive variance is different. The argument is the same as in eq. (3.23) and yields

$$\begin{aligned}
\mathbb{V}_q[f(\mathbf{x}_*)] \;=\;\; & k(\mathbf{x}_*, \mathbf{x}_*) - \mathbf{k}_m(\mathbf{x}_*)^\top K_{mm}^{-1}\mathbf{k}_m(\mathbf{x}_*) \\
& + \mathbf{k}_m(\mathbf{x}_*)^\top K_{mm}^{-1}\mathrm{cov}(\mathbf{f}_m|\mathbf{y})K_{mm}^{-1}\mathbf{k}_m(\mathbf{x}_*) \\
=\;\; & k(\mathbf{x}_*, \mathbf{x}_*) - \mathbf{k}_m(\mathbf{x}_*)^\top K_{mm}^{-1}\mathbf{k}_m(\mathbf{x}_*) \\
& + \sigma_n^2\mathbf{k}_m(\mathbf{x}_*)^\top(\sigma_n^2 K_{mm} + K_{mn}K_{nm})^{-1}\mathbf{k}_m(\mathbf{x}_*).
\end{aligned} \tag{8.27}$$

---

[3]There is no a priori reason why the m points chosen have to be a subset of the n points in $\mathcal{D}$—they could be disjoint from the training set. However, for our derivations below we will consider them to be a subset.

Notice that predictive variance is the sum of the predictive variance under the SR model (last term in eq. (8.27)) plus $k(\mathbf{x}_*, \mathbf{x}_*) - \mathbf{k}_m(\mathbf{x}_*)^\top K_{mm}^{-1} \mathbf{k}_m(\mathbf{x}_*)$ which is the predictive variance at $\mathbf{x}_*$ given $\mathbf{f}_m$. Thus eq. (8.27) is never smaller than the SR predictive variance and will become close to $k(\mathbf{x}_*, \mathbf{x}_*)$ when $\mathbf{x}_*$ is far away from the points in set I.

As for the SR model it takes time $\mathcal{O}(m^2 n)$ to carry out the necessary matrix computations. After this the prediction of the mean for a new test point takes time $\mathcal{O}(m)$, and the predictive variance takes $\mathcal{O}(m^2)$.

We have $q(\mathbf{y}|\mathbf{f}_m) = \mathcal{N}(\mathbf{y}|P^\top \mathbf{f}_m, \sigma_n^2 I)$ and $p(\mathbf{f}_m) = \mathcal{N}(\mathbf{0}, K_{mm})$. By integrating out $\mathbf{f}_m$ we find that $\mathbf{y} \sim \mathcal{N}(\mathbf{0}, K + \sigma_n^2 I_n)$. Thus the marginal likelihood for the projected process approximation is the same as that for the SR model eq. (8.17).

Again the question of how to choose which points go into the set I arises. Csató and Opper [2002] present a method in which the training examples are presented sequentially (in an "on-line" fashion). Given the current active set I one can compute the novelty of a new input point; if this is large, then this point is added to I, otherwise the point is added to R. To be precise, the novelty of an input $\mathbf{x}$ is computed as $k(\mathbf{x}, \mathbf{x}) - \mathbf{k}_m(\mathbf{x})^\top K_{mm}^{-1} \mathbf{k}(\mathbf{x})$, which can be recognized as the predictive variance at $\mathbf{x}$ given non-noisy observations at the points in I. If the active set gets larger than some preset maximum size, then points can be deleted from I, as specified in section 3.3 of Csató and Opper [2002]. Later work by Csató et al. [2002] replaced the dependence of the algorithm described above on the input sequence by an expectation-propagation type algorithm (see section 3.6).

As an alternative method for selecting the active set, Seeger et al. [2003] suggest using a greedy subset selection method as per Algorithm 8.1. Computation of the information gain criterion after incorporating a new site takes $\mathcal{O}(mn)$ and is thus too expensive to use as a selection criterion. However, an approximation to the information gain can be computed cheaply (see Seeger et al. [2003, eq. 3] and Seeger [2003, sec. C.4.2] for further details) and this allows the greedy subset algorithm to be run on all points in R on each iteration.

8.3.5 Bayesian Committee Machine

Tresp [2000] introduced the Bayesian committee machine (BCM) as a way of speeding up Gaussian process regression. Let $\mathbf{f}_*$ be the vector of function values at the test locations. Under GPR we obtain a predictive Gaussian distribution for $p(\mathbf{f}_*|\mathcal{D})$. For the BCM we split the dataset into p parts $\mathcal{D}_1, \ldots, \mathcal{D}_p$ where $\mathcal{D}_i = (X_i, \mathbf{y}_i)$ and make the approximation that $p(\mathbf{y}_1, \ldots, \mathbf{y}_p|\mathbf{f}_*, X) \simeq \prod_{i=1}^p p(\mathbf{y}_i|\mathbf{f}_*, X_i)$. Under this approximation we have

$$q(\mathbf{f}_*|\mathcal{D}_1, \ldots, \mathcal{D}_p) \propto p(\mathbf{f}_*) \prod_{i=1}^p p(\mathbf{y}_i|\mathbf{f}_*, X_i) = c \, \frac{\prod_{i=1}^p p(\mathbf{f}_*|\mathcal{D}_i)}{p^{p-1}(\mathbf{f}_*)}, \qquad (8.28)$$

where c is a normalization constant. Using the fact that the terms in the numerator and denomination are all Gaussian distributions over $\mathbf{f}_*$ it is easy to show (see exercise 8.7.1) that the predictive mean and covariance for $\mathbf{f}_*$ are given by

$$\mathbb{E}_q[\mathbf{f}_*|\mathcal{D}] = [\text{cov}_q(\mathbf{f}_*|\mathcal{D})] \sum_{i=1}^{p}[\text{cov}(\mathbf{f}_*|\mathcal{D}_i)]^{-1}\mathbb{E}[\mathbf{f}_*|\mathcal{D}_i], \tag{8.29}$$

$$[\text{cov}_q(\mathbf{f}_*|\mathcal{D})]^{-1} = -(p-1)K_{**}^{-1} + \sum_{i=1}^{p}[\text{cov}(\mathbf{f}_*|\mathcal{D}_i)]^{-1}, \tag{8.30}$$

where K_{**} is the covariance matrix evaluated at the test points. Here $\mathbb{E}[\mathbf{f}_*|\mathcal{D}_i]$ and $\text{cov}(\mathbf{f}_*|\mathcal{D}_i)$ are the mean and covariance of the predictions for $\mathbf{f}_*$ given $\mathcal{D}_i$, as given in eqs. (2.23) and (2.24). Note that eq. (8.29) has an interesting form in that the predictions from each part of the dataset are weighted by the inverse predictive covariance.

We are free to choose how to partition the dataset $\mathcal{D}$. This has two aspects, the number of partitions and the assignment of data points to the partitions. If we wish each partition to have size m, then $p = n/m$. Tresp [2000] used a random assignment of data points to partitions but Schwaighofer and Tresp [2003] recommend that clustering the data (e.g. with p-means clustering) can lead to improved performance. However, note that compared to the greedy schemes used above clustering does not make use of the target y values, only the inputs $\mathbf{x}$.

Although it is possible to make predictions for any number of test points n_*, this slows the method down as it involves the inversion of $n_* \times n_*$ matrices. Schwaighofer and Tresp [2003] recommend making test predictions on blocks of size m so that all matrices are of the same size. In this case the computational complexity of BCM is $\mathcal{O}(pm^3) = \mathcal{O}(m^2 n)$ for predicting m test points, or $\mathcal{O}(mn)$ per test point.

The BCM approach is *transductive* [Vapnik, 1995] rather than inductive, in the sense that the method computes a test-set dependent model making use of the test set input locations. Note also that if we wish to make a prediction at just one test point, it would be necessary to "hallucinate" some extra test points as eq. (8.28) generally becomes a better approximation as the number of test points increases.

8.3.6 Iterative Solution of Linear Systems

One straightforward method to speed up GP regression is to note that the linear system $(K + \sigma_n^2 I)\mathbf{v} = \mathbf{y}$ can be solved by an iterative method, for example conjugate gradients (CG). (See Golub and Van Loan [1989, sec. 10.2] for further details on the CG method.) Conjugate gradients gives the exact solution (ignoring round-off errors) if run for n iterations, but it will give an approximate solution if terminated earlier, say after k iterations, with time complexity $\mathcal{O}(kn^2)$. This method has been suggested by Wahba et al. [1995] (in the context of numerical weather prediction) and by Gibbs and MacKay [1997] (in the context of general GP regression). CG methods have also been used in the context

Method	m	SMSE	MSLL	mean runtime (s)
SD	256	0.0813 ± 0.0198	-1.4291 ± 0.0558	0.8
	512	0.0532 ± 0.0046	-1.5834 ± 0.0319	2.1
	1024	0.0398 ± 0.0036	-1.7149 ± 0.0293	6.5
	2048	0.0290 ± 0.0013	-1.8611 ± 0.0204	25.0
	4096	0.0200 ± 0.0008	-2.0241 ± 0.0151	100.7
SR	256	0.0351 ± 0.0036	-1.6088 ± 0.0984	11.0
	512	0.0259 ± 0.0014	-1.8185 ± 0.0357	27.0
	1024	0.0193 ± 0.0008	-1.9728 ± 0.0207	79.5
	2048	0.0150 ± 0.0005	-2.1126 ± 0.0185	284.8
	4096	0.0110 ± 0.0004	-2.2474 ± 0.0204	927.6
PP	256	0.0351 ± 0.0036	-1.6940 ± 0.0528	17.3
	512	0.0259 ± 0.0014	-1.8423 ± 0.0286	41.4
	1024	0.0193 ± 0.0008	-1.9823 ± 0.0233	95.1
	2048	0.0150 ± 0.0005	-2.1125 ± 0.0202	354.2
	4096	0.0110 ± 0.0004	-2.2399 ± 0.0160	964.5
BCM	256	0.0314 ± 0.0046	-1.7066 ± 0.0550	506.4
	512	0.0281 ± 0.0055	-1.7807 ± 0.0820	660.5
	1024	0.0180 ± 0.0010	-2.0081 ± 0.0321	1043.2
	2048	0.0136 ± 0.0007	-2.1364 ± 0.0266	1920.7

Table 8.1: Test results on the inverse dynamics problem for a number of different methods. Ten repetitions were used, the mean loss is shown $\pm$ one standard deviation.

of Laplace GPC, where linear systems are solved repeatedly to obtain the MAP solution $\tilde{\mathbf{f}}$ (see sections 3.4 and 3.5 for details).

One way that the CG method can be speeded up is by using an approximate rather than exact matrix-vector multiplication. For example, recent work by Yang et al. [2005] uses the improved fast Gauss transform for this purpose.

8.3.7 Comparison of Approximate GPR Methods

Above we have presented six approximation methods for GPR. Of these, we retain only those methods which scale linearly with n, so the iterative solution of linear systems must be discounted. Also we discount the Nyström approximation in preference to the SR method, leaving four alternatives: subset of regressors (SR), subset of data (SD), projected process (PP) and Bayesian committee machine (BCM).

Table 8.1 shows results of the four methods on the robot arm inverse dynamics problem described in section 2.5 which has $D = 21$ input variables, 44,484 training examples and 4,449 test examples. As in section 2.5 we used the squared exponential covariance function with a separate length-scale parameter for each of the 21 input dimensions.

Method	Storage	Initialization	Mean	Variance
SD	$\mathcal{O}(m^2)$	$\mathcal{O}(m^3)$	$\mathcal{O}(m)$	$\mathcal{O}(m^2)$
SR	$\mathcal{O}(mn)$	$\mathcal{O}(m^2n)$	$\mathcal{O}(m)$	$\mathcal{O}(m^2)$
PP	$\mathcal{O}(mn)$	$\mathcal{O}(m^2n)$	$\mathcal{O}(m)$	$\mathcal{O}(m^2)$
BCM	$\mathcal{O}(mn)$		$\mathcal{O}(mn)$	$\mathcal{O}(mn)$

Table 8.2: A comparison of the space and time complexity of the four methods using random selection of subsets. Initialization gives the time needed to carry out preliminary matrix computations before the test point $\mathbf{x}_*$ is known. Mean (resp. variance) refers to the time needed to compute the predictive mean (variance) at $\mathbf{x}_*$.

For the SD method a subset of the training data of size m was selected at random, and the hyperparameters were set by optimizing the marginal likelihood on this subset. As ARD was used, this involved the optimization of $D+2$ hyperparameters. This process was repeated 10 times, giving rise to the mean and standard deviation recorded in Table 8.1. For the SR, PP and BCM methods, the same subsets of the data and hyperparameter vectors were used as had been obtained from the SD experiments.[4] Note that the $m = 4096$ result is not available for BCM as this gave an out-of-memory error.

These experiments were conducted on a 2.0 GHz twin processor machine with 3.74 GB of RAM. The code for all four methods was written in MATLAB.[5]

A summary of the time complexities for the four methods are given in Table 8.2. Thus for a test set of size n_* and using full (mean and variance) predictions we find that the SD method has time complexity $\mathcal{O}(m^3) + \mathcal{O}(m^2n_*)$, for the SR and PP methods it is $\mathcal{O}(m^2n) + \mathcal{O}(m^2n_*)$, and for the BCM method it is $\mathcal{O}(mnn_*)$. Assuming that $n_* \geq m$ these reduce to $\mathcal{O}(m^2n_*)$, $\mathcal{O}(m^2n)$ and $\mathcal{O}(mnn_*)$ respectively. These complexities are in broad agreement with the timings in Table 8.1.

The results from Table 8.1 are plotted in Figure 8.1. As we would expect, the general trend is that as m increases the SMSE and MSLL scores decrease. Notice that it is well worth doing runs with small m so as to obtain a learning curve with respect to m; this helps in getting a feeling of how useful runs at large m will be. Both in terms of SMSE and MSLL we see (not surprisingly) that SD is inferior to the other methods, all of which have similar performance.

These results were obtained using a random selection of the active set. Some experiments were also carried out using active selection for the SD method (IVM) and for the SR method but these did not lead to significant improvements in performance. For BCM we also experimented with the use of p-means clustering instead of random assignment to partitions; again this did not lead to significant improvements in performance. Overall on this dataset our con-

---

[4]In the BCM case it was only the hyperparameters that were re-used; the data was partitioned randomly into blocks of size m.

[5]We thank Anton Schwaighofer for making his BCM code available to us.

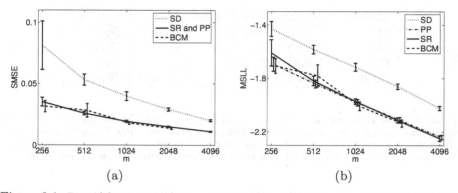

Figure 8.1: Panel(a): plot of SMSE against m. Panel(b) shows the MSLL for the four methods. The error bars denote one standard deviation. For clarity in both panels the BCM results are slightly displaced horizontally w.r.t. the SR results.

clusion is that for fixed m SR or PP are the methods of choice, as BCM has longer running times for similar performance. However, notice that if we compare on runtime, then SD for $m = 4096$ is competitive with the SR, PP and BCM results for $m = 1024$ on both time and performance.

In the above experiments the hyperparameters for all methods were set by optimizing the marginal likelihood of the SD model of size m. This means that we get a direct comparison of the different methods using the same hyperparameters and subsets. However, one could alternatively optimize the (approximate) marginal likelihood for each method (see section 8.5) and then compare results. Notice that the hyperparameters which optimize the approximate marginal likelihood may depend on the method. For example Figure 5.3(b) shows that the maximum in the marginal likelihood occurs at shorter length-scales as the amount of data increases. This effect has also been observed by V. Tresp and A. Schwaighofer (pers. comm., 2004) when comparing the SD marginal likelihood eq. (8.31) with the full marginal likelihood computed on all n datapoints eq. (5.8).

Schwaighofer and Tresp [2003] report some experimental comparisons between the BCM method and some other approximation methods for a number of synthetic regression problems. In these experiments they optimized the kernel hyperparameters for each method separately. Their results are that for fixed m BCM performs as well as or better than the other methods. However, these results depend on factors such as the noise level in the data generating process; they report (pers. comm., 2005) that for relatively large noise levels BCM no longer displays an advantage. Based on the evidence currently available we are unable to provide firm recommendations for one approximation method over another; further research is required to understand the factors that affect performance.

8.4 Approximations for GPC with Fixed Hyperparameters

The approximation methods for GPC are similar to those for GPR, but need to deal with the non-Gaussian likelihood as well, either by using the Laplace approximation, see section 3.4, or expectation propagation (EP), see section 3.6. In this section we focus mainly on binary classification tasks, although some of the methods can also be extended to the multi-class case.

For the subset of regressors (SR) method we again use the model $f_{\mathrm{SR}}(\mathbf{x}_*) = \sum_{i=1}^{m} \alpha_i k(\mathbf{x}_*, \mathbf{x}_i)$ with $\boldsymbol{\alpha}_m \sim \mathcal{N}(\mathbf{0}, K_{mm}^{-1})$. The likelihood is non-Gaussian but the optimization problem to find the MAP value of $\boldsymbol{\alpha}_m$ is convex and can be obtained using a Newton iteration. Using the MAP value $\hat{\boldsymbol{\alpha}}_m$ and the Hessian at this point we obtain a predictive mean and variance for $f(\mathbf{x}_*)$ which can be fed through the sigmoid function to yield probabilistic predictions. As usual the question of how to choose a subset of points arises; Lin et al. [2000] select these using a clustering method, while Zhu and Hastie [2002] propose a forward selection strategy.

The subset of datapoints (SD) method for GPC was proposed in Lawrence et al. [2003], using an EP-style approximation of the posterior, and the differential entropy score (see section 8.3.3) to select new sites for inclusion. Note that the EP approximation lends itself very naturally to sparsification: a sparse model results when some *site precisions* (see eq. (3.51)) are zero, making the corresponding likelihood term vanish. A computational gain can thus be achieved by ignoring likelihood terms whose site precisions are very small.

The projected process (PP) approximation can also be used with non-Gaussian likelihoods. Csató and Opper [2002] present an "online" method where the examples are processed sequentially, while Csató et al. [2002] give an expectation-propagation type algorithm where multiple sweeps through the training data are permitted.

The Bayesian committee machine (BCM) has also been generalized to deal with non-Gaussian likelihoods in Tresp [2000]. As in the GPR case the dataset is broken up into blocks, but now approximate inference is carried out using the Laplace approximation in each block to yield an approximate predictive mean $\mathbb{E}_q[\mathbf{f}_*|\mathcal{D}_i]$ and approximate predictive covariance $\mathrm{cov}_q(\mathbf{f}_*|\mathcal{D}_i)$. These predictions are then combined as before using equations 8.29 and 8.30.

8.5 Approximating the Marginal Likelihood and its Derivatives *

We consider approximations first for GP regression, and then for GP classification. For GPR, both the SR and PP methods give rise to the same approximate marginal likelihood as given in eq. (8.17). For the SD method, a very simple approximation (ignoring the datapoints not in the active set) is given by

$$\log p_{\mathrm{SD}}(\mathbf{y}_m | X_m) = -\tfrac{1}{2}\log|K_{mm}+\sigma^2 I| - \tfrac{1}{2}\mathbf{y}_m^\top (K_{mm}+\sigma^2 I)^{-1}\mathbf{y}_m - \tfrac{m}{2}\log(2\pi),$$
(8.31)

where $\mathbf{y}_m$ is the subvector of $\mathbf{y}$ corresponding to the active set; eq. (8.31) is simply the log marginal likelihood under the model $\mathbf{y}_m \sim \mathcal{N}(\mathbf{0}, K_{mm}+\sigma^2 I)$.

For the BCM, a simple approach would be to sum eq. (8.31) evaluated on each partition of the dataset. This ignores interactions between the partitions. Tresp and Schwaighofer (pers. comm., 2004) have suggested a more sophisticated BCM-based method which approximately takes these interactions into account.

For GPC under the SR approximation, one can simply use the Laplace or EP approximations on the finite-dimensional model. For SD one can again ignore all datapoints not in the active set and compute an approximation to $\log p(\mathbf{y}_m | X_m)$ using either Laplace or EP. For the projected process (PP) method, Seeger [2003, p. 162] suggests the following lower bound

$$\begin{aligned}
\log p(\mathbf{y}|X) &= \log \int p(\mathbf{y}|\mathbf{f})p(\mathbf{f})\,d\mathbf{f} = \log \int q(\mathbf{f})\frac{p(\mathbf{y}|\mathbf{f})p(\mathbf{f})}{q(\mathbf{f})}\,d\mathbf{f} \\
&\geq \int q(\mathbf{f})\log\left(\frac{p(\mathbf{y}|\mathbf{f})p(\mathbf{f})}{q(\mathbf{f})}\right)d\mathbf{f} \qquad\qquad (8.32) \\
&= \int q(\mathbf{f})\log q(\mathbf{y}|\mathbf{f})\,d\mathbf{f} - \mathrm{KL}(q(\mathbf{f})\|p(\mathbf{f})) \\
&= \sum_{i=1}^{n} \int q(f_i)\log p(y_i|f_i)\,df_i - \mathrm{KL}(q(\mathbf{f}_m)\|p(\mathbf{f}_m)),
\end{aligned}$$

where $q(\mathbf{f})$ is a shorthand for $q(\mathbf{f}|\mathbf{y})$ and eq. (8.32) follows from the equation on the previous line using Jensen's inequality. The KL divergence term can be readily evaluated using eq. (A.23), and the one-dimensional integrals can be tackled using numerical quadrature.

We are not aware of work on extending the BCM approximations to the marginal likelihood to GPC.

Given the various approximations to the marginal likelihood mentioned above, we may also want to compute derivatives in order to optimize it. Clearly it will make sense to keep the active set fixed during the optimization, although note that this clashes with the fact that methods that select the active set might choose a different set as the covariance function parameters $\boldsymbol{\theta}$ change. For the classification case the derivatives can be quite complex due to the fact that site parameters (such as the MAP values $\hat{\mathbf{f}}$, see section 3.4.1) change as $\boldsymbol{\theta}$ changes. (We have already seen an example of this in section 5.5 for the non-sparse Laplace approximation.) Seeger [2003, sec. 4.8] describes some experiments comparing SD and PP methods for the optimization of the marginal likelihood on both regression and classification problems.

8.6 Appendix: Equivalence of SR and GPR Using the Nyström Approximate Kernel *

In section 8.3 we derived the subset of regressors predictors for the mean and variance, as given in equations 8.14 and 8.15. The aim of this appendix is to show that these are equivalent to the predictors that are obtained by replacing $k(\mathbf{x}, \mathbf{x}')$ systematically with $\tilde{k}(\mathbf{x}, \mathbf{x}')$ in the GPR prediction equations 2.25 and 2.26.

First for the mean. The GPR predictor is $\mathbb{E}[f(\mathbf{x}_*)] = \mathbf{k}(\mathbf{x}_*)^\top (K + \sigma_n^2 I)^{-1} \mathbf{y}$. Replacing all occurrences of $k(\mathbf{x}, \mathbf{x}')$ with $\tilde{k}(\mathbf{x}, \mathbf{x}')$ we obtain

$$\mathbb{E}[\tilde{f}(\mathbf{x}_*)] = \tilde{\mathbf{k}}(\mathbf{x}_*)^\top (\tilde{K} + \sigma_n^2 I)^{-1} \mathbf{y} \tag{8.33}$$

$$= \mathbf{k}_m(\mathbf{x}_*)^\top K_{mm}^{-1} K_{mn} (K_{nm} K_{mm}^{-1} K_{mn} + \sigma_n^2 I)^{-1} \mathbf{y} \tag{8.34}$$

$$= \sigma_n^{-2} \mathbf{k}_m(\mathbf{x}_*)^\top K_{mm}^{-1} K_{mn} \left[I_n - K_{nm} Q^{-1} K_{mn} \right] \mathbf{y} \tag{8.35}$$

$$= \sigma_n^{-2} \mathbf{k}_m(\mathbf{x}_*)^\top K_{mm}^{-1} \left[I_m - K_{mn} K_{nm} Q^{-1} \right] K_{mn} \mathbf{y} \tag{8.36}$$

$$= \sigma_n^{-2} \mathbf{k}_m(\mathbf{x}_*)^\top K_{mm}^{-1} \left[\sigma_n^2 K_{mm} Q^{-1} \right] K_{mn} \mathbf{y} \tag{8.37}$$

$$= \mathbf{k}_m(\mathbf{x}_*)^\top Q^{-1} K_{mn} \mathbf{y}, \tag{8.38}$$

where $Q = \sigma_n^2 K_{mm} + K_{mn} K_{nm}$, which agrees with eq. (8.14). Equation (8.35) follows from eq. (8.34) by use of the matrix inversion lemma eq. (A.9) and eq. (8.37) follows from eq. (8.36) using $I_m = (\sigma_n^2 K_{mm} + K_{mn} K_{nm}) Q^{-1}$. For the predictive variance we have

$$\mathbb{V}[\tilde{f}_*] = \tilde{k}(\mathbf{x}_*, \mathbf{x}_*) - \tilde{\mathbf{k}}(\mathbf{x}_*)^\top (\tilde{K} + \sigma_n^2 I)^{-1} \tilde{\mathbf{k}}(\mathbf{x}_*) \tag{8.39}$$

$$= \mathbf{k}_m(\mathbf{x}_*)^\top K_{mm}^{-1} \mathbf{k}_m(\mathbf{x}_*) - \tag{8.40}$$

$$\mathbf{k}_m(\mathbf{x}_*)^\top K_{mm}^{-1} K_{mn} (K_{nm} K_{mm}^{-1} K_{mn} + \sigma_n^2 I)^{-1} K_{nm} K_{mm}^{-1} \mathbf{k}_m(\mathbf{x}_*)$$

$$= \mathbf{k}_m(\mathbf{x}_*)^\top K_{mm}^{-1} \mathbf{k}_m(\mathbf{x}_*) - \mathbf{k}_m(\mathbf{x}_*)^\top Q^{-1} K_{mn} K_{nm} K_{mm}^{-1} \mathbf{k}_m(\mathbf{x}_*) \tag{8.41}$$

$$= \mathbf{k}_m(\mathbf{x}_*)^\top \left[I_m - Q^{-1} K_{mn} K_{nm} \right] K_{mm}^{-1} \mathbf{k}_m(\mathbf{x}_*) \tag{8.42}$$

$$= \mathbf{k}_m(\mathbf{x}_*)^\top Q^{-1} \sigma_n^2 K_{mm} K_{mm}^{-1} \mathbf{k}_m(\mathbf{x}_*) \tag{8.43}$$

$$= \sigma_n^2 \mathbf{k}_m(\mathbf{x}_*)^\top Q^{-1} \mathbf{k}_m(\mathbf{x}_*), \tag{8.44}$$

in agreement with eq. (8.15). The step between eqs. (8.40) and (8.41) is obtained from eqs. (8.34) and (8.38) above, and eq. (8.43) follows from eq. (8.42) using $I_m = (\sigma_n^2 K_{mm} + K_{mn} K_{nm}) Q^{-1}$.

8.7 Exercises

1. Verify that the mean and covariance of the BCM predictions (equations 8.29 and 8.30) are correct. If you are stuck, see Tresp [2000] for details.

2. Using eq. (8.10) and the fact that $C_{\text{opt}} = K_{nm} K_{mm}^{-1}$ show that $E(C_{\text{opt}}) = \text{tr}(K - \tilde{K})$, where $\tilde{K} = K_{nm} K_{mm}^{-1} K_{mn}$. Now consider adding one datapoint into set I, so that K_{mm} grows to $K_{(m+1)(m+1)}$. Using eq. (A.12)

show that the change in E due to adding the extra datapoint can be computed in time $\mathcal{O}(mn)$. If you need help, see Schölkopf and Smola [2002, sec. 10.2.2] for further details.

Chapter 9

Further Issues and Conclusions

In the previous chapters of the book we have concentrated on giving a solid grounding in the use of GPs for regression and classification problems, including model selection issues, approximation methods for large datasets, and connections to related models. In this chapter we provide some short descriptions of other issues relating to Gaussian process prediction, with pointers to the literature for further reading.

So far we have mainly discussed the case when the output target y is a single label, but in section 9.1 we describe how to deal with the case that there are multiple output targets. Similarly, for the regression problem we have focussed on i.i.d. Gaussian noise; in section 9.2 we relax this condition to allow the noise process to have correlations. The classification problem is characterized by a non-Gaussian likelihood function; however, there are other non-Gaussian likelihoods of interest, as described in section 9.3.

We may not only have observations of function values, by also on derivatives of the target function. In section 9.4 we discuss how to make use of this information in the GPR framework. Also it may happen that there is noise on the observation of the input variable $\mathbf{x}$; in section 9.5 we explain how this can be handled. In section 9.6 we mention how more flexible models can be obtained using mixtures of Gaussian process models.

As well as carrying out prediction for test inputs, one might also wish to try to find the global optimum of a function within some compact set. Approaches based on Gaussian processes for this problem are described in section 9.7. The use of Gaussian processes to evaluate integrals is covered in section 9.8.

By using a scale mixture of Gaussians construction one can obtain a multivariate Student's t distribution. This construction can be extended to give a Student's t process, as explained in section 9.9. One key aspect of the Bayesian framework relates to the incorporation of prior knowledge into the problem formulation. In some applications we not only have the dataset $\mathcal{D}$ but also additional information. For example, for an optical character recognition problem we know that translating the input pattern by one pixel will not change the label of the pattern. Approaches for incorporating this knowledge are discussed in section 9.10.

In this book we have concentrated on supervised learning problems. However, GPs can be used as components in unsupervised learning models, as described in section 9.11. Finally, we close with some conclusions and an outlook to the future in section 9.12.

9.1 Multiple Outputs

Throughout this book we have concentrated on the problem of predicting a single output variable y from an input $\mathbf{x}$. However, it can happen that one may wish to predict multiple output variables (or channels) simultaneously. For example in the robot inverse dynamics problem described in section 2.5 there are really seven torques to be predicted. A simple approach is to model each output variable as independent from the others and treat them separately. However, this may lose information and be suboptimal.

One way in which correlation can occur is through a correlated noise process. Even if the output channels are *a priori* independent, if the noise process is correlated then this will induce correlations in the posterior processes. Such a situation is easily handled in the GP framework by considering the joint, block-diagonal, prior over the function values of each channel.

Another way that correlation of multiple channels can occur is if the prior already has this structure. For example in geostatistical situations there may be correlations between the abundances of different ores, e.g. silver and lead. This situation requires that the covariance function models not only the correlation structure of each channel, but also the cross-correlations between channels. Some work on this topic can be found in the geostatistics literature under the name of cokriging, see e.g. Cressie [1993, sec. 3.2.3]. One way to induce correlations between a number of output channels is to obtain them as linear combinations of a number of latent channels, as described in Teh et al. [2005]; see also Micchelli and Pontil [2005]. A related approach is taken by Boyle and Frean [2005] who introduce correlations between two processes by deriving them as different convolutions of the same underlying white noise process.

cokriging

9.2 Noise Models with Dependencies

The noise models used so far have almost exclusively assumed Gaussianity and independence. Non-Gaussian likelihoods are mentioned in section 9.3 below. Inside the family of Gaussian noise models, it is not difficult to model dependencies. This may be particularly useful in models involving time. We simply add terms to the noise covariance function with the desired structure, including

coloured noise

hyperparameters. In fact, we already used this approach for the atmospheric
carbon dioxide modelling task in section 5.4.3. Also, Murray-Smith and Girard
[2001] have used an autoregressive moving-average (ARMA) noise model (see   ARMA
also eq. (B.51)) in a GP regression task.

9.3 Non-Gaussian Likelihoods

Our main focus has been on regression with Gaussian noise, and classification
using the logistic or probit response functions. However, Gaussian processes can
be used as priors with other likelihood functions. For example, Diggle et al.
[1998] were concerned with modelling count data measured geographically using
a Poisson likelihood with a spatially varying rate. They achieved this by placing
a GP prior over the log Poisson rate.

Goldberg et al. [1998] stayed with a Gaussian noise model, but introduced
heteroscedasticity, i.e. allowing the noise variance to be a function of $\mathbf{x}$. This
was achieved by placing a GP prior on the log variance function. Neal [1997]
robustified GP regression by using a Student's t-distributed noise model rather
than Gaussian noise. Chu and Ghahramani [2005] have described how to use
GPs for the ordinal regression problem, where one is given ranked preference
information as the target data.

9.4 Derivative Observations

Since differentiation is a linear operator, the derivative of a Gaussian process
is another Gaussian process. Thus we can use GPs to make predictions about
derivatives, and also to make inference based on derivative information. In
general, we can make inference based on the joint Gaussian distribution of
function values and partial derivatives. A covariance function $k(\cdot, \cdot)$ on function
values *implies* the following (mixed) covariance between function values and
partial derivatives, and between partial derivatives

$$\operatorname{cov}\left(f_i, \frac{\partial f_j}{\partial x_{dj}}\right) = \frac{\partial k(\mathbf{x}_i, \mathbf{x}_j)}{\partial x_{dj}}, \qquad \operatorname{cov}\left(\frac{\partial f_i}{\partial x_{di}}, \frac{\partial f_j}{\partial x_{ej}}\right) = \frac{\partial^2 k(\mathbf{x}_i, \mathbf{x}_j)}{\partial x_{di} \partial x_{ej}}, \quad (9.1)$$

see e.g. Papoulis [1991, ch. 10] or Adler [1981, sec. 2.2]. With n datapoints in
D dimensions, the complete joint distribution of f and its D partial derivatives
involves $n(D+1)$ quantities, but in a typical application we may only have access
to or interest in a subset of these; we simply remove the rows and columns
from the joint matrix which are not needed. Observed function values and
derivatives may often have different noise levels, which are incorporated by
adding a diagonal contribution with differing hyperparameters. Inference and
predictions are done as usual. This approach was used in the context of learning
in dynamical systems by Solak et al. [2003]. In Figure 9.1 the posterior process
with and without derivative observations are compared. Noise-free derivatives
may be a useful way to enforce known constraints in a modelling problem.

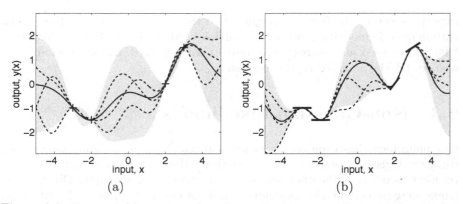

Figure 9.1: In panel (a) we show four data points in a one dimensional noise-free regression problem, together with three functions sampled from the posterior and the 95% confidence region in light grey. In panel (b) the same observations have been augmented by noise-free derivative information, indicated by small tangent segments at the data points. The covariance function is the squared exponential with unit process variance and unit length-scale.

9.5   Prediction with Uncertain Inputs

It can happen that the input values to a prediction problem can be uncertain. For example, for a discrete time series one can perform multi-step-ahead predictions by iterating one-step-ahead predictions. However, if the one-step-ahead predictions include uncertainty, then it is necessary to propagate this uncertainty forward to get the proper multi-step-ahead predictions. One simple approach is to use sampling methods. Alternatively, it may be possible to use analytical approaches. Girard et al. [2003] showed that it is possible to compute the mean and variance of the output analytically when using the SE covariance function and Gaussian input noise.

More generally, the problem of regression with uncertain inputs has been studied in the statistics literature under the name of errors-in-variables regression. See Dellaportas and Stephens [1995] for a Bayesian treatment of the problem and pointers to the literature.

9.6   Mixtures of Gaussian Processes

In chapter 4 we have seen many ideas for making the covariance functions more flexible. Another route is to use a mixture of different Gaussian process models, each one used in some local region of input space. This kind of model is generally known as a mixture of experts model and is due to Jacobs et al. [1991]. In addition to the local expert models, the model has a *manager* that (probabilistically) assigns points to the experts. Rasmussen and Ghahramani [2002] used Gaussian process models as local experts, and based their manager on another type of stochastic process: the Dirichlet process. Inference in this model required MCMC methods.

9.7 Global Optimization

Often one is faced with the problem of being able to evaluate a continuous function $g(\mathbf{x})$, and wishing to find the global optimum (maximum or minimum) of this function within some compact set $A \subset \mathbb{R}^D$. There is a very large literature on the problem of global optimization; see Neumaier [2005] for a useful overview.

Given a dataset $\mathcal{D} = \{(\mathbf{x}_i, g(\mathbf{x}_i)) | i = 1, \ldots, n\}$, one appealing approach is to fit a GP regression model to this data. This will give a mean prediction and predictive variance for every $\mathbf{x} \in A$. Jones [2001] examines a number of criteria that have been suggested for where to make the next function evaluation based on the predictive mean and variance. One issue with this approach is that one may need to *search* to find the optimum of the criterion, which may itself be multimodal optimization problem. However, if evaluations of g are expensive or time-consuming, it can make sense to work hard on this new optimization problem.

For historical references and further work in this area see Jones [2001] and Ritter [2000, sec. VIII.2].

9.8 Evaluation of Integrals

Another interesting and unusual application of Gaussian processes is for the evaluation of the integrals of a deterministic function f. One evaluates the function at a number of locations, and then one can use a Gaussian process as a posterior over functions. This posterior over functions induces a posterior over the value of the integral (since each possible function from the posterior would give rise to a particular value of the integral). For some covariance functions (e.g. the squared exponential), one can compute the expectation and variance of the value of the integral analytically. It is perhaps unusual to think of the value of the integral as being random (as it does have one particular deterministic value), but it is perfectly in line of Bayesian thinking that you treat all kinds of uncertainty using probabilities. This idea was proposed under the name of Bayes-Hermite quadrature by O'Hagan [1991], and later under the name of Bayesian Monte Carlo in Rasmussen and Ghahramani [2003].

Another approach is related to the ideas of global optimization in the section 9.7 above. One can use a GP model of a function to aid an MCMC sampling procedure, which may be advantageous if the function of interest is computationally expensive to evaluate. Rasmussen [2003] combines Hybrid Monte Carlo with a GP model of the log of the integrand, and also uses derivatives of the function (discussed in section 9.4) to get an accurate model of the integrand with very few evaluations.

combining GPs with MCMC

9.9 Student's t Process

scale mixture

A Student's t process can be obtained by applying the *scale mixture* of Gaussians construction of a Student's t distribution to a Gaussian process [O'Hagan, 1991, O'Hagan et al., 1999]. We divide the covariances by the scalar τ and put a gamma distribution on τ with shape α and mean β so that

$$\tilde{k}(\mathbf{x},\mathbf{x}') \;=\; \tau^{-1}k(\mathbf{x},\mathbf{x}'), \qquad p(\tau|\alpha,\beta) \;=\; \frac{\alpha^\alpha}{\beta^\alpha\Gamma(\alpha)}\tau^{\alpha-1}\exp\Big(-\frac{\tau\alpha}{\beta}\Big), \quad (9.2)$$

where k is any valid covariance function. Now the joint prior distribution of any finite number n of function values $\mathbf{y}$ becomes

$$
\begin{aligned}
p(\mathbf{y}|\alpha,\beta,\boldsymbol{\theta}) \;&=\; \int \mathcal{N}(\mathbf{y}|\mathbf{0},\tau^{-1}K_y)p(\tau|\alpha,\beta)d\tau \\
&=\; \frac{\Gamma(\alpha+n/2)(2\pi\alpha)^{-n/2}}{\Gamma(\alpha)|\beta^{-1}K_y|^{-1/2}}\Big(1+\frac{\beta\mathbf{y}^\top K_y^{-1}\mathbf{y}}{2\alpha}\Big)^{-(\alpha+n/2)},
\end{aligned}
\tag{9.3}
$$

which is recognized as the zero mean, multivariate Student's t distribution with 2α degrees of freedom: $p(\mathbf{y}|\alpha,\beta,\boldsymbol{\theta}) = \mathcal{T}(0,\beta^{-1}K_y,2\alpha)$. We could state a definition analogous to definition 2.1 on page 13 for the Gaussian process, and write

$$f \sim \mathcal{TP}(0,\beta^{-1}K,2\alpha), \tag{9.4}$$

cf. eq. (2.14). The marginal likelihood can be directly evaluated using eq. (9.3), and training can be achieved using the methods discussed in chapter 5 regarding α and β as hyperparameters. The predictive distribution for test cases are also t distributions, the derivation of which is left as an exercise below.

noise entanglement

Notice that the above construction is clear for noise-free processes, but that the interpretation becomes more complicated if the covariance function $k(\mathbf{x},\mathbf{x}')$ contains a noise contribution. The noise and signal get entangled by the common factor τ, and the observations can no longer be written as the sum of independent signal and noise contributions. Allowing for independent noise contributions removes analytic tractability, which may reduce the usefulness of the t process.

Exercise Using the scale mixture representation from eq. (9.3) derive the posterior predictive distribution for a Student's t process.

Exercise Consider the generating process implied by eq. (9.2), and write a program to draw functions at random. Characterize the difference between the Student's t process and the corresponding Gaussian process (obtained in the limit $\alpha \to \infty$), and explain why the t process is perhaps not as exciting as one might have hoped.

9.10 Invariances

It can happen that the input is apparently in vector form but in fact it has additional structure. A good example is a pixelated image, where the 2-d array of pixels can be arranged into a vector (e.g. in raster-scan order). Imagine that the image is of a handwritten digit; then we know that if the image is translated by one pixel it will remain the same digit. Thus we have knowledge of certain *invariances* of the input pattern. In this section we describe a number of ways in which such invariances can be exploited. Our discussion is based on Schölkopf and Smola [2002, ch. 11].

Prior knowledge about the problem tells us that certain transformations of the input would leave the class label invariant—these include simple geometric transformations such as translations, rotations,[1] rescalings, and rather less obvious ones such as line thickness transformations.[2] Given enough data it should be possible to learn the correct input-output mapping, but it would make sense to try to make use of these known invariances to reduce the amount of training data needed. There are at least three ways in which this prior knowledge has been used, as described below.

The first approach is to generate synthetic training examples by applying valid transformations to the examples we already have. This is simple but it does have the disadvantage of creating a larger training set. As kernel-machine training algorithms typically scale super-linearly with n this can be problematic.

synthetic training examples

A second approach is to make the predictor invariant to small transformations of each training case; this method was first developed by Simard et al. [1992] for neural networks under the name of "tangent prop". For a single training image we consider the manifold of images that are generated as various transformations are applied to it. This manifold will have a complex structure, but locally we can approximate it by a tangent space. The idea in "tangent prop" is that the output should be invariant to perturbations of the training example in this tangent space. For neural networks it is quite straightforward to modify the training objective function to penalize deviations from this invariance, see Simard et al. [1992] for details. Section 11.4 in Schölkopf and Smola [2002] describes some ways in which these ideas can be extended to kernel machines.

tangent prop

The third approach to dealing with invariances is to develop a representation of the input which is invariant to some or all of the transformations. For example, binary images of handwritten digits are sometimes "skeletonized" to remove the effect of line thickness. If an invariant representation can be achieved for all transformations it is the most desirable, but it can be difficult or perhaps impossible to achieve. For example, if a given training pattern can belong to more than one class (e.g. an ambiguous handwritten digit) then it is clearly not possible to find a new representation which is invariant to transformations yet leaves the classes distinguishable.

invariant representation

---

[1] The digit recognition problem is only invariant to small rotations; we must avoid turning a 6 into a 9.

[2] i.e. changing the thickness of the pen we write with within reasonable bounds does not change the digit we write.

9.11   Latent Variable Models

Our main focus in this book has been on supervised learning. However, GPs have also been used as components for models carrying out non-linear dimensionality reduction, a form of unsupervised learning. The key idea is that data which is apparently high-dimensional (e.g. a pixelated image) may really lie on a low-dimensional non-linear manifold which we wish to model.

Let $\mathbf{z} \in \mathbb{R}^L$ be a latent (or hidden) variable, and let $\mathbf{x} \in \mathbb{R}^D$ be a visible variable. We suppose that our visible data is generated by picking a point in $\mathbf{z}$-space and mapping this point into the data space through a (possibly non-linear) mapping, and then optionally adding noise. Thus $p(\mathbf{x}) = \int p(\mathbf{x}|\mathbf{z})p(\mathbf{z})d\mathbf{z}$. If the mapping from $\mathbf{z}$ to $\mathbf{x}$ is linear and $\mathbf{z}$ has a Gaussian distribution then this is the factor analysis model, and the mean and covariance of the Gaussian in $\mathbf{x}$-space can easily be determined. However, if the mapping is non-linear then the integral cannot be computed exactly. In the generative topographic mapping (GTM) model [Bishop et al., 1998b] the integral was approximated using a grid of points in $\mathbf{z}$-space. In the original GTM paper the non-linear mapping was taken to be a linear combination of non-linear basis functions, but in Bishop et al. [1998a] this was replaced by a Gaussian process mapping between the latent and visible spaces.

GTM

More recently Lawrence [2004] has introduced a rather different model known as the Gaussian process latent variable model (GPLVM). Instead of having a prior (and thus a posterior) distribution over the latent space, we consider that each data point $\mathbf{x}_i$ is derived from a corresponding latent point $\mathbf{z}_i$ through a non-linear mapping (with added noise). If a Gaussian process is used for this non-linear mapping, then one can easily write down the joint distribution $p(X|Z)$ of the visible variables conditional on the latent variables. Optimization routines can then be used to find the locations of the latent points that optimize $p(X|Z)$. This has some similarities to the work on regularized principal manifolds [Schölkopf and Smola, 2002, ch. 17] except that in the GPLVM one integrates out the latent-to-visible mapping rather than optimizing it.

GPLVM

9.12   Conclusions and Future Directions

In this section we briefly wrap up some of the threads we have developed throughout the book, and discuss possible future directions of work on Gaussian processes.

In chapter 2 we saw how Gaussian process regression is a natural extension of Bayesian linear regression to a more flexible class of models. For Gaussian noise the model can be treated analytically, and is simple enough that the GP model could be often considered as a replacement for the traditional linear analogue. We have also seen that historically there have been numerous ideas along the lines of Gaussian process models, although they have only gained a sporadic following.

One may indeed speculate, why are GPs not currently used more widely in applications? We see three major reasons: (1) Firstly, that the application of Gaussian processes requires the handling (inversion) of large matrices. While these kinds of computations were tedious 20 years ago, and impossible further in the past, even naïve implementations suffice for moderate sized problems on an anno 2005 PC. (2) Another possibility is that most of the historical work on GPs was done using fixed covariance functions, with very little guide as to how to choose such functions. The choice was to some degree arbitrary, and the idea that one should be able to *infer* the structure or parameters of the covariance function as we discuss in chapter 5 is not so well known. This is probably a very important step in turning GPs into an interesting method for practitioners. (3) The viewpoint of placing Gaussian process priors over functions is a Bayesian one. Although the adoption of Bayesian methods in the machine learning community is quite widespread, these ideas have not always been appreciated more widely in the statistics community.

Although modern computers allow simple implementations for up to a few thousand training cases, the computational constraints are still a significant limitation for applications where the datasets are significantly larger than this. In chapter 8 we have given an overview of some of the recent work on approximations for large datasets. Although there are many methods and a lot of work is currently being undertaken, both the theoretical and practical aspects of these approximations need to be understood better in order to be a useful tool to the practitioner.

The computations required for the Gaussian process classification models developed in chapter 3 are a lot more involved than for regression. Although the theoretical foundations of Gaussian process classification are well developed, it is not yet clear under which circumstances one would expect the extra work and approximations associated with treating a full probabilistic latent variable model to pay off. The answer may depend heavily on the ability to learn meaningful covariance functions.

The incorporation of prior knowledge through the choice and parameterization of the covariance function is another prime target for future work on GPs. In chapter 4 we have presented many families of covariance functions with widely differing properties, and in chapter 5 we presented principled methods for choosing between and adapting covariance functions. Particularly in the machine learning community, there has been a tendency to view Gaussian processes as a "black box"—what exactly goes on in the box is less important, as long as it gives good predictions. To our mind, we could perhaps learn something from the statisticians here, and ask how and why the models work. In fact the hierarchical formulation of the covariance functions with hyperparameters, the testing of different hypotheses and the adaptation of hyperparameters gives an excellent opportunity to understand more about the data.

We have attempted to illustrate this line of thinking with the carbon dioxide prediction example developed at some length in section 5.4.3. Although this problem is comparatively simple and very easy to get an intuitive understanding of, the principles of trying out different components in the covariance structure and adapting their parameters could be used universally. Indeed, the use of the isotropic squared exponential covariance function in the digit classification examples in chapter 3 is not really a choice which one would expect to provide very much insight to the classification problem. Although some of the results presented are as good as other current methods in the literature, one could indeed argue that the use of the squared exponential covariance function for this task makes little sense, and the low error rate is possibly due to the inherently low difficulty of the task. There is a need to develop more sensible covariance functions which allow for the incorporation of prior knowledge and help us to gain real insight into the data.

Going beyond a simple vectorial representation of the input data to take into account structure in the input domain is also a theme which we see as very important. Examples of this include the invariances described in section 9.10 arising from the structure of images, and the kernels described in section 4.4 which encode structured objects such as strings and trees.

As this brief discussion shows, we see the current level of development of Gaussian process models more as a rich, principled framework for supervised learning than a fully-developed set of tools for applications. We find the Gaussian process framework very appealing and are confident that the near future will show many important developments, both in theory, methodology and practice. We look forward very much to following these developments.

Appendix A

Mathematical Background

A.1 Joint, Marginal and Conditional Probability

Let the n (discrete or continuous) random variables $y_1, \ldots, y_n$ have a *joint* probability $p(y_1, \ldots, y_n)$, or $p(\mathbf{y})$ for short.[1] Technically, one ought to distinguish between probabilities (for discrete variables) and probability densities for continuous variables. Throughout the book we commonly use the term "probability" to refer to both. Let us partition the variables in $\mathbf{y}$ into two groups, $\mathbf{y}_A$ and $\mathbf{y}_B$, where A and B are two disjoint sets whose union is the set $\{1, \ldots, n\}$, so that $p(\mathbf{y}) = p(\mathbf{y}_A, \mathbf{y}_B)$. Each group may contain one or more variables.

joint probability

The *marginal* probability of $\mathbf{y}_A$ is given by

marginal probability

$$p(\mathbf{y}_A) \;=\; \int p(\mathbf{y}_A, \mathbf{y}_B) \, d\mathbf{y}_B. \tag{A.1}$$

The integral is replaced by a sum if the variables are discrete valued. Notice that if the set A contains more than one variable, then the marginal probability is itself a joint probability—whether it is referred to as one or the other depends on the context. If the joint distribution is equal to the product of the marginals, then the variables are said to be *independent*, otherwise they are *dependent*.

independence

The *conditional* probability function is defined as

conditional probability

$$p(\mathbf{y}_A | \mathbf{y}_B) \;=\; \frac{p(\mathbf{y}_A, \mathbf{y}_B)}{p(\mathbf{y}_B)}, \tag{A.2}$$

defined for $p(\mathbf{y}_B) > 0$, as it is not meaningful to condition on an impossible event. If $\mathbf{y}_A$ and $\mathbf{y}_B$ are independent, then the marginal $p(\mathbf{y}_A)$ and the conditional $p(\mathbf{y}_A | \mathbf{y}_B)$ are equal.

---

[1] One can deal with more general cases where the density function does not exist by using the distribution function.

Bayes' rule

Using the definitions of both $p(\mathbf{y}_A|\mathbf{y}_B)$ and $p(\mathbf{y}_B|\mathbf{y}_A)$ we obtain *Bayes' theorem*

$$p(\mathbf{y}_A|\mathbf{y}_B) = \frac{p(\mathbf{y}_A)p(\mathbf{y}_B|\mathbf{y}_A)}{p(\mathbf{y}_B)}. \qquad (A.3)$$

Since conditional distributions are themselves probabilities, one can use all of the above also when further conditioning on other variables. For example, in supervised learning, one often conditions on the inputs throughout, which would lead e.g. to a version of Bayes' rule with additional conditioning on X in all four probabilities in eq. (A.3); see eq. (2.5) for an example of this.

A.2   Gaussian Identities

Gaussian definition

The multivariate Gaussian (or Normal) distribution has a joint probability density given by

$$p(\mathbf{x}|\mathbf{m}, \Sigma) = (2\pi)^{-D/2}|\Sigma|^{-1/2}\exp\left(-\tfrac{1}{2}(\mathbf{x}-\mathbf{m})^\top\Sigma^{-1}(\mathbf{x}-\mathbf{m})\right), \qquad (A.4)$$

where $\mathbf{m}$ is the *mean* vector (of length D) and Σ is the (symmetric, positive definite) *covariance* matrix (of size $D \times D$). As a shorthand we write $\mathbf{x} \sim \mathcal{N}(\mathbf{m}, \Sigma)$.

Let $\mathbf{x}$ and $\mathbf{y}$ be jointly Gaussian random vectors

$$\begin{bmatrix} \mathbf{x} \\ \mathbf{y} \end{bmatrix} \sim \mathcal{N}\left(\begin{bmatrix} \boldsymbol{\mu}_x \\ \boldsymbol{\mu}_y \end{bmatrix}, \begin{bmatrix} A & C \\ C^\top & B \end{bmatrix}\right) = \mathcal{N}\left(\begin{bmatrix} \boldsymbol{\mu}_x \\ \boldsymbol{\mu}_y \end{bmatrix}, \begin{bmatrix} \tilde{A} & \tilde{C} \\ \tilde{C}^\top & \tilde{B} \end{bmatrix}^{-1}\right), \qquad (A.5)$$

conditioning and marginalizing

then the *marginal* distribution of $\mathbf{x}$ and the *conditional* distribution of $\mathbf{x}$ given $\mathbf{y}$ are

$$\mathbf{x} \sim \mathcal{N}(\boldsymbol{\mu}_x, A), \quad \text{and} \quad \mathbf{x}|\mathbf{y} \sim \mathcal{N}(\boldsymbol{\mu}_x + CB^{-1}(\mathbf{y}-\boldsymbol{\mu}_y), A - CB^{-1}C^\top)$$
$$\text{or} \quad \mathbf{x}|\mathbf{y} \sim \mathcal{N}(\boldsymbol{\mu}_x - \tilde{A}^{-1}\tilde{C}(\mathbf{y}-\boldsymbol{\mu}_y), \tilde{A}^{-1}). \qquad (A.6)$$

See, e.g. von Mises [1964, sec. 9.3], and eqs. (A.11 - A.13).

products

The product of two Gaussians gives another (un-normalized) Gaussian

$$\mathcal{N}(\mathbf{x}|\mathbf{a}, A)\mathcal{N}(\mathbf{x}|\mathbf{b}, B) = Z^{-1}\mathcal{N}(\mathbf{x}|\mathbf{c}, C) \qquad (A.7)$$
$$\text{where} \quad \mathbf{c} = C(A^{-1}\mathbf{a} + B^{-1}\mathbf{b}) \quad \text{and} \quad C = (A^{-1} + B^{-1})^{-1}.$$

Notice that the resulting Gaussian has a precision (inverse variance) equal to the sum of the precisions and a mean equal to the convex sum of the means, weighted by the precisions. The normalizing constant looks itself like a Gaussian (in $\mathbf{a}$ or $\mathbf{b}$)

$$Z^{-1} = (2\pi)^{-D/2}|A + B|^{-1/2}\exp\left(-\tfrac{1}{2}(\mathbf{a}-\mathbf{b})^\top(A+B)^{-1}(\mathbf{a}-\mathbf{b})\right). \qquad (A.8)$$

To prove eq. (A.7) simply write out the (lengthy) expressions by introducing eq. (A.4) and eq. (A.8) into eq. (A.7), and expand the terms inside the exp to verify equality. Hint: it may be helpful to expand C using the matrix inversion lemma, eq. (A.9), $C = (A^{-1} + B^{-1})^{-1} = A - A(A+B)^{-1}A = B - B(A+B)^{-1}B$.

To generate samples $\mathbf{x} \sim \mathcal{N}(\mathbf{m}, K)$ with arbitrary mean $\mathbf{m}$ and covariance matrix K using a scalar Gaussian generator (which is readily available in many programming environments) we proceed as follows: first, compute the Cholesky decomposition (also known as the "matrix square root") L of the positive definite symmetric covariance matrix $K = LL^\top$, where L is a lower triangular matrix, see section A.4. Then generate $\mathbf{u} \sim \mathcal{N}(\mathbf{0}, I)$ by multiple separate calls to the scalar Gaussian generator. Compute $\mathbf{x} = \mathbf{m} + L\mathbf{u}$, which has the desired distribution with mean $\mathbf{m}$ and covariance $L\mathbb{E}[\mathbf{u}\mathbf{u}^\top]L^\top = LL^\top = K$ (by the independence of the elements of $\mathbf{u}$).

generating multivariate Gaussian samples

In practice it may be necessary to add a small multiple of the identity matrix ϵI to the covariance matrix for numerical reasons. This is because the eigenvalues of the matrix K can decay very rapidly (see section 4.3.1 for a closely related analytical result) and without this stabilization the Cholesky decomposition fails. The effect on the generated samples is to add additional independent noise of variance ϵ. From the context ϵ can usually be chosen to have inconsequential effects on the samples, while ensuring numerical stability.

A.3 Matrix Identities

The *matrix inversion lemma*, also known as the Woodbury, Sherman & Morrison formula (see e.g. Press et al. [1992, p. 75]) states that

matrix inversion lemma

$$(Z + UWV^\top)^{-1} = Z^{-1} - Z^{-1}U(W^{-1} + V^\top Z^{-1}U)^{-1}V^\top Z^{-1}, \qquad \text{(A.9)}$$

assuming the relevant inverses all exist. Here Z is $n \times n$, W is $m \times m$ and U and V are both of size $n \times m$; consequently if Z^{-1} is known, and a low rank (i.e. $m < n$) perturbation is made to Z as in left hand side of eq. (A.9), considerable speedup can be achieved. A similar equation exists for determinants

determinants

$$|Z + UWV^\top| = |Z|\,|W|\,|W^{-1} + V^\top Z^{-1}U|. \qquad \text{(A.10)}$$

Let the invertible $n \times n$ matrix A and its inverse A^{-1} be partitioned into

inversion of a partitioned matrix

$$A = \begin{pmatrix} P & Q \\ R & S \end{pmatrix}, \qquad A^{-1} = \begin{pmatrix} \tilde{P} & \tilde{Q} \\ \tilde{R} & \tilde{S} \end{pmatrix}, \qquad \text{(A.11)}$$

where P and $\tilde{P}$ are $n_1 \times n_1$ matrices and S and $\tilde{S}$ are $n_2 \times n_2$ matrices with $n = n_1 + n_2$. The submatrices of A^{-1} are given in Press et al. [1992, p. 77] as

$$\left. \begin{aligned} \tilde{P} &= P^{-1} + P^{-1}QMRP^{-1} \\ \tilde{Q} &= -P^{-1}QM \\ \tilde{R} &= -MRP^{-1} \\ \tilde{S} &= M \end{aligned} \right\} \text{ where } M = (S - RP^{-1}Q)^{-1}, \qquad \text{(A.12)}$$

or equivalently

$$\left.\begin{array}{rcl} \tilde{P} & = & N \\ \tilde{Q} & = & -NQS^{-1} \\ \tilde{R} & = & -S^{-1}RN \\ \tilde{S} & = & S^{-1} + S^{-1}RNQS^{-1} \end{array}\right\} \text{ where } N = (P - QS^{-1}R)^{-1}. \qquad \text{(A.13)}$$

A.3.1   Matrix Derivatives

derivative of inverse

Derivatives of the elements of an inverse matrix:

$$\frac{\partial}{\partial\theta}K^{-1} = -K^{-1}\frac{\partial K}{\partial\theta}K^{-1}, \qquad \text{(A.14)}$$

derivative of log
determinant

where $\frac{\partial K}{\partial\theta}$ is a matrix of elementwise derivatives. For the log determinant of a positive definite symmetric matrix we have

$$\frac{\partial}{\partial\theta}\log|K| = \text{tr}\left(K^{-1}\frac{\partial K}{\partial\theta}\right). \qquad \text{(A.15)}$$

A.3.2   Matrix Norms

The Frobenius norm $\|A\|_F$ of a $n_1 \times n_2$ matrix A is defined as

$$\|A\|_F^2 = \sum_{i=1}^{n_1}\sum_{j=1}^{n_2}|a_{ij}|^2 = \text{tr}(AA^\top), \qquad \text{(A.16)}$$

[Golub and Van Loan, 1989, p. 56].

A.4   Cholesky Decomposition

The Cholesky decomposition of a symmetric, positive definite matrix A decomposes A into a product of a lower triangular matrix L and its transpose

$$LL^\top = A, \qquad \text{(A.17)}$$

solving linear systems

computational cost

where L is called the Cholesky factor. The Cholesky decomposition is useful for solving linear systems with symmetric, positive definite coefficient matrix A. To solve $A\mathbf{x} = \mathbf{b}$ for $\mathbf{x}$, first solve the triangular system $L\mathbf{y} = \mathbf{b}$ by forward substitution and then the triangular system $L^\top\mathbf{x} = \mathbf{y}$ by back substitution. Using the backslash operator, we write the solution as $\mathbf{x} = L^\top\backslash(L\backslash\mathbf{b})$, where the notation $A\backslash\mathbf{b}$ is the vector $\mathbf{x}$ which solves $A\mathbf{x} = \mathbf{b}$. Both the forward and backward substitution steps require $n^2/2$ operations, when A is of size $n \times n$. The computation of the Cholesky factor L is considered numerically extremely stable and takes time $n^3/6$, so it is the method of choice when it can be applied.

Note also that the determinant of a positive definite symmetric matrix can be calculated efficiently by

determinant

$$|A| = \prod_{i=1}^{n} L_{ii}^2, \quad \text{or} \quad \log|A| = 2\sum_{i=1}^{n} \log L_{ii}, \qquad (A.18)$$

where L is the Cholesky factor from A.

A.5   Entropy and Kullback-Leibler Divergence

The *entropy* $H[p(\mathbf{x})]$ of a distribution $p(\mathbf{x})$ is a non-negative measure of the amount of "uncertainty" in the distribution, and is defined as

entropy

$$H[p(\mathbf{x})] = -\int p(\mathbf{x})\log p(\mathbf{x})\,d\mathbf{x}. \qquad (A.19)$$

The integral is substituted by a sum for discrete variables. Entropy is measured in *bits* if the log is to the base 2 and in *nats* in the case of the natural log. The entropy of a Gaussian in D dimensions, measured in nats is

$$H[\mathcal{N}(\boldsymbol{\mu}, \Sigma)] = \tfrac{1}{2}\log|\Sigma| + \tfrac{D}{2}(\log 2\pi e). \qquad (A.20)$$

The Kullback-Leibler (KL) divergence (or relative entropy) $\mathrm{KL}(p\|q)$ between two distributions $p(\mathbf{x})$ and $q(\mathbf{x})$ is defined as

$$\mathrm{KL}(p\|q) = \int p(\mathbf{x})\log\frac{p(\mathbf{x})}{q(\mathbf{x})}\,d\mathbf{x}. \qquad (A.21)$$

It is easy to show that $\mathrm{KL}(p\|q) \geq 0$, with equality if $p = q$ (almost everywhere). For the case of two Bernoulli random variables p and q this reduces to

divergence of Bernoulli random variables

$$\mathrm{KL}_{\mathrm{Ber}}(p\|q) = p\log\frac{p}{q} + (1-p)\log\frac{(1-p)}{(1-q)}, \qquad (A.22)$$

where we use p and q both as the name and the parameter of the Bernoulli distributions. For two Gaussian distributions $\mathcal{N}(\boldsymbol{\mu}_0, \Sigma_0)$ and $\mathcal{N}(\boldsymbol{\mu}_1, \Sigma_1)$ we have [Kullback, 1959, sec. 9.1]

divergence of Gaussians

$$\begin{aligned}
\mathrm{KL}(\mathcal{N}_0\|\mathcal{N}_1) = &\tfrac{1}{2}\log|\Sigma_1\Sigma_0^{-1}| + \\
&\tfrac{1}{2}\operatorname{tr}\Sigma_1^{-1}\big((\boldsymbol{\mu}_0 - \boldsymbol{\mu}_1)(\boldsymbol{\mu}_0 - \boldsymbol{\mu}_1)^\top + \Sigma_0 - \Sigma_1\big).
\end{aligned} \qquad (A.23)$$

Consider a general distribution $p(\mathbf{x})$ on $\mathbb{R}^D$ and a Gaussian distribution $q(\mathbf{x}) = \mathcal{N}(\boldsymbol{\mu}, \Sigma)$. Then

minimizing KL$(p\|q)$ divergence leads to moment matching

$$\begin{aligned}
\mathrm{KL}(p\|q) = &\int \tfrac{1}{2}(\mathbf{x}-\boldsymbol{\mu})^\top\Sigma^{-1}(\mathbf{x}-\boldsymbol{\mu})p(\mathbf{x})\,d\mathbf{x} + \\
&\tfrac{1}{2}\log|\Sigma| + \tfrac{D}{2}\log 2\pi + \int p(\mathbf{x})\log p(\mathbf{x})\,d\mathbf{x}.
\end{aligned} \qquad (A.24)$$

Equation (A.24) can be minimized w.r.t. $\boldsymbol{\mu}$ and Σ by differentiating w.r.t. these parameters and setting the resulting expressions to zero. The optimal q is the one that matches the first and second moments of p.

The KL divergence can be viewed as the extra number of nats needed on average to code data generated from a source $p(\mathbf{x})$ under the distribution $q(\mathbf{x})$ as opposed to $p(\mathbf{x})$.

A.6   Limits

The limit of a rational quadratic is a squared exponential

$$\lim_{\alpha \to \infty} \left(1 + \frac{x^2}{2\alpha}\right)^{-\alpha} = \exp\left(-\frac{x^2}{2}\right).$$ (A.25)

A.7   Measure and Integration

Here we sketch some definitions concerning measure and integration; fuller treatments can be found e.g. in Doob [1994] and Bartle [1995].

Let Ω be the set of all possible outcomes of an experiment. For example, for a D-dimensional real-valued variable, $\Omega = \mathbb{R}^D$. Let $\mathcal{F}$ be a σ-field of subsets of Ω which contains all the events in whose occurrences we may be interested.[2] Then μ is a countably additive *measure* if it is real and non-negative and for all mutually disjoint sets $A_1, A_2, \ldots \in \mathcal{F}$ we have

$$\mu\left(\bigcup_{i=1}^{\infty} A_i\right) = \sum_{i=1}^{\infty} \mu(A_i).$$ (A.26)

finite measure
probability measure
Lebesgue measure

If $\mu(\Omega) < \infty$ then μ is called a *finite measure* and if $\mu(\Omega) = 1$ it is called a *probability measure*. The *Lebesgue measure* defines a uniform measure over subsets of Euclidean space. Here an appropriate σ-algebra is the Borel σ-algebra $\mathcal{B}^D$, where $\mathcal{B}$ is the σ-algebra generated by the open subsets of $\mathbb{R}$. For example on the line $\mathbb{R}$ the Lebesgue measure of the interval (a, b) is $b - a$.

We now restrict Ω to be $\mathbb{R}^D$ and wish to give meaning to integration of a function $f : \mathbb{R}^D \to \mathbb{R}$ with respect to a measure μ

$$\int f(\mathbf{x}) \, d\mu(\mathbf{x}).$$ (A.27)

We assume that f is *measurable*, i.e. that for any Borel-measurable set $A \in \mathbb{R}$, $f^{-1}(A) \in \mathcal{B}^D$. There are two cases that will interest us (i) when μ is the Lebesgue measure and (ii) when μ is a probability measure. For the first case expression (A.27) reduces to the usual integral notation $\int f(\mathbf{x}) d\mathbf{x}$.

---

[2]The restriction to a σ-field of subsets is important technically to avoid paradoxes such as the Banach-Tarski paradox. Informally, we can think of the σ-field as restricting consideration to "reasonable" subsets.

For a probability measure μ on $\mathbf{x}$, the non-negative function $p(\mathbf{x})$ is called the *density* of the measure if for all $A \in \mathcal{B}^D$ we have

$$\mu(A) = \int_A p(\mathbf{x}) \, d\mathbf{x}. \tag{A.28}$$

If such a density exists it is uniquely determined almost everywhere, i.e. except for sets with measure zero. Not all probability measures have densities—only distributions that assign zero probability to individual points in $\mathbf{x}$-space can have densities.[3] If $p(\mathbf{x})$ exists then we have

$$\int f(\mathbf{x}) \, d\mu(\mathbf{x}) = \int f(\mathbf{x}) p(\mathbf{x}) \, d\mathbf{x}. \tag{A.29}$$

If μ does not have a density expression (A.27) still has meaning by the standard construction of the Lebesgue integral.

For $\Omega = \mathbb{R}^D$ the probability measure μ can be related to the *distribution function* $F : \mathbb{R}^D \to [0,1]$ which is defined as $F(\mathbf{z}) = \mu(x_1 \leq z_1, \ldots x_D \leq z_D)$. The distribution function is more general than the density as it is always defined for a given probability measure. A simple example of a random variable which has a distribution function but no density is obtained by the following construction: a coin is tossed and with probability p it comes up heads; if it comes up heads x is chosen from $U(0,1)$ (the uniform distribution on $[0,1]$), otherwise (with probability $1-p$) x is set to $1/2$. This distribution has a "point mass" (or atom) at $x = 1/2$.

"point mass" example

A.7.1 L_p Spaces

Let μ be a measure on an input set $\mathcal{X}$. For some function $f : \mathcal{X} \to \mathbb{R}$ and $1 \leq p < \infty$, we define

$$\|f\|_{L_p(\mathcal{X},\mu)} \triangleq \left(\int |f(\mathbf{x})|^p \, d\mu(\mathbf{x}) \right)^{1/p}, \tag{A.30}$$

if the integral exists. For $p = \infty$ we define

$$\|f\|_{L_\infty(\mathcal{X},\mu)} = \operatorname*{ess\,sup}_{\mathbf{x} \in \mathcal{X}} |f(\mathbf{x})|, \tag{A.31}$$

where ess sup denotes the essential supremum, i.e. the smallest number that upper bounds $|f(\mathbf{x})|$ almost everywhere. The function space $L_p(\mathcal{X}, \mu)$ is defined for any p in $1 \leq p \leq \infty$ as the space of functions for which $\|f\|_{L_p(\mathcal{X},\mu)} < \infty$.

A.8 Fourier Transforms

For sufficiently well-behaved functions on $\mathbb{R}^D$ we have

$$f(\mathbf{x}) = \int_{-\infty}^{\infty} \tilde{f}(\mathbf{s}) e^{2\pi i \mathbf{s} \cdot \mathbf{x}} \, d\mathbf{s}, \qquad \tilde{f}(\mathbf{s}) = \int_{-\infty}^{\infty} f(\mathbf{x}) e^{-2\pi i \mathbf{s} \cdot \mathbf{x}} \, d\mathbf{x}, \tag{A.32}$$

---

[3]A measure μ has a density if and only if it is absolutely continuous with respect to Lebesgue measure on $\mathbb{R}^D$, i.e. every set that has Lebesgue measure zero also has μ-measure zero.

where $\tilde{f}(\mathbf{s})$ is called the *Fourier transform* of $f(\mathbf{x})$, see e.g. Bracewell [1986]. We refer to the equation on the left as the *synthesis* equation, and the equation on the right as the *analysis* equation. There are other conventions for Fourier transforms, particularly those involving $\boldsymbol{\omega} = 2\pi\mathbf{s}$. However, this tends to destroy symmetry between the analysis and synthesis equations so we use the definitions given above.

Here we have defined Fourier transforms for $f(\mathbf{x})$ being a function on $\mathbb{R}^D$. For related transforms for periodic functions, functions defined on the integer lattice and on the regular N-polygon see section B.1.

A.9   Convexity

Below we state some definitions and properties of convex sets and functions taken from Boyd and Vandenberghe [2004].

convex sets

A set C is convex if the line segment between any two points in C lies in C, i.e. if for any x_1, $x_2 \in C$ and for any θ with $0 \le \theta \le 1$, we have

$$\theta x_1 + (1 - \theta)x_2 \in C. \tag{A.33}$$

convex function

A function $f : \mathcal{X} \to \mathbb{R}$ is *convex* if its domain $\mathcal{X}$ is a convex set and if for all x_1, $x_2 \in \mathcal{X}$ and θ with $0 \le \theta \le 1$, we have:

$$f(\theta x_1 + (1 - \theta)x_2) \le \theta f(x_1) + (1 - \theta)f(x_2), \tag{A.34}$$

where $\mathcal{X}$ is a (possibly improper) subset of $\mathbb{R}^D$. f is *concave* if $-f$ is convex.

A function f is convex if and only if its domain $\mathcal{X}$ is a convex set and its Hessian is positive semidefinite for all $x \in \mathcal{X}$.

Appendix B

Gaussian Markov Processes

Particularly when the index set for a stochastic process is one-dimensional such as the real line or its discretization onto the integer lattice, it is very interesting to investigate the properties of Gaussian *Markov* processes (GMPs). In this Appendix we use $X(t)$ to define a stochastic process with continuous time parameter t. In the discrete time case the process is denoted $\ldots, X_{-1}, X_0, X_1, \ldots$ etc. We assume that the process has zero mean and is, unless otherwise stated, stationary.

A discrete-time autoregressive (AR) process of order p can be written as

$$X_t = \sum_{k=1}^{p} a_k X_{t-k} + b_0 Z_t, \qquad (B.1)$$

where $Z_t \sim \mathcal{N}(0,1)$ and all Z_t's are i.i.d. . Notice the order-p Markov property that given the history $X_{t-1}, X_{t-2}, \ldots$, X_t depends only on the previous p X's. This relationship can be conveniently expressed as a graphical model; part of an AR(2) process is illustrated in Figure B.1. The name autoregressive stems from the fact that X_t is predicted from the p previous X's through a regression equation. If one stores the current X and the $p-1$ previous values as a state vector, then the AR(p) scalar process can be written equivalently as a vector AR(1) process.

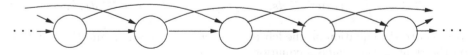

Figure B.1: Graphical model illustrating an AR(2) process.

Moving from the discrete time to the continuous time setting, the question arises as to how generalize the Markov notion used in the discrete-time AR process to define a continuoous-time AR process. It turns out that the correct generalization uses the idea of having not only the function value but also p of its derivatives at time t giving rise to the stochastic differential equation (SDE)[1]

AR process

SDE: stochastic differential equation

$$a_p X^{(p)}(t) + a_{p-1} X^{(p-1)}(t) + \ldots + a_0 X(t) = b_0 Z(t), \qquad \text{(B.2)}$$

where $X^{(i)}(t)$ denotes the ith derivative of $X(t)$ and $Z(t)$ is a white Gaussian noise process with covariance $\delta(t - t')$. This white noise process can be considered the derivative of the Wiener process. To avoid redundancy in the coefficients we assume that $a_p = 1$. A considerable amount of mathematical machinery is required to make rigorous the meaning of such equations, see e.g. Øksendal [1985]. As for the discrete-time case, one can write eq. (B.2) as a first-order vector SDE by defining the state to be $X(t)$ and its first $p - 1$ derivatives.

We begin this chapter with a summary of some Fourier analysis results in section B.1. Fourier analysis is important to linear time invariant systems such as equations (B.1) and (B.2) because $e^{2\pi i s t}$ is an eigenfunction of the corresponding difference (resp differential) operator. We then move on in section B.2 to discuss continuous-time Gaussian Markov processes on the real line and their relationship to the same SDE on the circle. In section B.3 we describe discrete-time Gaussian Markov processes on the integer lattice and their relationship to the same difference equation on the circle. In section B.4 we explain the relationship between discrete-time GMPs and the discrete sampling of continuous-time GMPs. Finally in section B.5 we discuss generalizations of the Markov concept in higher dimensions. Much of this material is quite standard, although the relevant results are often scattered through different sources, and our aim is to provide a unified treatment. The relationship between the second-order properties of the SDEs on the real line and the circle, and difference equations on the integer lattice and the regular polygon is, to our knowledge, novel.

B.1   Fourier Analysis

We follow the treatment given by Kammler [2000]. We consider Fourier analysis of functions on the real line $\mathbb{R}$, of periodic functions of period l on the circle $\mathbb{T}_l$, of functions defined on the integer lattice $\mathbb{Z}$, and of functions on $\mathbb{P}_N$, the regular N-polygon, which is a discretization of $\mathbb{T}_l$.

For sufficiently well-behaved functions on $\mathbb{R}$ we have

$$f(x) = \int_{-\infty}^{\infty} \tilde{f}(s) e^{2\pi i s x} \, ds, \qquad \tilde{f}(s) = \int_{-\infty}^{\infty} f(x) e^{-2\pi i s x} \, dx. \qquad \text{(B.3)}$$

We refer to the equation on the left as the *synthesis* equation, and the equation on the right as the *analysis* equation.

For functions on $\mathbb{T}_l$ we obtain the Fourier series representations

$$f(x) = \sum_{k=-\infty}^{\infty} \tilde{f}[k] e^{2\pi i k x / l}, \qquad \tilde{f}[k] = \frac{1}{l} \int_0^l f(x) e^{-2\pi i k x / l} \, dx, \qquad \text{(B.4)}$$

---

[1] The a_k coefficients in equations (B.1) and (B.2) are not intended to have a close relationship. An approximate relationship might be established through the use of finite-difference approximations to derivatives.

where $\tilde{f}[k]$ denotes the coefficient of $e^{2\pi ikx/l}$ in the expansion. We use square brackets [ ] to denote that the argument is discrete, so that X_t and $X[t]$ are equivalent notations.

Similarly for $\mathbb{Z}$ we obtain

$$f[n] = \int_0^l \tilde{f}(s)e^{2\pi isn/l}\,ds, \qquad \tilde{f}(s) = \frac{1}{l}\sum_{n=-\infty}^{\infty} f[n]e^{-2\pi isn/l}. \qquad (B.5)$$

Note that $\tilde{f}(s)$ is periodic with period l and so is defined only for $0 \le s < l$ to avoid aliasing. Often this transform is defined for the special case $l = 1$ but the general case emphasizes the duality between equations (B.4) and (B.5).

Finally, for functions on $\mathbb{P}_N$ we have the discrete Fourier transform

$$f[n] = \sum_{k=0}^{N-1} \tilde{f}[k]e^{2\pi ikn/N}, \qquad \tilde{f}[k] = \frac{1}{N}\sum_{n=0}^{N-1} f[n]e^{-2\pi ikn/N}. \qquad (B.6)$$

Note that there are other conventions for Fourier transforms, particularly those involving $\omega = 2\pi s$. However, this tends to destroy symmetry between the analysis and synthesis equations so we use the definitions given above.

In the case of stochastic processes, the most important Fourier relationship is between the covariance function and the power spectrum; this is known as the Wiener-Khintchine theorem, see e.g. Chatfield [1989].

B.1.1 Sampling and Periodization

We can obtain relationships between functions and their transforms on $\mathbb{R}$, $\mathbb{T}_l$, $\mathbb{Z}$, $\mathbb{P}_N$ through the notions of *sampling* and *periodization*.

Definition B.1 h-sampling: *Given a function f on $\mathbb{R}$ and a spacing parameter $h > 0$, we construct a corresponding discrete function ϕ on $\mathbb{Z}$ using*

h-sampling

$$\phi[n] = f(nh), \qquad n \in \mathbb{Z}. \qquad (B.7)$$
$\square$

Similarly we can discretize a function defined on $\mathbb{T}_l$ onto $\mathbb{P}_N$, but in this case we must take $h = l/N$ so that N steps of size h will equal the period l.

Definition B.2 Periodization by summation: *Let $f(x)$ be a function on $\mathbb{R}$ that rapidly approaches 0 as $x \to \pm\infty$. We can sum translates of the function to produce the l-periodic function*

periodization by
summation

$$g(x) = \sum_{m=-\infty}^{\infty} f(x - ml), \qquad (B.8)$$

for $l > 0$. Analogously, when ϕ is defined on $\mathbb{Z}$ and $\phi[n]$ rapidly approaches 0 as $n \to \pm\infty$ we can construct a function γ on $\mathbb{P}_N$ by N-summation by setting

$$\gamma[n] = \sum_{m=-\infty}^{\infty} \phi[n - mN]. \qquad (B.9)$$
$\square$

Let $\phi[n]$ be obtained by h-sampling from $f(x)$, with corresponding Fourier transforms $\tilde{\phi}(s)$ and $\tilde{f}(s)$. Then we have

$$\phi[n] = f(nh) = \int_{-\infty}^{\infty} \tilde{f}(s)e^{2\pi isnh}\,ds, \tag{B.10}$$

$$\phi[n] = \int_{0}^{l} \tilde{\phi}(s)e^{2\pi isn/l}\,ds. \tag{B.11}$$

By breaking up the domain of integration in eq. (B.10) we obtain

$$\phi[n] = \sum_{m=-\infty}^{\infty} \int_{ml}^{(m+1)l} \tilde{f}(s)e^{2\pi isnh}\,ds \tag{B.12}$$

$$= \sum_{m=-\infty}^{\infty} \int_{0}^{l} \tilde{f}(s'+ml)e^{2\pi inh(s'+ml)}\,ds', \tag{B.13}$$

using the change of variable $s' = s - ml$. Now set $hl = 1$ and use $e^{2\pi inm} = 1$ for n, m integers to obtain

$$\phi[n] = \int_{0}^{l} \Big(\sum_{m=-\infty}^{\infty} \tilde{f}(s+ml) \Big) e^{2\pi isn/l}\,ds, \tag{B.14}$$

which implies that

$$\tilde{\phi}(s) = \sum_{m=-\infty}^{\infty} \tilde{f}(s+ml), \tag{B.15}$$

with $l = 1/h$. Alternatively setting $l = 1$ one obtains $\tilde{\phi}(s) = \frac{1}{h}\sum_{m=-\infty}^{\infty} \tilde{f}(\frac{s+m}{h})$. Similarly if f is defined on $\mathbb{T}_l$ and $\phi[n] = f(\frac{nl}{N})$ is obtained by sampling then

$$\tilde{\phi}[n] = \sum_{m=-\infty}^{\infty} \tilde{f}[n+mN]. \tag{B.16}$$

Thus we see that sampling in x-space causes periodization in Fourier space.

Now consider the periodization of a function $f(x)$ with $x \in \mathbb{R}$ to give the l-periodic function $g(x) \triangleq \sum_{m=-\infty}^{\infty} f(x-ml)$. Let $\tilde{g}[k]$ be the Fourier coefficients of $g(x)$. We obtain

$$\tilde{g}[k] = \frac{1}{l}\int_{0}^{l} g(x)e^{-2\pi ikx/l}\,dx = \frac{1}{l}\int_{0}^{l} \sum_{m=-\infty}^{\infty} f(x-ml)e^{-2\pi ikx/l}\,dx \tag{B.17}$$

$$= \frac{1}{l}\int_{-\infty}^{\infty} f(x)e^{-2\pi ikx/l}\,dx = \frac{1}{l}\tilde{f}\Big(\frac{k}{l}\Big), \tag{B.18}$$

assuming that $f(x)$ is sufficiently well-behaved that the summation and integration operations can be exchanged. A similar relationship can be obtained for the periodization of a function defined on $\mathbb{Z}$. Thus we see that periodization in x-space gives rise to sampling in Fourier space.

B.2   Continuous-time Gaussian Markov Processes

We first consider continuous-time Gaussian Markov processes on the real line, and then relate the covariance function obtained to that for the stationary solution of the SDE on the circle. Our treatment of continuous-time GMPs on $\mathbb{R}$ follows Papoulis [1991, ch. 10].

B.2.1   Continuous-time GMPs on $\mathbb{R}$

We wish to find the power spectrum and covariance function for the stationary process corresponding to the SDE given by eq. (B.2). Recall that the covariance function of a stationary process $k(t)$ and the power spectrum $S(s)$ form a Fourier transform pair.

The Fourier transform of the stochastic process $X(t)$ is a stochastic process $\tilde{X}(s)$ given by

$$\tilde{X}(s) = \int_{-\infty}^{\infty} X(t)e^{-2\pi i s t}\,dt, \qquad X(t) = \int_{-\infty}^{\infty} \tilde{X}(s)e^{2\pi i s t}\,ds, \qquad \text{(B.19)}$$

where the integrals are interpreted as a mean-square limit. Let $*$ denote complex conjugation and $\langle \ldots \rangle$ denote expectation with respect to the stochastic process. Then for a stationary Gaussian process we have

$$\langle \tilde{X}(s_1)\tilde{X}^*(s_2) \rangle = \int_{-\infty}^{\infty} \int_{-\infty}^{\infty} \langle X(t)X^*(t') \rangle e^{-2\pi i s_1 t} e^{2\pi i s_2 t'}\,dt\,dt' \qquad \text{(B.20)}$$

$$= \int_{-\infty}^{\infty} dt' e^{-2\pi i (s_1 - s_2)t'} \int_{-\infty}^{\infty} d\tau\, k(\tau) e^{-2\pi i s_1 \tau} \qquad \text{(B.21)}$$

$$= S(s_1)\delta(s_1 - s_2), \qquad \text{(B.22)}$$

using the change of variables $\tau = t - t'$ and the integral representation of the delta function $\int e^{-2\pi i s t} dt = \delta(s)$. This shows that $\tilde{X}(s_1)$ and $\tilde{X}(s_2)$ are uncorrelated for $s_1 \neq s_2$, i.e. that the Fourier basis are eigenfunctions of the differential operator. Also from eq. (B.19) we obtain

$$X^{(k)}(t) = \int_{-\infty}^{\infty} (2\pi i s)^k \tilde{X}(s)e^{2\pi i s t}\,ds. \qquad \text{(B.23)}$$

Now if we Fourier transform eq. (B.2) we obtain

$$\sum_{k=0}^{p} a_k (2\pi i s)^k \tilde{X}(s) = b_0 \tilde{Z}(s), \qquad \text{(B.24)}$$

where $\tilde{Z}(s)$ denotes the Fourier transform of the white noise. Taking the product of equation B.24 with its complex conjugate and taking expectations we obtain

$$\left[\sum_{k=0}^{p} a_k (2\pi i s_1)^k \right]\left[\sum_{k=0}^{p} a_k (-2\pi i s_2)^k \right] \langle \tilde{X}(s_1)\tilde{X}^*(s_2) \rangle = b_0^2 \langle \tilde{Z}(s_1)\tilde{Z}^*(s_2) \rangle.$$
$$\text{(B.25)}$$

Let $A(z) = \sum_{k=0}^{p} a_k z^k$. Then using eq. (B.22) and the fact that the power spectrum of white noise is 1, we obtain

$$S_{\mathbb{R}}(s) = \frac{b_0^2}{|A(2\pi i s)|^2}. \tag{B.26}$$

Note that the denominator is a polynomial of order p in s^2. The relationship of stationary solutions of pth-order SDEs to rational spectral densities can be traced back at least as far as Doob [1944].

Above we have assumed that the process is stationary. However, this depends on the coefficients $a_0, \ldots, a_p$. To analyze this issue we assume a solution of the form $X_t \propto e^{\lambda t}$ when the driving term $b_0 = 0$. This leads to the condition for stationarity that the roots of the polynomial $\sum_{k=0}^{p} a_k \lambda^k$ must lie in the left half plane [Arató, 1982, p. 127].

AR(1) process

Example: AR(1) process. In this case we have the SDE

$$X'(t) + a_0 X(t) = b_0 Z(t), \tag{B.27}$$

where $a_0 > 0$ for stationarity. This gives rise to the power spectrum

$$S(s) = \frac{b_0^2}{(2\pi i s + a_0)(-2\pi i s + a_0)} = \frac{b_0^2}{(2\pi s)^2 + a_0^2}. \tag{B.28}$$

Taking the Fourier transform we obtain

$$k(t) = \frac{b_0^2}{2a_0} e^{-a_0|t|}. \tag{B.29}$$

This process is known as the Ornstein-Uhlenbeck (OU) process [Uhlenbeck and Ornstein, 1930] and was introduced as a mathematical model of the velocity of a particle undergoing Brownian motion. It can be shown that the OU process is the unique stationary first-order Gaussian Markov process.

AR(p) process

Example: AR(p) process. In general the covariance transform corresponding to the power spectrum $S(s) = ([\sum_{k=0}^{p} a_k (2\pi i s)^k][\sum_{k=0}^{p} a_k (-2\pi i s)^k])^{-1}$ can be quite complicated. For example, Papoulis [1991, p. 326] gives three forms of the covariance function for the AR(2) process depending on whether $a_1^2 - 4a_0$ is greater than, equal to or less than 0. However, if the coefficients $a_0, a_1, \ldots, a_p$ are chosen in a particular way then one can obtain

$$S(s) = \frac{1}{(4\pi^2 s^2 + \alpha^2)^p} \tag{B.30}$$

for some α. It can be shown [Stein, 1999, p. 31] that the corresponding covariance function is of the form $\sum_{k=0}^{p-1} \beta_k |t|^k e^{-\alpha|t|}$ for some coefficients $\beta_0, \ldots, \beta_{p-1}$. For $p = 1$ we have already seen that $k(t) = \frac{1}{2\alpha} e^{-\alpha|t|}$ for the OU process. For $p = 2$ we obtain $k(t) = \frac{1}{4\alpha^3} e^{-\alpha|t|}(1 + \alpha|t|)$. These are special cases of the Matérn class of covariance functions described in section 4.2.1.

Example: Wiener process. Although our derivations have focussed on *stationary* Gaussian Markov processes, there are also several important non-stationary processes. One of the most important is the Wiener process that satisfies the SDE $X'(t) = Z(t)$ for $t \geq 0$ with the initial condition $X(0) = 0$. This process has covariance function $k(t, s) = \min(t, s)$. An interesting variant of the Wiener process known as the Brownian bridge (or *tied-down* Wiener process) is obtained by conditioning on the Wiener process passing through $X(1) = 0$. This has covariance $k(t, s) = \min(t, s) - st$ for $0 \leq s, t \leq 1$. See e.g. Grimmett and Stirzaker [1992] for further information on these processes.

Wiener process

Markov processes derived from SDEs of order p are $p - 1$ times MS differentiable. This is easy to see heuristically from eq. (B.2); given that a process gets rougher the more times it is differentiated, eq. (B.2) tells us that $X^{(p)}(t)$ is like the white noise process, i.e. not MS continuous. So, for example, the OU process (and also the Wiener process) are MS continuous but not MS differentiable.

B.2.2 The Solution of the Corresponding SDE on the Circle

The analogous analysis to that on the real line is carried out on $\mathbb{T}_l$ using

$$X(t) = \sum_{n=-\infty}^{\infty} \tilde{X}[n]e^{2\pi int/l}, \qquad \tilde{X}[n] = \frac{1}{l} \int_0^l X(t)e^{-2\pi int/l}dt. \qquad \text{(B.31)}$$

As $X(t)$ is assumed stationary we obtain an analogous result to eq. (B.22), i.e. that the Fourier coefficients are independent

$$\langle \tilde{X}[m]\tilde{X}^*[n] \rangle = \begin{cases} S[n] & \text{if } m = n \\ 0 & \text{otherwise.} \end{cases} \qquad \text{(B.32)}$$

Similarly, the covariance function on the cirle is given by $k(t-s) = \langle X(t)X^*(s) \rangle = \sum_{n=-\infty}^{\infty} S[n]e^{2\pi in(t-s)/l}$. Let $\omega_l = 2\pi/l$. Then plugging in the expression $X^{(k)}(t) = \sum_{n=-\infty}^{\infty} (in\omega_l)^k \tilde{X}[n]e^{in\omega_l t}$ into the SDE eq. (B.2) and equating terms in $[n]$ we obtain

$$\sum_{k=0}^{p} a_k (in\omega_l)^k \tilde{X}[n] = b_0 \tilde{Z}[n]. \qquad \text{(B.33)}$$

As in the real-line case we form the product of equation B.33 with its complex conjugate and take expectations to give

$$S_{\mathbb{T}}[n] = \frac{b_0^2}{|A(in\omega_l)|^2}. \qquad \text{(B.34)}$$

Note that $S_{\mathbb{T}}[n]$ is equal to $S_{\mathbb{R}}\left(\frac{n}{l}\right)$, i.e. that it is a sampling of $S_{\mathbb{R}}$ at intervals $1/l$, where $S_{\mathbb{R}}(s)$ is the power spectrum of the continuous process on the real line given in equation B.26. Let $k_{\mathbb{T}}(h)$ denote the covariance function on the circle and $k_{\mathbb{R}}(h)$ denote the covariance function on the real line for the SDE. Then using eq. (B.15) we find that

$$k_{\mathbb{T}}(t) \;=\; \sum_{m=-\infty}^{\infty} k_{\mathbb{R}}(t - ml). \qquad (B.35)$$

1st order SDE

Example: 1st-order SDE. On $\mathbb{R}$ for the OU process we have $k_{\mathbb{R}}(t) = \frac{b_0^2}{2a_0} e^{-a_0|t|}$. By summing the series (two geometric progressions) we obtain

$$k_{\mathbb{T}}(t) \;=\; \frac{b_0^2}{2a_0(1 - e^{-a_0 l})} \left(e^{-a_0|t|} + e^{-a_0(l-|t|)} \right) = \frac{b_0^2}{2a_0} \frac{\cosh[a_0(\frac{l}{2} - |t|)]}{\sinh(\frac{a_0 l}{2})} \quad (B.36)$$

for $-l \le t \le l$. Eq. (B.36) is also given (up to scaling factors) in Grenander et al. [1991, eq. 2.15], where it is obtained by a limiting argument from the discrete-time GMP on $\mathbb{P}_n$, see section B.3.2.

B.3   Discrete-time Gaussian Markov Processes

We first consider discrete-time Gaussian Markov processes on $\mathbb{Z}$, and then relate the covariance function obtained to that of the stationary solution of the difference equation on $\mathbb{P}_N$. Chatfield [1989] and Diggle [1990] provide good coverage of discrete-time ARMA models on $\mathbb{Z}$.

B.3.1   Discrete-time GMPs on $\mathbb{Z}$

Assuming that the process is stationary the covariance function $k[i]$ denotes $\langle X_t X_{t+i} \rangle \ \forall t \in \mathbb{Z}$. (Note that because of stationarity $k[i] = k[-i]$.)

We first use a Fourier approach to derive the power spectrum and hence the covariance function of the AR(p) process. Defining $a_0 = -1$, we can rewrite eq. (B.1) as $\sum_{k=0}^{p} a_k X_{t-k} + b_0 Z_t = 0$. The Fourier pair for $X[t]$ is

$$X[t] \;=\; \int_0^l \tilde{X}(s) e^{2\pi i s t/l}\, ds, \qquad \tilde{X}(s) = \frac{1}{l} \sum_{t=-\infty}^{\infty} X[t] e^{-2\pi i s t/l}. \qquad (B.37)$$

Plugging this into $\sum_{k=0}^{p} a_k X_{t-k} + b_0 Z_t = 0$ we obtain

$$\tilde{X}(s) \Big(\sum_{k=0}^{p} a_k e^{-i\omega_l s k} \Big) + b_0 \tilde{Z}(s) \;=\; 0, \qquad (B.38)$$

where $\omega_l = 2\pi/l$. As above, taking the product of eq. (B.38) with its complex conjugate and taking expectations we obtain

$$S_{\mathbb{Z}}(s) \;=\; \frac{b_0^2}{|A(e^{i\omega_l s})|^2}. \qquad (B.39)$$

Above we have assumed that the process is stationary. However, this depends on the coefficients $a_0, \ldots, a_p$. To analyze this issue we assume a solution of the form $X_t \propto z^t$ when the driving term $b_0 = 0$. This leads to the condition for stationarity that the roots of the polynomial $\sum_{k=0}^p a_k z^{p-k}$ must lie *inside* the unit circle. See Hannan [1970, Theorem 5, p. 19] for further details.

As well as deriving the covariance function from the Fourier transform of the power spectrum it can also be obtained by solving a set of linear equations. Our first observation is that X_s is independent of Z_t for $s < t$. Multiplying equation B.1 through by Z_t and taking expectations, we obtain $\langle X_t Z_t \rangle = b_0$ and $\langle X_{t-i} Z_t \rangle = 0$ for $i > 0$. By multiplying equation B.1 through by X_{t-j} for $j = 0, 1, \ldots$ and taking expectations we obtain the *Yule-Walker* equations

Yule-Walker equations

$$k[0] = \sum_{i=1}^p a_i k[i] + b_0^2 \qquad (B.40)$$

$$k[j] = \sum_{i=1}^p a_i k[j-i] \qquad \forall j > 0. \qquad (B.41)$$

The first $p+1$ of these equations form a linear system that can be used to solve for $k[0], \ldots, k[p]$ in terms of b_0 and $a_1, \ldots, a_p$, and eq. (B.41) can be used to obtain $k[j]$ for $j > p$ recursively.

Example: AR(1) process. The simplest example of an AR process is the AR(1) process defined as $X_t = a_1 X_{t-1} + b_0 Z_t$. This gives rise to the Yule-Walker equations

AR(1) process

$$k[0] - a_1 k[1] = b_0^2, \quad \text{and} \quad k[1] - a_1 k[0] = 0. \qquad (B.42)$$

The linear system for $k[0], k[1]$ can easily be solved to give $k[j] = a_1^{|j|} \sigma_X^2$, where $\sigma_X^2 = b_0^2 / (1 - a_1^2)$ is the variance of the process. Notice that for the process to be stationary we require $|a_1| < 1$. The corresponding power spectrum obtained from equation B.39 is

$$S(s) = \frac{b_0^2}{1 - 2a_1 \cos(\omega_l s) + a_1^2}. \qquad (B.43)$$

Similarly to the continuous case, the covariance function for the discrete-time AR(2) process has three different forms depending on $a_1^2 + 4a_2$. These are described in Diggle [1990, Example 3.6].

B.3.2 The Solution of the Corresponding Difference Equation on $\mathbb{P}_N$

We now consider variables $\mathbf{X} = X_0, X_1, \ldots, X_{N-1}$ arranged around the circle with $N \geq p$. By appropriately modifying eq. (B.1) we obtain

$$X_t = \sum_{k=1}^p a_k X_{\text{mod}(t-k, N)} + b_0 Z_t. \qquad (B.44)$$

The Z_t's are i.i.d. and $\sim \mathcal{N}(0,1)$. Thus $\mathbf{Z} = Z_0, Z_1, \ldots, Z_{N-1}$ has density $p(\mathbf{Z}) \propto \exp -\frac{1}{2} \sum_{t=0}^{N-1} Z_t^2$. Equation (B.44) shows that $\mathbf{X}$ and $\mathbf{Z}$ are related by a linear transformation and thus

$$p(\mathbf{X}) \propto \exp\left(-\frac{1}{2b_0^2} \sum_{t=0}^{N-1} \left(X_t - \sum_{k=1}^{p} a_k X_{\mathrm{mod}(t-k,N)}\right)^2\right). \tag{B.45}$$

This is an N-dimensional multivariate Gaussian. For an AR(p) process the inverse covariance matrix has a circulant structure [Davis, 1979] consisting of a diagonal band $(2p+1)$ entries wide and appropriate circulant entries in the corners. Thus $p(X_t|\mathbf{X}\setminus X_t) = p(X_t|X_{\mathrm{mod}(t-1,N)}, \ldots, X_{\mathrm{mod}(t-p,N)}, X_{\mathrm{mod}(t+1,N)}, \ldots, X_{\mathrm{mod}(t+p,N)})$, which Geman and Geman [1984] call the "two-sided" Markov property. Notice that it is the zeros in the *inverse* covariance matrix that indicate the conditional independence structure; see also section B.5.

The properties of eq. (B.44) have been studied by a number of authors, e.g. Whittle [1963] (under the name of circulant processes), Kashyap and Chellappa [1981] (under the name of circular autoregressive models) and Grenander et al. [1991] (as cyclic Markov process).

As above, we define the Fourier transform pair

$$X[n] = \sum_{m=0}^{N-1} \tilde{X}[m] e^{2\pi i n m/N}, \qquad \tilde{X}[m] = \frac{1}{N} \sum_{n=0}^{N-1} X[n] e^{-2\pi i n m/N}. \tag{B.46}$$

By similar arguments to those above we obtain

$$\sum_{k=0}^{p} a_k \tilde{X}[m] (e^{2\pi i m/N})^k + b_0 \tilde{Z}[m] = 0, \tag{B.47}$$

where $a_0 = -1$, and thus

$$S_{\mathbb{P}}[m] = \frac{b_0^2}{|A(e^{2\pi i m/N})|^2}. \tag{B.48}$$

As in the continuous-time case, we see that $S_{\mathbb{P}}[m]$ is obtained by sampling the power spectrum of the corresponding process on the line, so that $S_{\mathbb{P}}[m] = S_{\mathbb{Z}}\left(\frac{ml}{N}\right)$. Thus using eq. (B.16) we have

$$k_{\mathbb{P}}[n] = \sum_{m=-\infty}^{\infty} k_{\mathbb{Z}}[n + mN]. \tag{B.49}$$

AR(1) process

Example: AR(1) process. For this process $X_t = a_1 X_{\mathrm{mod}(t-1,n)} + b_0 Z_t$, the diagonal entries in the inverse covariance are $(1 + a_1^2)/b_0^2$ and the non-zero off-diagonal entries are $-a_1/b_0^2$.

By summing the covariance function $k_{\mathbb{Z}}[n] = \sigma_X^2 a_1^{|n|}$ we obtain

$$k_{\mathbb{P}}[n] = \frac{\sigma_X^2}{(1 - a_1^N)} (a_1^{|n|} + a_1^{|N-n|}) \qquad n = 0, \ldots, N-1. \tag{B.50}$$

We now illustrate this result for $N = 3$. In this case the covariance matrix has diagonal entries of $\frac{\sigma_X^2}{(1-a_1^3)}(1 + a_1^3)$ and off-diagonal entries of $\frac{\sigma_X^2}{(1-a_1^3)}(a_1 + a_1^2)$. The inverse covariance matrix has the structure described above. Multiplying these two matrices together we do indeed obtain the identity matrix.

B.4   The Relationship Between Discrete-time and Sampled Continuous-time GMPs

We now consider the relationship between continuous-time and discrete-time GMPs. In particular we ask the question, is a regular sampling of a continuous-time $AR(p)$ process a discrete-time $AR(p)$ process? It turns out that the answer will, in general, be negative. First we define a generalization of AR processes known as autoregressive moving-average (ARMA) processes.

ARMA processes   The $AR(p)$ process defined above is a special case of the more general $ARMA(p, q)$ process which is defined as

$$X_t = \sum_{i=1}^{p} a_i X_{t-i} + \sum_{j=0}^{q} b_j Z_{t-j}. \qquad (B.51)$$

Observe that the $AR(p)$ process is in fact also an $ARMA(p, 0)$ process. A spectral analysis of equation B.51 similar to that performed in section B.3.1 gives

$$S(s) = \frac{|B(e^{i\omega_l s})|^2}{|A(e^{i\omega_l s})|^2}, \qquad (B.52)$$

where $B(z) = \sum_{j=0}^{q} b_j z^j$. In continuous time a process with a rational spectral density of the form

$$S(s) = \frac{|B(2\pi i s)|^2}{|A(2\pi i s)|^2} \qquad (B.53)$$

is known as a $ARMA(p, q)$ process. For this to define a valid covariance function we require $q < p$ as $k(0) = \int S(s)ds < \infty$.

Discrete-time observation of a continuous-time process   Let $X(t)$ be a continuous-time process having covariance function $k(t)$ and power spectrum $S(s)$. Let X_h be the discrete-time process obtained by sampling $X(t)$ at interval h, so that $X_h[n] = X(nh)$ for $n \in \mathbb{Z}$. Clearly the covariance function of this process is given by $k_h[n] = k(nh)$. By eq. (B.15) this means that

$$S_h(s) = \sum_{m=-\infty}^{\infty} S(s + \frac{m}{h}) \qquad (B.54)$$

where $S_h(s)$ is defined using $l = 1/h$.

Theorem B.1 *Let X be a continuous-time stationary Gaussian process and X_h be the discretization of this process. If X is an ARMA process then X_h is also an ARMA process. However, if X is an AR process then X_h is not necessarily an AR process.*   □

The proof is given in Ihara [1993, Theorem 2.7.1]. It is easy to see using the covariance functions given in sections B.2.1 and B.3.1 that the discretization of a continuous-time AR(1) process is indeed a discrete-time AR(1) process. However, Ihara shows that, in general, the discretization of a continuous-time AR(2) process is not a discrete-time AR(2) process.

B.5   Markov Processes in Higher Dimensions

We have concentrated above on the case where t is one-dimensional. In higher dimensions it is interesting to ask how the Markov property might be generalized. Let ∂S be an infinitely differentiable closed surface separating $\mathbb{R}^D$ into a bounded part S^- and an unbounded part S^+. Loosely speaking[2] a random field $X(\mathbf{t})$ is said to be *quasi-Markovian* if $X(\mathbf{t})$ for $\mathbf{t} \in S^-$ and $X(\mathbf{u})$ for $\mathbf{u} \in S^+$ are independent given $X(\mathbf{s})$ for $\mathbf{s} \in \partial S$. Wong [1971] showed that the only isotropic quasi-Markov Gaussian field with a continuous covariance function is the degenerate case $X(\mathbf{t}) = X(\mathbf{0})$, where $X(\mathbf{0})$ is a Gaussian variate. However, if instead of conditioning on the values that the field takes on in ∂S, one conditions on a somewhat larger set, then Gaussian random fields with non-trivial Markov-type structure can be obtained. For example, random fields with an inverse power spectrum of the form $\sum_{\mathbf{k}} a_{k_1,\ldots,k_D} s_1^{k_1} \cdots s_d^{k_d}$ with $\mathbf{k}^\top \mathbf{1} = \sum_{j=1}^D k_j \leq 2p$ and $C(\mathbf{s} \cdot \mathbf{s})^p \leq \left| \sum_{\mathbf{k}^\top \mathbf{1} = 2p} a_{k_1,\ldots,k_D} s_1^{k_1} \cdots s_D^{k_d} \right|$ for some $C > 0$ are said to be *pseudo-Markovian* of order p. For example, the D-dimensional tensor-product of the OU process $k(\mathbf{t}) = \prod_{i=1}^D e^{-\alpha_i |t_i|}$ is pseudo-Markovian of order D. For further discussion of Markov properties of random fields see the Appendix in Adler [1981].

If instead of $\mathbb{R}^D$ we wish to define a Markov random field (MRF) on a graphical structure (for example the lattice $\mathbb{Z}^D$) things become more straightforward. We follow the presentation in Jordan [2005]. Let $G = (X, E)$ be a graph where X is a set of nodes that are in one-to-one correspondence with a set of random variables, and E be the set of undirected edges of the graph. Let $\mathcal{C}$ be the set of all maximal cliques of G. A potential function $\psi_C(\mathbf{x}_C)$ is a function on the possible realizations $\mathbf{x}_C$ of the maximal clique $\mathbf{X}_C$. Potential functions are assumed to be (strictly) positive, real-valued functions. The probability distribution $p(\mathbf{x})$ corresponding to the Markov random field is given by

$$p(\mathbf{x}) \;=\; \frac{1}{Z} \prod_{C \in \mathcal{C}} \psi_C(\mathbf{x}_C), \qquad\qquad (\text{B.55})$$

where Z is a normalization factor (known in statistical physics as the partition function) obtained by summing/integrating $\prod_{C \in \mathcal{C}} \psi_C(\mathbf{x}_C)$ over all possible as-

---

[2]For a precise formulation of this definition involving σ-fields see Adler [1981, p. 256].

signments of values to the nodes X. Under this definition it is easy to show that a local Markov property holds, i.e. that for any variable x the conditional distribution of x given all other variables in X depends only on those variables that are neighbours of x. A useful reference on Markov random fields is Winkler [1995].

A simple example of a Gaussian Markov random field has the form

$$p(\mathbf{x}) \propto \exp\left(-\alpha_1 \sum_i x_i^2 - \alpha_2 \sum_{i,j:j\in N(i)} (x_i - x_j)^2\right), \tag{B.56}$$

where $N(i)$ denotes the set of neighbours of node x_i and α_1, $\alpha_2 > 0$. On $\mathbb{Z}^2$ one might choose a four-connected neighbourhood, i.e. those nodes to the north, south, east and west of a given node.

Appendix C

Datasets and Code

The datasets used for experiments in this book and implementations of the algorithms presented are available for download at the website of the book:

http://www.GaussianProcess.org/gpml

The programs are short stand-alone implementations and not part of a larger package. They are meant to be simple to understand and modify for a desired purpose. Some of the programs allow specification of covariance functions from a selection provided, or to link in user defined covariance code. For some of the plots, code is provided which produces a similar plot, as this may be a convenient way of conveying the details.

Bibliography

Abrahamsen, P. (1997). A Review of Gaussian Random Fields and Correlation Functions. Technical Report 917, Norwegian Computing Center, Oslo, Norway. `http://publications.nr.no/` `917_Rapport.pdf`. p. 82

Abramowitz, M. and Stegun, I. A. (1965). *Handbook of Mathematical Functions.* Dover, New York. pp. 84, 85

Adams, R. (1975). *Sobolev Spaces.* Academic Press, New York. p. 134

Adler, R. J. (1981). *The Geometry of Random Fields.* Wiley, Chichester. pp. 80, 81, 83, 191, 218

Amari, S. (1985). *Differential-Geometrical Methods in Statistics.* Springer-Verlag, Berlin. p. 102

Ansley, C. F. and Kohn, R. (1985). Estimation, Filtering, and Smoothing in State Space Models with Incompletely Specified Initial Conditions. *Annals of Statistics*, 13(4):1286–1316. p. 29

Arató, M. (1982). *Linear Stochastic Systems with Constant Coefficients.* Springer-Verlag, Berlin. Lecture Notes in Control and Information Sciences 45. p. 212

Arfken, G. (1985). *Mathematical Methods for Physicists.* Academic Press, San Diego. pp. xv, 134

Aronszajn, N. (1950). Theory of Reproducing Kernels. *Trans. Amer. Math. Soc.*, 68:337–404. pp. 129, 130

Bach, F. R. and Jordan, M. I. (2002). Kernel Independent Component Analysis. *Journal of Machine Learning Research*, 3(1):1–48. p. 97

Baker, C. T. H. (1977). *The Numerical Treatment of Integral Equations.* Clarendon Press, Oxford. pp. 98, 99

Barber, D. and Saad, D. (1996). Does Extra Knowledge Necessarily Improve Generalisation? *Neural Computation*, 8:202–214. p. 31

Bartle, R. G. (1995). *The Elements of Integration and Lebesgue Measure.* Wiley, New York. p. 204

Bartlett, P. L., Jordan, M. I., and McAuliffe, J. D. (2003). Convexity, Classification and Risk Bounds. Technical Report 638, Department of Statistics, University of California, Berkeley. Available from `http://www.stat.berkeley.edu/tech-reports/638.pdf`. Accepted for publication in Journal of the American Statistical Association. p. 157

Berger, J. O. (1985). *Statistical Decision Theory and Bayesian Analysis.* Springer, New York. Second edition. pp. 22, 35

Bishop, C. M. (1995). *Neural Networks for Pattern Recognition*. Clarendon Press, Oxford.   p. 45

Bishop, C. M., Svensen, M., and Williams, C. K. I. (1998a). Developments of the Generative Topographic Mapping. *Neurocomputing*, 21:203–224.   p. 196

Bishop, C. M., Svensen, M., and Williams, C. K. I. (1998b). GTM: The Generative Topographic Mapping. *Neural Computation*, 10(1):215–234.   p. 196

Blake, I. F. and Lindsey, W. C. (1973). Level-Crossing Problems for Random Processes. *IEEE Trans Information Theory*, 19(3):295–315.   p. 81

Blight, B. J. N. and Ott, L. (1975). A Bayesian Approach to Model Inadequacy for Polynomial Regression. *Biometrika*, 62(1):79–88.   p. 28

Boyd, S. and Vandenberghe, L. (2004). *Convex Optimization*. Cambridge University Press, Cambridge, UK.   p. 206

Boyle, P. and Frean, M. (2005). Dependent Gaussian Processes. In Saul, L. K., Weiss, Y., and Bottou, L., editors, *Advances in Neural Information Processing Systems 17*, pages 217–224. MIT Press. p. 190

Bracewell, R. N. (1986). *The Fourier Transform and Its Applications*. McGraw-Hill, Singapore, international edition.   pp. 83, 206

Caruana, R. (1997). Multitask Learning. *Machine Learning*, 28(1):41–75.   p. 115

Chatfield, C. (1989). *The Analysis of Time Series: An Introduction*. Chapman and Hall, London, 4th edition.   pp. 82, 209, 214

Choi, T. and Schervish, M. J. (2004). Posterior Consistency in Nonparametric Regression Problems Under Gaussian Process Priors. Technical Report 809, Department of Statistics, CMU. http://www.stat.cmu.edu/tr/tr809/tr809.html.   p. 156

Choudhuri, N., Ghosal, S., and Roy, A. (2005). Nonparametric Binary Regression Using a Gaussian Process Prior. Unpublished. http://www4.stat.ncsu.edu/~sghosal/papers.html.   p. 156

Chu, W. and Ghahramani, Z. (2005). Gaussian Processes for Ordinal Regression. *Journal of Machine Learning Research*, 6:1019–1041.   p. 191

Collins, M. and Duffy, N. (2002). Convolution Kernels for Natural Language. In Diettrich, T. G., Becker, S., and Ghahramani, Z., editors, *Advances in Neural Information Processing Systems 14*. MIT Press.   p. 101

Collobert, R. and Bengio, S. (2001). SVMTorch: Support Vector Machines for Large-Scale Regression Problems. *Journal of Machine Learning Research*, 1:143–160. http://www.idiap.ch/~bengio/projects/SVMTorch.html.   pp. 69, 72

Cornford, D., Nabney, I. T., and Williams, C. K. I. (2002). Modelling Frontal Discontinuities in Wind Fields. *Journal of Nonparameteric Statsitics*, 14(1-2):43–58.   p. 85

Cox, D. D. (1984). Multivariate Smoothing Spline Functions. *SIAM Journal on Numerical Analysis*, 21(4):789–813.   p. 156

Cox, D. D. and O'Sullivan, F. (1990). Asymptotic Analysis of Penalized Likelihood and Related Estimators. *Annals of Statistics*, 18(4):1676–1695.   p. 156

Craven, P. and Wahba, G. (1979). Smoothing Noisy Data with Spline Functions. *Numer. Math.*, 31:377–403. p. 112

Cressie, N. A. C. (1993). *Statistics for Spatial Data*. Wiley, New York. pp. 30, 137, 190

Cristianini, N. and Shawe-Taylor, J. (2000). *An Introduction to Support Vector Machines*. Cambridge University Press. p. 141

Cristianini, N., Shawe-Taylor, J., Elisseeff, A., and Kandola, J. (2002). On Kernel-Target Alignment. In Diettrich, T. G., Becker, S., and Ghahramani, Z., editors, *Advances in Neural Information Processing Systems 14*. MIT Press. p. 128

Csató, L. (2002). *Gaussian Processes—Iterative Sparse Approximations*. PhD thesis, Aston University, UK. p. 179

Csató, L. and Opper, M. (2002). Sparse On-Line Gaussian Processes. *Neural Computation*, 14(3):641–668. pp. 180, 185

Csató, L., Opper, M., and Winther, O. (2002). TAP Gibbs Free Energy, Belief Propagation and Sparsity. In Diettrich, T. G., Becker, S., and Ghahramani, Z., editors, *Advances in Neural Information Processing Systems 14*, pages 657–663. MIT Press. pp. 180, 185

Daley, R. (1991). *Atmospheric Data Analysis*. Cambridge University Press, Cambridge, UK. p. 30

David, H. A. (1970). *Order Statistics*. Wiley, New York. pp. 169, 170

Davis, P. J. (1979). *Circulant Matrices*. Wiley, New York. p. 216

Dawid, A. P. (1976). Properties of Diagnostic Data Distributions. *Biometrics*, 32:647–658. p. 34

Dellaportas, P. and Stephens, D. A. (1995). Bayesian Analysis of Errors-in-Variables Regression Models. *Biometrics*, 51:1085–1095. p. 192

Devroye, L., Györfi, L., and Lugosi, G. (1996). *A Probabilistic Theory of Pattern Recognition*. Springer, New York. pp. 156, 166

Diaconis, P. and Freedman, D. (1986). On the Consistency of Bayes Estimates. *Annals of Statistics*, 14(1):1–26. p. 156

Diggle, P. J. (1990). *Time Series: A Biostatistical Introduction*. Clarendon Press, Oxford. pp. 214, 215

Diggle, P. J., Tawn, J. A., and Moyeed, R. A. (1998). Model-based Geostatistics (with discussion). *Applied Statistics*, 47:299–350. p. 191

Doob, J. L. (1944). The Elementary Gaussian Processes. *Annals of Mathematical Statistics*, 15(3):229–282. p. 212

Doob, J. L. (1994). *Measure Theory*. Springer-Verlag, New York. p. 204

Drineas, P. and Mahoney, M. W. (2005). On the Nyström Method for Approximating a Gram Matrix for Improved Kernel-Based Learning. Technical Report YALEU/DCS/TR-1319, Yale University. http://cs-www.cs.yale.edu/homes/mmahoney. p. 174

Duchon, J. (1977). Splines Minimizing Rotation-Invariant Semi-norms in Sobolev Spaces. In Schempp, W. and Zeller, K., editors, *Constructive Theory of Functions of Several Variables*, pages 85–100. Springer-Verlag. p. 137

Duda, R. O. and Hart, P. E. (1973). *Pattern Classification and Scene Analysis*. John Wiley, New York. p. 146

Edgeworth, F. Y. (1887). On Observations Relating to Several Quantities. *Hermathena*, 6:279–285. p. 146

Faul, A. C. and Tipping, M. E. (2002). Analysis of Sparse Bayesian Learning. In Dietterich, T. G., Becker, S., and Ghahramani, Z., editors, *Advances in Neural Information Processing Systems 14*, pages 383–389, Cambridge, Massachussetts. MIT Press. p. 149

Feldman, J. (1958). Equivalence and Perpendicularity of Gaussian Processes. *Pacific J. Math.*, 8:699–708. Erratum in *Pacific J. Math.* 9, 1295-1296 (1959). p. 157

Ferrari Trecate, G., Williams, C. K. I., and Opper, M. (1999). Finite-dimensional Approximation of Gaussian Processes. In Kearns, M. S., Solla, S. A., and Cohn, D. A., editors, *Advances in Neural Information Processing Systems 11*, pages 218–224. MIT Press. p. 152

Fine, S. and Scheinberg, K. (2002). Efficient SVM Training Using Low-Rank Kernel Representations. *Journal of Machine Learning Research*, 2(2):243–264. pp. 47, 174

Fowlkes, C., Belongie, S., and Malik, J. (2001). Efficient Spatiotemporal Grouping Using the Nyström Method. In *Proceedings of the IEEE Conference on Computer Vision and Pattern Recognition, CVPR 2001*. p. 172

Freedman, D. (1999). On the Bernstein-Von Mises Theorem with Infinite-Dimensional Parameters. *Annals of Statistics*, 27(4):1119–1140. p. 156

Frieze, A., Kannan, R., and Vempala, S. (1998). Fast Monte-Carlo Algorithms for Finding Low-Rank Approximations. In *39th Conference on the Foundations of Computer Science*, pages 370–378. p. 174

Geisser, S. and Eddy, W. F. (1979). A Predictive Approach to Model Selection. *Journal of the Americal Statistical Association*, 74(365):153–160. p. 117

Geman, S. and Geman, D. (1984). Stochastic Relaxation, Gibbs Distributions, and the Bayesian Restoration of Images. *IEEE Trans. Pattern Analysis and Machine Intellligence*, 6(6):721–741. p. 216

Gibbs, M. N. (1997). *Bayesian Gaussian Processes for Regression and Classification*. PhD thesis, Department of Physics, University of Cambridge. p. 93

Gibbs, M. N. and MacKay, D. J. C. (1997). Efficient Implementation of Gaussian Processes. Unpublished manuscript. Cavendish Laboratory, Cambridge, UK. http://www.inference.phy.cam.ac.uk/mackay/BayesGP.html. p. 181

Gibbs, M. N. and MacKay, D. J. C. (2000). Variational Gaussian Process Classifiers. *IEEE Transactions on Neural Networks*, 11(6):1458–1464. p. 41

Gihman, I. I. and Skorohod, A. V. (1974). *The Theory of Stochastic Processes*, volume 1. Springer Verlag, Berlin. p. 82

Girard, A., Rasmussen, C. E., Quiñonero-Candela, J., and Murray-Smith, R. (2003). Gaussian Process Priors With Uncertain Inputs: Application to Multiple-Step Ahead Time Series Forecasting. In Becker, S., Thrun, S., and Obermayer, K., editors, *Advances in Neural Information Processing Systems 15*. MIT Press. p. 192

Girosi, F. (1991). Models of Noise and Robust Estimates. Technical Report AI Memo 1287, MIT AI Laboratory. p. 146

Girosi, F., Jones, M., and Poggio, T. (1995). Regularization Theory and Neural Networks Architectures. *Neural Computation*, 7(2):219–269. p. 25

Goldberg, P. W., Williams, C. K. I., and Bishop, C. M. (1998). Regression with Input-dependent Noise: A Gaussian Process Treatment. In Jordan, M. I., Kearns, M. J., and Solla, S. A., editors, *Advances in Neural Information Processing Systems 10*. MIT Press, Cambridge, MA. p. 191

Golub, G. H. and Van Loan, C. F. (1989). *Matrix Computations*. Johns Hopkins University Press, Baltimore. Second edition. pp. 172, 173, 174, 181, 202

Gradshteyn, I. S. and Ryzhik, I. M. (1980). *Tables of Integrals, Series and Products*. Academic Press. Corrected and enlarged edition prepared by A. Jeffrey. pp. 98, 103

Green, P. J. and Silverman, B. W. (1994). *Nonparametric Regression and Generalized Linear Models*. Chapman and Hall, London. p. 138

Grenander, U., Chow, Y., and Keenan, D. M. (1991). *Hands: A Pattern Theoretic Study of Biological Shapes*. Springer-Verlag, New York. pp. 214, 216

Grimmett, G. R. and Stirzaker, D. R. (1992). *Probability and Random Processes*. Oxford University Press, Oxford, England, second edition. pp. 94, 213

Grünwald, P. D. and Langford, J. (2004). Suboptimal Behaviour of Bayes and MDL in Classification Under Misspecification. In *Proc. Seventeenth Annual Conference on Computational Learning Theory (COLT 2004)*. p. 156

Györfi, L., Kohler, M., Krzyżak, A., and Walk, H. (2002). *A Distribution-Free Theory of Nonparametric Regression*. Springer, New York. p. 156

Hajek, J. (1958). On a Property of Normal Distributions of Any Stochastic Process (In Russian). *Czechoslovak Math. J.*, 8:610–618. Translated in *Selected Trans. Math. Statist. Probab. 1* 245-252 (1961). Also available in *Collected Works of Jaroslav Hajek*, eds. M. Hušková, R. Beran, V. Dupač, Wiley, (1998). p. 157

Hand, D. J., Mannila, H., and Smyth, P. (2001). *Principles of Data Mining*. MIT Press. p. 100

Hannan, E. J. (1970). *Multiple Time Series*. Wiley, New York. p. 215

Hansen, L. K., Liisberg, C., and Salamon, P. (1997). The Error-Reject Tradeoff. *Open Sys. & Information Dyn.*, 4:159–184. p. 36

Hastie, T. J. and Tibshirani, R. J. (1990). *Generalized Additive Models*. Chapman and Hall. pp. 24, 25, 95

Haussler, D. (1999). Convolution Kernels on Discrete Structures. Technical Report UCSC-CRL-99-10, Dept of Computer Science, University of California at Santa Cruz. p. 101

Hawkins, D. L. (1989). Some Practical Problems in Implementing a Certain Sieve Estimator of the Gaussian Mean Function. *Communications in Statistics—Simulation and Computation*, 18(2):481–500.   p. 97

Hoerl, A. E. and Kennard, R. W. (1970). Ridge Regression: Biased Estimation for Nonorthogonal Problems. *Technometrics*, 12(1):55–67.   p. 11

Hornik, K. (1993). Some New Results on Neural Network Approximation. *Neural Networks*, 6(8):1069–1072.   p. 90

Ihara, S. (1993). *Information Theory for Continuous Systems*. World Scientific, Singapore.   p. 218

Jaakkola, T. S., Diekhans, M., and Haussler, D. (2000). A Discriminative Framework for Detecting Remote Protein Homologies. *Journal of Computational Biology*, 7:95–114.   pp. 101, 102, 104

Jaakkola, T. S. and Haussler, D. (1999). Probabilistic Kernel Regression Models. In Heckerman, D. and Whittaker, J., editors, *Workshop on Artificial Intelligence and Statistics 7*. Morgan Kaufmann. p. 41

Jacobs, R. A., Jordan, M. I., Nowlan, S. J., and Hinton, G. E. (1991). Adaptive Mixtures of Local Experts. *Neural Computation*, 3:79–87.   p. 192

Johnson, N. L., Kotz, S., and Balakrishnan, N. (1995). *Continuous Univariate Distributions volume 2*. John Wiley and Sons, New York, second edition.   p. 45

Jones, D. R. (2001). A Taxonomy of Global Optimization Methods Based on Response Surfaces. *J. Global Optimization*, 21:345–383.   p. 193

Jordan, M. I. (2005). An Introduction to Probabilistic Graphical Models. Draft book.   p. 218

Journel, A. G. and Huijbregts, C. J. (1978). *Mining Geostatistics*. Academic Press.   p. 30

Kailath, T. (1971). RKHS Approach to Detection and Estimation Problems—Part I: Deterministic Signals in Gaussian Noise. *IEEE Trans. Information Theory*, 17(5):530–549.   p. 131

Kammler, D. W. (2000). *A First Course in Fourier Analysis*. Prentice-Hall, Upper Saddle River, NJ.
                                                                                                p. 208

Kashyap, R. L. and Chellappa, R. (1981). Stochastic Models for Closed Boundary Analysis: Representation and Reconstruction. *IEEE Trans. on Information Theory*, 27(5):627–637.   p. 216

Keeling, C. D. and Whorf, T. P. (2004). Atmospheric CO_2 Records from Sites in the SIO Air Sampling Network. In *Trends: A Compendium of Data on Global Change*. Carbon Dioxide Information Analysis Center, Oak Ridge National Laboratory, Oak Ridge, Tenn., U.S.A.   p. 119

Kent, J. T. and Mardia, K. V. (1994). The Link Between Kriging and Thin-plate Splines. In Kelly, F. P., editor, *Probability, Statsitics and Optimization*, pages 325–339. Wiley.   p. 137

Kimeldorf, G. and Wahba, G. (1970). A Correspondence between Bayesian Estimation of Stochastic Processes and Smoothing by Splines. *Annals of Mathematical Statistics*, 41:495–502.   p. 136

Kimeldorf, G. and Wahba, G. (1971). Some Results on Tchebycheffian Spline Functions. *J. Mathematical Analysis and Applications*, 33(1):82–95.   p. 132

Kohn, R. and Ansley, C. F. (1987). A New Algorithm for Spline Smoothing based on Smoothing a Stochastic Process. *SIAM J. Sci. Stat. Comput.*, 8(1):33–48.   p. 141

Kolmogorov, A. N. (1941). Interpolation und Extrapolation von stationären zufäligen Folgen. *Izv. Akad. Nauk SSSR*, 5:3–14.   p. 29

König, H. (1986). *Eigenvalue Distribution of Compact Operators*. Birkhäuser.   p. 96

Kullback, S. (1959). *Information Theory and Statistics*. Dover, New York.   pp. 158, 203

Kuss, M. and Rasmussen, C. E. (2005). Assessing Approximations for Gaussian Process Classification. In Weiss, Y., Schölkopf, B., and Platt, J., editors, *Advances in Neural Information Processing Systems 18*. MIT Press.   pp. 72, 73

Lanckriet, G. R. G., Cristianini, N., Bartlett, P. L., El Ghaoui, L., and Jordan, M. I. (2004). Learning the Kernel Matrix with Semidefinite Programming. *Journal of Machine Learning Research*, 5(1):27–72.
                                                                                          p. 128

Lauritzen, S. L. (1981). Time Series Analysis in 1880: A Discussion of Contributions Made by T. N. Thiele. *International Statistical Review*, 49:319–333.   p. 29

Lawrence, N. (2004). Gaussian Process Latent Variable Models for Visualization of High Dimensional Data. In Thrun, S., Saul, L., and Schölkopf, B., editors, *Advances in Neural Information Processing Systems 16*, pages 329–336. MIT Press.   p. 196

Lawrence, N., Seeger, M., and Herbrich, R. (2003). Fast Sparse Gaussian Process Methods: The Informative Vector Machine. In Becker, S., Thrun, S., and Obermayer, K., editors, *Advances in Neural Information Processing Systems 15*, pages 625–632. MIT Press.   pp. 178, 185

Leslie, C., Eskin, E., Weston, J., and Stafford Noble, W. (2003). Mismatch String Kernels for SVM Protein Classification. In Becker, S., Thrun, S., and Obermayer, K., editors, *Advances in Neural Information Processing Systems 15*. MIT Press.   pp. 100, 101, 104

Lin, X., Wahba, G., Xiang, D., Gao, F., Klein, R., and Klein, B. (2000). Smoothing Spline ANOVA Models for Large Data Sets With Bernoulli Observations and the Randomized GACV. *Annals of Statistics*, 28:1570–1600.   p. 185

Lindley, D. V. (1985). *Making Decisions*. John Wiley and Sons, London, UK, second edition.   p. 111

Lodhi, H., Shawe-Taylor, J., Cristianini, N., and Watkins, C. J. C. H. (2001). Text Classification using String Kernels. In Leen, T. K., Diettrich, T. G., and Tresp, V., editors, *Advances in Neural Information Processing Systems 13*. MIT Press.   p. 101

Luo, Z. and Wahba, G. (1997). Hybrid Adaptive Splines. *J. Amer. Statist. Assoc.*, 92:107–116. p. 176

MacKay, D. J. C. (1992a). A Practical Bayesian Framework for Backpropagation Networks. *Neural Computation*, 4(3):448–472.   pp. 109, 166, 167

MacKay, D. J. C. (1992b). Bayesian Interpolation. *Neural Computation*, 4(3):415–447. pp. xiii, xvi, 109

MacKay, D. J. C. (1992c). Information-Based Objective Functions for Active Data Selection. *Neural Computation*, 4(4):590–604.   p. 178

MacKay, D. J. C. (1992d). The Evidence Framework Applied to Classification Networks. *Neural Computation*, 4(5):720–736.   p. 45

MacKay, D. J. C. (1998). Introduction to Gaussian Processes. In Bishop, C. M., editor, *Neural Networks and Machine Learning*. Springer-Verlag.   pp. 84, 92

MacKay, D. J. C. (1999). Comparison of Approximate Methods for Handling Hyperparameters. *Neural Computation*, 11(5):1035–1068.   p. 110

MacKay, D. J. C. (2003). *Information Theory, Inference, and Learning Algorithms*. Cambridge University Press, Cambridge, UK.   pp. xiv, 167

Malzahn, D. and Opper, M. (2002). A Variational Approach to Learning Curves. In Diettrich, T. G., Becker, S., and Ghahramani, Z., editors, *Advances in Neural Information Processing Systems 14*. MIT Press.   p. 161

Mandelbrot, B. B. (1982). *The Fractal Geometry of Nature*. W. H. Freeman, San Francisco.   p. 137

Mardia, K. V. and Marshall, R. J. (1984). Maximum Likelihood Estimation for Models of Residual Covariance in Spatial Regression. *Biometrika*, 71(1):135–146.   p. 115

Matérn, B. (1960). *Spatial Variation*. Meddelanden från Statens Skogsforskningsinstitut, 49, No.5. Almänna Förlaget, Stockholm. Second edition (1986), Springer-Verlag, Berlin.   pp. 85, 87, 89

Matheron, G. (1973). The Intrinsic Random Functions and Their Applications. *Advances in Applied Probability*, 5:439–468.   p. 30

Maxwell, J. C. (1850). Letter to Lewis Campbell; reproduced in L. Campbell and W. Garrett, *The Life of James Clerk Maxwell*, Macmillan, 1881.   p. v

McAllester, D. (2003). PAC-Bayesian Stochastic Model Selection. *Machine Learning*, 51(1):5–21.   p. 164

McCullagh, P. and Nelder, J. (1983). *Generalized Linear Models*. Chapman and Hall.   pp. 37, 38, 138

Meinguet, J. (1979). Multivariate Interpolation at Arbitrary Points Made Simple. *Journal of Applied Mathematics and Physics (ZAMP)*, 30:292–304.   p. 137

Meir, R. and Zhang, T. (2003). Generalization Error Bounds for Bayesian Mixture Algorithms. *Journal of Machine Learning Research*, 4(5):839–860.   p. 164

Micchelli, C. A. and Pontil, M. (2005). Kernels for Multi-task Learning. In Saul, L. K., Weiss, Y., and Bottou, L., editors, *Advances in Neural Information Processing Systems 17*, pages 921–928. MIT Press.   p. 190

Micchelli, C. A. and Wahba, G. (1981). Design Problems for Optimal Surface Interpolation. In Ziegler, Z., editor, *Approximation Theory and Applications*, pages 329–348. Academic Press.   p. 161

Minka, T. P. (2001). *A Family of Algorithms for Approximate Bayesian Inference*. PhD thesis, Massachusetts Institute of Technology.   pp. 41, 52

Minka, T. P. (2003). A Comparison of Numerical Optimizers for Logistic Regression. http://research.microsoft.com/~minka/papers/logreg.   p. 38

Minka, T. P. and Picard, R. W. (1999). Learning How to Learn is Learning With Point Sets. `http://research.microsoft.com/~minka/papers/point-sets.html`. p. 116

Mitchell, T. M. (1997). *Machine Learning*. McGraw-Hill, New York. pp. 2, 165

Murray-Smith, R. and Girard, A. (2001). Gaussian Process priors with ARMA noise models. In *Irish Signals and Systems Conference*, pages 147–153, Maynooth. `http://www.dcs.gla.ac.uk/~rod/publications/MurGir01.pdf`. p. 191

Neal, R. M. (1996). *Bayesian Learning for Neural Networks*. Springer, New York. Lecture Notes in Statistics 118. pp. xiii, 30, 90, 91, 106, 166, 167

Neal, R. M. (1997). Monte Carlo Implementation of Gaussian Process Models for Bayesian Regression and Classification. Technical Report 9702, Department of Statistics, University of Toronto. `http://www.cs.toronto.edu/~radford`. p. 191

Neal, R. M. (1999). Regression and Classification using Gaussian Process Priors. In Bernardo, J. M., Berger, J. O., Dawid, A. P., and Smith, A. F. M., editors, *Bayesian Statistics 6*, pages 475–501. Oxford University Press. (with discussion). pp. 41, 47

Neal, R. M. (2001). Annealed Importance Sampling. *Statistics and Computing*, 11:125–139. p. 72

Neumaier, A. (2005). Introduction to Global Optimization. `http://www.mat.univie.ac.at/~neum/glopt/intro.html`. p. 193

O'Hagan, A. (1978). Curve Fitting and Optimal Design for Prediction. *Journal of the Royal Statistical Society B*, 40:1–42. (with discussion). pp. 28, 30, 94

O'Hagan, A. (1991). Bayes-Hermite Quadrature. *Journal of Statistical Planning and Inference*, 29:245–260. pp. 193, 194

O'Hagan, A., Kennedy, M. C., and Oakley, J. E. (1999). Uncertainty Analysis and other Inference Tools for Complex Computer Codes. In Bernardo, J. M., Berger, J. O., Dawid, A. P., and Smith, A. F. M., editors, *Bayesian Statistics 6*, pages 503–524. Oxford University Press. (with discussion). p. 194

Øksendal, B. (1985). *Stochastic Differential Equations*. Springer-Verlag, Berlin. p. 208

Opper, M. and Vivarelli, F. (1999). General Bounds on Bayes Errors for Regression with Gaussian Processes. In Kearns, M. S., Solla, S. A., and Cohn, D. A., editors, *Advances in Neural Information Processing Systems 11*, pages 302–308. MIT Press. p. 160

Opper, M. and Winther, O. (2000). Gaussian Processes for Classification: Mean-Field Algorithms. *Neural Computation*, 12(11):2655–2684. pp. 41, 44, 52, 127, 128

O'Sullivan, F., Yandell, B. S., and Raynor, W. J. (1986). Automatic Smoothing of Regression Functions in Generalized Linear Models. *Journal of the American Statistical Association*, 81:96–103. pp. 132, 138

Paciorek, C. and Schervish, M. J. (2004). Nonstationary Covariance Functions for Gaussian Process Regression. In Thrun, S., Saul, L., and Schölkopf, B., editors, *Advances in Neural Information Processing Systems 16*. MIT Press. pp. 93, 94

Papoulis, A. (1991). *Probability, Random Variables, and Stochastic Processes*. McGraw-Hill, New York. Third Edition. pp. 79, 153, 154, 191, 211, 212

Plaskota, L. (1996). *Noisy Information and Computational Complexity*. Cambridge University Press, Cambridge.   pp. 161, 169

Plate, T. A. (1999). Accuarcy versus Interpretability in Flexible Modeling: Implementing a Tradeoff using Gaussian Process Models. *Behaviourmetrika*, 26(1):29–50.   p. 95

Platt, J. C. (1999). Fast Training of Support Vector Machines Using Sequential Minimal Optimization. In Schölkopf, B., Burges, C. J. C., and Smola, A. J., editors, *Advances in Kernel Methods*, pages 185–208. MIT Press.   p. 144

Platt, J. C. (2000). Probabilities for SV Machines. In Smola, A., Bartlett, P., Schölkopf, B., and Schuurmans, D., editors, *Advances in Large Margin Classifiers*, pages 61–74. MIT Press.
                                                                              pp. 69, 70, 145, 147, 148

Poggio, T. and Girosi, F. (1990). Networks for Approximation and Learning. *Proceedings of IEEE*, 78:1481–1497.   pp. 89, 133, 134, 135, 147, 176

Poggio, T., Voorhees, H., and Yuille, A. (1985). A Regularized Solution to Edge Detection. Technical Report AI Memo 833, MIT AI Laboratory.   p. 154

Pontil, M., Mukherjee, S., and Girosi, F. (1998). On the Noise Model of Support Vector Machine Regression. Technical Report AI Memo 1651, MIT AI Laboratory.   p. 146

Press, W. H., Teukolsky, S. A., Vetterling, W. T., and Flannery, B. P. (1992). *Numerical Recipes in C*. Cambridge University Press, Second edition.   pp. 96, 99, 201

Quiñonero-Candela, J. (2004). *Learning with Uncertainty—Gaussian Processes and Relevance Vector Machines*. PhD thesis, Informatics and Mathematical Modelling, Technical Univeristy of Denmark.
                                                                                              p. 177

Rasmussen, C. E. (1996). *Evaluation of Gaussian Processes and Other Methods for Non-linear Regression*. PhD thesis, Dept. of Computer Science, University of Toronto. http://www.kyb.mpg.de/publications/pss/ps2304.ps.   p. 30

Rasmussen, C. E. (2003). Gaussian Processes to Speed up Hybrid Monte Carlo for Expensive Bayesian Integrals. In Bernardo, J. M., Bayarri, M. J., Berger, J. O., Dawid, A. P., Heckerman, D., Smith, A. F. M., and West, M., editors, *Bayesian Statistics 7*, pages 651–659. Oxford University Press. p. 193

Rasmussen, C. E. and Ghahramani, Z. (2001). Occam's Razor. In Leen, T., Dietterich, T. G., and Tresp, V., editors, *Advances in Neural Information Processing Systems 13*, pages 294–300. MIT Press. p. 110

Rasmussen, C. E. and Ghahramani, Z. (2002). Infinite Mixtures of Gaussian Process Experts. In Diettrich, T. G., Becker, S., and Ghahramani, Z., editors, *Advances in Neural Information Processing Systems 14*. MIT Press.   p. 192

Rasmussen, C. E. and Ghahramani, Z. (2003). Bayesian Monte Carlo. In Suzanna Becker, S. T. and Obermayer, K., editors, *Advances in Neural Information Processing Systems 15*, pages 489–496. MIT Press.   p. 193

Rasmussen, C. E. and Quiñonero-Candela, J. (2005). Healing the Relevance Vector Machine through Augmentation. In *Proc. 22nd International Conference on Machine Learning*.   pp. 150, 176

Rifkin, R. and Klautau, A. (2004). In Defense of One-Vs-All Classification. *Journal of Machine Learning Research*, 5:101–141.   pp. 146, 147

Ripley, B. (1981). *Spatial Statistics*. Wiley, New York.   p. 30

Ripley, B. (1996). *Pattern Recognition and Neural Networks*. Cambridge University Press, Cambridge, UK.   p. 35

Ritter, K. (2000). *Average-Case Analysis of Numerical Problems*. Springer Verlag. pp. 159, 161, 169, 193

Ritter, K., Wasilkowski, G. W., and Woźniakowski, H. (1995). Multivariate Integration and Approximation of Random Fields Satisfying Sacks-Ylvisaker Conditions. *Annals of Applied Probability*, 5:518–540.
                                                                                                p. 97

Rousseeuw, P. J. (1984). Least Median of Squares Regression. *Journal of the American Statistical Association*, 79:871–880.   p. 146

Sacks, J., Welch, W. J., Mitchell, T. J., and Wynn, H. P. (1989). Design and Analysis of Computer Experiments. *Statistical Science*, 4(4):409–435.   pp. 16, 30

Saitoh, S. (1988). *Theory of Reproducing Kernels and its Applications*. Longman, Harlow, England.
                                                                                                p. 129

Salton, G. and Buckley, C. (1988). Term-weighting Approaches in Automatic Text Retrieval. *Information Processing and Management*, 24:513–523.   p. 100

Sampson, P. D. and Guttorp, P. (1992). Nonparametric Estimation of Nonstationary Covariance Structure. *Journal of the American Statistical Association*, 87:108–119.   p. 92

Santner, T. J., Williams, B. J., and Notz, W. (2003). *The Design and Analysis of Computer Experiments*. Springer, New York.   p. 30

Saunders, C., Gammerman, A., and Vovk, V. (1998). Ridge Regression Learning Algorithm in Dual Variables. In Shavlik, J., editor, *Proceedings of the Fifteenth International Conference on Machine Learning (ICML 1998)*. Morgan Kaufmann.   p. 30

Saunders, C., Shawe-Taylor, J., and Vinokourov, A. (2003). String Kernels, Fisher Kernels and Finite State Automata. In Becker, S., Thrun, S., and Obermayer, K., editors, *Advances in Neural Information Processing Systems 15*. MIT Press.   p. 101

Schoenberg, I. J. (1938). Metric Spaces and Positive Definite Functions. *Trans. American Mathematical Society*, 44(3):522–536.   p. 86

Schoenberg, I. J. (1964). Spline Functions and the Problem of Graduation. *Proc. Nat. Acad. Sci. USA*, 52:947–950.   pp. 132, 138

Schölkopf, B. and Smola, A. J. (2002). *Learning with Kernels*. MIT Press.
                                pp. xvi, 73, 89, 90, 91, 129, 130, 133, 141, 144, 147, 173, 188, 195, 196

Schölkopf, B., Smola, A. J., and Müller, K.-R. (1998). Nonlinear Component Analysis as a Kernel Eigenvalue Problem. *Neural Computation*, 10:1299–1319.   p. 99

Schwaighofer, A. and Tresp, V. (2003). Transductive and Inductive Methods for Approximate Gaussian Process Regression. In Becker, S., Thrun, S., and Obermayer, K., editors, *Advances in Neural Information Processing Systems 15*. MIT Press.   pp. 181, 184

Scott, D. W. (1992). *Multivariate Density Estimation*. Wiley, New York.   p. 25

Seeger, M. (2000). Bayesian Model Selection for Support Vector Machines, Gaussian Processes and Other Kernel Classifiers. In Solla, S. A., Leen, T. K., and Müller, K.-R., editors, *Advances in Neural Information Processing Systems 12*. MIT Press, Cambridge, MA.   pp. 41, 54, 145

Seeger, M. (2002). PAC-Bayesian Generalisation Error Bounds for Gaussian Process Classification. *Journal of Machine Learning Research*, 3:322–269.   pp. 161, 164, 165

Seeger, M. (2003). *Bayesian Gaussian Process Models: PAC-Bayesian Generalisation Error Bounds and Sparse Approximations*. PhD thesis, School of Informatics, University of Edinburgh. http://www.cs.berkeley.edu/~mseeger.   pp. 46, 145, 161, 162, 163, 179, 180, 186

Seeger, M. (2005). Expectation Propagation for Exponential Families. http://www.cs.berkeley.edu/~mseeger/papers/epexpfam.ps.gz.   p. 127

Seeger, M. and Jordan, M. I. (2004). Sparse Gaussian Process Classification With Multiple Classes. Technical Report TR 661, Department of Statistics, University of California at Berkeley.   p. 50

Seeger, M., Williams, C. K. I., and Lawrence, N. (2003). Fast Forward Selection to Speed Up Sparse Gaussian Process Regression. In Bishop, C. and Frey, B. J., editors, *Proceedings of the Ninth International Workshop on Artificial Intelligence and Statistics*. Society for Artificial Intelligence and Statistics.   pp. 178, 180

Shawe-Taylor, J. and Williams, C. K. I. (2003). The Stability of Kernel Principal Components Analysis and its Relation to the Process Eigenspectrum. In Becker, S., Thrun, S., and Obermayer, K., editors, *Advances in Neural Information Processing Systems 15*. MIT Press.   p. 99

Shepp, L. A. (1966). Radon-Nikodym Derivatives of Gaussian Measures. *Annals of Mathematical Statistics*, 37(2):321–354.   p. 139

Silverman, B. W. (1978). Density Ratios, Empirical Likelihood and Cot Death. *Applied Statistics*, 27(1):26–33.   p. 138

Silverman, B. W. (1984). Spline Smoothing: The Equivalent Variable Kernel Method. *Annals of Statistics*, 12(3):898–916.   pp. 25, 153, 154

Silverman, B. W. (1985). Some Aspects of the Spline Smoothing Approach to Non-parametric Regression Curve Fitting (with discussion). *J. Roy. Stat. Soc. B*, 47(1):1–52.   pp. 170, 175

Simard, P., Victorri, B., Le Cun, Y., and Denker, J. (1992). Tangent Prop—A Formalism for Specifying Selected Invariances in an Adaptive Network. In Moody, J. E., Hanson, S. J., and Lippmann, R. P., editors, *Advances in Neural Information Processing Systems 4*, pages 895–903. Morgan Kaufmann.
                                                                                      pp. 73, 195

Smola, A. J. and Bartlett, P. L. (2001). Sparse Greedy Gaussian Process Regression. In Leen, T. K., Diettrich, T. G., and Tresp, V., editors, *Advances in Neural Information Processing Systems 13*, pages 619–625. MIT Press.   p. 176

Smola, A. J. and Schölkopf, B. (2000). Sparse Greedy Matrix Approximation for Machine Learning. In *Proceedings of the Seventeenth International Conference on Machine Learning*. Morgan Kaufmann. pp. 173, 174

Solak, E., Murray-Smith, R., Leithead, W. E., Leith, D., and Rasmussen, C. E. (2003). Derivative Observations in Gaussian Process Models of Dynamic Systems. In Becker, S., S. T. and Obermayer, K., editors, *Advances in Neural Information Processing Systems 15*, pages 1033–1040. MIT Press. p. 191

Sollich, P. (1999). Learning Curves for Gaussian Processes. In Kearns, M. S., Solla, S. A., and Cohn, D. A., editors, *Neural Information Processing Systems, Vol. 11*. MIT Press. pp. 160, 161

Sollich, P. (2002). Bayesian Methods for Support Vector Machines: Evidence and Predictive Class Probabilities. *Machine Learning*, 46:21–52. pp. 145, 150, 161

Sollich, P. and Williams, C. K. I. (2005). Using the Equivalent Kernel to Understand Gaussian Process Regression. In Saul, L. K., Weiss, Y., and Bottou, L., editors, *Advances in Neural Information Processing Systems 17*. MIT Press. p. 154

Stein, M. L. (1991). A Kernel Approximation to the Kriging Predictor of a Spatial Process. *Ann. Inst. Statist. Math*, 43(1):61–75. p. 154

Stein, M. L. (1999). *Interpolation of Spatial Data*. Springer-Verlag, New York. pp. 82, 83, 85, 86, 87, 115, 137, 157, 158, 161, 212

Steinwart, I. (2005). Consistency of Support Vector Machines and Other Regularized Kernel Classifiers. *IEEE Trans. on Information Theory*, 51(1):128–142. p. 157

Stitson, M. O., Gammerman, A., Vapnik, V. N., Vovk, V., Watkins, C. J. C. H., and Weston, J. (1999). Support Vector Regression with ANOVA Decomposition Kernels. In Schölkopf, B., Burges, C. J. C., and Smola, A. J., editors, *Advances in Kernel Methods*. MIT Press. p. 95

Sundararajan, S. and Keerthi, S. S. (2001). Predictive Approaches for Choosing Hyperparameters in Gaussian Processes. *Neural Computation*, 13:1103–1118. p. 117

Suykens, J. A. K. and Vanderwalle, J. (1999). Least Squares Support Vector Machines. *Neural Processing Letters*, 9:293–300. p. 147

Szeliski, R. (1987). Regularization uses Fractal Priors. In *Proceedings of the 6th National Conference on Artificial Intelligence (AAAI-87)*. pp. 135, 137

Teh, Y. W., Seeger, M., and Jordan, M. I. (2005). Semiparametric Latent Factor Models. In Cowell, R. G. and Ghahramani, Z., editors, *Proceedings of Tenth International Workshop on Artificial Intelligence and Statistics*, pages 333–340. Society for Artificial Intelligence and Statistics. p. 190

Thomas-Agnan, C. (1996). Computing a Family of Reproducing Kernels for Statistical Applications. *Numerical Algorithms*, 13:21–32. p. 154

Thompson, P. D. (1956). Optimum Smoothing of Two-Dimensional Fields. *Tellus*, 8:384–393. p. 30

Tikhonov, A. N. (1963). Solution of Incorrectly Formulated Problems and the Regularization Method. *Soviet. Math. Dokl.*, 5:1035–1038. p. 133

Tikhonov, A. N. and Arsenin, V. Y. (1977). *Solutions of Ill-posed Problems*. W. H. Winston, Washington, D.C. p. 133

Tipping, M. E. (2001). Sparse Bayesian Learning and the Relevance Vector Machine. *Journal of Machine Learning Research*, 1:211–244. p. 149

Tipping, M. E. and Faul, A. C. (2003). Fast Marginal Likelihood Maximisation for Sparse Bayesian Models. In Bishop, C. M. and Frey, B. J., editors, *Proceedings of Ninth International Workshop on Artificial Intelligence and Statistics*. Society for Artificial Intelligence and Statistics. p. 149

Tresp, V. (2000). A Bayesian Committee Machine. *Neural Computation*, 12(11):2719–2741. pp. 180, 181, 185, 187

Tsuda, K., Kawanabe, M., Rätsch, G., Sonnenburg, S., and Müller, K.-R. (2002). A New Discriminative Kernel from Probabilistic Models. *Neural Computation*, 14(10):2397–2414. p. 102

Uhlenbeck, G. E. and Ornstein, L. S. (1930). On the Theory of Brownian Motion. *Phys. Rev.*, 36:823–841. pp. 86, 212

Valiant, L. G. (1984). A Theory of the Learnable. *Communications of the ACM*, 27(11):1134–1142. p. 161

Vapnik, V. N. (1995). *The Nature of Statistical Learning Theory*. Springer Verlag, New York. pp. 36, 141, 181

Vapnik, V. N. (1998). *Statistical Learning Theory*. John Wiley and Sons. p. 140

Vijayakumar, S., D'Souza, A., and Schaal, S. (2005). Incremental Online Learning in High Dimensions. Accepted for publication in *Neural Computation*. pp. 22, 24

Vijayakumar, S., D'Souza, A., Shibata, T., Conradt, J., and Schaal, S. (2002). Statistical Learning for Humanoid Robots. *Autonomous Robot*, 12(1):55–69. p. 22

Vijayakumar, S. and Schaal, S. (2000). LWPR: An $O(n)$ Algorithm for Incremental Real Time Learning in High Dimensional Space. In *Proc. of the Seventeenth International Conference on Machine Learning (ICML 2000)*, pages 1079–1086. p. 22

Vishwanathan, S. V. N. and Smola, A. J. (2003). Fast Kernels for String and Tree Matching. In Becker, S., Thrun, S., and Obermayer, K., editors, *Advances in Neural Information Processing Systems 15*. MIT Press. p. 101

Vivarelli, F. and Williams, C. K. I. (1999). Discovering Hidden Features with Gaussian Processes Regression. In Kearns, M. S., Solla, S. A., and Cohn, D. A., editors, *Advances in Neural Information Processing Systems 11*. MIT Press. p. 89

von Mises, R. (1964). *Mathematical Theory of Probability and Statistics*. Academic Press. p. 200

Wahba, G. (1978). Improper Priors, Spline Smoothing and the Problem of Guarding Against Model Errors in Regression. *Journal of the Royal Statistical Society B*, 40(3):364–372. p. 139

Wahba, G. (1985). A Comparison of GCV and GML for Choosing the Smoothing Parameter in the Generalized Spline Smoothing Problem. *Annals of Statistics*, 13:1378–1402. p. 29

Wahba, G. (1990). *Spline Models for Observational Data.* Society for Industrial and Applied Mathematics, Philadelphia, PA. CBMS-NSF Regional Conference series in applied mathematics.
pp. 95, 112, 117, 118, 129, 131, 137, 138, 157, 176

Wahba, G., Johnson, D. R., Gao, F., and Gong, J. (1995). Adaptive Tuning of Numerical Weather Prediction Models: Randomized GCV in Three-and Four-Dimensional Data Assimilation. *Monthly Weather Review*, 123:3358–3369.
p. 181

Watkins, C. J. C. H. (1999). Dynamic Alignment Kernels. Technical Report CSD-TR-98-11, Dept of Computer Science, Royal Holloway, University of London.
p. 101

Watkins, C. J. C. H. (2000). Dynamic Alignment Kernels. In Smola, A. J., Bartlett, P. L., and Schölkopf, B., editors, *Advances in Large Margin Classifiers*, pages 39–50. MIT Press, Cambridge, MA.
p. 100

Wegman, E. J. (1982). Reproducing Kernel Hilbert Spaces. In Kotz, S. and Johnson, N. L., editors, *Encyclopedia of Statistical Sciences*, volume 8, pages 81–84. Wiley, New York.
pp. 129, 130

Weinert, H. L., editor (1982). *Reproducing Kernel Hilbert Spaces.* Hutchinson Ross, Stroudsburg, Pennsylvania.
p. 129

Wendland, H. (2005). *Scattered Data Approximation.* Cambridge Monographs on Applied and Computational Mathematics. Cambridge University Press.
p. 88

Whittle, P. (1963). *Prediction and Regulation by Linear Least-square Methods.* English Universities Press.
pp. 30, 216

Widom, H. (1963). Asymptotic Behavior of the Eigenvalues of Certain Integral Equations. *Trans. of the American Mathematical Society*, 109(2):278–295.
p. 97

Widom, H. (1964). Asymptotic Behavior of the Eigenvalues of Certain Integral Equations II. *Archive for Rational Mechanics and Analysis*, 17:215–229.
p. 97

Wiener, N. (1949). *Extrapolation, Interpolation and Smoothing of Stationary Time Series.* MIT Press, Cambridge, Mass.
p. 29

Williams, C. K. I. (1998). Computation with Infinite Neural Networks. *Neural Computation*, 10(5):1203–1216.
p. 91

Williams, C. K. I. and Barber, D. (1998). Bayesian Classification with Gaussian Processes. *IEEE Transactions on Pattern Analysis and Machine Intelligence*, 20(12):1342–1351.
pp. 41, 45, 48, 49

Williams, C. K. I. and Rasmussen, C. E. (1996). Gaussian Processes for Regression. In Touretzky, D. S., Mozer, M. C., and Hasselmo, M. E., editors, *Advances in Neural Information Processing Systems 8*, pages 514–520. MIT Press.
pp. 30, 107

Williams, C. K. I., Rasmussen, C. E., Schwaighofer, A., and Tresp, V. (2002). Observations on the Nyström Method for Gaussian Process Prediction. Technical report, University of Edinburgh. http://www.dai.ed.ac.uk/homes/ckiw/online_pubs.html.
p. 177

Williams, C. K. I. and Seeger, M. (2001). Using the Nyström Method to Speed Up Kernel Machines. In Leen, T. K., Diettrich, T. G., and Tresp, V., editors, *Advances in Neural Information Processing Systems 13*, pages 682–688. MIT Press.
pp. 173, 177

Williams, C. K. I. and Vivarelli, F. (2000). Upper and Lower Bounds on the Learning Curve for Gaussian Proccesses. *Machine Learning*, 40:77–102.   pp. 31, 161, 168

Winkler, G. (1995). *Image Analysis, Random Fields and Dynamic Monte Carlo Methods*. Springer, Berlin.   p. 219

Wong, E. (1971). *Stochastic Processes in Information and Dynamical Systems*. McGraw-Hill, New York.
                                                                                                    p. 218

Wood, S. and Kohn, R. (1998). A Bayesian Approach to Robust Binary Nonparametric Regression. *J. American Statistical Association*, 93(441):203–213.   p. 45

Yaglom, A. M. (1987). *Correlation Theory of Stationary and Related Random Functions Volume I: Basic Results*. Springer Verlag.   p. 89

Yang, C., Duraiswami, R., and David, L. (2005). Efficient Kernel Machines Using the Improved Fast Gauss Transform. In Saul, L. K., Weiss, Y., and Bottou, L., editors, *Advances in Neural Information Processing Systems 17*. MIT Press.   p. 182

Ylvisaker, D. (1975). Designs on Random Fields. In Srivastava, J. N., editor, *A Survey of Statistical Design and Linear Models*, pages 593–608. North-Holland.   p. 159

Yuille, A. and Grzywacz, N. M. (1989). A Mathematical Analysis of Motion Coherence Theory. *International Journal of Computer Vision*, 3:155–175.   p. 134

Zhang, T. (2004). Statistical Behaviour and Consistency of Classification Methods based on Convex Risk Minimization (with discussion). *Annals of Statistics*, 32(1):56–85.   p. 157

Zhu, H., Williams, C. K. I., Rohwer, R. J., and Morciniec, M. (1998). Gaussian Regression and Optimal Finite Dimensional Linear Models. In Bishop, C. M., editor, *Neural Networks and Machine Learning*. Springer-Verlag, Berlin.   p. 97

Zhu, J. and Hastie, T. J. (2002). Kernel Logistic Regression and the Import Vector Machine. In Diettrich, T. G., Becker, S., and Ghahramani, Z., editors, *Advances in Neural Information Processing Systems 14*, pages 1081–1088. MIT Press.   p. 185

Author Index

Subject Index